Professional Practices in Association Management

Executive Editor
John B. Cox, CAE

Richie Jacobs

asae | american society of
association executives

Washington, DC

The authors have worked to ensure that all information in this book is accurate as of the time of publication and consistent with standards of good practice in the general management community. As research and practice advance, however, standards may change. For this reason, it is recommended that readers evaluate the applicability of any recommendation in light of particular situations and changing standards.

Elissa M. Myers, CAE, ASAE Vice President and Publisher
Linda Munday, ASAE Director of Book Publishing

Reviewers: Elaine Kotell Binder, CAE; Gary LaBranche, CAE; Elissa M. Myers, CAE; and Linda J. Shinn, CAE

Editorial and Production Manager: Marianna Nunan, Gravel Hill Communications, Beltsville, MD

Editor: Sandra R. Sabo, Mendota Heights, MN

Designer: Anita Dahlman, DahlmanMiddourDesign, McLean, VA

Printed in the United States of America

American Society of Association Executives
1575 I Street, N.W.
Washington, DC 20005
(202) 626-2723
Fax (202) 408-9634
e-mail address: books@asae.asaenet.org

ISBN 0-88034-113-0 (paper)   0-88034-137-8 (cloth)

This book is available at a special discount when ordered in bulk quantities. For information, contact ASAE Member Services at (202) 371-0940.

A complete catalog of titles is available on the ASAE home page at http://www.asaenet.org

CONTENTS

PROGRAMS AND SERVICES

PREFACE

This book represents a happy confluence of collaborative events.

In the early 1990s the American Society of Association Executives (ASAE) brought together a group of the best and brightest in our profession to examine and define what every well-rounded association management professional needs to know to function successfully in this field. This group's effort, known as the Body of Knowledge, went on to literally define the borders, the boundaries of knowable skills, activities, and requisite background and/or experience in association management.

At the same moment that this project was nearing completion and an outline of its substantial findings was being prepared, the author approached ASAE's publications staff to propose a new kind of book.

Based on years of teaching Certified Association Executive (CAE) courses, as well as mentoring CAE candidates, the author became convinced that a comprehensive book was required that provided an overview of every topic encompassed in association management. Further, I knew from participating in numerous ASAE association peer evaluations that many smaller, geographically isolated associations, and their executives, needed an omnibus reference work in order to function professionally.

In still another serendipitous turn, ASAE's CAE Commission began redesigning and/or examining the entire CAE program, including personal data forms, the examination, and, of course, test preparation. Although the new exam would no longer be based on information derived from books, printed reference materials would still be needed for those not versed in every particular of association management.

At that point, all three dynamics came together: the Body of Knowledge Report, later known as the role delineation study, with its five broad domains in association management knowledge, was quickly adopted as the Table of Contents for this work, which in turn, will be used as one of the four major reference books for future classes of CAE candidates. Ultimately, though, this book is intended to serve many masters: aspiring CAE candidates, to be sure, but also executives who, while perhaps not seeking the CAE designation, need the best composite source of knowledge in association management. Additionally, it can serve as an overview of nonprofit organizational management in college courses, and though designed with associations in mind, it can also serve as a highly useful reference tool for any nonprofit organization, for it can accurately be said that, at present, there is no broader compilation of working knowledge in this profession than *Professional Practices in Association Management.*

I want to thank the numerous authors, contributors, reviewers, and editors who worked so selflessly to produce the high-utility information contained in this work. Though literally too numerous to mention individually, they deserve serious recognition and praise; they devoted their most precious commodity—time—so that others might prosper from their wisdom.

—John B. Cox, CAE

CHAPTER 1

ASSOCIATION GOVERNANCE AND STRUCTURE

WAYNE E. LEROY, CAE

Volunteers are the lifeblood of any association. Their commitment to and efforts on behalf of the association make it possible to not only establish a mission and goals that respond to members' needs but also implement programs and services that fulfill those objectives.

Within an association's structure, form follows function. In other words, an organization's mission and goals determine how those volunteers serve and govern. For instance, a trade association, whose members are companies or businesses, may be structured differently from a professional society or fraternal organization, whose members are individuals.

But regardless of whether its governing body is a board of directors or a house of delegates, an association delineates the decision-making authority in its bylaws. This is the formal, internal document that provides the operational framework regarding the establishment, integration, and maintenance of an effective and representative governance system. The bylaws may, for instance, specify the size and composition of the governing body as well as how many times that group meets per year. Changes to bylaws typically require either a member referendum or a vote of the governing body.

By the Book

Association bylaws vary in their length and complexity, but most have the following common elements:

1. Statement of purpose(s).
2. Forms, types, and qualifications of membership.
3. Dues structure (but not dues amounts).
4. List of elected offices, including terms, powers, duties, and rules for filling vacancies.
5. The role of the chief executive officer.
6. Voting qualifications, including procedures, proxies, and quorum provisions.
7. General assembly and special meeting criteria.
8. Descriptions of standing committees.
9. Accounting, fiscal, and reporting procedures.
10. Designation of corporate seal.
11. Procedures for amending bylaws and dissolution.

Rather than being detailed and prescriptive, bylaws should be general statements; more detailed management and operational items belong in a separate document that focuses on administrative policies and procedures (See Chapter 2).

The bylaws may also contain information mandated by state law, such as where the association's offices are located and whether it is incorporated. Because state laws vary, it may be advantageous for an association to be located in one geographic area while being incorporated in another; legal counsel can assist in exploring the various options.

The legal process of incorporation has both advantages and disadvantages; the balance, however, tips in favor of the former.

An association's bylaws should also specify its tax-exempt purpose (for example, business league, scientific organization, or educational group). This statement of purpose, however, does not constitute designated tax-exempt status under United States Tax Code Section 501(c)(3) (scientific or education) or Section 501(c)(6) (business league).

Association, Inc.

According to *Policies and Procedures in Association Management*, the vast majority of associations (95 percent) are incorporated. Incorporation provides several advantages. For instance, it:

- Eliminates personal liability of volunteer leaders.

- Establishes continuity of the association.

- Creates psychological benefits, such as stability and a business-like environment.

- Provides protection under applicable laws.

- Has guidelines regarding formation, administration, and organization (for instance, who can sue or be sued).

- Gives the association the ability to own real estate.

- Makes it easier to obtain liability insurance for officers and directors.

On the other hand, unincorporated nonprofit associations have no separate existence or legal identity of their own, are subject to wide fluctuations of government interpretations, and can be dissolved by the will of the membership.

Organizational Units

Approximately three out of four associations (77 percent) grant their members direct voting privileges. Submitting every decision to the entire membership, however, would soon prove unwieldy. Instead, associations establish a structure of organizational units to make the decisions that lead to the implementation of their missions and goals.

Those organizational units may include the following:

- **Board of directors.** Board sizes vary, with the average association having 27 voting members. In addition, more than half of associations (56 percent) have *ex-officio* board members who do not vote; those people tend to be the chief executive officer (CEO) or the chief elected officer who just completed his or her term.

A variety of methods are used to select board members, ranging from direct election by the membership, to selection by various constituency groups within the association (such as regions, chapters, or special interest groups), to selection by a nominating committee. The most common length of board tenure, preferred by two out of five associations (44 percent), is three years; one-fourth of associations favor two-year terms.

To ensure stability and continuity, while at the same time injecting new ways of thinking into a board, most associations use a rotation method for selecting board members. A three-year cycle, for instance, allows for one out of three board members to be new each year, while two-thirds remain experienced board members. Still, a majority of associations (78 percent) allow a board member to succeed himself or herself for an additional term or two.

Leading the board's work are officers, whose duties are typically specified in the association bylaws. The number of board officers usually ranges between four and seven, including these positions:

— *President/Chair(man) of the Board.* This is the chief elected or appointed volunteer position which, in three out of four associations (74 percent), has a one-year term. (To avoid confusion, associations often assign the title of chairman to the chief elected officer if the chief executive officer carries the title of president).

— *First Vice President/Vice Chair(man)/Chair(man)-Elect.* This person is next in succession for becoming the chief volunteer officer.

— *Secretary/Treasurer.* This officer is responsible for maintaining the fiscal and official written records of the association. Instead of combining this office, some organizations treat it as two separate positions. Others designate the chief executive officer as the secretary, thus removing that position from elective office.

— *Vice Presidents/Directors.* These positions are usually designated by program or service functions (for example, Director of Education or Membership Vice President) or by geographic designation (for example, Vice President of Professional Development or Eastern Regional Director).

- **Executive committee.** This smaller governing body, which averages seven members, has the authority to act on behalf of the entire board of directors. It may comprise the board officers, or it may include other members of the board in the interest of achieving balance and harmony. In about 40 percent of associations, for instance, members of the executive committee include the chief executive officer, the incoming chief elected officer, and the immediate past elected officer. Most associations use executive committee meetings as an interim decision-making measure between meetings of the full board of directors.

- **House (or assembly) of delegates.** Some associations, usually individual membership organizations, mirror the legislative branch of the United States government by having a delegate representation system that may be based on geography, special interest area, or other appropriate criteria. For instance, a national association of attorneys might have a delegate from each affiliated state association, as well as delegates who represent the interests of a particular region or type of legal practice. Because of the larger size of this organizational unit, it may convene only once or twice a year.

- **Standing committees.** On average, associations have 11 standing committees—ongoing groups that continue from one year to the next. Usually described in the bylaws, these committees focus on the long-term needs of the association as identified in the mission statement or strategic plan. According to *Policies and Procedures in Association Management*, the most common standing committees, in addition to the Executive Committee described above, are: budget or finance, nominating, membership, government affairs, and education.

A committee's composition should reflect the association's membership. If committee membership isn't representative of the general membership, either the committee or the members at large might feel disenfranchised from the association. This balance is especially important for the nominating committee, which is charged with identifying future leaders who reflect the organization's constituencies.

As on the board of directors, terms of service may last three years, with about one-third of the committee turning over each year. Some associations make annual appointments, with the provision that effective and productive committee members can be re-appointed for multiple years. To emphasize the committee's importance and accountability to the board of directors, many associations appoint a board member to chair each standing committee.

- **Ad hoc groups.** To keep pace with today's rapidly changing environment, many associations have increased their use of ad hoc groups, such as task forces or teams. They are often appointed by the chief elected officer, with input from the executive committee or board of directors.

These groups are self-limiting in both time and scope; they focus on short-term, specific needs—such as generating a solution to an organizational problem or the association's response to an emerging issue—and then disband when their work is complete. In fact, those characteristics make it somewhat easier to recruit volunteers who may be unable to make a greater commitment to the organization.

Because most ad hoc groups are formed for special purposes or functions, they require detailed objectives and desired outcomes. Electronic communications such as e-mail and conference calls can enable ad hoc groups to accomplish their short-term tasks without time-consuming, face-to-face meetings. This conserves the association's financial resources while involving more of the membership.

- **Special interest groups.** These groups represent a specialized or focused area of the industry or profession represented by the association. Special interest groups are usually transitional: They relate to a newly identified need or perhaps to an area where membership or interest is declining. By serving as an incubator, the association provides the support, resources, and volunteers that the group needs to identify and fulfill its mission.

Once that mission has been achieved, the special interest group and its leaders are often absorbed into other organizational structures of the association. But if the association hasn't supported the group, such as by assisting with meetings and providing a staff liaison, the group may break away and form a separate organization or form an alliance with a competing association.

- **Membership sections.** A special interest group may evolve into a permanent membership section that represents a geographic or functional area—for instance, a U.S.-based trade association may maintain an international section for its members who do business abroad. In some associations, sections operate much like an "association within an association," with their own elected leaders, budgets, and designated staff. Volunteer leaders may represent the section's interest within the association's overall governing body.

Strengthening the Volunteer Relationship

Associations depend upon volunteers to provide leadership within their organizational structures as well as to assist with events and programs, such as contributing articles to the association's publication, giving a presentation at its annual conference, or helping raise funds for its educational foundation. Activities related to attracting—and keeping—those valuable volunteers must be incorporated not only into the strategic plan but also into the culture of the association.

Those activities include:

- **Recruitment.** Getting involved in the association by attending or helping with events can get someone noticed, but it may take some effort to encourage that person to assume a leadership role. Current leaders—especially those who serve on the nominating committee—should always be on the lookout for knowledgeable, talented, and enthusiastic people who could eventually take over the responsibilities of top-ranking volunteers. By meeting and talking with members, both staff and current leaders will get some idea of their leadership potential and availability.

- **Volunteer Orientation.** Once potential leaders have agreed to become part of the governance structure, the association must acquaint them with their new roles and responsibilities. The board of directors, for instance, may have the responsibility of approving the association's financial and investment statements; an introduction to how those documents are organized and what they communicate would enable new board members to make well-informed decisions.

Three types of documents prove useful for providing volunteers with an understanding of the association's structure and operations:

1. *Legal,* including articles of incorporation and bylaws.

2. *Management,* such as association policies and procedures, financial reports, minutes of past meetings, and job descriptions for both volunteers and staff.

3. *Internal,* such as the association's code of ethics, organizational chart, and strategic plan.

What It Takes

Although by no means a complete list of leadership attributes and characteristics, the following list serves as a starting point for selecting volunteers to lead the association:

- **Proven performance.** Leadership requires knowledge, talent, skill, vitality, and the ability to make a difference. In the association environment, that translates into a solid track record of contributing to the success of programs, events, or projects.

- **Commitment.** Serving as an association leader is an honor and a reward—but it requires a demonstrated commitment to the organization and its mission and goals.

- **Time to serve.** Participating fully in association activities requires extra time to prepare for, travel to, and attend meetings.

- **Good health.** The often hectic and strenuous pace of volunteer leadership requires a good mental and physical condition.

- **Understanding of team work.** Many people contribute their efforts toward the realization of an association's goals and objectives—no one does it alone. Well-developed interpersonal and communication skills are essential to effective team work.

- **Sound judgment and integrity.** In many instances, popularity brings potential leaders into the limelight of the association. But popularity must be tempered with good judgment and integrity: Decisions may need to be made that are not popular among the members.

- **Communication and "teaching" skills.** By virtue of their position, current leaders serve as mentors and teachers to future leaders. Enthusiasm—a zest for serving the association—is an important ingredient that leaders must be able to pass along to their successors.

- **Ability to subordinate special interests.** Leaders often emerge because of their special expertise or effective representation of a specific membership constituency. Leadership, however, may require subordinating those special interests for the greater good of the entire association.

- **Exemplary personal conduct.** Leaders' behavior and attitudes can greatly influence others in the association. As a result, it's vital for them to have and exhibit a sensitivity to race, ethnic, gender, age, and other human differences.

- **Support systems.** The extra efforts required of volunteer leaders involve a substantial time commitment. Not only does this need to be understood by the person's employer but also by his or her family and friends.

The final consideration relates to the end of a volunteer's leadership tenure: the ability to bow out gracefully. Nothing can be more fractious to an association than a leader who continues to lead after his or her term has concluded.

Although many associations rely on staff and current leaders to conduct orientation and training, some are increasingly turning to outside consultants who have a working knowledge of governance structures and systems. In fact, a number of association chief executive officers trade the function of training one another's volunteer leaders. Whether the trainer comes from another association or a consulting firm, the rationale is that someone from the "outside" can deliver appropriate messages with a greater degree of objectivity.

Also gaining in popularity is mentoring—pairing an experienced board member with a newly elected one to answer questions, provide information, and simply serve as a friendly face in a possible sea of strangers.

While training is more task oriented, orientation provides an overview of the association and identifies how and where the new leader fits into the picture. Orientation—whether handled by one person or by a team of experienced leaders and staff—should provide new leaders with guidance on the specific task their committee, task force, or other organizational unit is to accomplish during their tenure.

- **Recognition.** For the many hours association volunteers spend away from their families, friends, and jobs—not to mention the weekends in airplanes or hotel rooms—they deserve recognition. Of course, volunteers gain recognition among their peers and even the public by contributing to association publications, giving presentations at conferences, and serving as a spokesperson for the association. Still, all leaders should be formally recognized for their service and contributions when their volunteer commitment ends.

The award need not be elaborate or expensive but should be appropriate and presented with sincerity. Recognition may be as simple as providing a special ribbon for all volunteer leaders to wear at the convention. Or, it might entail arranging upgraded accommodations or special in-room amenities for those who travel to association meetings. One association might provide volunteers with desk items (mugs, letter openers, and so forth) carrying its logo, while another might host a thank-you reception and give engraved plaques to volunteers.

Because many volunteers serve in order to make a contribution to their fellow members, recognition of their efforts should take place in the presence of their peers—the association's members.

- **Support.** As *Policies and Procedures in Association Management* points out, more than half of associations don't reimburse committee members for the travel, food, and lodging expenses incurred to attend meetings (the majority, however, do reimburse those expenses for the chief elected officer). Yet associations that aren't in the position to reimburse expenses can still demonstrate support of their volunteers.

For instance, volunteers accept the risk of personal liability when they accept a position as an officer or director. Although successful legal action against association officers and directors is rare, the potential consequences of an action initiated in today's litigious society might warrant the purchase of professional liability insurance. A comprehensive insurance plan can shield volunteers from being held personally liable for actions taken on behalf of the association.

The most visible means of volunteer support, however, is staff assistance. In addition to serving as the liaison to the chief executive officer, staff can lighten a volunteer leader's load by preparing meeting materials; handling logistics for meetings; drafting and distributing minutes; and providing information on association policies, procedures, and programs.

The Staff-Volunteer Relationship

A balance between volunteer and staff involvement is needed for the overall mission and goals of the association to be achieved. Volunteers have "real world" experience and expertise because they operate in—and are therefore sensitive to—the environment that influences members' needs. Staff has the experience and expertise needed to administer and operate the association so it can meet those needs.

To put it simply:

- The role of volunteers is to ensure that the association serves the needs of its members, by establishing direction and policies for programs, products, and services. They focus on longer term, strategic issues.
- The role of staff is to keep the association moving ahead in the direction and according to the policies established by volunteers, by implementing procedures that deliver the programs, products, and services to the members. They focus on shorter term, operational issues.

In some associations, achieving an appropriate balance between the volunteer and staff roles and responsibilities is fraught with anxiety and causes much consternation and frustration to both volunteers and staff. As noted above, a delineation that clarifies the value and appropriate role of each party can help avoid or alleviate such situations.

Role clarification, for instance, should emphasize that committees, task forces, sections, special interest groups, and the chief executive officer are accountable to the board of directors. In turn, the board answers to the membership for how the association is governed and managed.

Open and frequent communication—through newsletters, periodicals, annual meetings, chapter or section gatherings, and so forth—provides accountability back to the membership. An increasing number of associations now provide fax-on-demand services and a web site, not only as a means of disseminating information but also to ensure that they remain accountable to members who depend upon receiving certain products and services. In addition, some associations have turned to issuing annual and quarterly reports, long used by business and industry, to communicate their financial and strategic decisions to their stakeholders—their members.

Partners in Leadership

Achieving open communication depends greatly on appointing a liaison between the board of directors and the various organizational units. The chief executive officer typically assumes this role of liaison along with his or her other responsibilities to ensure that the board receives timely and accurate information regarding the activities of the various organizational units.

The chief executive officer may channel much of that information through the chief elected officer, which is why the two people should function as a true team for the association to remain on a positive and forward course. If, for example, one withholds information from the other, or if the two have widely differing opinions about the association's strategic direction, confusion may result among the volunteers as well as the staff.

Working as a team entails learning about one another's strengths, weaknesses, hopes, and aspirations. That may be accomplished by attending seminars aimed at building partnerships between the chief elected and executive officers or by observing one another in action. For instance, some associations have a tradition of inviting the newly elected officer to their offices to meet staff and observe how board policies are carried out at the operational level. Likewise, other organizations routinely send the chief executive officer to visit the chief elected officer in his or her work environment.

On an ongoing basis, many chief elected and chief executive officers spend several hours on the phone every week or two—or trade frequent e-mail messages—to coordinate their schedules, discuss upcoming activities and emerging concerns, and brainstorm solutions to problems that may have arisen. By becoming familiar with the other's personality, working style, and decision-making preferences—and by remaining in frequent contact—the two parties can build a partnership that avoids power struggles and advances the work of the association.

References and Suggested Reading

Able, Edward H., Jr., *Future Perspectives*, Foundation of the American Society of Association Executives, Washington, D.C., 1985.

Conners, Tracy D., *The Nonprofit Organization Handbook*, McGraw-Hill Board Co., New York, 1980.

Drucker, Peter F., *Management*, Harper & Row, New York, 1973.

Dunlop, James J., *Leading the Association: Striking the Right Balance Between Staff and Volunteers*, Foundation of the American Society of Association Executives, Washington, D.C., 1989.

Eadie, Douglas C., *Boards That Work: A Practical Guide to Building Effective Association Boards*, American Society of Association Executives, Washington, D.C., 1995.

Foundation of the American Society of Association Executives, *Critical Competencies of Association Executives*, Washington, D.C., 1979.

Greif, Joseph, *Managing Membership Societies*, Foundation of the American Society of Association Executives, Washington, D.C., 1979.

Imming, Bernard J., *Fundamentals of Association Management: The Volunteer*, American Society of Association Executives, Washington, D.C., 1982.

——, *Getting Involved: The Challenge of Committee Participation*, American Society of Association Executives, Washington, D.C., 1980.

——, *A Special Responsibility*, Foundation of the American Society of Association Executives, Washington, D.C., 1984.

Jacobs, Jerald A., *Association Law Handbook*, American Society of Association Executives, Washington, D.C., 1996.

Levitt, Theodore, *The Third Sector: New Tactics for a Responsive Society*, AMACOM, New York, 1973.

Schlegel, John F., *Enhancing Committee Effectiveness*, American Society of Association Executives, Washington, D.C., 1994.

Snyder, David Pearce, and Gregg Edwards, *Future Forces*, Foundation of the American Society of Association Executives, Washington, D.C., 1984.

Webster, George D., *The Law of Associations*, Mathew Bender Company, New York, 1982.

Wayne E. Leroy, CAE , is executive vice president of the Association of Higher Education Facilities Officers, Alexandria, Virginia.

CHAPTER 2

DEVELOPING POLICIES AND PROCEDURES

JONE R. SIENKIEWICZ, CMP, CAE

Associations without policies and procedures are like ships without rudders. They may experience smooth sailing on calm days, but the minute a storm begins brewing they risk losing their way in troubled waters. Policies and procedures keep an association on course by giving members and staff the guidelines for making consistent and logical decisions as critical issues arise.

Understanding the difference between the two is essential to ensuring an association's success:

- *Policies*, which spell out standards of conduct and decision making, articulate the strategy and philosophy of an organization's governing body, be it a board of directors, executive council, or assembly of delegates. Developed and adopted by volunteer leaders, policies provide the framework upon which the association builds its procedures.

- *Procedures* delineate how to administer the policy; in other words, they spell out the steps needed to turn a particular concept into reality. Both volunteers and staff can develop procedures, although staff implements them as part of the association's operations.

For example, an association's board of directors may propose and adopt a policy stating that the annual convention will take place every year on the third weekend in May. The corresponding procedures, which provide staff with a plan of action to follow, might dictate that the meeting occur in a particular type of facility (urban hotel, suburban conference center, or resort), over a particular set of days or hours, and with a particular schedule (general sessions, educational seminars, recreational activities, and so forth).

Involving officers, board members, committee leaders, and staff in the development and review process helps shape usable, enforceable policies. To provide consistency as staff and volunteer leadership changes—and to lessen the possibility of misinterpretation—written procedures should accompany each policy. Although they can be elaborate, written procedures don't have to be complicated to get the job done.

Once supporting procedures have been drafted and approved—by either the governing body or, more likely, by the chief executive officer—legal counsel should review the total package to ensure that the policies and applicable procedures comply with all applicable federal and state laws.

In general, association policies and procedures address three areas: governance, management and operations, and public image and public policy.

Governance

Policies in this area relate to how the governing body governs both itself and the association. They include the following:

- **Membership and organizational structure.** Such policies define the categories of membership (regular, associate, affiliate, and so forth) and corresponding dues structures, as well as such things as whether the association is incorporated, its nonprofit tax code, and whether legal counsel is hired, retained, or used as needed.

  Because the Internal Revenue Service (IRS) has begun to question whether associate members are truly members—as opposed to vendors buying access to a specialized market or services—more associations are refining their membership policies to spell out what roles associate members may fill within the governance structure. The more involved associate members are in leadership roles, the less likely the IRS seems to tax their membership dues.

Guidelines for Development

Having a list of questions to answer will help define policy concerns and set the stage for drafting the supporting procedures. Additionally, developing a format for a written policy manual will provide consistency throughout the association.

Here is a simple, six-step methodology for setting policies and procedures; the smallest organization can use it to develop and maintain guidelines, or a larger organization with more complicated needs can expand upon it. To illustrate the process, consider the example of the Anything For A Buck Association (AFABA):

1. **Define the question or problem requiring a policy statement.** AFABA wants to form a foundation to award college scholarships to the children of members.

2. **Analyze the alternative solutions.** Questions might include: Should students be entering freshmen in college, or can they be at any level? Is the scholarship based solely on academics, or does community service play a role? What is the timetable for receiving and reviewing applications? How many scholarships should be given? In what amount? Will the money be paid directly to the college or to the student?

3. **Select the most reasonable alternative.** After analyzing the alternatives and choosing the answers that best suit the association's needs, drafting the policy and related procedures is easy.

4. **Develop the policy that speaks to the accepted alternative.** For instance, AFABA's policy statement might read: The AFABA Scholarship will be awarded to entering college freshmen. The children of all members will

be eligible for this award. The scholarship will be awarded in May. Deadline for receipt of applications will be the last Friday in March.

5. **Develop procedures that will implement the policy.** In this example, the procedures might read as follows:

- AFABA staff will design an announcement and application that incorporate the criteria for the scholarship.
- The draft application and announcement will be sent to the AFABA Scholarship Committee for review and comment.
- Upon approval from the committee, AFABA staff will proceed with production of the application and announcement.
- Scholarship announcements and applications will be sent to all members with the January issue of the *AFABA Journal* and again in a stand-alone mailing in February.
- Scholarship applications received in the AFABA office will be date-stamped on the cover and held for forwarding to the Scholarship Committee for its April meeting.
- Completed applications will be sent to the committee for review not later than two weeks before its meeting.

6. **Evaluate the results to identify the need for change.** AFABA might build this step into its procedure as follows:

- AFABA staff and the Scholarship Committee will review the policy and administrative procedures for this scholarship annually.
- Changes in this policy require the approval of the AFABA Board of Directors.
- Changes in administration require the approval of the Scholarship Committee.

- **Volunteer leadership.** Associations use these policies to spell out terms of office, explain the selection or election process (including guidelines for campaigning or the role of the nominating committee in preparing a slate of candidates), and describe any reimbursements available to volunteers for board or committee service.

- **Related entities.** Many associations establish for-profit subsidiaries for generating nondues revenue or set up nonprofit foundations for advancing the industry or profession through research and educational activities. In either case, the parent association should develop separate policies and procedures for governing and operating the spin-off organization, such as the size and composition of its governing body. Keeping records—and possibly personnel—exclusive to the subsidiary or foundation will facilitate compliance with tax-code regulations and minimize confusion in day-to-day operations.

In addition, the parent association should establish a set of policies that explain the relationship between it and the subsidiary or foundation. Especially helpful are policies that outline the management fee, if any, paid to the parent organization; the percentage of shared overhead; the amount of dividends or royalties to be paid and to whom; and reporting responsibilities.

- **Association management.** The chief executive officer is accountable to the association's governing body; it, in turn, reviews his or her performance and determines the appropriate compensation and benefits. To ensure consistency in the review process as volunteer leaders change, governance policies often outline the volunteer positions that participate in the process—for example, the chief elected officer and his or her successor may conduct the review each year on behalf of the entire board.

    Although not often discussed, a succession policy helps protect the association in the event of the death or abrupt termination of the chief executive officer. It would cover areas such as which staff person, department vice president, or director would be in charge on a interim basis; what salary or benefit payments would be paid to the estate of the departed executive; and what procedure would be followed to seek the services of another executive. (Note: a succession policy must be consistent with the terms of any employment contract that exists between the association and chief executive officer, primarily in the area of severance or death benefits.)

    It's helpful to have policies in place to guide the work of a search committee, even though the committee is ad hoc in nature. The policy may, for example, designate the incoming elected chairman or president as the head of the group charged with finding and evaluating the next chief staff executive. The accompanying procedures should spell out the time frame for the search, how the candidates will be presented to the board, and any reimbursement of volunteer expenses associated with the search.

- **Finance.** At the governance level, policies generally address the association's fiscal year, the amount of money targeted for or maintained in reserves, what types of investments are to be considered, and who has the authority to invest the funds.

Operations and Management

These policies, which deal with day-to-day operations of the association, include the following:

- **Credentialing.** Many associations offer a credentialing program—either accreditation, certification, licensure, or standardization—as a means of ensuring professional competence in the field they represent or to establish standards. Policies must spell out eligibility requirements (such as the minimum number of years working in the industry or profession or passing an exam), as well as any criteria for renewal of the credential (such as attending a specific number of continuing education seminars within a certain number of years).

    Legal counsel should review the policies with an eye toward antitrust concerns and the potential for legal or tax liability.

- **Finances.** Sound financial policies can reduce costs by putting effective accounting practices in place. Topics addressed are the method of accounting used (cash, accrual, or a combination of the two), the number of signatures needed on checks (and who can sign them), the content of and schedule for financial reports presented to the governing body, and the method of reporting annually to the general membership.

- **Government affairs.** These policies encompass such issues as who serves as the lead lobbyist for the association, at what levels the association monitors legislation or regulatory actions, and whether the association operates a political action committee (PAC). In the latter case, procedures might cover how the PAC is administered, at what level PAC contributions could be made, and how contributions are acknowledged.

- **Meetings/Conventions.** Policy issues include the number and type of meetings to be held, whether an exhibition or trade show will take place in conjunction with one or more meetings, the geographic pattern of site selection, and who has the authority to select the site. Other issues of concern might be the design and content of the educational program, related activities (golf tournaments, family programs, and so forth), and who has the authority to enter into contracts on behalf of the association.

Policies for international meetings or world congresses must take into consideration the secretariat of those events. For instance, the host organization's meeting policies may not coincide with those of the co-sponsoring association. The production of a world congress can be time-consuming and nerve-racking. Imagine planning an annual meeting in three, four, or five different countries for people of such diversity that the most innocent of remarks, slights, or omissions can ruin the event. Policies established for these events must transcend those of any single organization within the secretariat. To achieve a balance that provides the most advantageous position for all groups involved, tact and diplomacy are essential.

The host organization might naturally assume a leadership role in not only contracting with vendors but also in setting the policies and procedures for administration of the congress itself. A trap to avoid is assuming that the policies and procedures in place for the host organization's annual event(s) are acceptable to the co-hosts.

For example, the host organization may have a policy that allows exhibitors to set up their booths on Saturday and Sunday for a Monday opening. One of the co-hosts may not allow such practices on the basis of religious beliefs. In order to have the exhibits set up and ready for Monday, a compromise may have to be reached that, while the activity will be allowed, it will not be posted or publicly announced. In other words, those who need to know will know, and those who may be offended and need not know would not be included in the informational loop. Another example might be the use of first names or nicknames on badges. Some cultures welcome this informality as a way of "breaking the ice." Other cultures consider it an insult to call people by their first names before you become well-acquainted.

In addition to discussing cultural likes and dislikes, it might be appropriate to simply designate which group's policies take precedence in instances where cultural considerations are not part of the equation.

- **Membership and dues.** While governance policies outline who members are, operational policies outline how those individuals or companies are treated. For instance, an association may have a policy of answering a member's question within 24 hours or communicating with all members at least once a month.

  Associations with chapters require policies for serving and communicating with them. Items for consideration include the costs of services provided by the national to each chapter, which level has the responsibility for invoicing or rebating membership dues, and how chapters are represented at national meetings.

  Some associations stipulate that their members pay dues based on a calendar year; others tie dues payments to their fiscal year or to the member's anniversary date. The amount of dues can be flat, sliding, or a percentage of some tangible number related to the industry (such as sales volume, number of employees, and so forth).

  Whatever dues criteria are established, supporting procedures should outline how the association handles late-paying or nonrenewing members. For example, procedures might address when and how many times dues will be billed, how to accommodate members who wish to stretch dues payments over several months or quarters of the year, and when non-paying members will be removed from the active membership list.

- **Office administration.** Issues range from the hours of operation to the use of computer equipment by staff, from the way the phone is answered to which employees are covered by liability insurance.

- **Personnel.** These policies set the tone of the workplace: If they're strict and unyielding, they may alienate employees. On the other hand, liberal policies can weaken the position of management and jeopardize professionalism. Personnel policies usually cover sick and annual leave (how it's accrued, the number of paid holidays, and so forth); insurance benefits; reimbursement of staff travel expenses; and grounds for termination, leaves of absence, outplacement services, and severance pay.

  Because this area is heavily regulated, it's best to consult with both a human resources professional and an attorney to ensure policies comply with both federal and state laws.

- **Publishing.** The vast majority of associations publish at least one periodical. Whether it's a one-page, one-color newsletter or a slick, four-color magazine or journal, the print vehicle requires policies such as whether advertising is accepted and from whom, how sales representatives are compensated, how—and whether—members review material before it's printed, and the requirements for submitting material for publication.

- **Services.** Policies in this area might spell out who can have access to the association's information services, library, fax-on-demand service, referral program, or group insurance plan. Antitrust concerns dictate that associations consult with legal counsel when drafting policies that relate to pricing structures and participation in group-purchasing plans.

If the association maintains relationships with suppliers through affinity programs, this area would also include guidelines for selecting the suppliers, promoting or marketing the product or service, and determining royalties.

Public Image and Public Policy

Every association serves or comes into contact with a number of publics, ranging from its elected leaders to its general membership, from the narrow niche of the specialized trade press to the general public. With that in mind, policies typically cover the following:

- **Media relations.** The designation of an official spokesperson for the association is, unfortunately, often omitted from the policy manual. Many associations limit the role of spokesperson to the CEO or the chief elected officer—either exclusively or in tandem. For instance, a trade association might designate the CEO to speak on issues affecting the industry, while the top elected leader addresses association-related issues. Another policy might identify exceptions, such as when other staff members or volunteers take on the role of association spokespeople while testifying before a regulatory or legislative body.

  Media relations policies may also spell out what media receive which type of news. For instance, some association news releases may be appropriate for distribution to the trade press exclusively, while other news with more affect on the general public would warrant releases to the national media.

- **Crisis management.** Most associations, at one time or another, face a negative situation within their industry or profession—or perhaps within the organization itself. Having a crisis-management policy, coupled with a set of procedures that define what to do in specific circumstances, not only helps maintain the association's image but also assists staff in fulfilling their roles. Policies need to designate a spokesperson, describe who will serve on the task force that sets the ground rules for a response, and list who must be contacted immediately and in what order.

  Supporting procedures should outline which board and staff positions do what and, more important, which ones should do nothing at all.

Under Review

After policies have been developed and put in place, it's important to ensure they continue to serve the association's ever-changing needs. Some guidelines to consider are:

1. Set an annual date to review all existing policies and procedures—and stick to it. An obvious time might be during the annual review of the bylaws. In most cases, if bylaws changes are needed or recommended, policies and procedures will be affected and may need to be modified or even abolished.

2. Involve staff in reviewing the association's policies and procedures. The people who must enforce, carry out, and be responsible for and to the policies are the ones who can most efficiently and effectively see the needed changes. The end result is not only better policies and procedures but also a staff "buy-in" to facilitate adherence to them.

3. Consider using past presidents to review policies and procedures that affect external entities, such as members, the general public, and the industry or profession.

4. Set aside a short period of time to try out the new policies and procedures before finalizing them. It is easier to change something that is temporary than to revise something the board has approved and made a permanent part of the association's structure.

Jone R. Sienkiewicz, CMP, CAE, is president and CEO of the Washington Group, Inc., an association management company in Fairfax, Virginia.

CHAPTER 3

STRATEGIC MANAGEMENT

BRUCE BUTTERFIELD, CAE

Alice: Would you tell me, please, which way I ought to go from here?

Cheshire Cat: That depends a good deal on where you want to get to.

Alice: I don't much care where.

Cheshire Cat: Then it doesn't matter which way you go.

— *Alice in Wonderland,* by Lewis Carroll

Many organizations are like Alice. They have no idea where they are going, so any way will do. Unfortunately, this approach leads to disorganization, misuse of resources, and dissatisfied members and customers.

Strategic management can resolve these problems. It's the process by which an association assesses its strengths and weaknesses, identifies present and future member needs, and empowers volunteers and staff to provide excellent products and services that respond to those needs. Strategic management involves monitoring and evaluating environmental opportunities and problems in light of the organization's strengths and weaknesses and then shaping a coherent set of strategies, programs, and budgets to take advantage of these circumstances.

Strategic management has four steps:

1. **Strategic thinking** assesses the future effects of outside forces on the organization. A key component is gathering information and opinions from important constituencies to give planners a solid basis for decision making.

2. **Strategic planning** creates the association's future based on strategic thinking. It includes developing a vision of the future and identifying what the association needs to do today to achieve the vision.

3. **Strategic implementation** translates the strategic plan into detailed programs and budgets—the work plan of the association—and evaluates them to ensure that they meet member or customer needs.

4. **Evaluation and feedback,** based on data and activity reports, determine how closely performance matches the plan.

Strategic management involves asking a set of basic questions: Where is the association now, and how does it fit into its environment? What is the association's vision of its desired future? If no changes are made, where will the association be in one year, two years, five years, and ten years? Are the answers acceptable? If not, what specific steps need to be taken now to bring about the desired future? What are the risks and payoffs of those steps? What evaluation and control mechanisms are needed to ensure that the steps are carried out? What provisions should be made for reconsideration if circumstances change?

Strategic management and strategic planning are *not* synonymous. Strategic planning is only one step in developing a strategic-management action plan that is practical, serves the best interests of the organization, and can be implemented (see Chapter 4). Unless it's an integral part of the association's overall management structure, a strategic plan represents an exercise in futility.

When asked for a copy of their strategic plan, many association executives mistakenly pull out their long-range plan. Strategic planning, however, is not long-range planning. The latter addresses what to do in the future, while strategic planning is what you do now to achieve your vision of the future.

Although many associations do long-range planning, few engage in strategic planning. Even when they claim to have a strategic plan, many associations have nothing more than a multi-year budget document. But extrapolating the current year's budget figures or extending a historic growth curve into the future is not planning: Basing decisions principally on budgetary considerations doesn't prepare an association to cope successfully with future challenges. Many associations begin their planning process with their budget, but budgeting should be virtually the last step in the planning process.

Long-range plans rarely work. Strategic plans do, when they are part of the institutionalized strategic-management process outlined below.

Step 1: Strategic Thinking

Strategic thinking begins with an *environmental scan*—a look at the future world in which the association must operate. An environmental scan enables the association to base its decisions on fact and substance rather than conjecture and serves as a baseline for consensus on the board and within the staff.

Every association operates within two environments—the external (the world outside the association) and the internal (volunteer leadership, membership, staff). An environmental scan needs to encompass each of these in terms of the current situation and alternative future scenarios as they affect the association's history, culture, and traditions.

No association can hope to respond to members' needs and earn their continued support unless it regularly learns what they think of the issues that concern them. It's unrealistic to expect elected leaders to serve as an accurate barometer of member views. Instead, an association must use member-needs research to judge how well it meets three "fitness tests":

1. **Fitness to standard:** determining what members consider to be standards of excellence in products and services currently offered and ensuring those standards are met.
2. **Fitness to need:** asking members what new services they would value and fulfilling those needs with excellence.

3. **Fitness to future needs:** staying a step ahead of members by identifying emerging trends and critical issues and responding with excellent new products and services before members realize they need them.

THE EXTERNAL ENVIRONMENT

Five forces affect the general external environment in which an association operates. These "spheres" can influence the association but are difficult for the association to influence in return:

- **Econosphere**—the world market for products and services, gross national product trends, interest rates, inflation/deflation, and financial markets. This sphere also encompasses regional conditions, employment/unemployment, energy, monetary policy, income, skill requirements, defense/budget priorities, and new-business formation.

- **Sociosphere**—lifestyle changes, consumer activism, education, career expectations, demographics, values, role models, and mass communications. Population growth/decline also falls within this category, as do family formation, population shifts, family stability, life expectancy, birth rates, literacy, crime, and drug use.

- **Technosphere**—automation, productivity, the Internet and World Wide Web, biotechnology, and new products. Also included are laboratory-to-market transfers, federal research and development, patents, international technology transfer, and building-code developments.

- **Politisphere**—in addition to the current occupant of the White House, this sphere includes control of federal, state, and local governments; the justice system; environmental protection; antitrust regulations; tax and employment laws; discrimination; foreign trade regulations; government stability; federal/state balance; and international conditions (for example, terrorism).

- **Biosphere**—conditions in the natural environment that may limit the association's freedom of action, such as air and water pollution, depletion of natural resources (for instance, rain forests and petroleum), global warming, endangered species, erosion of farm land, and water shortages.

As with any gaze into the crystal ball, simply making assumptions about the likely shape of the future is likely to be wrong. Making assumptions based on *alternative futures*, however, enables the association to frame contingency plans that better prepare it to shape the future to its liking and to deal successfully with any outcomes. An alternative-futures assessment uses information from the five spheres and drafts scenarios that could develop.

This exercise offers the best way to deal with crises—which is to prevent them or, if that's not possible, to have contingency plans in place to deal with them. In fact, after analyzing 50,000 news stories, the Institute for Crisis Management determined that only 14 percent of business crises are unexpected; 86 percent are "smoldering"—trends that could have been identified before becoming crises.

Many clues to possible futures have already emerged. For example:

- The young, middle-aged, and elderly people of the next decade are already available to study. Projections of their behavior can be made from current data.
- Worldwide economic trends often take years to change direction, so current indicators can provide a glimpse of the emerging economy of the 21st century.
- Political trends already in place may determine the shape of government for many years, such as a relatively youthful Supreme Court, the collapse of the Soviet Union, and the emergence of China, to name a few.
- Emerging technologies might be extrapolated into new products and services.

Some managers shrug off alternative-futures assessment as too theoretical. But the five forces have brought about profound changes in the closing years of the 20th century, including the worst stock market crash in 50 years and an unprecedented bull market (econosphere); the aging of America and the dramatic increase in working mothers (sociosphere); the explosive growth of the Internet and wireless personal communications (technosphere); the United States' shift from a creditor nation to a debtor nation and the collapse of Communism in much of the world (politisphere); and the destruction of tropical forests and the worldwide decline of lakes from acid rain (biosphere).

An association that had used alternative-futures assessment to prepare for any of these developments would have been in a highly advantageous position.

Scanning the general environment will identify the association's principal opportunities and threats. But while the general external environment has a powerful effect on the association, it is difficult to influence or change. In contrast, the *specific* external environment—those forces in society that directly affect and are directly affected by the association—can be changed.

Another term for those forces are an association's key "publics" or audiences. They include:
- Government officials and regulators
- Communities served by the organization and its members
- The news media
- Special interest or consumer groups
- Competing organizations
- Suppliers
- Customers

THE INTERNAL ENVIRONMENT

Scanning the internal environment—the association's leadership, members, management, and staff—will identify its strengths and weaknesses so that it can successfully address external opportunities and threats. The internal environment encompasses three areas:

1. **Structure**—how the association is organized in terms of communications, authority, and work flow. This area deals with the chain of command: the relationship between volunteer leaders and staff, the relationships among departments and peer groups, and the relationships with members.

2. **Culture**—the beliefs, expectations, and values that predominate within the association. For example, the organization may have strong top-down direc-

tion or be consensus-driven; it may value innovation and risk taking or favor a conservative course of action.

3. **Resources**—the association's financial, human, and capital assets. These include volunteer leadership, staff, and managerial talent; dues, contributions, earnings, and investments; and physical assets, buildings, and reserves.

A Clear Direction

The environmental scan sets the framework for a possible future by examining scenarios that may possibly emerge. Once it's complete, the board of directors and the chief executive officer have the necessary information to identify the association's future opportunities as limited by future threats.

Next, the leadership must articulate an organizational vision that is possible within the emerging reality. This process is known as "visioning." Identifying an inspirational vision around which everyone can rally helps create a strong association culture. Without such a vision, leaders, staff, and members will inevitably wander off in different directions.

Step 2: Strategic Planning

This step uses the environmental scan to develop a mission statement, identify goals and objectives, and adopt a strategy for achieving them. It's best accomplished by a strategic management committee that's appointed annually and chaired by the person next in line to become the chief elected officer. This choice of committee chair ensures that the plan will serve as the basis for the association's activities during the ensuing year and those that follow.

Ideally, the committee is small enough to function easily, with a maximum of 15 members (a board of directors could perform this function as well). It should include representatives from the board and the chief executive officer (CEO), all of whom should have participated in the environmental scanning process. Staggered terms ensure that there's no gap in institutional memory.

The committee has the responsibility for developing a multi-year strategic plan. This entails making decisions based on the association's overall needs, not on personal, chapter, regional, or sectional considerations. Committee members must focus on the future, not on the past or present, and avoid overcommitting the association's resources. The strategic planning they undertake must do the following:

- **Focus on meeting core member or customer needs.** After all, planning is done to ensure that resources are being applied effectively to produce the products and services desired by members and customers.

- **Be a process, not an event.** To be the force that drives the association, planning must be more than just an exercise.

- **Be continuous.** The forces affecting associations are constantly changing. Leaders must continually revisit planning assumptions to make sure they're current and still valid.

- **Address outcomes.** Getting something accomplished is the whole point of planning.
- **Be based on research, not opinions of the few.** Although it's tempting to assume that elected leaders know what is best for members, such an assumption is tantamount to a doctor's self-diagnosis.
- **Be done by small groups with large-group input.** Large planning groups tend to focus on parochial interests (chapter, region, or section) rather than the broad interests of the association. They also tend to create "wish books" rather than plans.

ON A MISSION

An association's *mission* identifies its most critical priorities in realizing its vision by addressing the opportunities and threats identified in the environmental scan.

Many associations have mission statements that, unfortunately, often consist of pious platitudes or have become obsolete. But the mission statement is a living document that should address the association's most important current challenges and opportunities. In short, an association's mission statement describes the businesses it's in.

Goals grow out of the mission. In fact, goals often restate the principal activities identified in the mission. Strategic planning involves program goals (which describe what the association does) and management goals (which describe what the association needs to carry out its programs). Program goals address products and services, while management goals address structure, culture, and resources. Form follows function, meaning that an association must determine program goals before developing management goals.

> ## A Point of Clarification
>
> Associations often confuse purpose and mission. The association's purpose is *why* it exists. Its mission describes *what* it does—what businesses it is in.
>
> As illustrated by this example of a fictitious association, here's how the two differ:
>
> - **Purpose:** The purpose of the Scuba Divers Association is to bring together recreational scuba divers from all walks of life to share and promote their common interest in sport diving.
> - **Mission:** The mission of the Scuba Divers Association is to support protection of the underwater environment, promote safe and responsible diving, give recreational divers a unified voice in matters that affect them, and enhance opportunities to engage in the sport.

Ideally, goals are:
- **Results oriented**—an outcome is stated.
- **A definition of general results**—the outcome is stated in broad, rather than specific, terms.
- **Long term**—no specific deadline is set for accomplishment.
- **Ranked**—goals must be listed in order of priority as determined by research and strategic thinking. This is helpful when the time comes to allocate resources.

Objectives and Strategies

A strategic plan is like a funnel—large at the top, small at the bottom. Objectives (which describe specific outcomes) and strategies (which describe the steps for achieving those outcomes) move the plan from the top to the bottom, from the general to the specific.

Objectives and strategies must be measurable and have deadlines for accomplishment that staff have helped develop—because staff carry out strategic implementation. The deadline for an objective is within a particular year; the deadline for a strategy is within a particular month in that year. Strategic management requires that each goal and objective list not only supporting strategies but also the person (or position) accountable for results.

Here's an example of how a goal leads to objectives and strategies:

Goal: Become the industry's principal resource for professional development.

Objective: Provide six new business management courses by (year); responsibility—director of education.

Strategy: Develop partnering opportunities with a leading university business

---

What's the Plan?

A useful strategic plan exhibits several characteristics. Specifically, it should be:

- **A set of priorities.** Everything the association wants to do is not of equal importance. By setting priorities, the plan can be adjusted according to changing needs or resources without doing harm to the programs and services that members value most.

- **Achievable, measurable, and time sensitive.** Keeping in mind that it's better to do a few important things well than many things poorly, planners must ensure that the association can realistically accomplish all it plans. The strategic plan also needs to be measurable and contain deadlines so that it is clear when activities have been accomplished.

- **Flexible and responsive to changing conditions.** The plan is a road map for the association's future, but sometimes a detour may be necessary if a crisis looms, a new opportunity arises, or resources change.

- **Short and simple.** Plans that fill up a thick three-ring binder will sit on a shelf. The plan needs to focus on the most important things to accomplish.

- **A unit, not a menu.** The strategic plan is not a wish book that leaders pore over before picking out their personal choices. Everything in the plan needs to be accomplished—unless a good and justifiable reason arises to change it. Conversely, the association should not do things that are not in its plan.

- **The means to an end, not an end in itself.** The plan enables the association to reach its destination; it is not the destination. Creating a plan simply for the sake of creation is a wasteful and futile activity.

- **Based on a three-year period.** The strategic plan needs to be a rolling plan. In other words, one year should drop off the plan and a new year be added annually so the plan always covers a three-year time line.

school by (month and year); responsibility—assistant director of education.

Policies flow directly from strategic planning and provide both volunteers and staff with a framework for decision making. They provide limitations on action but do not specify actions, which empowers people to be innovative and to do their best.

Well-designed policies express the association culture so thoroughly and are so well-understood that everyone in the association instinctively adheres to them. They relieve elected officers and senior staff from constantly providing detailed direction and guidance to others in the association and can help prevent crises (see Chapter 2).

Step 3: Strategy Implementation

In this step, the association puts its strategies and policies into action through allocation of the association's resources. Whereas volunteer leaders—assisted by staff—have the responsibility for strategic planning, staff—with the assistance of volunteers—carry out strategy implementation.

Strategy implementation has three components:

1. **Programs.** These serve as the step-by-step blueprints for converting objectives and strategies into concrete realities. Association programs (encompassing products, services, and events) fall into one of two categories:

   • **Those that directly support its mission,** such as the government relations function—representing members' political views to legislators and policy makers. These programs exist to achieve outcomes defined in the strategic plan. As a result, they should appear under the appropriate objective in the strategic plan and be listed in priority order, according to how directly each helps to achieve that objective.

   • **Those that are primarily sources of revenue,** such as trade shows and affinity programs. These programs are designed primarily to supplement dues and support the programs directly related to the association's mission.

2. **Procedures.** Procedures are specific, sequential steps for the tasks required to complete the programs.

3. **Budgets.** Budgets express the association's programs in monetary terms. Associations should draw up budgets to fund programs, which are the tangible result of the mission and strategic plan. Instead, many draw up programs based on their budget; in other words, they're budget-driven rather than strategy-driven.

Staying Focused

When translating a strategic plan into a work plan and budget, the association must focus on each program through a *strategic prism*—a succinct statement summarizing the association's business strategy. Take, for example, this strategic prism: "The association will be sharply focused on core issues that are vital to the broad base of its membership." During a time of cutbacks and scarce resources, putting programs to this test will screen out the ones that aren't essential to most of the association's members.

Other prisms can be applied to specific products and services. For example:

- If we were not doing this, would we start doing it now?
- Are we working in the right areas?
- Do we need to change our focus?
- What does this look like when we do it?
- Is it important?
- Can we afford it?

In many associations, an ongoing clash of wills occurs over the proper roles of volunteers and staff. Volunteers often think they have an unlimited right to tell staff what to do. Staff often believe that they are better informed and should play a greater role in policy making and deciding on goals and objectives.

Volunteers and staff have complementary and equally important roles, but a Great Wall of China needs to be erected between them that neither should cross. The role of volunteers is to create a future for the association by developing its mission, objectives, and policies. Staff can provide input, but the governing body makes the decisions.

On the other side of the wall, the roles are reversed: Staff implements what the governing body has decided. They may call upon volunteers to assist in carrying out the programs they develop to reach the board's objectives. Programs, budgets, and procedures are the job of first-line and middle management, with evaluation and control by senior management.

Step 4: Evaluation and Feedback

Successful strategic management depends on prompt, unbiased feedback. Every manager should receive performance data and activity reports that compare actual performance with what's called for in the plan. This step requires an evaluation of results, not activities. Volunteer leaders and staff executives who supervise and evaluate daily activities have their eyes on the wrong ball; instead, they should concern themselves with whether staff is reaching strategic objectives.

An approach called *management by exception* can help in this regard. It encourages responsible staff and others to develop their own plans to achieve the goals and objectives established by the board of directors. Through feedback, staff receive information on how well they're meeting their goals and adhering to the budget. This allows each person to use his or her unique personality style and skills to achieve the desired results. Management need only be notified when an exception to the agreed-upon plan arises. Notification is done in time to make necessary adjustments to keep the plan on target.

These plans then serve as the basis for performance evaluations. Management by exception releases the creativity of all members of the association and ensures that evaluation and recognition programs are tied to results. In turn, those results are directly related to the association's strategic objectives.

Putting Programs to the Test

Programs that financially support an association's mission-related activities require the same kind of rigorous market analysis that any private-sector business venture might endure. Even mission-driven activities can benefit from *portfolio analysis* to ensure that they're either self-supporting or operated cost effectively.

Portfolio analysis considers each product, strategic business unit (SBU), or division of the association separately for purposes of strategy formulation. (An SBU is a discrete, independent, product-market segment that has been given primary responsibility and authority for management of its functional areas.) Even associations involved in only one business—professional development, for instance—might benefit from a separate handling of several business segments. For example, it might manage national conferences, self-instructional programs, and regional meetings as separate and distinct market segments.

Portfolio analysis encourages managers to evaluate the association's businesses individually and to set objectives and allocate resources for each one. It stimulates the use of externally oriented data to supplement management's judgment. It also raises the issue of cash-flow availability for use in expansion and growth.

The effect of portfolio analysis is to serve the association's members with a small number of strong services and excellent products rather than with a large number of fragmented products and services that compete for limited dollars. Ian C. MacMillan, a professor at the Wharton School, has observed that it's preferable to provide good service to a focused market rather than to provide mediocre or poor service to too large a market. In other words, associations should concede mediocre programs to better competitors and wrest away promising programs from weaker competitors.

As part of portfolio analysis, MacMillan urges that an association evaluate each program in this way:

- Is it a good fit with our organization's mission and goals?
- Is it easy or difficult to implement?
- Is there much or little competition (high or low market coverage)?
- Is our competitive position strong or weak?

If there's a good fit, the program will relate to the mission and purpose of the association, have the ability to draw on existing skills within the association, and be able to share resources and coordinate activities with other programs. Ideally, an association has two types of programs: well-fitting, easy programs where the association has a strong position and competes aggressively for a dominant position; and well-fitting, difficult programs with low coverage that the association has the unique capability to provide to stakeholders.

Low coverage exists if comparable programs are few and far between. High coverage exists if many similar programs are offered elsewhere. "Easy" means the business appeals to groups capable of providing current and future support; has a stable source of funding; experiences market demand from a large, concentrated, and growing client base; appeals to volunteer leaders; and has measurable and reportable results.

ANNUAL UPDATING

Most plans, no matter how good, tend to end up gathering dust on a forgotten shelf. They may fail because they lack a strategy-implementation phase after the strategy-formulation phase. Or they may fail simply because they become obsolete. The moment a plan is drafted, the assumptions on which it is based start to change. That's why ongoing environmental scanning, feedback, and adjustments are necessary.

A "rolling" strategy, rather than a multi-year plan, ensures that the association always has an updated plan for a three-year period. As each year is completed, the second year is adjusted in light of the experience gained during the previous year. Then an additional year is added to the end of the plan. In this way, each incoming group of board members also participates in the planning process.

The future of associations is filled with uncertainty and difficult challenges. As in society generally, everything about associations is being questioned—programs, governance, and costs, to name a few. Members demand constant proof of value, increasingly view dues as a tax, and have little time to volunteer.

Associations principally are in the information business, and new, powerful competitors have emerged to provide a rich choice of information on new communications systems such as the World Wide Web. The speed of change leaves no time for reaction and little room for error. The accelerated pace of change demands that associations do strategic thinking, planning, and implementation concurrently. This parallel planning is imperative to an association's survival and success.

The Perils of Not Planning

In the absence of strategic management, these misfortunes often overtake associations:

- **Lack of institutional memory.** Repeated turnover of volunteer leadership leads to constantly shifting priorities and agendas. Because the association is constantly being reinvented, its mission remains vague and little agreement is found on vision, goals, and objectives.

- **Lack of organizational definition.** Confusion exists about the varied responsibilities of board and staff, as well as their relationship to one another and to chapters and members.

- **Budget-driven decisions rather than needs-driven.** When no clear vision or sense of direction prevails, leaders tend to base decisions on budgetary, rather than strategic, considerations.

- **Crisis-driven management.** Many associations tend to be reactive instead of proactive. They don't have an effective, formal strategy in place for anticipating and preventing crises or undesirable developments or for coping with them once they occur.

- **Shifting priorities.** These are a natural consequence of the lack of vision, mission, and purpose.

- **Membership restlessness or dissatisfaction.** If the association has no common vision of the future and no clearly defined, generally understood mission, goals, and objectives, continual quarreling will occur over what direction programming should take. Members may not know what to expect in return for the dollars invested.

References and Suggested Reading

Forbes, Paul S., "The Strategic Management Process: A Model for Associations, *A Sharing of Expertise and Experience*, Vol. 6, American Society of Association Executives, Washington, D.C., 1988.

——, "Avoiding the Strategic Implementation Trap," *Association Trends*, August 27, 1993.

——, "Change Will Push Associations to Think Like Businesses," *Association Trends*, September 2, 1994.

——, "The Changing Role for Association Boards: Thinking Strategically," *Association Trends*, March 4, 1994.

——, "Closing the Gap Between Your Strategic and Work Plans." *Association Trends*, April 1, 1994.

——, "Dissecting the Future: 3 Scenarios," *Association Trends*, October 27, 1995.

——, "Everything Is up for Grabs," *Association Trends*, November 4, 1994.

——, "Focus on Strategic Budgeting," *Association Trends*, June 3, 1994.

——, "Monitoring of These 5 Future Spheres Eases Strategic Planning," *Association Trends*, November 11, 1991.

——, "Rapid Changes Force Associations to Prepare for Alternative Futures," *Association Trends*, October 11, 1991.

——, "Strategic Management Will Prevent Amnesia from Affecting Associations," *Association Trends*, September 13, 1991.

——, "Update: Strategic Planning Is Dead," *Association Trends*, July 14, 1995.

——, "Use Scenarios to Take Control of Your Association's Future," *Association Trends*, September 8, 1995.

——, "Who Is Driving Your Association?," *Association Trends*, March 13, 1992.

Forbes, Paul S., and Bruce Butterfield, "Reshaping Your Association for the 21st Century," *Association Management*, March 1993.

Schwartz, Peter, *The Art of the Long View: Planning for the Future in an Uncertain World*, Doubleday, New York, 1991.

Bruce Butterfield, CAE, Fellow, PRSA, has nearly three decades of association and public relations management experience. As president and chief operating officer of The Forbes Group and its Mayet Research Division, he guides organizations through alternative futures, scenario building, and strategic planning and work plan development.

CHAPTER 4

STRATEGIC PLANNING

JAMES G. DALTON, CAE

Since its advent in associations during the mid-1960s, strategic planning has risen to such a level of importance that virtually every association possesses a plan, even if it doesn't use it.

In some associations, the strategic plan is paraded about occasionally but spends most of its time on a dusty shelf. Leaders in successful associations, however, see strategic planning as the means by which they get members and staff to think about the future in such a way that everyone arrives at similar conclusions about what needs to be done. The disparity between these two outcomes lies in the distinction between process and product. A process orientation strives for a system through which people think strategically every day; a product orientation simply works toward a document.

Most definitions of strategic planning make the following points: It is a consensus-seeking process through which organizations define their purpose, describe a future state they want to achieve, identify barriers and opportunities in reaching that destination, and decide how they intend to get there.

Missing from many definitions is the clear acknowledgment of the ultimate reference point in strategic planning: It's about customer satisfaction, not organizational prose. Also frequently missing is the context in which strategic planning occurs. Strategic planning sets objectives and allocates resources. Management planning (implementation) deals with obtaining and effectively using the resources. Operational planning (evaluation) ensures that the specific tasks are completed on time and on budget.

Preparing to Plan

Strategic planning is a cyclical process that requires a good beginning. One key to ultimate success may lie in the image that association leaders have in mind before they begin the planning process. One appropriate image would be a motion picture—people who genuinely and continuously engage in strategic thinking, with a consensus document as the script that keeps them acting in unison.

The process can become an exercise in futility if leaders aren't willing to share information, listen to one another, and exhibit flexibility. Strategic planning should focus on the most productive opportunities and create expectations that require additional resources usually at the expense of other activities. That means the organization must be prepared to shift resources.

These four elements are needed to initiate and sustain the planning process:

- **A champion.** Typically this is a free-thinking former elected officer who has no need to defend the past or a potential officer. Alternately, this person might be a "name" in the industry or the profession—someone who never will be part of the elected leadership but is willing to help define the association's future. The champion must have organizational credibility and be smart, articulate, and trustworthy. When the board, committees, and staff see these characteristics, they feel safe in letting go of their current assumptions long enough to consider alternatives.

- **Team commitment.** While the champion leads the charge, others with credibility within the organization must convince their peers that the effort will be sustained over time. The team typically includes the chief executive officer (CEO), members of the executive committee, and senior staff members.

  Advocates of strategic planning and the planning team itself are not necessarily synonymous, although some overlap may occur. The planning team is a carefully selected group of creative thinkers drawn from the same organizational levels as the advocates. Although the CEO and incoming chief elected officer typically serve on the team, it should also include representatives of key elements of the association, such as chapters and operating divisions.

  Demographics—including length of membership, years of experience in the industry or profession, level of association involvement, gender, and ethnicity—should also come into play. The team's composition should imply some strategic assumptions about the current situation and the desired future. For example, if few students are association members yet are well-represented within the population of potential members—and if balance is a desired outcome for the future—then students should be well-represented on the team.

- **Resources.** Because the strategic planning process arrives at a fairly generic set of guidelines, it's possible to construct a method, schedule, and affordable budget from an initial review of the human and capital resources needed. On average, establishing a strategic planning process and completing the first full cycle take one year.

- **Consultants.** An outside consultant brings impartiality, pointed questions, and the facilitation skills needed to balance differences of opinion. Even if an association decides against using a consultant to guide it through the strategic planning process, simply interviewing consultants can prove educational. For instance, each consultant will take a slightly different approach to strategic planning because no one, "right" way exists. Some may serve as facilitators, while others may take an active leadership role in the process.

  Hiring a consultant can be expensive, but he or she will significantly accelerate the association's learning curve and help ensure that the process, once initiated, will complete one full cycle. If the budget can't accommodate such assistance, it's possible to use a consultant for the initial sessions, where an objective assessment of the association's current status is highly recommended.

Steps in Strategic Planning

Once preparation is complete, the planning team embarks upon at least five sequential steps. The number varies by expert but typically includes the following:

1. **Process Definition.** After agreeing upon the process it will follow, the planning team needs to inform people within the organization and obtain approval from those who have the power to accept or reject the eventual outcome. Those who approve the process in advance buy into a portion of the outcome—they become vested stakeholders. Likewise, acceptance—or at least acknowledgment—should be obtained from those who will be affected by the outcome.

For instance, Perlov (1995) describes a "collaborative planning" process that solicits information from all sectors of the association. This approach produces valuable information while informing people about the process, which in turn establishes a favorable attitude toward the outcome.

The process, however defined, requires the following elements:

- *Input* from as many people affected by the outcome as possible. Surveys, open meetings, focus groups, and interviews can be used to invite and gather information.
- *Feedback* built into the process at various points. This ensures that recommendations (mission statements, goals, and objectives) are approved as they evolve, not when they are delivered.
- A final outcome that is more a *system* than a document. That system should be connected to other organization functions, such as program evaluation, budgeting, and committee charges.

2. **Research and Analysis.** The research phase includes a look at the following:

- **Association history,** including the organization's original purpose and the stages apparent in its development. To avoid a biased interpretation, a subcommittee of the planning team—in other words, more than one person—should review early documents, including the initial constitution and bylaws, newsletters, meeting minutes, proceedings, and correspondence from the founding officers.

The committee might also scan minutes and publications that span the full spectrum of the association's existence to identify any major issues addressed in the past. A report summarizing this history helps others in the planning process know why the association was founded and where it has succeeded.

- **Member demographics,** as drawn from the membership database or acquired through surveys. For instance, associations that provide statistical reports on the industry or profession are well-positioned to understand what they are and where they stand. Demographic analysis generally includes what is known about current and potential members, with comparisons that point out any distinctions between the two groups.

- **Member psychographics,** typically a compilation of surveys that tell what the members think about a given subject. At a minimum, the planning team should have an inventory of all available surveys and a summation of what each says about member needs and expectations. If this information is sparse, a formal research program might be in order.

  Although effective member research is a topic of its own (see Chapter 15), strategic planning can benefit from several focus groups in which rank-and-file members describe why they think the organization exists and how it should direct its resources. A member survey should then be undertaken to confirm their answers.

- **Future trends** that could affect the association typically fall into these key categories: demographics, social changes, information technology, science, technology and the environment, and government regulation. Developing "scanning" skills is essential because the exercise should be repeated annually.

  After reviewing the research findings in these categories, the planning team engages in a brainstorming session, often using the SWOT approach—which stands for Strengths, Weaknesses, Opportunities, and Threats. Their goal is to generate a comprehensive list for each of the four headings and then focus on the most significant ones.

  The SWOT exercise is a means to an end: identifying the critical issues that the organization must deal with in order to succeed. Once the SWOT lists are completed, the planning team culls through the lists to create one-sentence issues statements that spell out what the organization should address (for example, communications technology is changing the way committees are organized). These issue statements should be circulated widely to create agreement on the most significant issues.

  This step concludes with the development of a document often referred to as the "environmental assessment." Organized either around the SWOT elements or the issue statements that grew out of them, this document should reflect the association's current state of being, blemishes and all.

3. **Reasons for Being.** Based on the information assembled through research and analysis, the planning team fabricates three elements to articulate why an association exists and to describe the future it hopes to create. Those elements are:

- **Values**—the beliefs at the heart of the organization. One-sentence value statements may be thought of as the hot buttons that motivate people to advocate the organization's purpose. Take, for example, one of these values statements: "The XYZ Industry believes effective public policy requires citizen involvement and the active participation of knowledgeable sources" or "Professional XYZs believe that continuing education is a life-long obligation."

  Although the values statements may not appear in the final plan, knowing them—and being able to articulate them succinctly—focuses the planning team's attention on what is important and helps build agreement on the mission statement to follow.

- **Vision**—the image or state to which the association aspires. While values statements describe the motivations that people bring to the organization, the vision articulates what they see when they come together.

  One function of leadership is to present a vision of a future state of being so desirable that it motivates people to passionately work toward its achievement. As a general rule of thumb, the length of the vision statement is inversely proportional to the interest it will raise. Powerful imagery demands short prose.

- **Mission**—the organization's purpose as stated in a memorable phrase. The ideal mission statement is not only memorable but also motivating and descriptive. People remember a mission statement when it contains key words that evoke the energy contained in the association's vision—but not when it's so detailed that it repeats goals and objectives. Yet the mission should be descriptive enough that it could be used to determine which program receives funding should a dispute arise during resource allocation.

  The mission statement of the Salvation Army stands as the classic example: "To make citizens of the rejected." Bingo! It can ring a bell in the dead of winter.

  Group techniques such as brainstorming help the planning committee translate the findings of opinion surveys into value statements. Brainstorming can also evoke images of what the world would be like if the organization accomplished what it set out to do. Once the many images have been gathered together, a unifying element or several key words usually emerge. Those can form the basis for a mission statement.

  At this point, the planning committee should ask others to react to the preliminary values, vision, and mission. Documenting the reactions received—and recording the reasons why certain issues weren't addressed—becomes important evidence when seeking final approval. It demonstrates involvement and thoughtful consideration of rejected ideas.

4. **Actions.** Values, vision, and mission arouse interest, set direction, and ensure commitment. In short, they appeal to the heart. Conversely, action items appeal to the head. They spell out the logical steps to follow to bring the mission to fruition. The mission tells *why*; action items tell *how*.

   Terms such as *strategies* and *tactics* are often used to define the levels of action in this phase of strategic planning. The more classical terms are *goals* and *objectives*. Whatever the language adopted, the planning committee next focuses on developing strategic statements of intent and describing the outcomes that will result.

   Goals are functional statements that translate the mission into tangible endpoints that all other activities strive to achieve. Goal statements are usually related to the specific issues identified in the research and analysis step. In fact, they're the logical outcome of accurately identified issues.

   Each goal sets a clear target by describing one tangible facet of the perfected state of being implied in the mission statement. Taken together, the goal statements constitute an organizational framework for all work activities.

Here are some examples:

- Achieve funding for and expand the scientific base of physical therapy (American Physical Therapy Association).
- Provide information and educational opportunities on state-of-the-art technologies and practices that advance landscape architecture (American Society of Landscape Architects).
- The contributions to society of associations as voluntary organizations will be publicly recognized and highly valued (American Society of Association Executives).

The goals constitute a transition point in the strategic planning. Up to this point, the planning committee has taken the initiative by making proposals that others have responded to. Now, with the more permanent parts of the strategic plan turned into action items, others will take the initiative to accomplish them.

While goals express a perfected state, *objectives* define the near-term outcome of a work activity specifically put in place to achieve the goal. An objective typically pertains to one budget year and should be constructed in measurable terms—even if the measurement is as simple as a yes or no reply regarding whether it was accomplished.

For example, an objective developed to support the third goal noted above might read as follows: "Increase positive recognition among targeted audiences of the contributions and value of associations to society—such as setting standards, providing education, conducting research, and gathering statistics—as measured by the number of times that major media highlight associations and their programs."

Objectives open a dialogue between those who do the work and those who ensure that all the work taken together achieves the organization's goals in the most efficient manner. Typically this dialogue occurs between the board and committees and between the CEO and staff.

5. **Recycling.** Initiating a strategic plan and sustaining it over time are very different activities. The work of the planning committee changes significantly once the association has launched its initial plan.

   Assuming the process has been designed so that the board and committees have the annual responsibility for maintaining objectives that achieve goals, the planning committee focuses exclusively on research and analysis. The committee's primary job is to stay focused on the long-term future and anticipate issues that will affect the organization's ability to achieve its goals. This is often accomplished through an annual analysis using the SWOT (Strengths, Weaknesses, Opportunities, and Threats) technique.

Related Functions

An association's strategic plan is likely to end up on a shelf if it's not hard-wired to the budget and a program-evaluation process.

- **Budget.** When all is said and done, despite the lip service frequently given to strategic planning, the operating budget is the plan. The question then becomes, "Is the organization planning its budget or budgeting its plan?" To maintain a functional relationship between the plan and the budget, with the plan leading the way, the two documents should have structural compatibility—in other words, each should be organized in a fashion that allows for easy and logical reference to the other.

A project-based budget can achieve this by listing discrete work activities on separate lines; each budget line has an objective statement describing the outcome of this investment by the end of the year. Adding words to the numbers produces an operating plan, which becomes both a text version of budget intentions and an explanation of the relationship between the strategic plan and allocation of resources.

For example, assume the XYZ Association has a goal to "Expand the scientific base of information." This goal has several objectives, including, "Increase demand for research findings through increased dissemination of the results to the profession's client groups." In the operational plan, an objective (or strategy) for the conference marketing project might be to promote heavily to selected client groups. At the same time, the editorial objective of XYZ's magazine could be to send complimentary editions to carefully selected members of the same client groups. In this manner, two different project lines in the budget demonstrate their contributions to the same objective in the strategic plan.

This example illustrates how leaders such as the board of directors can set strategic direction without getting into project micromanagement: The board sets the strategies, and the committees determine how they will be accomplished by developing objectives.

- **Evaluation.** If properly stated, the objectives for each project in the budget provide the focal point for determining program effectiveness. Association leaders should apply two questions to each objective at the end of the budget year: "Was the objective accomplished?" and "Did it contribute substantially to the strategic plan?" These two questions constitute the evaluation dialogue between the board and committees. Each committee might address these questions in evaluation reports, which the board would comment on during a review session.

Results of the evaluation process might prompt the association to consider adjusting either the strategies or project objectives or both. It's possible, for instance, that an objective was accomplished yet contributed to a weak strategy. Another outcome of evaluation is information that the planning committee can use during its next round of research and analysis. Program information is especially helpful in identifying an association's strengths and weaknesses.

Activities undertaken throughout the year keep a strategic plan off the shelf and the subject of continuous evaluation. Those activities include reviewing the plan at monthly staff meetings, documenting each strategic task, measuring and interpreting data, obtaining feedback from involved groups, appraising job performance in light of the plan, and providing periodic progress reports to the board.

References and Suggested Reading

Berry, Lionel, and Eve W. Yeargain, "Turnaround Tool Kit for Association Managers," *A Sharing of Expertise & Experience*, vol. 8, American Society of Association Executives, Washington, D.C., 1990.

——, "Using Culture to Maximize Organizational Results: A Primer for CEOs," *A Sharing of Expertise & Experience*, vol. 9, American Society of Association Executives, Washington, D.C., 1991.

Bryson, J.M., *Strategic Planning for Public and Nonprofit Organizations*, Jossey-Bass, San Francisco, 1989.

Burke, Christine E., CAE, and Diana McCauley, "The Planning Process: More Than Just Deciding What to Do," *Membership Marketer*, June 1992, American Society of Association Executives, Washington, D.C.

Coughlan, William D., "Develop an Effective Strategic and Vision Process," *Long Range Planning*, American Society of Association Executives, Washington, D.C.

Edgley, Gerald J., "Strategic Planning," *Association Management*, March 1990.

Forbes, Paul S., "Separate Winners from Losers in Your Workplan," *A Sharing of Expertise & Experience*, vol. 11, American Society of Association Executives, Washington, D.C., 1993.

Jarratt, Jennifer, Joseph F. Coates, John B. Mahaffie, and Andy Hines, "Focusing on the Future," *Leadership*, 1995.

Miller, John A., and Henry L. Ernstthal, CAE, "Strategic Planning," *Long Range Planning*, American Society of Association Executives, Washington, D.C., 1995.

Perlov, Dadie, CAE, "The Strategic Plan," *Leadership*, 1995.

Rogers, Thomas, and James Alvino, "The Strategic Action Management Model: Getting Your Association Back on Track," *A Sharing of Expertise & Experience*, vol. 11, American Society of Association Executives, Washington, D.C., 1993.

Schlegel, John F., CAE, "The Power of the Plan," *Association Management*, April 1995.

Vovsi, Edgar A., "Planning: Making the Vision a Reality," *A Sharing of Expertise & Experience*, vol. 9, American Society of Association Executives, Washington, D.C., 1991.

James G. Dalton, CAE, is executive vice president of the American Society of Landscape Architects in Washington, D.C.

CHAPTER 5

LEGAL ISSUES

PART I.
PRACTICAL STEPS AND PROCESSES TO HELP MINIMIZE LEGAL RISK TO ASSOCIATIONS

JAMES H. EWALT, CAE

PART II.
AN OVERVIEW OF IMPORTANT LEGAL ISSUES FOR ASSOCIATIONS

JEFFERSON C. GLASSIE

Part I. Practical Steps and Processes to Help Minimize Legal Risk to Associations

Orderly governance of an association requires compliance with state, local, and federal laws, and there are a number of practical steps association executives can take to help avoid legal risk. Developing sound policies and procedures, maintaining key documents and records, and obtaining appropriate insurance will go a long way toward protecting the interests of the association, its members, and its staff. Each of these processes is important and demands close attention by the association. However, each also is complicated enough to require expert assistance. Therefore, at a minimum, a broad understanding of them is essential. A summary of some of the practical considerations in this area is provided here.

Developing Policies and Procedures

Associations and most of the activities they engage in are subject to myriad local, state, and federal laws. Compliance with these laws is required, but also can create valuable benefits for the association, such as tax-exempt status for the organization and limited liability for its members. Violations can lead to a variety of penalties, including fines and—under the tax laws—loss of exempt status. Thus associations should develop policies and procedures ensuring full compliance with laws so that they, their professional staff, and their volunteers can maximize benefits and avoid legal problems, including costly litigation.

It is important, at the outset, to recognize the complex and broad array of legal obligations incurred by associations. The list of applicable laws can indeed be daunting. For instance, most associations are incorporated and must comply with the nonprofit corporate laws, which vary from state to state, governing corporations. Associations also can enjoy tax-exempt status if they meet and follow certain provisions of the tax laws. Employment laws govern the association's relationship with its employees and even those who seek to be employees. Federal and state lobbying laws impose registration and reporting requirements on associations that engage in lobbying activities. Contract law controls agreements made between the association and others. Association publications, meetings, and other activities are subject to libel and copyright laws. And, most important, antitrust laws closely govern association activities that impart competition in the industry or profession.

Understanding what is required of the association to comply with applicable laws can be even more difficult. Some laws require that the association take affirmative actions, such as maintaining corporate records or filing annual tax statements. Others prohibit certain activities, such as conspiring to limit competition or discriminating in the selection and treatment of employees. And the requirements of some laws differ depending on the legal structure of the association. For example, Section 501 (c)(3) charitable and educational associations, under the tax laws, may not engage in lobbying activities to the same extent as Section 501 (c)(6) trade associations or business leagues. In addition, the legal landscape in which the association operates is constantly changed by the enactment of new laws and by courts and other government bodies, such as administrative agencies, that regularly announce decisions changing the way a law is applied or enforced.

Because it is so difficult, yet critically important, to know and fully understand an association's legal obligations, it usually is best to engage the services of someone who has expert knowledge about associations and the body of laws governing them. This may be an experienced association professional, but most often it is an attorney who specializes in association law. Attorneys who practice in this area are best suited to help identify laws specifically applicable to nonprofit, tax-exempt associations and their activities as well as develop policies and procedures to ensure legal compliance.

Policies and procedures need to be written, detailed, and specific to the association covering important areas of potential legal liability. At the very least, they need to include a record-retention program, procedures for conducting meetings, and an antitrust compliance program. The association's governing body should discuss and approve the approximate policies, procedures, and guidelines. Many associations include broad formal policy statements of compliance in their bylaws and record the more detailed procedures in a manual of association policies and procedures or some less formal document.

Associations should circulate policies and procedures among the staff, officers, directors, and members, along with sufficient additional information, so they can recognize the legal obligations and potential problems pertaining to any association activity in which they are involved. They also should ensure that legal counsel is readily available to answer questions or give advice. In some instances, this may mean having counsel in attendance at an association activity, for example, at a meeting where the expected discussion could stray into subjects prohibited by antitrust laws. Policies and procedures must be strictly implemented throughout the association and continuously reviewed in conjunction with ongoing association activities to maintain their relevance and effectiveness.

Maintaining Key Documents

Various state and federal laws require that certain association documents be maintained for stipulated periods of time. On the other hand, practical reasons, such as physical space, administrative costs, and litigation strategy, dictate that associations maintain certain files and records only as long as absolutely necessary. Thus, the association needs to establish and follow a clear record-retention program that details what is to be kept, as well as time periods for retaining and purging each kind of association file and record. Strict adherence to a record-retention program will ensure that current and useful information, as well as that which is legally required, will not be inadvertently destroyed.

A record-retention program begins with cataloging documents the association is required by law to retain. It also needs to specify the periods of time for holding certain categories of files and records. It usually is best to secure the services of legal counsel familiar with state and federal laws applicable to associations to ensure the list of required documents is complete and appropriate procedures for retaining and for destroying the documents are established.

Here are some examples of records that generally should be kept in permanent association files:

- The association's organizing and governing documents, including articles of incorporation, bylaws, the tax-exempt determination letter from the Internal Revenue Service (IRS), and minutes of meetings—all of which generally require permanent maintenance. State law often also requires that the association's financial books, records of accounts, and lists of its members' names be maintained.

- Documents required by the IRS for tax-exempt status, including details of receipts and disbursements, gross income, unrelated business income, and exempt association activities. The association also needs to keep canceled checks and other supporting documentation for income and expenses to substantiate its annual informational returns, such as IRS Form 990. Finally, records regarding the association's employees' wages and taxes withheld from wages, unemployment tax records, and records of Social Security taxes paid should be maintained for four years.

- Various employment records in addition to those required for tax purposes are required to be maintained by the Labor Department, the Fair Labor Standards Act, the Age Discrimination Act, Americans with Disabilities Act, and the Occupational Safety Health Act.

- Association contracts, insurance policies, deeds, leases, trademark or patent registration certificates, and similar documents need to be maintained while in effect and for a short period of time after they expire to protect the rights of the association.

- Once an association has any knowledge of a possible pending antitrust investigation, it needs to exercise extreme caution—proceeding only with the advice of informed legal counsel—before destroying any files or records. Even if no specific penalty for destruction of material exists, adverse legal inferences may be drawn in any litigation where it can be shown that the association failed to maintain, or willfully purged, pertinent files and records.

- Federal and state laws require documentation to support time and expenses attributed to lobbying activities. These include registration and reporting documents.

Once the list of records and procedures is complete, it needs to be rigorously followed with exceptions only for good reason and on authority of senior association staff.

Securing Appropriate Insurance Coverage

Broad insurance protection is vital to protecting the fiduciary interests of the association, its members, and its staff. Although no two associations are alike and insurance needs differ greatly, there are still some basic elements of coverage that should be included in nearly every association's checklist. Attention to insurance coverage can help safeguard the association's future.

Essentially, there are two types of insurance coverage associations need to consider: property and liability. Property insurance protects the association's physical assets, such as the headquarters building and its contents. Liability insurance protects it from losses resulting from a real or alleged wrongful action on the part of the insured whether it be the directors, officers, staff, volunteers, or the organization itself. Examples of liability claims are as numerous as there are association activities. Property and liability coverage also must extend beyond the association's headquarters to such "off premise" activities as seminars, conventions, and trade shows.

Securing appropriate property insurance is relatively straightforward. First, identify the different categories of association property. These generally include real property, personal property, computers, off premises, valuable papers and records, fine arts, money, boiler and machinery, and improvements. Next, take an inventory of everything in each category. And, finally, estimate how much it would cost to replace, at current replacement costs, everything the association owns. Once this process is complete, an insurance policy providing sufficient coverage can be secured.

Securing appropriate liability insurance is not as simple. A wide variety of liability claims may be brought against the officers, directors, staff, or other volunteers for acts they perform on behalf of the association. Associations can guard against liability in two ways:

1. By becoming informed—understanding the different types of liabilities that

exist, against whom legal challenges can be made, and what typical policies or programs of associations most often become the bases of claimed liability.

2. By securing broad appropriate insurance protection.

There are two general categories of liability claims:

1. Criminal claims—those brought by the government to obtain jail sentences or fines for serious violations of the law.

2. Civil claims—those usually brought by the government for less serious violations of law or by individuals or companies on their own behalf to obtain damages for antitrust, breach of contract, copyright infringement, injury from negligence, and so forth.

Liability claims involving an association most often are brought against the association itself. The claimant seeks financial remuneration for losses based on alleged organizational liability. When considering association liability, one is ordinarily concerned with organizational liability. However, liability claims also may be brought against the association's officers, directors, staff, and other volunteers for their activities on behalf of the association. These claims are the exception rather than the rule, and successful assertion of personal claims is rare. Nevertheless, they are of such sufficient concern that associations need to provide adequate insurance protection for persons who might be named in such a lawsuit.

There are three general areas of possible personal liability:

- Ultra vires acts are those where the individual is obviously acting beyond the scope of his or her authority.

- Torts are those acts where the activities—other than breaches of contract—damage or injure others. If they intentionally cause injury or damage to persons or property, they can give rise to personal liability even though the activities were carried on at the behest of the association.

- Criminal acts are those where there is participation in or conscious approval of activities that constitute serious violations of state or federal law.

In most circumstances, however, there is no personal liability if the person has acted using ordinary care and diligence in carrying out his or her association activity. The principal test of personal liability is whether individuals acted in "good faith":

- Did they knowingly perform or approve association activities that are beyond the association's appropriate sphere of authority?

- Did they intentionally cause injury or damage to persons or property while in the course of association work?

- Did they commit or facilitate acts while representing the association that violate antitrust provisions or other laws?

A wide variety of liability claims may be brought against the association as an entity, and its directors, officers, staff, or other individuals for acts they perform on behalf of the association or against the association itself as an organization. Moreover, allegations of wrongdoing, whether true or not, can lead to extraordinary expense particularly in legal costs. Sources of liability include contracts, publications, employment relationships, membership requirements and services, meetings, and activities covered by antitrust laws. The most frequent are those related to employment and personal injury, such as libel, slander, and defamation. Increasingly, associations also are receiving claims of damages alleged to have resulted from inadequate association-issued standards or certification; inaccurate association-promulgated advice on technical or medical issues; or the association's failure to correct or warn the public of a hazard.

The most essential element of any association insurance portfolio is general liability insurance, which provides important safeguards for claims arising from bodily injury and property damage. Often it includes an assortment of liability coverage, such as fire, personal injury, automobile, and libel and slander. Associations often elect to increase their general liability insurance by purchasing an umbrella policy, which is an additional amount of insurance, as excess coverage beyond the association's general and automobile liability coverage or limits, without increasing coverage for each individual.

Associations also should provide safeguards to minimize the exposure of their officers, directors, staff, and other volunteers for personal liability. Most states have volunteer protection laws, but often these provide less-than-adequate protection. Personal liability protection is best provided through indemnification by the association and, most important, by purchasing coverage from a private insurance carrier.

Many state laws permit a nonprofit corporation, such as an association, to indemnify its officers and directors, and sometimes staff and other volunteers as well, against claims made against them if the claims are based on individuals' activities conducted on behalf of the association. Through indemnification, the organization agrees to pay for any claims against individuals based on their activities conducted on behalf of the organization, but indemnification is limited as a source of protection to the extent of the assets of the association. State laws typically prohibit indemnification activities that involve criminal activity, gross negligence, or fraud. Indemnification usually can be accomplished by resolution, contract, or bylaws provisions, depending on state law.

Separate from providing its own indemnification, an association should also purchase professional liability insurance to protect named individuals against claims of personal liability while acting on behalf of the association by providing payment for damages and costs of defense in claims against them. This type of insurance, sometimes referred to as directors and officers insurance, is more correctly called association professional liability (APL) insurance.

APL insurance is tailored to the specific circumstances of the association and protects the association itself, as well as the officers and directors, staff, and other volunteers. Most APL policies cover only money damage losses and exclude coverage for bodily injury and property damage claims, because they are assumed to be covered in the association's basic comprehensive general liability policy (which may cover liability for accidents in the association's offices, etc.). Associations that may have more than the usual exposure to liability often purchase additional liability policies for those activities (i.e., publishing, errors and omissions, fiduciary, and employee-benefit liability).

A limitation on insurance is that some types of activities, for example, antitrust violations or certification programs, may not be covered. Another is that premiums have risen while policy coverage and limits have been reduced.

Insurance can be an extremely complicated subject and the assistance of a knowledgeable consultant is ordinarily essential to obtain the broadest possible coverage for the association at the lowest possible premiums. For example, some policies depend on the existence of indemnification provisions by the association. Others do not. Some cover only the association's officers and directors while others are more inclusive and also cover staff and other volunteers. Virtually all kinds of detailed limitations and qualifications exist. Terms, exclusions, conditions, definitions, deductibles, premiums, and endorsements can vary widely among different insurance carriers.

In particular, antitrust coverage needs to be carefully analyzed. Some policies exclude antitrust coverage entirely or when claims exceed a certain amount. Associations need to seriously consider if there is any significant value to policies that exclude antitrust coverage in whole or in part because of the potential that many association activities have for raising antitrust claims.

Diverse operations mean that associations may be exposed to liability in ways that they may not be able to recognize without the aid of an insurance broker who is familiar with association operations. Before purchasing insurance, associations need to carefully analyze the coverage afforded by policies under consideration, as well as applicable premiums for each policy. They should not assume that insurance is available only on a take-it-or-leave-it basis. Associations may be able to negotiate additional coverage, terms, or other provisions in standard insurance policies.

James H. Ewalt, CAE, is executive vice president of the Cable Telecommunications Association in Fairfax, Virginia. Ewalt began his career in 1972 as an attorney in the Cable Television Bureau of the Federal Communications Commission.

Part II. An Overview of Important Legal Issues for Associations

I n this litigious society, chief executive officers (CEOs) and all staff must
remain on alert to protect their associations from risks of liability. Lawsuits and
government enforcement actions can be devastating—financially and organi-
zationally—particularly if the association doesn't have proper legal risk-protec-
tion measures in place.

Legal Audits

In a perfect world, every association would commission a formal and comprehensive legal audit to review all aspects of its programs and activities to determine whether significant legal exposure existed. Then, in that perfect world, the
association would undertake a routine "legal check-up" every year or so to review
ongoing and developing legal issues and problems.

Like a financial audit, a legal audit can help protect an association against
unexpected liability. In addition, a legal audit can point out trouble spots that
deserve board or staff attention and may even trigger the development and implementation of key association policies that will help minimize potential liability
(for instance, an antitrust compliance policy).

Undertaking a legal audit of association activity also demonstrates the
board's or CEO's good faith and due diligence in taking reasonable steps to identify and avoid potential liability. Even a less formal but thorough legal review of
specific high-profile areas, such as certification programs, can highlight some of
the more problematic risks and generate recommendations for minimizing those
risks.

Of course, it is often not possible to have outside counsel conduct a full legal
audit. Both seasoned veterans and those new to association management can use
the following summary to review legal considerations important to most associations. (Note that this is not an exhaustive review and cannot replace legal advice,
counsel, or a formal legal audit; it may, however, help avoid some of the legal pot-
holes associations may encounter.)

Corporate Status

The association's corporate status offers a good starting point for a legal
review. An incorporated association has Articles of Incorporation on file with the
state or jurisdiction (such as the District of Columbia) in which incorporation
occurred. Periodically, association staff or the relevant volunteer committee should
review the Articles of Incorporation to ensure that they remain consistent with
current activities. For instance, changes made in the bylaws or other structural
aspects of the association—such as the number of directors and officers, membership criteria, and voting requirements—may make Articles of Incorporation out
of date.

In addition, the legal status of the association in its state of incorporation must be up to date—otherwise known as keeping the corporation in "good standing." Most states require the filing of annual or other periodic reports in order for associations to obtain the limited liability protection available through the corporate form.

An association incorporated in one state but with offices in another state usually needs to file reports in the other state, too. Failure to file the annual reports can result in revocation of corporate status or authority, with subsequent liability exposure to the individual officers, directors, and staff members of the association. Therefore, all annual corporate filings in any jurisdictions where the association is incorporated or has offices should be made routinely and on time.

The bylaws—the general governing document that applies primarily to day-to-day association activities—should be consistent with state law and the Articles of Incorporation. The bylaws usually cover such organizational aspects as membership, meetings, voting, officers, directors, and committees. Provisions authorizing the existence of chapters also may be included.

Many associations have specific committees charged with ensuring that the bylaws are up to date and consistent with the association's current practices and procedures. In turn, it's important for associations to follow their bylaws. For example, membership voting and proper notice of meetings should be accomplished in accordance with the bylaws. Otherwise, failure to follow the policies and procedures of the association as outlined in the bylaws and other governing documents can result in challenges by members. Legal counsel can review preparation of notices for meetings, voting materials, and agendas to ensure compliance with legal requirements.

Finances

Practically speaking, strong and healthy finances greatly influence the success of an association. Legally speaking, strong policies that protect against improper financial activities are essential as well. Legal liability can arise if association finances are mishandled, whether through incompetence, inadvertence, or deliberate fraud or embezzlement.

The board of directors generally has the responsibility for overseeing the development of budgets and for reviewing the finances. In fact, directors owe certain fiduciary duties to the organization to manage its affairs in good faith and in its best interests. The board, however, must remain apprised of important financial developments and receive periodic financial reports. Otherwise, the CEO or staff could possibly be accused of misleading the board, and liability could be imposed on individual staff members.

Accountants can help develop procedures and policies to prevent against embezzlement or other misuse or misappropriation of association funds (for instance, employees who handle funds should be bonded). Other useful policies relate to the investment of operating and surplus funds and the routine handling of deposits and writing of checks.

The preparation of audited financial reports also is recommended for associations. These reports give the board, members, and the general public confidence that the association's finances have been carefully and professionally prepared and audited. If the cost of hiring an outside professional (specifically, a certified public accountant) seems cost-prohibitive, the association should have an independent third party review its accounting and financial policies and procedures to ensure that appropriate protections are in place.

Tax

Carefully, correctly, and accurately compiled financial information must form the basis for annual reports to the Internal Revenue Service (IRS). Tax-exempt associations with annual revenues that exceed $25,000 per year must file an annual information report with the IRS on Form 990.

The majority of trade associations and professional societies are exempt from federal income tax under Section 501(c)(6) or 501(c)(3) of the Internal Revenue Code. Section 501(c)(6) covers membership organizations with professional industry interests, such as business leagues, boards of trade, and other organizations that exist to promote a specific profession or line of commerce. Section 501(c)(3) organizations have primary purposes that are charitable, educational, or scientific; because donations to such organizations are tax-deductible to the donors, additional legal requirements apply.

The determination letter from the IRS granting (c)(3), (c)(6), or other 501(c) tax status should remain part of the association's permanent records. In the absence of a determination letter, the association should immediately seek legal counsel to ensure that it fulfills appropriate filing and reporting requirements. In addition, most states require tax-exempt organizations to file annual reports, and some (such as California and the District of Columbia) even require that an association submit a formal application to obtain such an exemption.

If tax-exempt organizations fail to conduct their activities in accordance with the tax-exempt purposes described under the Internal Revenue Code, they may face the imposition of taxes, penalties, or even revocation of their tax-exempt status. In addition, if an association's nonexempt activities—such as marketing particular services for members or selling nonrelated products—become substantial, they may jeopardize the organization's tax exemption. More commonly, activities that are unrelated to the association's purpose or mission, are "regularly carried on," and constitute a "trade or business" under IRS definitions will result in unrelated business income subject to tax (UBIT).

If unrelated revenues subject to UBIT rise to within 30 or 40 percent of the association's annual budget, the IRS may question its tax-exempt status. Associations in that situation often spin off some of their activities into a for-profit subsidiary (see Chapter 7).

One way to avoid UBIT is to structure activities in such a manner that they will not be subjected to tax. For example, many association affinity programs can be appropriately characterized in legal agreements as generating "royalty" income for associations: Passive revenues, such as dividends, interest, and royalties, are exempt from UBIT provided certain rules are observed. In addition, sponsorships of activities can generate tax-free revenues if the association recognizes and acknowledges the sponsor in accordance with IRS guidance.

Insurance

Associations can take many steps to reduce potential liability. Yet, in the current legal environment, there is no way to prevent an aggrieved member or other person from suing the association to seek compensation or relief from allegedly harmful behavior. Therefore, associations must have adequate insurance coverage to protect against liability arising from a wide variety of legal claims. Given the sophisticated insurance policies on the market, associations do well to turn to a knowledgeable insurance agent or broker with experience in the association field for help in obtaining adequate and appropriate coverage.

Comprehensive general liability (CGL) insurance protects against basic theft, "slip and fall," or other activities that can occur in the association's office environment. Of perhaps greater value in protecting against liability that may arise from association programs is association professional liability insurance (APLI), often referred to as directors and officers (D&O) insurance. (The two policies are different, however; the traditional form of D&O isn't sufficient in today's environment.) APLI policies protect against negligence and other allegedly wrongful acts of the association, which provisions of CGL policies don't cover.

It's important to adequately disclose all association activities to the insurance company when obtaining insurance and to carefully review any endorsements or exclusions in the policy. For example, the policy may exclude damages or losses from antitrust, certification or standardization programs, or even employment practices. It often is worth paying additional amounts to ensure the coverage for the association is broad and without significant loopholes; the extra protection can pay off if a lawsuit is filed.

Litigation

Given the potentially high cost and time-intensity of litigation, ignoring any claims made against the association can prove foolhardy. Legal counsel must be involved in the analysis and handling of any claims that might lead to litigation. The CEO or other appropriate staff person should carefully monitor, with legal counsel, any litigation in process against the association. He or she can then ensure that all aspects of the litigation are handled carefully and in a timely manner, not only to avoid potentially serious damages but also to manage legal costs.

When litigation is either expected or in progress, it's important to have policies and procedures that preserve the association's confidences and "attorney/client privilege." Association boards of directors also should be kept informed of the status of any significant claims or litigation, but board members must be clearly warned against inadvertent disclosures that may harm the association's case.

Although insurance policies tailored to association activities should cover the costs of litigation, the insurer will require proper and timely notice of any claim to obtain coverage.

Contracts

A written contract or agreement should memorialize any important legal obligation owed by, or to, an association. This is important not simply from the legal perspective, but also to confirm that the parties entering into arrangements for the sale or purchase of goods or services know exactly what is required of each. Most associations have policies stating that legal counsel must review and approve all contracts, which can be signed only by authorized officers.

All contracts are subject to negotiation. In other words, an association doesn't have to accept the exact contracts submitted by hotels, vendors, or others. In fact, it's helpful for associations to develop standard-form contracts to use with hotels, vendors, affinity program sponsors, and other vendors. A standard form makes it easier to always include contractual provisions that protect the association.

Important provisions include the following: warranties or specifications with respect to the goods or services to be provided, licenses for any use of intangible property (such as trademarks or copyrights), payment terms, indemnification or limited liability provisions, and termination or cancellation clauses. An "out" clause always is advisable because a vendor relationship—no matter how good it appears at the start—can turn sour. It's better to think about contract termination before the contract is signed than have to fend off claims of loss or damage if a contract is terminated inappropriately without adequate terms.

Personnel

Personnel- or employment-related claims often present a difficult area for associations because personal relationships may become bitter when employees depart on the association's terms rather than on their own. Allegations of discrimination based on age, sex, or race are commonplace, whether in fact any discrimination occurred.

A well-written, clear, and legally sufficient employee manual offers the best protection against difficult disputes with employees. Courts look to a manual as the basis for the terms and conditions of the relationship between employer and employee. As such, it should govern all aspects of employment, including termination, and be kept up to date to reflect the current practices of the association. The association should also conduct objective and consistent personnel evaluations and maintain them in appropriate files.

Employment-related claims may arise in a number of areas other than discrimination. For example, some associations have been subject to legal liability for failing to pay proper overtime for nonexempt employees, instead substituting compensatory time. Vacation policies also are important; in most circumstances, unused vacation time must be paid upon termination.

A well-written employee manual, followed closely, can minimize the potential for long, expensive, and divisive suits based on employment practices. At least one association employee should be specially trained in employment matters, including proper methods of hiring and firing, as well as employee benefits. Legal advice should be sought in advance of any proposals to terminate employees.

Intellectual Property

What is the most important property held by an association? Perhaps an office building—but many lease space. And most associations are not likely to own cars, boats, or extensive art collections. Therefore, "intellectual property" often represents an association's most valuable property.

Also referred to as "intangible property," intellectual property consists of patents, trademarks, service marks, trade names, certification marks, copyrights, and mailing lists (which can be considered trade secrets). From a legal standpoint, the association should take all reasonable steps to protect its intangible property, such as filing registrations with appropriate state and government authorities. Registrations can enhance the value of intangible property and provide important procedural protections in the event of any litigation.

In addition to ensuring that they use proper copyright or trademark notices, file registration applications, and properly attribute sources in association publications, staff must also make sure that the association has all rights to use anyone else's copyrighted materials that it includes in its publications or other materials. For instance, articles submitted by independent authors or speeches made at association meetings and published in conference proceedings have to be handled in a manner that grants the association adequate rights to use the material as it wishes.

For copyrighted publications, the general recommendation is to obtain full copyright assignments so that the association *owns* the rights to the materials. Otherwise, it is sufficient for the holder of the copyrighted work (usually the author) to grant a release or license that is broad enough to cover any potential uses by the association. It's preferable that all who write for association publications or make presentations at association meetings submit standard-form copyright assignments or releases. Also, any agreements with independent contractors should include provisions assigning copyright to the association.

Intellectual property rights command increased attention as associations move further into the world of cyberspace by creating web sites, home pages, bulletin boards, and e-mail systems. Special legal issues apply to Internet activities, particularly in connection with intangible property rights, so associations should consult legal counsel before embarking on such activities.

Association Programs

The wide range of association activities and programs, different for each profession and industry, makes a full legal review of such programs impossible here. However, several themes run through the general collection of association programs and activities:

- **Antitrust.** The Sherman Act and other federal and state antitrust laws prohibit anticompetitive acts in restraint of trade. Among these are several commonly recognized illegal activities, such as price fixing, allocation of markets, and boycotting of competitors. But any activities considered unreasonably exclusionary or anticompetitive may give rise to problems. For instance, antitrust issues can crop up with respect to membership eligibility criteria, certification programs, availability of products and services to nonmembers, standard settings, promulgation of codes of conduct, statistical programs, and credit-reporting activities.

To avoid potential problems, associations need strong antitrust compliance policies that they routinely announce to members, particularly at association meetings. It's always advisable for legal counsel to attend meetings where sensitive topics are on the agenda and to remain apprised of any activities that potentially come within the jurisdiction of antitrust laws.

- **Due Process.** Association actions that are inherently exclusionary or may adversely affect members and others must be taken in accordance with basic due-process principles. In other words, association programs must be substantively and procedurally fair and reasonable.

  Furthermore, professional or product certification programs, standards setting, and other self-regulation programs should be developed in a fair and reasonable manner. They must not unfairly exclude those who should be entitled to participate or to receive credentials or other recognition from the association.

- **Membership.** Membership eligibility decisions and any disciplinary actions, particularly expulsion, must be undertaken in accordance with relevant due-process principles. It is recommended that members have the opportunity to appeal decisions to a neutral appeal panel.

- **Political and Lobbying Activities.** Special rules apply in this area. For instance, organizations that are exempt under Section 501(c)(3) of the Internal Revenue Code are absolutely prohibited from any political activities, such as supporting or opposing a particular candidate during an election campaign. Section 501(c)(3) also limits the amount of lobbying that organizations can conduct; lobbying cannot exceed an "insubstantial amount" or the specific limits established under Section 501(h) of the Internal Revenue Code.

  Although Section 501(c)(6) organizations have more freedom to lobby, they're subject to new lobbying dues nondeductibility laws, whereby the portion of member dues allocated to fund lobbying activities are nondeductible. Alternatively, the association can pay a "proxy" tax on such lobbying expenditures. (The American Society of Association Executives continues to challenge this law.)

  In addition, Congress in 1996 enacted a Lobbying Disclosure Act that requires registration of those lobbying the federal or executive branches of the United States government. The definitions of lobbying found in both the legislation and the Internal Revenue Code are broad and complex. To ensure compliance, associations may wish to seek the assistance of legal counsel.

Finally, under the Federal Election Campaign Act, it is illegal for corporations to participate in federal elections, except through political action committees (PACs). The rules for participation in federal elections and solicitations for PAC contributions are complex, and some states have laws with similar restrictions. Any associations engaging in political activity should consult legal counsel—except Section 501(c)(3) organizations for which such activities are not permitted.

Appropriate Protection

Association executives face numerous legal issues and obstacles in the daily course of their activities. That's why it's important for CEOs and staff to ensure that appropriate policies and procedures are in place to protect the association against potential liability. In situations where numerous, complicated, and often-times convoluted rules and regulations apply, however, CEOs may wish to seek legal counsel for assistance in devising appropriate steps or responses. In some cases, responding in the wrong manner may be worse than doing nothing.

Like it or not, one of the hats an association executive must wear says "Legal" on it, and he or she needs an adequate knowledge of legal issues to handle the job professionally and competently.

References and Suggested Reading

CCH Exempt Organizations Reporter.

CH Federal Election Campaign Financing Guide.

Hopkins, B., *The Law of Tax-Exempt Organizations,* 6th ed., John Wiley & Sons, 1992.

Jacobs, Jerald, *Association Law Handbook,* 3rd ed., American Society of Association Executives, Washington, D.C., 1996.

———, *Certification and Accreditation Law Handbook,* American Society of Association Executives, Washington, D.C., 1992.

———, *Federal Lobbying Law Handbook,* 2nd ed., American Society of Association Executives, Washington, D.C., 1993.

Jacobs, Jerald, and D. Ogden, *Legal Risk Management for Associations,* American Psychological Association, Washington, D.C., 1995.

Oleck, H., and M. Stewart, *Nonprofit Corporations, Organizations & Associations,* 6th ed., Prentice-Hall, Inc., Englewood Cliffs, N.J., 1994.

Webster, George, *Law of Associations,* Mathew Bender, New York, 1996.

Jefferson C. Glassie, J.D., is a partner at the law firm of Jenner & Block in Washington, D.C. He specializes in association and non-profit matters, working on a variety of legal matters. He is former chairman of the Law and Legislative Committee of the Greater Washington Society of Association Executives.

CHAPTER 6

POSITIVE PARENT/CHAPTER RELATIONSHIPS

RICHARD A. POPPA, CAE, AAI

Healthy, positive relationships don't just happen. They require hard work, mutual respect, and an understanding of the interdependence between the parties.

This recipe for success in personal relationships applies equally well to relations between national organizations and their chapters. In fact, relationships between related organizations share many of the same characteristics as relationships among people. The Golden Rule in this area of association management might well be: "Do unto your related organizations as you would have your related organizations do unto you."

Three key elements characterize a strong national/chapter relationship: clarity of role and purpose, open communication, and mutual commitment.

Element #1: Clarity of Role and Purpose

Each organization must clearly understand its own role and purpose, as well as how it is connected to the roles of related organizations. For example, do the national organization and its chapters equally share the responsibility of direct communications with members, or does the primary responsibility for this activity exist only at one level? The same level of understanding is equally important when it comes to delivering educational programs, conventions, insurance programs, and other services.

Clarity can be achieved by examining the following:

- **Organizational Documents.** The corporate charter, bylaws, and constitution of the component organizations will spell out the legal relationships that exist.

  For example, a chapter may come under the corporate entity of the national organization; therefore, the chapter's income, expenses, and liability all flow to the national organization. This is sometimes referred to as an *integrated chapter*. An *affiliated chapter*, on the other hand, refers to a relationship in which the chapter is a separate entity and operates independently.

- **Culture.** Often overlooked in the evaluation of national/chapter relations, culture refers to the norms of expectations and performance among the organizations.

For example, some organizations may emphasize state or local control of the organization's activities. Although it may not manifest itself in documents or agreements, this emphasis is still a critical component of the organizational culture that, if violated, may create ill will. Ideally, the documents that formally establish the relationship should explain the culture of the organization as well.

- **Planning and Operating Roles.** In many cases, one organization will have the primary responsibility in an area—such as membership recruitment—while the other has backup responsibility. In the bottom-up organization, for example, membership recruitment as well as dues collection and primary contact with members remain at the state or local level; the role of the national is to support that activity.

Organizational documents rarely establish such a specific operating relationship. Instead, this delineation can be accomplished through joint planning: The national organization would provide a sense of its overall direction, while each chapter would identify its individual strengths and the role it sees for itself. In practice, however, joint planning is difficult to achieve because of the diverse nature of organizations. At a minimum, each level of the organization should share its own plan and strategic direction with the others to ensure that significant conflicts do not exist.

A second approach is to create a document that describes the roles of each organization involved. This can enhance orientation processes as well as day-to-day operations.

The most successful organizations pinpoint the level at which a strength lies and then play to that strength. In most instances, the closer the organization is to the members, the better able it is to deliver those products and services that have a high degree of interaction with members. For instance, it's typically more economical (and more meaningful to members) for a local or state entity to conduct educational programs and seminars. (An exception might be a program featuring a nationally recognized speaker whose fees are too expensive for the chapter.)

No right or wrong approach exists. The correct approach is the one that best meets the needs of the members by assigning an activity to the level of the organization that's best-suited to support it.

Element #2: Open Communication

In *Organizational Communication: The Essence of Effective Management,* Philip V. Lewis writes, "Today's manager is a combination coach, teacher, judge, specialist, generalist, coordinator, planner and motivator. Fulfilling these roles requires a clearer understanding of the fundamentals of communication because communications is the very essence of any organization."

Role Call

Here's how an organization might define its roles in the area of chapter relations to minimize competition and duplication of services:

The role of the chapter is to:

- Work with national to regularly review and update national/chapter roles.
- Participate in the annual planning and budgeting process with national.
- Participate in joint planning and policy-making opportunities offered by national.
- Expand on research provided by national to evaluate member needs and association successes in meeting those needs.
- Regularly provide national directors an opportunity for a meaningful discussion of national activities during chapter board meetings.
- Support national programs and services with the members, and communicate them as an added value of membership in the chapter.
- Provide national with a copy of its annual plan.
- Endeavor to not compete with existing programs at the national level.

The role of the national is to:

- Conduct an annual planning process that invites chapter input.
- Provide ongoing, cost-effective research to evaluate member needs—and chapter successes in meeting those needs for use in developing annual national/chapter strategic plans.
- Provide chapters with cost-effective models, facilitators, time lines, bibliographies, and structures for planning.
- Organize national activities in a manner that minimizes duplication and competition with chapters.
- Avoid competing with chapters in offering products, programs, or services to members.
- Visit each chapter office regularly to conduct a joint evaluation of national's and the chapter's performance in meeting member needs.
- Assist chapters in improving performance, where they are failing to adequately meet member needs.

National/chapter relations aptly illustrate this axiom. While communication—transferring an idea, thought, or attitude—is certainly important between an organization and its membership, it's also critical among an organization's various entities. Inadequate or ineffective communication can seriously undermine efforts undertaken by one or all of the parties involved in the national/chapter relationship.

As Lewis notes, "An organization is a system of overlapping and interdependent groups. Consequently, if all things are equal, people will communicate most frequently to those individuals that are geographically closest to them." With that in mind, the components of open communication include:

- **Orientation.** The first step in building a strong communications foundation is to develop and implement an orientation program for volunteer leaders and for national and chapter employees. How orientation is managed either at the national or local level depends greatly on the structure and culture of the organization. Either way, information needs to be available at both the chapter and national level.

  Orientation works best as a stand-alone program; this positioning underscores the importance of the orientation process and prevents participants from being distracted by other events. An effective orientation program devotes significant time to the relationship between the organizations and also gives volunteers and association professionals the tools with which to deal with each organization.

- **Regular, Concise Information.** Regular, timely, and concise communications build upon a solid orientation program. The audience's characteristics will dictate the format and content of the communication, but conciseness is a key factor for all audiences given the information overload that everyone faces today.

  Another effective approach to national/chapter communication is to segment the audience; this enables messages to be targeted to the appropriate people at the appropriate time. Electronic forms of communication such as e-mail, the Internet, and the World Wide Web can increase the speed by which such targeted messages are delivered.

  An organization typically serves many publics, which range from association leaders to the general membership, from the trade press to the general media. Both the national and chapter will benefit from a clear understanding of who will communicate with each of these publics and how that communication will occur.

Resolving Conflicts

Within any healthy relationship, conflict will arise on occasion. In the parent/chapter situation, it's critical to recognize these conflicts and take appropriate steps to minimize them. Here are some ideas for conflict resolution:

1. Have both partners write a one- or two-paragraph description of their understanding of the conflict and their desired solution. Submit these two descriptions to a three-person panel comprising one representative of the national, one representative of the chapter, and a neutral third party. Use this as the basis for a meeting among the organizational leadership.

2. Determine who is primarily responsible for the particular activity that generated the conflict; let that organization take the lead in resolving it.

3. If the conflict is of a significant nature, the best solution may be to engage the respective boards of directors in a discussion about the situation. Frequently, significant conflicts are the result of problems inherent in the relationship among the partners. The best way to resolve those is in open and honest discussion.

Element #3: Mutual Commitment

The commitment of each partner to making the relationship work is characterized by respect for the other partner. Mutual respect requires each component of the organization to have a positive feeling about the value and the role the other partner brings to the relationship. Too often in national/chapter relations, distrust or even contempt arises among the groups; this is counterproductive to the overall good the association does in behalf of its members.

Of course, from time to time, component organizations will disagree on direction, policy, or implementation of programs. But when mutual respect exists, those disagreements focus on the issue at hand, not on whether one party has the right to be "at the table" or has questionable motives.

Declaration of Interdependence

Inherent in the national/chapter relationship is interdependency: Each organization has a stake in the results of the other. No matter what the operating structure of the organizations involved, this interdependency makes the end user—the association member—feel good about the organization and the value that he or she receives.

Imagine, for instance, that an executive receives a mailing from the chapter of a national organization to which she belongs. Does she limit her reaction, either favorably or unfavorably, exclusively to the chapter? Probably not. Most people transfer the value of a component organization to the value of the entire group.

As another example of interdependence, a state-based organization might do an excellent job of communicating to its members about a particular issue, thereby generating goodwill. This achievement, however, could be nullified in a moment if the national organization's mailing to the same members takes a different position.

In short, the way one partner chooses to do business affects the way the other partner is perceived. For better or for worse, members and the public measure chapters by the actions of the national organization. This was vividly illustrated in the early 1990s when leaders of the national United Way organization were accused of wrongdoing. Local United Way organizations may have had no connection with the allegations made against the national leaders, but many still suffered from the fallout in terms of decreased contributions.

With a commitment to maximize the individual strengths of the component organizations—and to make the relationship work in the best way possible for members—the national/chapter association family will prosper.

Glossary

The following terms can enhance understanding of the issues concerning national/chapter relations:

Affiliated group: Autonomous organization that has some formal relationship with a parent organization. (Example: allied societies of the American Society of Association Executives)

Bottom-up federation: Arrangement among contingent federations (mandatory membership at all levels) that gives the local organization a primary role in enrolling members, providing the focus for programming, or collecting dues for upward distribution.

Chapter: Group, organization, or association that has a formal relationship with a parent or umbrella organization and has jurisdiction over a geographic area rather than an area of special interest.

Coalition: Alliance between or among organizations, usually centering on a single, well-defined issue or concern.

Combination association: Organization composed of at least two of the following memberships: individuals, firms, and associations (also known as a conglomerate association).

Contingent membership: Arrangement between an organization and its chapters that requires members to belong to two or more levels (for example, by joining the national association you automatically become a member of a state chapter).

Council: Group, organization, or association that has jurisdiction over an area of interest (industry or professional skills) rather than a geographic area.

Federation: Organization in which associations are the principal organizational elements or members. (Examples: National Retail Federation and American Nurses Association)

Horizontal organization: Federation or organization organized around similar (but not the same) issues. (Example: American Recreation Coalition)

National organization: Central group within a federation to which all members relate or belong (also known as an umbrella organization).

Reciprocal membership: Arrangement between an umbrella organization and a chapter in which membership is not mandatory at all levels. (Examples: United States Chamber of Commerce and the American Medical Association)

Special interest section: Group or organization (but not an association) that operates with a limited amount of autonomy and has jurisdiction over an area of professional or business interest (see *Council*).

Top-down federation: Arrangement among contingent associations (mandatory membership at all levels) that gives the national organization a primary role in enrolling members, providing the focus for programming, or collecting dues for downward distribution.

Vertical organization: Federation or organization organized at each level around a central issue.

Source: Dennis Brown, Wayne L. Campbell, and Judith Pyke, *A Sharing of Expertise & Experience, 1991.*

References and Suggested Reading

Brown, Dennis, Wayne L. Campbell, and Judith Pyke, "National-State-Local Cooperation: The Winning Combination," *A Sharing of Expertise & Experience,* vol. 9, American Society of Association Executives, Washington, D.C., 1991.

Brown, Robert J., "Structuring Association Chapters," *The National-Chapter Partnership,* American Society of Association Executives, Washington, D.C., 1993.

Chaloupka, Marla, "Education and Awareness: Communications with Chapters," *A Sharing of Expertise & Experience,* vol. 8, American Society of Association Executives, Washington, D.C., 1990.

Cotter, Jennifer, "How to Develop a Quality Awards Program," *Chapter Relations,* March/April 1995, American Society of Association Executives, Washington, D.C.

Daly, Nancy R., and Nora L. Gambo, "How a Financial Education Program Improved Chapter Relations," *Dollars + Cents,* April 1992, American Society of Association Executives, Washington, D.C.

Downey, Melissa, and Ann L. Oliveri, "Support Systems Keeping the Lines Open," *A Sharing of Expertise & Experience,* vol. 8, American Society of Association Executives, Washington, D.C., 1990.

Estok, Marcy A., "Increasing Member/Customer Satisfaction Through Chapters," *A Sharing of Expertise & Experience,* vol. 11, American Society of Association Executives, Washington, D.C., 1994.

Fadik, Becky L., "A Manual that Benefits Volunteer Officers," *Chapter Relations,* March/April 1994, American Society of Association Executives, Washington, D.C.

——— and Brian Taylor, "Serving Your Association's Chapters/Sections with Field Service Representatives," *A Sharing of Expertise & Experience,* vol. 9, American Society of Association Executives, Washington, D.C., 1991.

Forbes, Paul S., "Together at the Takeoff: National/Chapter Strategic Planning," *A Sharing of Expertise & Experience,* vol. 8, American Society of Association Executives, Washington, D.C., 1990.

Gable, Ty E., and Charles E. Hawkins III, "National/Chapter Relations: For Better or Worse, 'Til Death Do Us Part," *A Sharing of Expertise & Experience,* vol. 10, American Society of Association Executives, Washington, D.C., 1992.

Geracie, Kathy, and James S. Schaming, "Growing Chapters with TQM," *Chapter Relations,* May/June 1995, American Society of Association Executives, Washington, D.C.

Gossett, James F., "Legal Aspects of Chapter Relations," *Association Law & Policy,* January 15, 1995.

Hannah, Sharon, "Encouraging Chapter Excellence Through an Awards Program," *A Sharing of Expertise & Experience,* vol. 8, American Society of Association Executives, Washington, D.C., 1990.

Hauschild, Beverly E., Ann C. Kenworthy, and Connie C. Wallace, "Everybody's Talking: Preventing and Resolving Conflict Between National and Chapters," *A Sharing of Expertise & Experience*, vol. 5, American Society of Association Executives, Washington, D.C., 1987.

Karelitz, Carolyn, "Creating and Maintaining a New Chapter Support Package," *A Sharing of Expertise & Experience*, vol. 10, American Society of Association Executives, Washington, D.C., 1992.

Jacobvitz, Robert, "Does the National Staff Know Who You Are and How to Effectively Work with You?," *A Sharing of Expertise & Experience*, vol. 8, American Society of Association Executives, Washington, D.C., 1990.

Murphy, John M., "National/Chapter Strategic Partnering: A Four-Question Model for Planning Success," *A Sharing of Expertise & Experience*, vol. 11, American Society of Association Executives, Washington, D.C., 1994.

Newton, Patricia M., "Goals and Roles: National Support for Chapter Leaders," *A Sharing of Expertise & Experience*, vol. 9, American Society of Association Executives, Washington, D.C., 1991.

Osina, Thomas C., "Making the Field Office an Integral Part of the Association," *A Sharing of Expertise & Experience*, vol. 11, American Society of Association Executives, Washington, D.C., 1994.

——, "Follow the Four 'Rs' When Working with Chapters," *Chapter Relations*, November/December 1994, American Society of Association Executives, Washington, D.C.

Pendley, Donald L., "Coaching Chapters in Public Relations," *Communication News*, July 1995, American Society of Association Executives, Washington, D.C.

Petrick, Annette E., "Looking at Things a Different Way," *A Sharing of Expertise & Experience*, vol. 7, American Society of Association Executives, Washington, D.C., 1989.

Riska, Stacey, "Tackling a Membership Campaign: Chapters Score New Members in Sporty Recruitment Game," *Membership Marketer*, April 1993, American Society of Association Executives, Washington, D.C.

Siegel, Patricia A., "How to Get 7,000 Members in One Month," *Membership Developments*, November 1993, American Society of Association Executives, Washington, D.C.

Sroge, Marian R., "Expanding Your Membership: Build Chapters One Member at a Time," *Membership Developments*, December 1993, American Society of Association Executives, Washington, D.C.

——, "Expansion is Not a 4-Letter Word: The Exciting Process of Forming New Chapters," *A Sharing of Expertise & Experience*, vol. 11, American Society of Association Executives, Washington, D.C., 1993.

Shinn, Linda J., and Martha L. Orr, "Forging an Effective State National Partnership and Making It Work," *A Sharing of Expertise & Experience*, vol. 11, American Society of Association Executives, Washington, D.C., 1994.

Toth, Lorili, "5,000 New Members for as Little as $2 Each," *Chapter Relations*, July/August 1995, American Society of Association Executives, Washington, D.C.

Wisniewski, Joseph, "Why You Need a Chapter Financial Handbook," *Dollars + Cents*, May 1994, American Society of Association Executives, Washington, D.C.

Richard A. Poppa, CAE, AAI, serves as executive vice president and secretary of the Independent Insurance Agents Association of New York, in Syracues. He formerly served as senior vice president and chief operating officer for the Independent Insurance Agents of America, in Alexandria, Virginia.

CHAPTER 7

SUBSIDIARY CORPORATIONS

WILLIAM T. ROBINSON, CAE

When associations wish to expand their scope of activities—by offering group-purchasing arrangements, insurance programs, investment services, books and journals, or travel services to name just a few possibilities—they often establish a subsidiary or an affiliate organization. The difference is mainly one of ownership: Subsidiaries are owned, while affiliates are independent corporations.

In either case, the association's legal counsel must be involved in establishing the corporation because of the many federal, state, and possibly foreign laws and regulations that may pertain. For instance, a general business corporation in Delaware is substantially different from one in California or from a captive insurance company in Vermont.

Generally speaking, associations form subsidiary corporations for five reasons. They are to:

1. **Allow the association to engage in activities not permitted by its purpose, charter, or bylaws.** The Internal Revenue Service (IRS) does not exempt from taxes non-related business income of trade associations and individual membership societies that fall under Section 501(c)(6) of the Internal Revenue Code. Nor can these organizations receive tax-deductible contributions from donors. One solution is to form an affiliate and qualify it as a 501(c)(3) organization, which *can* receive gifts or grants that are tax-deductible to the donor.

   Similarly, state and federal regulatory agencies have long maintained authority over certain businesses and would prevent an association from engaging in those businesses directly. One example is insurance underwriting—the association itself could not be an actual insurance company, but it can form a separate corporation to act as one.

2. **Enable the association to offer services to niche markets.** A specific set of members may express a desire for something that other members aren't interested in, such as a geographic-based facility or service. Rather than use all members' dues to fund something that not all would benefit from, an association could establish a subsidiary to meet those specific needs. Only those using the service would pay for it, and the association would charge related staff time to the subsidiary's budget, not its own.

3. **Provide additional revenue sources.** Some members might argue that associ-

ation dues are similar to a tax, and there's a limit to how much they're willing to be taxed. Rather than increase membership dues, associations can generate revenues through profit-seeking, tax-paying enterprises. (Because these association-related enterprises usually compete with tax-paying businesses, they are also subject to taxes, according to the IRS.)

4. **Increase the association's capacities and scope.** An association that can provide a wide range of additional services makes itself more valuable to members. Although additional staff are often needed to manage and operate an association's various business enterprises, they bring an expertise that can be of great value in other areas.

5. **Protect the association from the consequences of an activity's financial failure.** Any activity has a risk associated with it. Financial risks, in particular, increase with an activity's size and complexity. This is especially true when significant capital expenditures are required, along with expert (and expensive) personnel. But if an association carries on its high-risk activities through a separate corporation, the bankruptcy of one won't necessarily damage the financial viability of other activities or of the association itself.

Patterns of Governance

Generally speaking, an association can choose from four patterns of control or governance. Each has its pluses and minuses, as explained below:

1. **After forming the new company, the association turns it over to the participating members.** The association may maintain a presence by having its chief executive officer (CEO) or an elected leader sit on the subsidiary board.

   Advantages: The association will have performed a service for its members by establishing the company. Turning the new organization over to participants enables the association to avoid further operational responsibility and to remain focused on its principal mission.

   Disadvantages: The association will eventually lose identification with the enterprise, along with its ability to use the company for new purposes. Additionally, the association loses a potential source of additional revenue and staff expertise.

2. **The association board serves as the board of the subsidiary.** The two boards may be identical, or the subsidiary's board may have a few of the same officers and directors.

   Advantages: All the necessary business of the subsidiaries can be conducted at regular meetings of the association's board. In this way, board members become familiar with the activities of the subsidiaries, and the association avoids the additional costs of separate board meetings for the subsidiary.

   Disadvantages: As the subsidiary grows in size, the number of issues requiring attention by the governing board increases. These can reach the point where time is not available to accommodate the agendas of both the association and its subsidiaries. More important, the experience required to serve on an association board is not necessarily the same as that required to serve on the board of a complex subsidiary, such as an insurance company.

Lastly, by design, association governing boards have a regular turnover in membership. The same rate of turnover, however, is not necessarily good for subsidiary boards, where stability and accumulated experience are valuable from a business perspective.

3. **The association appoints the board of the subsidiary.** Usually selected are people with experience in the subsidiary's activities—perhaps some from the participating members—plus a representative of the association's governing board or executive committee and the CEO. This pattern is frequently used when an association has more than one subsidiary or when its subsidiary has a high level of activity.

Advantages: The subsidiary company is free to take on a life of its own, often independent of the association. The potentially heavy hand of over-governance by the association's board is avoided.

Disadvantages: The association incurs additional expenses to hold separate board meetings. Also, taking on "a life of its own" can so distance a subsidiary from its parent association that control issues emerge; subsidiary real estate operations or insurance companies, for instance, can have financial statements that dwarf the association's other resources.

4. **The association creates a holding company to oversee the subsidiaries' work.** The governing board of the holding company may be drawn from the association's executive committee or from the boards of the subsidiaries. Or, it might include senior staff officers of the association and the CEOs of the subsidiaries.

Advantages: When subsidiaries have become numerous, a holding company can summarize all activities in one report to the association's board. This permits the board to devote its time and attention to the normal association business.

Disadvantages: Subsidiary activities can become increasingly remote from the functions of the association, as perceived by its governing board.

For any of these structures, the parent organization can exert additional control by appointing its CEO, chief financial officer, or general counsel to serve in the same capacity for the subsidiary.

Management and Staffing

If a subsidiary engages in a minor activity, the association may assign managerial responsibility to a current staff member on an "additional duties" basis. If the subsidiary operates within a complex or fast-changing field, however, an expert in that area is required. He or she will eventually come to understand the parent association and associations in general, while providing valuable expertise.

One large professional association tried to sidestep the need for such expertise by appointing its executive committee as the board of the subsidiary company and its public relations director as the subsidiary company's manager. The public relations director's duties included liaison with the parent association's local societies, which were the intended beneficiaries of the subsidiary. The company manager did not report to the subsidiary company's board but to executives within the association.

While the company manager was learning about the subsidiary's business, the new company missed major opportunities for service and growth. A few years later, the manager retired and was succeeded by an executive experienced in the subsidiary's field. At this point, the subsidiary's business markets collapsed due to external forces. The association's subsidiary was financially unprepared for this, and the new executive requested large infusions of capital.

The executive committee of the association, however, in its role as the subsidiary's governing board, had turned over several times and had gradually lost interest in the affairs of the company. No one on the board recalled the crisis that had resulted in the subsidiary's formation. As a result the board did not provide additional capital. The company failed.

This example illustrates the necessity of employing trained personnel for each major subsidiary activity, as well as the importance of continuity among members of the subsidiary's governing board. Additional considerations for staffing subsidiaries include the following:

- **Experts should receive compensation based on the industry from which they have been recruited.** Compensation of association staff tends to reflect the patterns within the industry or profession represented, with modifications based on the association's locale, size, and scope. The same is true of compensation within the industry of the subsidiary.

  Often the two systems clash, causing difficulties for the association's CEO. For example, incentives for attracting new business, prizes, bonuses for achievement of management objectives, and stock options are common in industry but seldom found in associations. Yet the association may need to offer these to subsidiary employees to aid in their recruitment and retention.

- **Experts need to continue associating with colleagues and events in their industry.** A subsidiary's specialized employees maintain their expertise by associating with their colleagues. The related expenses may exceed those for employees of the association, especially where extensive or international travel is involved. This situation may create jealousy, or perhaps a sense of unequal treatment, on the part of association employees. The association CEO should be prepared to address any morale problem that may arise.

- **"Outside" experts may find the association world confusing or less interesting than their own fields.** Associations are usually deliberative and feature committee-based decision making, which people from some industries may find unfamiliar. Generally speaking, associations are also risk averse. These differences can be a source of difficulty, especially in the early stages of a new enterprise.

Potential Perils

These three perils may affect associations that operate subsidiaries:

1. **Failure of the enterprise.** In establishing a new activity, it is often difficult to find members who are willing to take the risks associated with it—especially in areas where growth is essential to success.

   In other words, it's easy to find the people willing to go second but difficult to find those willing to go first. If growth is essential to the subsidiary's financial viability but doesn't occur, it's wiser to discontinue the effort and accept the early loss to avoid a constant drain on the association's resources.

   Association subsidiaries can also fail for lack of sufficient start-up capital or overly optimistic assumptions of early success.

2. **Failure to recognize the enterprise's obsolescence.** Members will seek the best price of a product or service. Even loyalty to the association eventually takes a back seat to better prices. When an outside agency can perform the services of an association subsidiary better or cheaper—usually because of the economies of greater volume or more sophisticated systems—it's wiser to discontinue the effort. Sometimes the association can sell its subsidiary to its more successful competitor.

3. **Turnover on the governing board or the arrival of "second guessers."** New members of the association's governing board bring different experiences from those in leadership positions when the subsidiary was established. In addition, the subsidiary may have solved a problem that existed years earlier but is no longer evident to new board members.

   To avoid the surprise of opposition surfacing at a meeting, the orientation of new board members should devote sufficient time to reviewing the nature, purpose, and activities of each subsidiary. Any antipathy on the part of a new board member can be identified early on and accommodated with additional information.

Are subsidiaries worth the effort and the risk? The answer lies not in a simple yes or no but on individual circumstances. Timing, opportunity, finances, association leadership—even ambition—all play a role in the decision-making process.

On balance, subsidiaries can increase the value of an association to its members, expand the capacities and scope of the association, build up the association's revenue and wealth, and position the association to accommodate unforeseen challenges and opportunities.

William T. Robinson, CAE, is a retired senior vice president of the American Hospital Association. He currently serves the American Society of Association Executives (ASAE) as chair of the ASAE Insurance Company.

CHAPTER 8

LEADING THE WAY TO A HEALTHY ORGANIZATION

ELAINE KOTELL BINDER, CAE

> Once more unto the breach, dear friends, once more…
> Follow your spirit, and upon this charge
> Cry "God for Harry, England and Saint George!"
>
> —William Shakespeare, *The Life of King Henry V*

L ike Henry V, who exhorted his soldiers to follow him into battle at Agincourt, a leader must inspire others to participate in fulfilling a vision of what is possible. In addition to this charismatic spark, association executives must understand the skills and processes of leadership so they can enhance their existing capacities and develop those areas that are found wanting.

As the center of leadership for the organization (Herman and Heimovics 1991), the chief executive officer (CEO) influences the behaviors of both staff and volunteer leaders. The leadership processes discussed below focus on relationships with staff, yet the concepts apply equally well to relationships with volunteer leaders.

Warren Bennis (1989) identifies five basic ingredients of leadership: a guiding vision, passion, integrity, curiosity, and daring. While these intangible assets contribute enormously to their charisma, leaders must exhibit additional and more concrete behaviors to guide, facilitate, mentor, and coach others to carry out the work of the association. For instance, they must:

- **Be strategic thinkers.** Intuitive and interpretative skills enable leaders to understand the people around them, internalize the data they receive, recognize the relationships that exist between the systems within their world, and integrate all these elements into a coherent whole.

- **Have credibility.** In addition to professional expertise, leaders must exhibit an authenticity between their words and deeds. They need to be able to build trust so that those around them will have faith in their leadership and follow the path carved out, even through difficult terrain.

- **Be skilled communicators.** Emphasizing the importance of two-way communications ensures that leaders are not only being heard themselves but also are hearing from others. An open communication process provides leaders with knowledge about constituent groups within the association and substantive issues that affect its existence. This process enables them to better understand the diversity of opinions and behaviors within the organization, while providing opportunities for others to feel valued.

- **Have clear expectations.** Those who can establish well-defined parameters for performance—while giving sufficient latitude for individual differences—exhibit a consistency of expectations that increases the likelihood of excellent performance. When a leader demonstrates respect for individuals and a commitment to developing the leadership potential of others, staff have an increased sense of being valued. As a result, their loyalty to the association and to the leader intensifies.

In sum, leaders need to create and sustain a healthy community in which an equilibrium exists between the many forces within the organization. Positioned at the fulcrum of a seesaw, the leader must balance the personal and the professional, the competitive and the collaborative, the individual and the group, the needs of the volunteer and those of the staff, and the pressures of competing goals. Associations in which leaders manifest these qualities and behaviors are more likely to be competitive in the marketplace of ideas and more likely to attract both employees and members.

Sharing the Vision

The ability to exercise leadership competencies begins with an understanding of human behavior and a knowledge of the processes and techniques that contribute to and complement these competencies.

In the *Fifth Discipline Fieldbook,* Peter Senge writes that "a system is a perceived whole whose elements 'hang together' because they continually affect each other over time and operate toward a common purpose." Systems thinking can be applied to all aspects of an organization, most notably to its reason for being: An association's mission is central to and affects all other systems within the organization.

A nonprofit organization's mission serves as the basis for developing the criteria by which success will be measured over time (Wolf 1984). The organization's ability to carry out that mission depends on the degree to which all the groups and operations within it join together and move toward a common destination. The mission of the association must become a dynamic concept that staff incorporates into every aspect of their work. All activities of the association must be organized around the goals and objectives that move the association toward accomplishing its mission.

The effective association will be led by someone who has a clear vision of how to organize resources around the mission—the central defining reason for the association's existence and the work carried out in its name. However, that vision cannot be created in isolation from those who will be responsible for implementing it. Building and supporting a shared vision requires an ongoing process of discussing and sharing the meaning of the association's work and an individual's participation in it (Senge 1994). While volunteer leaders determine the association's mission as part of the strategic planning process, the staff leader creates multiple opportunities for staff to support and share that mission and ensures its integration into every aspect of the association.

In associations with a carefully constructed approach to generating shared commitment, staff members recognize that their perspectives are valued. They make a commitment to behaviors that support the organization's ability to accomplish its goals; they see a relationship between their professional satisfaction and the organization's success.

Building that commitment requires ongoing communication from the top leadership not only to the staff but also to every other component of the association, including members and committee leaders. Creating an open, deliberative forum that encourages the expression of ideas sets the stage for commitment by all parties.

The mission continues to influence the staff's work when they consistently examine its implications on their responsibilities, work plans, and performance reviews. Guiding employees through a process of developing all-staff goals linked to the association's mission and the strategic plan results in the staff setting performance expectations as a group. The development of individualized staff goals and objectives then flows out of this process.

Both of these exercises generate criteria that the group and individual staff members can use for evaluation purposes. For example, a staff performance-review process that parallels the board evaluation of the association's progress in meeting its goals creates a partnership between staff and the top leadership. It also gives purpose and coherence to staff performance.

Communicating for Results

In their book *Successful Association Leadership*, Glenn Tecker and Marybeth Fidler describe five broad competency areas needed for 21st century leaders:

1. Employing interpersonal skills.

2. Understanding complex relationships.

3. Acquiring and using information.

4. Valuing and using technology.

5. Deploying key resources.

Their concept of a superior leader is someone who has considerable intellectual capital as well as extraordinary human relations capabilities; these enable that leader to steer successfully through the "permanent whitewater" that characterizes today's business environment. At a minimum, leaders must demonstrate a level of knowledge and expertise that commands the respect of their colleagues and peers.

While behavior is the best indicator of competency, however, communicating effectively is a mark of excellence. Leaders need skills of both diagnosis and communication (Herman and Heimovics 1991). Listening, interpreting, and understanding what is being heard will enable leaders to understand the needs of their constituents, as well as the effect of their own behavior on others (Bolton 1979). Integrating what they have learned with the vision that has emerged helps leaders shape messages and stimulate processes and behaviors that inspire others to follow their guidance.

Resolving Interpersonal Conflict

An association can be viewed as a micro-community where a small group of people are expected to collaborate and feel mutually responsible for accomplishing their common goals. To ensure that this micro-community functions effectively, processes must be in place to resolve any conflicts that arise among community members. An overall philosophy of conflict resolution—and having steps in place to handle conflicts—contributes to the health and vitality of the community and reduces the likelihood of disagreements impeding work.

Because conflict seems an inevitable part of the human condition—one that can sap the energy of those faced with it regularly—it is important for leaders to establish a variety of systems that distribute the responsibility for conflict resolution. The tendency of most people dealing with interpersonal conflict is to employ either "fight or flight" methods. Therefore, training staff in more effective conflict-resolution techniques can be beneficial.

For example, developing language and techniques for defining behaviors and for handling the emotional components of conflict (Bolton 1979) will increase a person's ability to develop more rational approaches to the situation. Skills training that provides staff with insights into their own and others' behavior will lead to higher levels of proficiency in resolving conflicts; it will also contribute to staff's personal and professional development.

While most associations hold staff training sessions that focus on working with volunteer committees, the tendency is to avoid staff-to-staff conflict resolution training and to individually coach staff when conflicts arise. A more effective approach is to plan regular staff development training that includes discussions about the ways in which staff members approach and solve problems, their reactions to criticism, and how they handle pressure.

Interpersonal conflicts often escalate the longer they remain unresolved. One strategy for reducing this likelihood is to insist that staff members who have a conflict with one another first attempt to negotiate a resolution themselves. In other words, supervisors should resist the temptation to step in and solve the problem.

When an association has such rules, training becomes imperative: The staff needs the skills to fulfill the expectations. Furthermore, being a coach is an important role for a leader in these situations. Coaching staff members through the process of resolving interpersonal conflicts often enables leaders to facilitate a resolution without being directly involved.

Creating association-wide opportunities to identify problems and generate solutions is another effective technique for resolving differences. For instance, discussing issues becomes more natural when staff meetings regularly include time for discussing problems and possible solutions. In addition to providing leaders with a better understanding of the issues surrounding problems, this gives them an opportunity to demonstrate and model facilitative behaviors. Two other tactics can make rational conflict resolution a normal part of an association's life: Holding meetings devoted solely to evaluation and decision making or developing implementation strategies for decisions that have already been made.

Group Facilitation

Being an expert facilitator of a group requires three types of competencies: informative, interpretive, and intuitive (Zimmerman and Evans).

By employing *informative* skills, a leader ensures that the discussion has structure and is directed toward the goal. Strategies include clarifying the purpose of the group; establishing a process for the discussion by having an agenda; developing, along with the group, ground rules for behavior (for example, be concise and respect everyone's contribution); and periodically evaluating the effectiveness of the group discussion and process.

The more complex *interpretive* skills enable the leader to translate concepts that group members have articulated and reframe the discussion to take it to the next level of understanding. In addition, being able to manage the emotions that may arise requires an understanding and interpretation of people's hidden agendas.

The most complex group-facilitation skills are *intuitive*. They require the leader to synthesize ideas into understandable concepts and integrate these into the larger whole. Intuition is defined as the power of knowing things without conscious reasoning. While much of intuitive thinking is the result of experience, listening to the "inner messages" that accompany that experience is essential.

Everyone Wins

One effective way to resolve conflict is the "no lose" method (Gordon 1977). This problem-solving process works well with conflicts that involve as few as two people or large groups, because it produces solutions that result in mutual-needs satisfaction. It includes these six steps:

1. Identify and define the problem.
2. Generate alternative solutions.
3. Evaluate the alternatives.
4. Make the decision.
5. Implement the decision.
6. Follow up to evaluate the solution.

While such a structured approach may not be suitable for every conflict, a skilled facilitator will find that the process helps the parties navigate through highly emotional situations. A no-lose decision, however, does not necessarily mean that all members of a group agree with the decision. Instead, it refers to all parties being willing to accept a particular decision because sufficient agreements have been reached to convince each group that it did not lose.

Leaders who build on intuition in the group process can take a group to higher levels of functioning.

Clearly, effective leaders require an understanding of both individual behavior and of group dynamics. Within a group, the members will play two types of positive roles that enable work to progress. *Task roles* focus on accomplishing the substantive goals of the meeting; they include such behaviors as seeking and giving information, summarizing, and testing the feasibility of ideas. *Maintenance roles* concentrate on interpersonal elements and are characterized by behaviors such as encouraging others, showing a willingness to compromise, expressing the feelings of the group, or helping the group to stay focused on the issues at hand. When the facilitator or other members of the group affirm those who play positive roles, the group can become more productive.

On the other hand, some members of a group may adopt negative roles such as dominating, blocking, and seeking recognition. To counteract these behaviors, which can have an adverse effect on the group's work, the group leader must draw on a range of techniques. One effective strategy is to focus attention on the group process itself; this can be done by introducing into the agenda an examination of what is occurring within the group and discussing the roles that affect the group's work. This technique makes each participant aware of and responsible for the entire group's effectiveness.

Association executives typically hold "post mortems" after board meetings to brief staff on the outcomes. Many associations use these sessions to identify issues related to implementing board decisions and to develop general strategies for implementation. This approach provides an excellent opportunity for the executive to set in motion a process whereby small work groups or teams develop specific objectives, timetables for implementation, and a plan to monitor progress and evaluate outcomes. The process of planning, monitoring, and evaluating the implementation of specific board decisions thus sets the stage for staff to adapt these behaviors to all association projects and activities.

Inspiring Staff

While leaders cannot be held accountable for the internal qualities that motivate people, they *are* responsible for creating an environment that stimulates motivated behavior. In his classic work on employee motivation, Frederick Herzberg (1975) describes the factors that lead to the highest level of job satisfaction: achievement, recognition, the work itself, responsibility, advancement, and growth. Although generational differences may appear to influence employee motivation, experience has demonstrated that Herzberg's factors continue to be highly related to satisfaction.

Leaders who focus on these motivational factors will seek opportunities for recognizing staff contributions and for enhancing personal and professional growth. They will establish a climate that values and rewards innovation, experimentation, and risk-taking. In so doing, they will inspire others to strive to achieve their greatest potential.

Because leaders are role models, they will want to actively mentor—teach, coach, and help pave the way for—staff members who demonstrate potential. Under the tutelage of such mentors, staff members can take advantage of opportunities to develop their leadership skills and position themselves for the future. Leaders who have high self-esteem, are personally secure, and have confidence in their own abilities recognize that developing future leaders is a legacy that reflects positively on them.

Building Consensus

Max DePree, an authority on leadership, believes that "…every vital organization thrives because it depends more on commitment and enthusiasm than on the letter of the contract" and that "an open, participative structure or system of management most often elicits good performance…" (DePree 1992). One criterium of participative leadership is welcoming staff input into the association's decision-making process.

A leader can make a decision with or without input from the group, or the group can make the decision by vote or by consensus. While leaders are often required to make decisions independently or after consultation with others, numerous situations would benefit from gaining the commitment of others through a consensus-building process. That consensus often makes the difference between the successful and unsuccessful implementation of a decision.

Consensus does not require everyone to agree with the outcome; no vote is taken. Consensus *does* require that participants have sufficient time to express their opinions and can be moved to the point where they are ready to accept the group's general agreements.

Creating consensus requires a leader to build agreements around issues related to the particular decision. Using an expanding and contracting process of communications in which ideas are generated, summarized, and then returned to the group for continued discussion, the leader interprets and reinterprets the issues. He or she narrows down any areas of disagreement until the people involved reach consensus.

While this process is most often carried out in face-to-face encounters, it is also effective when the parties are not convened. In that case, the leader solicits input from multiple sources over time, crafts and refines the issues, and sends them to the entire group for review. This process continues until the group reaches consensus.

While this takes considerably more time than other forms of decision making, being part of the process increases commitment by the participants. This becomes critical when the issue requires participants to be involved in implementation. One caveat exists to the consensus building approach: Participants must agree at the outset how the decision will be made if the group fails to come to consensus.

Developing Individual Potential

One characteristic that defines an effective leader is his or her ability to select highly qualified staff and then create a learning environment in which all employees challenge themselves to develop to their fullest potential.

Some effective ways of enabling people to become active participants in the organization and to grow personally and professionally include:

- **Delegating responsibility,** which implies trust in the person's ability to make appropriate decisions and act effectively on them. Furthermore, it sends the message that the success of the association depends upon the accumulated actions of individual staff members.

- **Setting and communicating performance standards.** If, for example, the association expects excellence, leaders must communicate well-defined criteria for evaluating performance on that basis.

- **Giving immediate, specific, and honest feedback.** This enables staff to understand the expectations and recognize the existence of an environment that supports and encourages them to achieve the expected level of performance.

- **Working with staff to identify areas where training and education would be beneficial** and structuring work situations to maximize personal strengths and minimize weaknesses. This helps staff strive for the excellence that is desired and stimulates staff to plan for long-term career goals. The leader can provide insights about opportunities, within both the organization and the profession, where the staff member can develop his or her own leadership skills.

A Commitment to Diversity

The workforce of the 21st century will be truly heterogeneous—a mosaic of people who differ by gender, race, ethnic background, sexual preference, and physical ability (Jarratt and Coates 1994). Association leaders, who are already expected to be skilled communicators, must also develop the ability to understand and accept a wide range of human behaviors, particularly those based on cultural diversity.

Culture, also known as a "world view," refers to a set of basic assumptions that reflect the patterns of thoughts, feelings, and behaviors of the different identity groups to which people belong. Just as each association has a distinctive culture, so, too, does each person within that association; each brings his or her own world view to bear on that of the entire community.

In preparation for the future, today's leaders must develop strategies for ensuring that people of diverse backgrounds can work together productively. This necessitates an understanding of the differences in human behavior based on culture as well as personality. It requires *creating a climate* where staff will learn to understand one another, respect individual differences, and see different world views as important contributions toward the achievement of the association's goals. This is best accomplished when the executive is clear about his or her values and models the desired behaviors, when staff develop agreements about core values, and when performance is evaluated not only on the achievement of association goals but also on the qualitative elements of interpersonal relationships.

If an organization has agreed-upon norms and standards of behavior—for example, "Our goals in hiring will be to seek out individuals of varying ages, gender, and background in order to have a workforce that is diverse"—it's more likely to value individual differences. Because diversity extends beyond staff concerns and is reflected in the association's approach to its members, it is critical that staff pay attention to this issue. Ongoing human relations and diversity training programs that emphasize the value of soliciting and integrating different opinions can promote and reinforce a culture that truly values diversity. Educating staff members about holidays and customs celebrated by their colleagues moves the issue into a more social arena that is less emotionally charged and promotes camaraderie.

Workplace inclusiveness requires the total commitment of leaders and a plan of action that contains tangible strategies aimed at identifying and eliminating workplace barriers and enabling staff to work effectively and productively. Attention to diversity and inclusiveness is not just a "feel good" phenomenon; it is responsible behavior that addresses the realities of the workplace. The leader's challenge is to balance the needs of individuals with the needs of the organization. Associations that focus on inclusiveness find that they are better able to understand and meet the needs of their members.

As Norris and Lofton (1995) note, "The capacity to capitalize on changing demographic conditions in the marketplace becomes a fundamental competency of the organization."

Working in Teams

The complexity of association challenges and economic pressures require staff to work together effectively. Some associations rely on teams to carry out all work; others create teams for specific projects. One organization may appoint a special team to redesign its marketing plan, while another may have an ongoing team that determines how to evaluate performance.

According to Katzenbach and Smith (1993), "A team is a small number of people with complementary skills who are committed to a common purpose, a common set of performance goals and a common approach for which they hold themselves mutually accountable." Teams differ from other types of groups: Although someone may serve as the team's designated leader, other members will share the maintenance and task roles described above. The team leader's role is facilitative; he or she keeps the group on track and manages relationships with the rest of the organization.

While conventional wisdom states that teams can range in size from 2 to 25, larger teams often divide into subteams for efficiency. The charge given to the team must have sufficiently broad parameters to permit team members to translate the general purpose into specific performance goals in which they will have ownership. The process of clarifying and specifying these goals also gives team members their first opportunity to communicate clearly with one another and to develop constructive approaches to resolving conflicts that may arise.

Early on, high-performing teams decide how to complete their job. Through this exercise they develop a work plan that includes an allocation of responsibilities among the team members, a schedule of deadlines, agreements about how to handle missed deadlines, and the process used for making decisions. Teams also should analyze their needs and request additional training, consultation, or other assistance that may be necessary. Finally, in addition to individual accountability, members have a mutual accountability to fellow teammates for their collective work. Therefore, they need to determine a process for evaluating both their individual and group performance.

When selecting team members, a leader has the responsibility of ensuring that the team has the resources—technical, problem-solving, and interpersonal skills—plus the expertise needed to fulfill the charge. In some instances, leaders might help staff acquire the necessary knowledge and skills by providing appropriate reading material, offering training, and serving as a coach and mentor.

Recognizing and Rewarding Performance

Many people find personal satisfaction through achieving performance excellence. Those whose attainments are further rewarded will continue contributing to the organization. Economic constraints may limit rewards in the form of salary increases and bonuses, yet other ways of acknowledging achievements can be effective. They range from the tangible—attendance at a professional seminar or flexible working arrangements—to the intangible, such as a public thank-you for someone's contribution. Leaders who can identify which rewards are important to which person will inspire additional loyalty and commitment.

Creating a Healthy Organization

A healthy organization exhibits a synergy between values that nurture, challenge, and empower people and behaviors that support commitment to the organization and its mission. A healthy organization takes a holistic view of staff, giving equal importance to their personal and professional lives.

Viewing people as its most valuable asset, a healthy organization reflects a humanistic philosophy through the roles and responsibilities articulated for its staff, the processes by which decisions are made, and the policies and practices that are implemented. A vitality and spirit permeate settings where this congruence between philosophy and behavior exists, which motivates staff to focus on and attain exceptional performance (Rosen and Berger 1991).

Associations face a unique challenge because they must concentrate on meeting the needs of their members. In other words, leaders must focus attention

What It Takes

Leadership is about challenging the process, inspiring a shared vision, empowering others to act, modeling the way, and encouraging the heart (Kouzes and Posner 1988). Leaders are willing and able to recognize the potential of others and to create opportunities for others to succeed. In addition, leaders:

- Take risks and support ideas that may challenge the status quo.
- Expect to learn from their mistakes as well as from their successes.
- Spend much of their time peering into the future and creating a vision of how to move toward that future. They do not command adherence to their vision but rather use the full range of their skills to inspire commitment to it.
- Use the word "we" instead of "I". They recognize they cannot achieve their vision without the commitment of others.
- Create a participative environment, finding multiple opportunities for followers to be involved through collaboration, mutual communication processes, and team work.
- Set the example for others by being consistent and by conveying congruence between their beliefs and their behavior.
- Behave ethically and with integrity. Through their actions, they create a climate that engenders respect and trust.
- Recognize and reward those around them, understanding and supporting the needs of others to be treated with dignity and respect.

"The challenge for leaders is to live up to their fundamental responsibility as human beings: to treat others as themselves"

— (Nair 1994).

on staff without losing sight of the members. Maintaining that delicate balance so vital to the health of an association requires leaders to create and sustain a spirit of partnership within the staff, between staff and leaders, and between staff and members. All must believe they are working together toward common goals.

Along with instituting processes and systems designed to maximize individual performance and commitment to the association's purpose, effective leaders attend to their staff's psychological and physical needs. Staff burnout occurs in environments where the pressure to perform is unrelenting or where no one pays attention to the varying needs that result from family and personal commitments. Most employees will tolerate long days and weekend work in times of organizational crisis or need. But when such practices become commonplace, staff's effectiveness will diminish and discontent will grow, no matter how many other humanistic work processes are in place.

Association leaders also need to be aware of how their behaviors are interpreted. "You can't create quality on the job if you don't create it equally in your personal life" (McGee-Cooper and Trammel 1994). Modeling the ability to balance personal and professional needs is critical. For instance, an association may have personnel policies that spell out a 35-hour work week and adequate vacation and leave time, yet the leaders may not make it easy for staff to take either the vacation or the compensatory time they have earned for additional work. To overcome the detrimental effects of an overworked and exhausted staff, association leaders should encourage employees to use their allotted time off. In the long run, the association will be better served by a staff that is refreshed and committed to work.

References

Bennis, Warren, *On Becoming a Leader,* Addison-Wesley Publishing Company, Inc., Reading, Massachusetts, 1989.

Bethel, Sheila, *Beyond Management to Leadership,* American Society of Association Executives Foundation, Washington, D.C.

Bolton, Robert, *People Skills,* Prentice-Hall, Englewood Cliffs, New Jersey, 1979.

DePree, Max, *Leadership Jazz,* Doubleday, New York, 1992.

Gordon, Thomas, *Leader Effectiveness Training,* Wyden Books, New York, 1977.

Herman, Robert D., and Richard D. Heimovics, *Executive Leadership in Nonprofit Organizations,* Jossey-Bass, San Francisco, 1991.

Herzberg, Frederick, "One More Time: How Do You Motivate Employees?" *Business Classics: Fifteen Key Concepts for Managerial Success,* Harvard Business Review, Boston, Massachusetts, 1975.

Jarratt, Jennifer, and Joseph F. Coates, *Managing Your Future as an Association,* American Society of Association Executives, Washington, D.C., 1994.

Katzerbach & Smith, *The Wisdom of Teams,* Harvard Business School Press, Boston, Massachusetts, 1993.

Kouzes, James M., and Barry Z. Posner, *The Leadership Challenge,* Jossey-Bass Publishers, San Francisco, 1988.

McGee-Cooper, Ann, with Duane Trammel, *Time Management for Unmanageable People,* Bantam Books, New York, 1993, 1994.

Nair, Keshavan, *A Higher Standard of Leadership,* Berrett-Koehler Publishers, San Francisco, 1994.

Norris, Donald M., and M.C. Joelle Fignole Lofton, *Winning with Diversity,* American Society of Association Executives Foundation, Washington, D.C., 1995.

Rosen, Robert H., with Lisa Berger, *The Healthy Organization,* The Putnam Publishing Group, New York, 1991.

Senge, Peter, *The Fifth Discipline Fieldbook,* Doubleday, New York, 1994.

Tecker, Glenn, and Marybeth Fidler, *Successful Association Leadership: Dimensions of 21st Century Competency for the CEO,* American Society of Association Executives Foundation, Washington, D.C., 1993.

Wolf, Thomas, *Managing a Nonprofit Organization,* Prentice Hall Press, New York, 1984.

Zimmerman, A.L., and Carol J. Evans, *Facilitation: From Discussion to Decision,* Nichols Publishing, East Brunswick, New Jersey.

Elaine Kotell Binder, CAE, is a principle partner with Tecker Consultants in Trenton, New Jersey, and president of Binder Associates in Bethesda, Maryland. Prior to founding her firm, Binder served for nine years as executive director of B'nai B'rith Women. She is a Fellow of the American Society of Association Executives.

CHAPTER 9

NEGOTIATING MORE EFFECTIVELY

JACK W. KAINE

Any time two or more people are exchanging information with the intent of changing the relationship, they are negotiating. Some people are natural negotiators; those who aren't can still master the skill of negotiating. It begins with an understanding of the three requirements of a successful negotiation:

1. **The terms can be varied.** If the terms are all-or-nothing, take-it-or-leave-it, then it is not negotiating. It is selling. And any association chief executive officer (CEO) who is perceived as trying to sell the board on anything is headed for trouble.

2. **It centers on a scarce resource**—or what is perceived as scarce, such as money, time, talent, or information. In the association environment, where there never seems to be enough money, budgets and salaries must be negotiated. Too, because time always is in short supply, the CEO constantly negotiates priorities.

3. **Each party must have something to gain.** People often think of negotiation as a competition. When they feel as if they are competing with one another, people do not share any information—or if they do, the information is intended to mislead the other party. Another common problem is that some negotiators take too narrow a view of the negotiations: People see the negotiation as something that is done to simply reach agreement on an issue.

Negotiating is actually a process of getting and keeping agreements. A successful negotiation produces not just an agreement but one that will work for all parties. Getting an agreement is the easy part—keeping it is harder. An agreement that works only for one side ultimately works for neither side. If one side perceives itself as the loser, that person or group has no desire to keep the agreement and the negotiation fails. It then becomes the source of further conflict and negotiation.

A successful negotiation is win-win which should never be confused with "equal win." The term *win-win* means mutual gain; very seldom can each party win equally. Following a principled approach to negotiations, however, ensures that all parties come out of the negotiation ahead.

Five Traits of Effective Negotiators

These are the five traits necessary to negotiate successfully:

- **Be a good planner.** Good negotiators do their homework, preparing a wide-ranging list of alternatives. The more alternatives that are available, the better the chance of finding a position that all parties find favorable.

  Preparation also builds confidence, which is an important element for establishing power in negotiations. In the association environment, the strategic planning process offers an excellent example of good planning—and of negotiation.

- **Have high expectations.** Executives who expect more, get more. Entering a negotiation with high goals and a positive attitude greatly influences the final result. Negative attitudes and grudges can be easily revealed during the negotiation process, so it's important to set a positive tone from the start.

- **Have a high energy level.** It takes a great deal of energy and concentration to negotiate effectively. The tension involved in reaching a position can quickly drain one's levels of energy and alertness. As a result, always enter a negotiation rested and, conversely, never commit to a course of action when fatigued.

- **Be a good listener.** Negotiation involves the exchange of information to change a relationship. Information is power, and the most important way to gain information is to listen. Negotiators who listen to the other side's desires have a better understanding of what it will take to make a deal; they understand what will satisfy the other party's needs.

- **Be persistent.** Persistence—the ability to retain resilience after rejections and setbacks—is to negotiating as carbon is to steel: It's essential to building a solid agreement. Executives who are not satisfied with an impasse and continue to negotiate are able to move the discussion toward a positive outcome for everyone.

Principles of Negotiation

- **The person who speaks first sets the tone for the negotiation.** Don't worry about getting in the last word; work hard to get in the first word, and make it positive. The opening remarks represent the one part of a negotiation that must be scripted and rehearsed to the point of seeming spontaneous. Why? As Will Rogers, the American humorist, said, "You never get a second chance to make a first impression."

- **The person who asks the most questions determines the content and direction of the negotiation.** Questions provide information as well as a safeguard: It's impossible to say something wrong when listening. If you ask a question, however, you must listen to the answer. And note that there's a difference between questioning and interrogating; the former helps you understand the other party's real interest, while the latter makes the other party defensive and suspicious.

- **People do things for their reasons, not yours.** Most people prepare for the negotiation from their point of view. However, all good negotiators must be able to state the other party's case—and answer it as well. Leverage is important, and it cannot be gained without viewing the negotiation from all points of view.

---

11 Golden Rules

These rules apply to every negotiation:

Rule 1: Begin from a position of trust. When people are angry or do not trust one another, they communicate poorly and don't share their information. Or, if information is shared, it will be designed to deceive or mislead the other party.

It is a lot easier to get a negotiation off on a positive note than to overcome a bad start.

Rule 2: Avoid escalating a conflict. Conflict is inevitable. It can be positive, negative, or irrelevant; what makes the difference is how the conflict is handled. Like steam, conflict can be used to generate energy or cause an explosion.

Negotiations often become heated when the parties have a desire to win at any cost. This common mistake is fueled by biased perceptions and judgments, as well as egos, pride, and emotion. But when people get angry or do not trust one another, negotiations become stalled.

Many people view negotiations as a competitive endeavor where one party wins and the other party loses. As soon as a negotiation becomes competitive, the negotiator should stop it and reframe the discussion in a positive light. This can be done, for example, by saying, "How do you feel about this discussion we're having right now?" If the other party is being honest, he or she will probably reply, "I'm very uncomfortable." This opens the door to an agreement, if the first party acknowledges, "I am very uncomfortable as well."

In this way, agreement can grow out of argument. This situation would also give you an opportunity to take the lead in the negotiation by then saying, "I would like to suggest that we refocus our thinking on all the areas we agree on, and then let's build from there to see if we both cannot get more of what we need."

If repeated attempts to reframe the negotiation do not work, a cooling-off period in the form of a break may be necessary. A good rule of thumb is to break off negotiations for at least 12 hours; after that amount of time, it will be much easier to focus on the facts and not on the emotions. The cooling-off period, however, should not exceed 48 hours; conflict does not age gracefully.

Rule 3: Know when to walk away. Some people start a negotiation by seeing how far they can push the other party. If these bullies get away with their behavior, they will continue it. In other words, difficult people may never change because they have been rewarded for being difficult. They may have to change, however, if you resist the pressure to make a bad deal—generally by walking away.

To be able to do this, you must assess—*before* the negotiation begins—what you will do if you don't reach agreement. This is known as your walk-away position. Any agreement that is of higher value than your walk-away position is better than an impasse.

You also must be able to assess what the other party will do if an agreement is not reached. The party with the best walk-away position has a decided advantage in the negotiation.

Rule 4: Be a careful communicator. Expert negotiators are clear, concise communicators. One technique they use is "labeling" their communications.

Labeling signals a change of direction, much like using turn signals when driving a car. This makes it easier for the other party to follow and understand the conversation.

For example, before making a point, the expert negotiator says, "I would like to make a point." He or she also says, "May I ask a question?"—and then asks the question. Likewise, if the person has a concern, he or she will preface it by saying, "I have a concern." This technique not only clarifies the discussion but also creates receptivity. If you say, "May I ask a question?" the other person sounds rude if he or she says no. By asking for permission, you create a more receptive environment.

Good negotiators, however, do not label their disagreements. They do not say, "I disagree with you because. . . ." When stated in that form, the disagreement comes first and the reasons for it second. What is being said is, "Here I come. Get ready to disagree with me in return." The other person then starts listening for points to argue about. Instead, ask questions about the points of disagreement. These questions will weaken the other person's position by pinpointing flaws. Then you can make your proposal.

Another effective way to handle disagreement is to say, "I have this point I would like to discuss with you. It is. . ., and as a result, I disagree." In this case, reason comes first, then disagreement.

Saving Face

One night, the CEO of a large trade association received a telephone call from a member who said, "Now before you say no, let me tell you about a great idea I have for a television commercial that the association should produce." He went on to describe a scene that was guaranteed to generate lots of awareness for the association—all bad, from the CEO's perspective.

Rather than argue with the member by telling him how wrong the idea was, the CEO asked questions: How long would it take to build a set for shooting the commercial? Where would it be built? How much would it cost? After some discussion, the real problem surfaced: The member had gotten tired of the association's commercials. The CEO proposed some research to determine whether the commercials were effective in gaining more business for the association's members. The results showed they were, so the commercials continued to be televised.

This is but one example of the "4-F" approach that you can employ when you disagree with someone yet don't want them to dislike you for it. The four Fs represent Feel, Felt, Found, and Facts. After listening to the other person's comments, you might say, "I can appreciate why you would feel that way. I felt that way myself, until I found out the following. . . ." At this point, share the facts that prompted you to change your mind. In essence, you're saying, "I felt just like you until I learned the real facts. When I got them I changed my mind, and you will want to change yours as well." The 4-F method of disagreeing allows someone to change their mind without losing face.

Rule 5: Lead by questioning. The way to control a negotiation, board meeting, or conversation is not by talking but by questioning: The person who asks the most questions controls the content and direction of the discussion. Questioning also produces information and gives you time to think—while depriving the other person of thinking time.

At times you may be called upon to negotiate without adequate preparation time. One technique that will gain you some time is to ask questions you already know the answers to. This also enables you to assess the honesty of the person answering: Proceed cautiously if the answers are not correct. In addition, asking questions may make it appear as if you are not well-informed—and people may tell you a lot if they believe they know more than you do.

In preparation for a negotiation, list all the questions that could be asked. Decide who will answer each question on the list, as well as the unanticipated questions that arise during the negotiation. This responsibility may fall to the CEO or chief elected officer, depending on who directs the negotiating team.

Next, develop an answer for each question. That helps control your response; the more you talk during a negotiation, the more likely you are to overexplain and thus weaken your position. Developing answers is best done as a group and with a tape recorder. The person to whom the question has been assigned answers it on the tape, which is then played back so the group can critique the response. The question is repeated and the group again critiques the revised response. This process continues until everyone is satisfied with the answer.

In this way, the person who is responsible for that question has a tape-recorded version of the perfected answer. He or she can review the answer repeatedly in preparation for the negotiation.

Rule 6: Avoid making counterproposals. Most negotiators put their proposals on the table too soon, in opposition to the other party's proposal. For example, an association may start with a low salary figure and the CEO with a high one.

When the other negotiator has advanced a proposal or taken an opposite position, he or she is in the least receptive frame of mind to hear your proposal. Rather than offer a counterproposal, ask questions about what was presented: How would this work? What does this mean? What would happen if. . . ? After clearly identifying the proposal's shortcomings, make suggestions to resolve the problems that have become evident. Advance proposals not in opposition to the other side's proposal but as solutions to problems identified in the discussion.

This technique helps establish an atmosphere of trust and cooperation. Good negotiators do not think of themselves as negotiators but rather as problem solvers.

Rule 7: Focus on your strongest positions. Most people are taught that the more reasons they can find to support a position, the stronger it becomes. When most people negotiate, however, they advance too many reasons: Every argument put forth that isn't as persuasive as the strongest argument simply weakens their position.

Develop as many reasons as possible to support your position. However, use only the strongest ones during the negotiation. Here's the typical scenario: After the other party in a negotiation offers a reason to support his or her position, ask, somewhat skeptically, "Is that your only reason?" The other party then will offer a half dozen more supporting reasons. As soon as you hear one reason that sounds weak, say, "Now, just a minute, let's examine the last thing you said." At this point, the power in the negotiation switches, all because of the weak point that was advanced.

Rule 8: Settle on an agreement that is workable. An agreement that will not stand up to close examination will not last. Instead, it will become the source of further conflict and negotiation.

To ensure an agreement is workable, frequently summarize the negotiation's proceedings to make sure all the parties involved understand it. Otherwise, the parties may both think they have an agreement, only to find out that their understanding of what had been agreed to was different. Testing understanding and summarizing can help avoid problems in the future.

In addition, skilled negotiators know it is not in their best interests to slip anything past the other party. In fact, if you believe that the other party has agreed to something not in its best interest, mention it. This not only helps build trust but also puts the obligation on the other party to make a concession in return to move the negotiation forward.

For instance, after the board or staff has agreed to something, ask, "Now if we are going to have a problem with this agreement, what do you think it will be?" At the moment of agreement, the trust level will be high because all parties want the agreement to work. It is at this point that people will bring out their hidden agendas. When a concern surfaces, agree that the point is valid and ask what other concerns the person may have. Also express any concerns you may have and then pose this question: "If this does occur (taking the concerns one at a time) how will we handle it?"

What makes this rule so powerful is that any solution worked out before a problem occurs will be fairer to the parties concerned. "Pre-negotiating" solutions allows you to be hard on problems yet soft on people.

Rule 9: Develop a power position. Power is a function of having options and being willing to take risks. Options give you the ability to make choices; risk is variously described as mental toughness, backbone, or fortitude.

In general, negotiators do not realize their full power when they:

- Focus on their limitations. What you think about in a negotiation is what you realize.
- Feel powerless. Power is very illusive: If you think you are powerful, you are.
- Are unwilling to take a risk. The party willing to take the greatest informed risk in a negotiation always has a decided advantage.
- Are intimidated by the power of the other party. To generate power, you must understand the limits of the other negotiator's power.

It's best to prepare for a negotiation as a group, because groups tend to take greater and more informed risks than individuals. In addition, a group can generate and anticipate more options and alternatives. The Japanese have an expression that's good to keep in mind for negotiations: "None of us is as smart as all of us."

Rule 10: Time is power. Every negotiation has a deadline that is either stated or implied. Deadlines pressure people to make decisions; without deadlines, very little movement would occur in a negotiation.

Although important, time is one of the least understood elements in a negotiation. The party with the longest deadline in a negotiation always has a decided advantage because time buys more options.

Before a negotiation begins, ask yourself these three time-related questions:

- What self-imposed or association deadlines am I under that will make it hard for me to negotiate?
- Are these deadlines real, or can I negotiate an extension with my own team? Most of the pressure a negotiator feels is generated internally.
- What deadlines make it difficult for the other party to negotiate? You cannot generate leverage in a negotiation until you can look at it from the other party's point of view.

Rule 11: Create a positive climate. Climate can best be described as what you do that makes people want to negotiate with you. It includes where you meet, when you meet, how you dress, who you bring, and any number of other factors. Good negotiators create a positive climate that is conducive to information exchange.

Where you meet depends on where you are in the negotiation. During the information collection stage, it is better to meet at the other party's place of business and to take as many people as possible with you. Members of the group should attempt to meet independently with the other party—people will share information when given a chance, especially if their boss is not present. If you're in the final stage of a negotiation, however, meet in your office. This gives you control: The door can be shut, the phones turned off, refreshments brought in at your request, and the room set up to your liking.

Power is an important element in negotiation, and it starts with dress. It is better to be overdressed than underdressed; you can take off a coat and tie, but it is hard to put one on at the last minute. A good rule is to dress like the other party, but marginally better.

Never negotiate without an agenda, which is the guiding force behind the information exchange. It keeps you organized and the negotiation on track. It does not have to be a formalized agenda—a checklist works fine—nor does it have to be shared with the other party.

If a formalized agenda is used, ask the other party to provide a list of the items they would like to discuss. At the same time, make your own list, then draft the agenda in the order you wish to maintain control. What appears on the agenda is as important as what isn't on it. Remember that one way to make issues nonnegotiable is to never allow them to reach the agenda.

Common Mistakes

Several pitfalls can doom negotiations and result in an undesirable agreement. The most common mistakes are:

1. **Believing that one person wins and the other loses.** This is called distributive negotiation and typically involves a single issue or a "fixed pie." Yet it's a misconception that only one party can win at the expense or loss of another. Very seldom is negotiating a zero-sum game.

Rather than divide the "pie," focus on enlarging it. There always are things that you can do for the other party that will have a high value to them and a low cost to you. Likewise, the other party can do things that will cost them very little but mean a lot to you.

2. **Ego.** More negotiations are destroyed by ego than any other single factor. Ego comes into play when one of the parties starts acting emotionally—angry, hurt, insecure, or frightened—and not rationally. If you feel that either you or the other party has allowed emotions to take control of the negotiation, call for a break or cooling-off period.

3. **Being inflexible.** The negotiator who holds to an initial position or belief and fails to adjust as the negotiation proceeds doesn't achieve the best agreement. This type of negotiation often results in an all-or-nothing settlement where neither party is satisfied.

   The secret of a good negotiator is flexibility. There always is a better deal for all parties involved in a negotiation than is apparent at first.

4. **A negative approach.** The way a negotiation is framed can affect each party's willingness to reach an agreement. Presenting negotiations in a favorable light for the other party will build trust and understanding and help to achieve a sound agreement.

5. **Dissecting information.** Know the amount and the reliability of the information that is available. Learning to distinguish information that is relevant will improve the quality and success of the negotiation.

6. **Having a narrow point of view.** Negotiators who take the other party's perspective into account are more likely to reach a successful agreement.

7. **Making assumptions.** You must make assumptions to negotiate. Those assumptions, however, do not always hold up to reality. In preparing for a negotiation, list all your assumptions, as well as those you believe the other party will make. Test these assumptions for validity, and change any that don't ring true.

8. **Overconfidence.** Many biases can combine to inflate a negotiator's confidence and judgment. Assumptions, prejudices, and egos can impede the process. Minimize overconfidence by effective information gathering and never taking anything for granted. Most people believe they have more control over the outcomes of negotiation than they really do.

9. **Negotiating with yourself.** Most negotiators are harder on themselves than on the party across the table. If, in preparation for a negotiation, you write down your starting position but think, "They'll never buy that," you'll probably lower your position. That's negotiating with yourself.

   When you do this, you give away your "bottom line." The other side always will ask for concessions, some of which will have no value to you. When you give concessions before the other side asks for them, you deprive yourself of room to negotiate. An impasse often occurs as a result.

10. **Poor concession making.** Good negotiators know how to make concessions.

Too quick a concession is viewed as a sign of weakness by a competitive win-lose negotiator. In addition, it will not bring you closer to agreement but will elevate the competitive negotiator's goals.

Never give a concession the minute you realize that you can give it. When you do concede a point, always explain what new information led you to change your position. The stock and trade of a good negotiator is credibility, which will diminish quickly if you make concessions without explaining why.

Practice Makes Perfect

Sound negotiation skills can be learned and refined, most often through everyday business conduct. Practice these fundamentals to become a better negotiator and a more effective representative of your association:

- **Use direct, clear communications.** Good negotiators are easy to follow and are clear in their discussions.
- **Ask a lot of questions.** Use questions to gain information, establish the credibility of the other party, reframe an issue, and gain thinking time at the expense of the other party.
- **Test and summarize understanding.** All sides in a negotiation must understand what has been agreed to and be satisfied with the agreement. A successful agreement will stand the test of time.
- **Anticipate and plan how to handle problems before they arise.** Thinking ahead and addressing potential situations early during the negotiations creates a more solid agreement.

Redefining the Issue

It's often possible to remove an issue from a negotiation by asking a good question. For example, one association called a consultant when it became clear that board members were divided over whether to relocate the organization's headquarters. Upon hearing the consultant's fee, however, the association's executive director expressed concern about the cost.

In response, the consultant asked, "What will happen to you and your association if you do nothing?" The CEO responded, "We'd lose the entire West Coast membership. They are talking about starting another association if we do not make a move." The consultant replied that he couldn't leave the executive director and the association in a worse position than that. The consultant made price a nonissue by asking a question—and the association hired him.

By getting people to confront their most dreaded fear, you may convince them to accept a change you want. In 1988, for instance, Jim Baker was negotiating the formalities for the presidential television debates on behalf of George Bush. The staff of Michael Dukakis wanted their candidate to stand on a box behind the podium so he'd appear taller and more presidential. Baker simply asked if they planned to take a box along for Dukakis to stand on when he negotiated with Gorbachev. His question made the box a nonissue and quickly took it off the agenda for the debate.

Jack W. Kaine is a consultant who specializes in teaching negotiating skills to the leaders of associations and corporations worldwide. Prior to forming his consulting firm, he was vice president and principal human relations consultant for Lawrence-Leiter and Company, a management and association consulting firm.

CHAPTER 10

ETHICAL CONDUCT

LOUIE V. LARIMER

E mployee misconduct is on the rise, litigation is pervasive, attorney's fees are outrageous, and juries return judgments in amounts overwhelming to most organizations. In this hostile environment, ethical conduct is more critical than ever and requires more than cosmetic efforts.

The United Way experience of the early 1990s when the CEO was charged with mismanagement of funds—is a haunting reminder of what can happen when an association's staff and board do not make it a priority to define and inculcate responsible conduct. Associations face daily ethical dilemmas that range from conflicts of interest and kickbacks to misuse of association property, diversion of association funds, and incomplete financial reporting.

One association's CEO, for example, lobbied his board to relocate the national office. The board approved buying out the CEO's residence based on an independent appraisal. When the appraisal arrived, the executive disagreed with the designated value, suppressed the report, and arranged for an appraisal that met his expectations. The new figure was significantly higher than the first, and the board did not learn of the first appraisal until several years later when the CEO retired. This occurred despite the association's code of ethics.

Ethical dilemmas do not always involve money. The coach of a national sports organization was dismissed for allegedly having sex with three of his young female players. The coach admits he had sex with these females but contends that the acts were consensual and occurred after the women were of age. Assuming the acts were legal, do they constitute ethical and responsible conduct? The organization's board did not think so and now faces a $1 million lawsuit for wrongfully dismissing the coach.

Ethical Initiatives

Many associations have developed a code of ethics and made a commitment to ethical leadership. Some even have created an ethics committee to address concerns as they arise. Beyond these initial efforts, however, most associations probably lack a written plan outlining how to encourage ethical behavior. Furthermore, financial resources committed to the ethics initiative most likely are nominal.

Certainly, ethics codes and committees are necessary and desirable. In fact, any association that does not have a code and committee needs to create them. But these two steps alone do not constitute a complete and effective organizational ethics program. Nor does distributing posters, brochures, or videos that simply encourage everyone to act ethically. What's also needed are examples of ethical dilemmas and how the association's response reflected a responsible decision.

Due Diligence

The consequences of improper behavior by an association include:

- Debarment from participation in federal programs.
- Multimillion-dollar judgments.
- High attorney's fees.
- Public humiliation and lost member confidence.
- Tarnished reputations and careers.

Another compelling reason for effective ethics programs is found within the United States Sentencing Guidelines. Federal district court judges use these when sentencing organizations convicted of federal crimes. The guidelines provide for significant reductions in fines and penalties if an organization has implemented an effective program of ethics and legal compliance.

To obtain a reduction in a fine or penalty, prior to an offense, the organization must have made a genuine institutional commitment and exercised due diligence to prevent and detect violations of law. Under the guidelines, due diligence at a minimum requires that the organization take the following steps:

1. Establish compliance standards and procedures capable of reducing the prospect of criminal conduct.
2. Assign high-level personnel to oversee compliance with standards.
3. Use due care not to delegate substantial discretionary authority to individuals who the organization knew—or should have known—had a propensity to engage in illegal activities.
4. Communicate standards to all employees by requiring participation in training programs or by disseminating publications that explain in a practical manner what is required.
5. Use monitoring and auditing systems reasonably designed to detect criminal conduct and install a reporting system whereby employees can report unlawful activity by others within the organization.
6. Consistently discipline those who violate the standards.
7. Respond appropriately to violations and act to prevent further similar offenses, including any necessary modifications to the organization's ethics program.

Steps to Follow

The challenge is to implement the sentencing guidelines' recommendations so that an organizational ethics program reflects the association's unique needs and character. The following steps are crucial to the success of any organizational ethics initiative.

Taking the High Road

A well-developed ethics program will have these benefits:

- Demonstrate and reflect the association's commitment to and expectation of ethical behavior.
- Encourage ethical decisions and responsible behavior.
- Preserve the public's confidence in the organization and its products and services.
- Provide an organizational conscience that helps staff and volunteers responsibly face and overcome the ethical challenges they encounter in the association's service.
- Improve morale by strengthening the association's relationship with employees, members, and the governing body.
- Mitigate possible fines and penalties under the United States Sentencing Guidelines.
- Provide a framework for resolving ethical dilemmas before they develop into serious litigation, fraud, or corruption.
- Protect the organization's profitability.
- Reduce the threat of employee misconduct, fraud, scandal, corruption, and litigation.

1. Ensure that the governing body makes a genuine commitment to the ethics initiative and devotes enough financial resources to develop and maintain the program.
2. Assign a single senior manager who reports directly to the CEO to oversee day-to-day aspects of the ethics program. This person also should be familiar to the board.
3. Commission an independent assessment of the organization's current ethical climate. Confidential personal interviews, focus groups, and an anonymous written survey will answer such questions as:
- What types of ethical dilemmas do staff and volunteers commonly face?
- How are these dilemmas resolved?
- Has unethical or unlawful conduct ever occurred?
- What was the nature of that conduct, and why did it occur?
- How frequent was it, and does it still occur?
- What are staff perceptions about the organization's ethical climate?
4. Next, commission an independent ethics audit to compare the organization's existing ethics program to state-of-the-art possibilities and determine program effectiveness.
5. Create an ethics task force to review assessment and audit findings. The task

force uses this information to develop recommendations for an ethics initiative, incorporating United States Sentencing Guidelines suggestions.

6. Include in the ethics program a strong training component focused on common ethical dilemmas faced by staff and volunteers, reasons for unethical conduct, the process of ethical reasoning, and the organization's ethical values.

7. Have each supervisor develop an action plan addressing how he or she will promote ethical conduct.

8. Create an ethics advisory hotline so that employees and volunteers can seek guidance confidentially.

9. Institute a reporting system that encourages staff to come forward with ethical concerns or violation reports. Prompt resolutions can avert full-scale crises.

10. Publicize the ethics program throughout the organization using media such as e-mail, brochures, videos, posters, and newsletters.

11. Ensure that the governing board reviews the ethics program at least quarterly.

Employee and volunteer misconduct, fraud, scandal, corruption, and litigation are real threats to every association. But an affirmative, active approach—spreading the message and taking charge—will greatly minimize these threats.

Louie V. Larimer is the founder and president of the Larimer Center for Ethical Leadership, Inc., a Colorado Springs, Colorado, ethics consulting firm. He consults, speaks, and writes extensively about the practical and applied aspects of ethics.

CHAPTER 11

HIGH-YIELD TACTICAL PLANNING

BY JOHN B. COX, CAE

Strategic planning must be a wonderful thing. All associations seem to do it. But if strategic plans are so good, why don't they consistently yield the stellar results their creators intend?

The answer is obvious and simple: The associations creating these plans did not take them to the next step, neglecting to design the tactical planning required to achieve the goals and objectives identified in the strategic planning process.

Time and again the author has either evaluated or consulted to associations that have developed glittering, sometimes brilliant strategic plans. These plans contain admirable goals, attainable objectives, and remarkable vision. Each association had the goal to be the number-one representative of the widget industry or profession, with the objectives of presenting a loud and unified voice to elected representatives, capturing additional dues revenue, and—ultimately—providing still more benefits, programs, products, and services to members. And in each case, a carefully crafted vision statement said this will happen by 2005, 2010, or 2020.

When asked for the steps, methods, actions, and activities—in short, the tactics—that will accomplish these enviable goals, objectives, and visions, association staff and volunteers most often respond with a blank stare. Like retirement planning for too many people, it was almost quite enough just to have the idea. The details would somehow, sometime, take care of themselves.

It doesn't have to be this way.

By taking the next logical steps after achieving vision, establishing goals, and defining objectives—by developing the tactical machinery to drive the dream—every association can realize its full potential and attain the promise established in its strategic planning.

All Roads Lead to Rome

There are as many different approaches to tactical planning as there are associations. As long as they lead to the same result, they are worth the effort. The following model is proffered because in use after use, it has yielded the absolutely highest return on the investment of association time and human and financial resources. It is what the sciences call radially adaptive (i.e., highly malleable); it can be freely employed for almost any application an association needs, with or without a strategic plan backing it up. It can be used for a single purpose or program, or expanded to encompass an entire association wish list of goals and objectives. It is in the latter regard, moreover, that the tactical plan is most valuable. In its creation, obvious synergies between various operational functions, programs, and activities will surface, and it is in recognizing and cross-fertilizing these opportunities that the highest yields will occur. Stated simply, no association activity occurs in a vacuum. When various operations such as continuing education, annual meetings, publications, political activities, and press and communications programs are linked together in a tactical plan, a multiplier effect kicks in and the return on investment is far greater than on any activity undertaken alone.

Keep that multiplier effect in mind as you read the planning steps below. You will rapidly see that periodic and nonperiodic publications are as integral to member recruitment and retention as are continuing education and conventions. They redouble when combined with political or representational activities, and compound with public and media relations. Once you begin to think tactically, you'll realize that you can expand every beneficial program to serve four or six masters, and these expansions will interlock and cross-fertilize to produce even greater activity and return.

A thought or two before examining the linear steps in tactical planning.

More than one thoughtful association professional has noted that the problem with this whole enterprise is that most people don't plan to plan. That is, they simply don't set aside the time or the ideation that thoughtful, involved, and productive planning demands. Don't make that mistake. Tactical planning requires a serious commitment and continuity; it is not an occasional thing. The yield will so far exceed the effort expended that any time allocated for it will be more than well spent. It will, quite literally, transform the association.

There are no bad ideas. Time and again, the author has heard one or another idea shot down during planning sessions as too risky, tried before, not right for the association's members, too advanced, too retro, too something. Nonsense! These same ideas, in the proper context, went on to become the engines that drove or accelerated successful tactical plans. You are about to read several references to "blue sky" thinking. Heed them. Most often, it is the blue-sky idea—the thought from left field—that allows you to break out of the box.

"If you don't know where you're going, it doesn't matter which road you take."

Perhaps the White Rabbit didn't say it exactly that way to Alice during her travels. But he would have if he had been describing tactical planning. Besides, it's a nice segue to our first step. Because, if you don't know what you want or where you want to go, why do tactical planning at all? So. . .

I. Setting Goals and Objectives

This step will already be accomplished in the aforementioned (and much abused) strategic planning exercise that many associations engage in. But if not, the reader needs to understand that it is the prerequisite to tactical planning. Quite simply, it must answer questions such as, what does the association want to accomplish? Why? What strategies will take it there?

Stand by for blue-sky reference number one. If you haven't already defined your goal and objectives, do so. Now. Even if you have, revisit them. Ignore the obvious. Kick your way out of the box. In other words, avoid the predictable, easy-to-attain goals. Maybe it's time to think of a global presence. Of starting a for-profit subsidiary. Of opening that branch office in Tierra del Fuego.

In any case, in step one you define what you want to attain, your goal(s) in planning. Then you define why you think you want to achieve them, and what your objectives are for goal attainment. Finally, you think of the gross strategies to get you there. For example:

- The World Wide Widgets Association (WWWA) establishes a goal to have the greatest possible number of members, to represent the entire industry.
- Its objectives are to generate a lot of additional revenue to increase its political clout, to become the real voice of the industry, and to provide more programs, services, benefits, and activities to its constituents.
- WWWA's strategy will be to design and implement a major, ongoing member recruitment and retention program.

Now, that was easy, wasn't it?

In a couple of steps or so, we'll look at how tactics are required to drive strategies. But first this important announcement: Please plan to plan. Setting goals and objectives is best done in an atmosphere devoted to the enterprise. A retreat is usually the best venue and vehicle. Wherever and whenever, allow thinking to roam free. That's when breakthroughs occur.

II. Situation Analysis/Problem Definition

Remember those initial references to tactical planning as being linear and sequential? Here is where it begins to become obvious.

WWWA now has goals and objectives. Before it can set about attaining them, it needs to carefully analyze its current status, its market position, the impediments to goal and objectives attainment, its strengths, and, most important, its weaknesses. Does it have the resources to proceed? If not, can it acquire them? What will be required to succeed, to realize its potential?

As, and after, it has analyzed and defined its current status, WWWA needs to define its problem areas—those impediments to achieving its goals. This is actually a two-part exercise:

INTERNAL PROBLEMS

What elements will preclude realizing its goals? It is absolutely imperative to be brutally honest in this exercise. Anything less will doom the enterprise. In a nutshell, if there are roadblocks, identify them.

Typical references here include insufficient staff, insufficient financial resources, lack of an integrated computer database that would make coordination of a member campaign possible, lack of real time to devote to the effort, and so on. If you don't candidly identify the barriers here, don't proceed with planning. The effort won't be successful.

EXTERNAL PROBLEMS

Surprisingly, these are less problematic than internal problems, but they must be recognized and overcome nonetheless. In marketing, it can be thought of as identifying and measuring the competition. Suppose there is a larger, stronger, longer-established association that predominates in member share, or there is a lack of recognition in the marketplace. Perhaps the association didn't prevail in an important political battle. Possibly, its dues are considered too high by potential and former members. Whatever the problems are, they must be identified, confronted, and, if possible, overcome to clear the way for any success with stated goals.

Something important will have transpired at this point. The association has established its goals and knows why it wants to achieve them. It knows the strategies it will take to get there and has analyzed its current status including what is going right and where there are challenges. And, it has identified the problems, internal and external, that it must address to realize its dreams. In short, the association's leadership and staff probably know more about the organization at this moment than has been identified in years, if ever. And if ever there was a case of knowledge being power, this is it! Armed with the knowledge gained to this point, those engaged in the planning exercise can quite literally create the future of this association.

First, of course, must come the next essential and once again sequential steps in tactical planning.

III. Identification of Key Audiences

Audiences in our context may also be thought of as publics, markets, and targets. In brief, these are the buyers, nonmembers, potential members, legislators, funders, and consumers of products, services, benefits, and programs that the association wants and needs to reach.

On a global scale, listing the audiences includes virtually everyone with whom the association wants or needs to interact. For a specific, single-purpose campaign, the list would be narrowed to those audiences relevant to the purpose or goal at hand.

A side note here. The author has regularly been surprised at how narrowly many associations define their universe. When asked how many media would be on a key audiences or target list for a public information program, they will respond with six or eight; a minimal list could include more than 20, and the author has seen successful and ambitious media lists with 40 separate kinds of media targets. Similarly, a membership recruitment and retention campaign target list might yield a half dozen different types of audiences. But, there are so many different audiences involved in a proactive campaign, any good list should extend well into double digits.

The same point could be extended to lists of audiences for fund-raising campaigns, legislative and governmental initiatives, conference and meeting development plans, and more. Far too many associations allow their grasp to exceed their reach. Here is another place where blue sky thinking on the part of all involved can produce surprising results. And only when an association defines all its possible audiences for any given outreach can it achieve the full potential envisioned in its campaign. No one has ever erred in identifying too many potential buyers.

Okay, then, the association has identified all possible audiences, buyers, consumers, publics, targets, and markets for its intended purposes. Now, how does it go about reaching them? That would be step four, logically enough.

IV. Identification and Development of Vehicles and Tactics

In our tactical-planning context, the ideas of vehicles and tactics are almost interchangeable. Once an association has defined all of its audiences, it must define and determine the best ways, the best vehicles and approaches, for reaching them. And as with audience definition, on a global tactical plan the association must list every possible, conceivable method of reaching the targets in its plan. Newsletters, meetings, workshops, e-mail, fax, testimony, letters, speeches, trade press coverage, general interest media, annual conferences, and so on ad infinitum must be listed. Even if an approach or vehicle isn't being used currently, it should nonetheless be listed; it is something to be aspired to and may eventually prove to be a key element in achieving success.

On a cautionary note, the same concern expressed in step three pertains in step four. Namely, associations regularly underestimate the number, breadth, and range of vehicles and tactics for reaching their intended audiences. If a list of audiences can extend well into double digits for any given tactical campaign, the methods, tactics, and vehicles possible for reaching these publics should, at the minimum, match it. Too often the author has asked an association to list the vehicles it needs to reach a given audience, say, the media. After consideration, staff will list perhaps six vehicles. With a little prodding and some free thinking, the list expands to 26 or 28 different vehicles and approaches.

The only limits here are self-imposed. There are those who could argue quite successfully that there are literally no limits when it comes to reaching essential publics. Doing so will certainly increase the margins of success.

To this point, the association has set goals, objectives, and strategies. It has analyzed its current status and defined its problems. It knows its audiences and the vehicles and tactics it must use to reach them. Very powerful information. Now to put it all together.

V. Creating the Tactical Plan: "A Matrix of Opportunities"

Flush with all the knowledge gained to this point, you will discover that the rest is simplicity itself. Actually, it is all rather mechanical.

If an association has set its goals and objectives, knows what it has to overcome, has identified its audiences and the vehicles needed to reach them, it need only match column A with column B, calendar the activities, and put a cost line on the enterprise.

Let's look at three brief examples of single-purpose tactical campaign planning. It is important to bear in mind that if we were looking at a global, organization-wide plan, the audiences and vehicles would be integrated in their respective steps, or columns, and that all activities would be intertwined synergistically. This, of course, would produce the aforementioned multiplier effect; i.e., when one or two elements in audiences and vehicles are cross-linked with others, they become worth four or five times their value alone.

EXAMPLE ONE

The Ozone Society decides it wants to create a tactical membership recruitment/retention plan. It has conducted all the preliminary steps outlined to this point. In items three and four it identified its key audiences and the vehicles/tactics required to reach them as

Step III	Step IV
Audiences/Publics	*Vehicles/Tactics*
potential members	personal letters to best prospects
former members	direct mail letters to remainder of list
students	telephone calls to best prospects
affiliated organizations	telemarketing to remainder of list
those ineligible, but, nonetheless interested	member-get-a-member and other campaigns
corporations	personal visits
foundations	special offers
auxiliary members	inducements
retired	incentives
inactive members	discounts for joining in conjunction with book purchases, workshops, and annual meeting attendance
	special campaign-only rates
	World Wide Web informational/target messages

EXAMPLE TWO

The American Ethereal Association wants to design and mount a major fund raising/endowment building campaign. It successfully navigated all steps to this point and has identified its targets and methods as

Step III	Step IV
all members	individualized letters
foundations	direct marketing
corporation	funding proposals
potential donors	grant proposals

former donors	telemarketing
known benefactors	campaign and collateral theme
most likely individual contributors	personal visits
medium-to-least-likely contributors	participation/contributions, "gifts" and/or acknowledgments
program sponsors, e.g., annual meetings, workshops	formal recognitions programs electronic campaign information and targeting

EXAMPLE THREE

The National Sea Shells League (NSSL) wants to pump attendance at its annual conference. It has identified its key publics and tactical methods as:

Step III	Step IV
current members	meetings program promotions and brochures
interested nonmembers	letters
those who always attend	magazines
those medium-to-least likely to attend	newsletters
NSSL book and periodicals buyers and subscribers	telemarketing
all workshop attendees	Home Page, World Wide Web, Internet, member bulletin board systems
current exhibitors	state and chapter newsletters
potential exhibitors	press releases
former exhibitors	media wires
members of affinity organizations	feature articles targeted to interested publications
members of affiliated organizations	postage-meter cancellations/indicias
general public	buck slips
press	stuffers/flyers for book orders
students	blow-ins and tip-ins for NSSL publications
spouses	stationery legends/logos
	and so on, ad infinitum

At this point, the tactical planners would simply draw "synergy" lines between the audiences, targets, and publics identified in Step III with the vehicles, tactics, and methods needed to reach them as listed in Step IV. For ease of purpose, it can be helpful to create a "Matrix of Opportunities" with audiences listed on one axis and vehicles on the other; contacts and activities would then fall into the grid of the matrix. In Step IV, it is important to remember that some vehicles will reach only one public, others will reach all. Similarly, some audiences are continuously key, while others have value only once or twice. Identifying who is to be targeted and when, and with what vehicle can produce the earlier referenced multiplier effect, where multiple vehicle hits with various target publics can produce results disproportionate with efforts.

VI. Scheduling the Plan

The difficult part of the planning is now complete. Not incidentally, the association is probably armed with more useful knowledge about itself, its audiences, and how to reach them than it has known for years.

Having identified the who, what, where, and how, the planning association need only identify the when. In years past, strategic planning—along with the tactics needed to support it—could be thought of in multiyear terms, with typical plans stretching out four or five years and beyond. That is no longer practical or wise today. Events simply move too rapidly. A good tactical plan will be in the 24-month range, with a top-end max of 36 months.

Many associations use the "NASA" approach to tactical plan calendaring, i.e., identifying the goal and then working backward on the steps it will take to get there. In real terms, if the WWWA wants to increase membership attendance at its August annual meeting, it needs to identify its target audiences several months earlier, perhaps October or November of the preceding year, and then begin applying its tactical steps and employing its vehicles at calendared intervals, say, January, March, May, and so on.

There is a very important consideration in the calendaring step. All tactical plans should contain a lot of "air." Do not think of any tactical plan as a finished document. Rather, with ongoing evaluation, the plan will be continuously tweaked. Certain vehicles will be dropped while others are being added, and new or additional target audiences will replace existing ones. Most important, with sufficient malleability or air built into the plan, it will be possible to add and maximize opportunities not thought of or included in the plan during its design phase. More about this later.

VII. Budgeting to the Plan

In the not-too-distant past, tactical and strategic plans were stand-alone enterprises, almost entities unto themselves, whose implementation—though demanding the serious commitment of staff, volunteer, and financial resources—simply wasn't viewed in economic terms.

Fortunately, that is no longer the case today.

In fact, in the current climate, everything is thought of in economic terms, including and especially planning. And that is precisely the way it should be. So, to add the validity a serious tactical plan will require, a column should be added to the right of the matrix of opportunity, and in every place where an action is being calendared—where a vehicle or tactic is being used to reach a targeted audience—its economic impact must be indicated. On a happy note, not every reference connotes cost. Rather, when the tactical plan is being used to generate greater meeting attendance, hype book sales, promote membership, or whatever, its positive economic consequences should be listed as well.

Not only will you have an accurate idea of what your effort will cost in human and financial resources, you will also be able to show the benefit to be derived. And that promotes buy-in by all the stakeholders in the plan, including other staff, boards, leadership, and interested volunteers.

A final benefit of budgeting to the plan is that it forces the planner(s) to focus and prioritize. When costs are added to the wish lists, those involved usually become a little more serious and begin to look at such things as return on investment before expending precious association resources.

VIII. Evaluation

Evaluation is the sine qua non of tactical planning. It separates the professionals from the amateurs. It is the essential step. Everything to this point would be, in fact, pointless if some measure of the plan's progress weren't used.

In prior days, evaluation checkpoints could be built into a plan at longer intervals. In today's rapidly evolving climate, opportunities present themselves at a moment's notice, and the longest possible interval between evaluation points should be six months and preferably at three months on shorter, 12- to18-month plans.

In brief, evaluation is a snapshot of your progress at a given moment. It tells you where you've been, where you are, and where you appear to be going. It can tell you what to add, what to drop, what needs additional reworking, and where some tuning would help. It allows you to prevent failure and to measure success.

Most important, periodic evaluation guarantees that your tactical plans won't suffer the fate of most strategic and/or tactical plans: growing dust on a shelf. As noted at the outset, many associations think it is quite enough just to create the plan; somehow, implementation will take care of itself. By evaluating the plan at specific intervals and making the changes required to ensure its success, you also ensure that the plan becomes a living, working blueprint for accomplishments. You institutionalize accountability, and that is a powerful motivator.

Well all of this sounds fine and good. A matrix of opportunity. Budgeting to plan. Vehicles and audiences. Accountability.

But does it all work? The author has working, personal experience with either the planning just described, or derivative variations on it and can respond with an emphatic yes! In one association, such planning increased net revenues on member professional development from $150,000 to $800,000 in a three-year period, and more than doubled annual meeting attendance—from 4500 to 9700—in the same window. In another association, it produced a 10 percent increase in membership that costs three figures each year, and in still another association, generated a 6 percent increase in membership that costs four figures a year. A fourth association quadrupled its nonperiodic publishing output and income within a four-year period, while tripling its advertising revenues. The list goes on, but the point is already made.

Everyone can plan *strategically*, and many quite frequently do. It is those association professionals who knowledgeably back up their strategic plans with *tactical planning* who guarantee achievement. In a nutshell, high-yield tactical planning is the engine that can drive an association's success. And, everybody wins: the planners, the association, its members, volunteers, and leaders! Very few other association activities can make that claim.

So go forth, do some tactical planning, and prosper!

John B. Cox, CAE, is executive director of the American Association of Pharmaceutical Scientists in Alexandria, Virginia. He has more than a quarter century experience working with, consulting to, and/or evaluating nonprofit and member-based organizations, ranging from trade associations to professional societies.

CRISIS MANAGEMENT

It would be nice to believe that strategic and/or tactical planning would obviate the need for all other plan development. It would be nice, but it would be foolish. Regardless of how well an association professionalizes its planning, structures its messages, and achieves its objectives, crises will occur. Witness the rash of crises that have affected entire industries and professions in the past several years and, ultimately, the associations and societies representing them. In every case, associations became the focal point for information and response to the issue.

It is a wise association that presumes sometime in its future it will face a major crisis, with all attendant scrutiny.

There are probably as many crisis management strategies as there are crises. All will see an association through a rough period of forced response.

It is recommended that an association use the most simple, effective formula for dealing with a crisis, and that it insist on strict compliance with the crisis policy for all involved leadership, members, and staff. Following is a three-phase process that should help any association deal with any crisis.

Phase I: Precrisis

• Plan for crisis
  –Assume that at some future point a crisis will occur.
  –Identify possible or probable crises and how membership will be affected.
  –Identify essential vehicles for reaching critical publics during a crisis.

• Establish policy
  –Determine spokesperson(s).
  –Determine essential message-clearance procedures.
  –Inform those concerned—especially all staff—about clearance procedures and designated spokesperson(s).
  –Develop fact sheets on the assumption of crises, tailored to specific need.

• Establish a crisis information function (typically in the Communications or Public Affairs offices).
  –Ensure that all inquiries and information will be directed to and from this office.
  –Ensure that staff is knowledgeable, with access to essential contact numbers for clearances and spokesperson(s).
  –Keep this function current at all times; crises have a way of occurring when least expected.

Phase II: The Crisis

• Define the crisis
  –Assemble every knowable fact about the crisis.
  –Determine which members, if not all, are affected.
  –Determine which publics are affected.
  –Determine whether the crisis is national, local, or regional.
  –Determine whether the crisis is of short or long duration.
  –Determine what other associations, industries, or professions are involved.
  –Can and should they be allied with for response(s)?

- Access existing crisis plan
  - Determine if it is adequate to meet the crisis, or will it more probably have to be modified.
  - Determine if all key personnel are alerted and know their roles. Are response policies in place and adequate? Is the response procedure, including clearances, functional and ready?
- Respond professionally
  - Prepare a fact sheet about the crisis with all information verified and essential clearances obtained and distribute it to all concerned publics—particularly the media.
  - Do not speculate about the crisis, at any point or with any public; stick to the facts at all times.
  - Be accessible to the media.
  - Schedule regular briefings as appropriate, and stick to the schedule.
  - Document every aspect of the crisis while it is in progress, including statements, fact sheets, legal reviews and clearances, interviews, media coverage, public response, and final resolution, if possible.

Phase III: Post Crisis

- Review the association's crisis performance
  - Did the generic precrisis planning help?
  - Did spokesperson(s) and clearance procedures function properly?
  - Did the internal mechanisms, especially the crisis information, function perform correctly?
  - Was the association blindsided by any aspect of the crisis?
- Plan for the next crisis
  - Use information and experience gained during the process to build an even more successful response procedure for the next occurrence.

The following tips should help both knowledgeable and inexperienced association professionals when confronting media during a crisis.

- Never say "no comment." It is an admission of guilt to contemporary publics.

- Do not be afraid to say that not all the facts are available, and a response can only be forthcoming when they are. Media are always on deadline, and will try to force a speculative response. The only safe response is possible when all knowable facts are available.

- Never go "off the record" with media during a crisis. There is no such thing to a deadline-oriented press in a crisis situation. Even if direct attribution is not made, careless remarks can and will easily be traced back to their source.

- Anticipate a media ambush. It is a sad but true fact of life in the Information Age that media will go to great and not so attractive lengths to get stories during a crisis. There is an old but accurate adage in professional communications: "The only kind of visibility you will get without proper planning is the kind you don't want."

The underlying theme, the most common word, is planning. Planning is not the ultimate panacea. It is not the miracle cure. It is the only way professional management can take place in an association. Indeed, planning separates the amateurs from the professionals. When activity is professionally planned, everyone—members, publics, the industry or profession, and the association—profits. It is an exercise well worth the effort.

CHAPTER 12

BUDGET AND FINANCE

VELMA R. HART, CAE

The terms *budget, finance,* and *accounting* mean different things to different associations. Small associations often view these terms as a means to an end or a project that, once complete, can be filed away; larger associations generally view the budgeting aspect in particular as a necessary tool for managing their projects and general operations. In these larger environments, managing to the budget on a monthly, quarterly, or yearly basis is usually a performance objective of the staff responsible for budget administration.

The way in which financial information is communicated can often be the difference between understanding and chaos. Good financial reporting has three major components: accuracy, clarity, and a firm understanding of when to use detail versus summary reporting. These components, combined with good internal and external financial controls, will ensure that your financial reports will be well-received and understood.

Long-Range Planning

The need to accurately forecast into the future is critical to an organization's continued growth and advancement. To successfully perform this function, you must understand the direction in which the organization is going and the special needs that must be addressed to get there. (For information on long-range and strategic planning, see Chapters 3 and 4).

When planning for the future, an organization's financial resources should not limit its scope; rather, develop the overall plan and then find creative ways to make sure the funding will be in place when it is needed. Put simply, an association's overall long-range plan should always precede its financial long-range plan.

Depending on how your organization views its strategic plan, you may be required to link it to the budget. If, for instance, the strategic plan has a goal of increasing the association's net surplus in three years, in order to fund future projects or to build a reserve balance, the budget should include detailed revenue and expense strategies aimed at meeting the target set for each year.

It is always more difficult to link the budget and strategic plan at a detailed level than in a general way. Before you attempt this challenge, answer these questions: "How do we as an organization view the strategic plan?" and "What does our audience want to learn from linking the plan?" Most organizations choose a text-based linkage—the response to the strategic objective is written next to the corresponding budgeted dollars. Other organizations use project codes to cross-reference budget items and strategic objectives.

Budget

In its simplest terms, a budget is an estimate of future events. Because it is often computed from proven historical data, it is deemed credible as a forecast of what will transpire. A budget also establishes objectives, which provide the basis for measuring performance.

Associations most often use the *operating budget* and the *cash budget*. The operating budget (or *earnings budget* as it is sometimes called) attempts to forecast the earnings of an organization into a future period. Usually, this type of budget consists of "sub-budgets" such as sales, administration, advertising, and so forth. The accuracy of each individual budget determines the accuracy of the overall operating budget.

On the other hand, the cash budget tries to forecast use of the organization's cash resources. It projects anticipated cash expenditures and income for a specified period. A cash budget depends heavily on the organization's ability to project its sale—should sales or revenue fall far short of expectations, the organization's operations will be greatly affected.

You can ensure the accuracy of your budget projections by forecasting sales, performing accurate market analysis, ensuring adequate pricing policies are in place, and—after the budget is complete—measuring actual performance against the budget.

Some organizations also use a *capital expenditures budget*. The capital budget, as it is commonly called, helps identify opportunities to acquire equipment such as copiers and postage machines, which have a useful life that exceeds one year. By viewing capital expenditures within the context of a separate budget, an association can avoid overspending on equipment. For instance, a capital budget should point out the effect of such expenditures on the cash position of the association and on future earnings. A lack of necessary working capital could have serious repercussions on internal operations.

If you prepare a capital budget, use it in the calculation of the *depreciation expense budget*. Because depreciable items such as computers and desks will have varying depreciation schedules, double check your math before finalizing the depreciation expense budget.

Other concepts include *incremental budgeting* and *zero-based budgeting*. Incremental budgeting refers to adjusting the base budget during the fiscal or calendar year. Although there has been much debate about the value of adjusting the base budget once the year has started, scheduled and controlled adjustments can help an association react to the changing environment and allow it to be flexible and responsive.

As its name implies, zero-based budgeting assumes a starting point of zero on every budget being developed and requires detailed justification for every dollar requested. This concept, while frequently discussed in the association community, is not widely used because much of an association's budget is repetitive from year to year. For instance, expense categories related to serving members, such as printing, postage, telephone, and supplies, do not vary; the main variable in the membership budget would be the number of members served (is the population growing, level, or declining?). Therefore, most associations base their budgets on past performance and activity, using history as a basis for developing future years' budgets.

Whatever the budgeting approach taken, it's important to classify costs based on how they behave in accordance with changes in volume and as a means of measuring activity. *Variable costs* vary in direct proportion to changes in activity. In other words, variable costs are not stable—if activity in a budget area increases, so will the associated costs. Examples of variable costs are those related to producing publications and products for sale, such as printing, binding, and consultant costs. *Fixed costs* remain fairly stable regardless of whether activity increases or decreases. These costs—such as rent, insurance, and taxes—tend not only to be consistent but also recurring.

Financial Reporting

When you are confident that your financial data are accurate, the next step is to prepare it for disclosure to internal management, the treasurer, the finance committee, the board, or the members. The way in which the information is disclosed and the degree of detail provided depend largely on the audience and the level of financial knowledge it possesses.

In general, the group with the level of day-to-day responsibility receives the most detailed report. Most associations provide their staff with very detailed and regular financial reports (usually monthly). On the other extreme, the board may require only consolidated information while members may need only the basics—financial information that answers, "Where are we?" and "Are we doing OK?" A good rule of thumb to apply when preparing material for any audience is to make sure every heading and comparison is not in financial jargon.

Regardless of the audience, the material being presented should have three characteristics:

- **Clear**. Based on your knowledge and understanding of the readers, prepare information that is easy for them to understand. Avoid information that goes over their heads or is not concise in its presentation.
- **Accurate**. Reviewers of financial information will look for items in the report that appear to be inconsistent or do not make sense to them. Should they find an error in the report, no matter how small, it can call into question the validity of the entire financial presentation.
- **Complete**. Take the time to understand the needs of the audience—anticipate their questions based on previous reporting inquiries and interest in new projects and activities. Including variance reporting against current budget, actuals for the same period last year, and a comparison to future budget usually provides good comparison data. A notes section that outlines anything unusual is also a welcome addition to any financial report. While numbers usually speak for themselves, having a text-based supplement can help those reviewers who are not accustomed to interpreting numbers.

Accounting Standards and Procedures

In the *accrual method* of accounting, which is the most widely used, revenue is recorded when it is earned. For instance, if an ad is placed in your monthly magazine, the recording of that revenue takes place after the invoice has been issued but before the check has been received. On the other hand, if the income was not recorded until the check was actually received, the organization would be operating on the *cash method* of accounting.

The Financial Accounting Standards Board (FASB), established in 1973, sets the standards that govern financial accounting and reporting. Known as Generally Accepted Accounting Principles (GAAP), these standards and procedures represent the accounting profession's efforts to establish a body of theory and common practice. It is unethical for an accountant to state that a financial statement conforms with GAAP if the statement significantly departs from those accounting principles.

Accurate and timely financial statements that comply with official reporting guidelines clarify the financial position of an organization. The only element the FASB does not outline in GAAP is the routine—how financial reporting is done to ensure its accuracy and timeliness. But whether it be monthly, bimonthly, or quarterly, distribution of financial information must occur more than once during a fiscal period.

Financial reporting comes in many shapes and sizes. It can include detailed information such as encumbrance (expenses not yet billed but contracted or committed for) or stick to a basic three-column comparison format (current budget, current year-to-date actual, and variance of the two columns). Some reports you prepare may not comply with GAAP requirements but still may be used in reporting financial information. The difference is that your association's auditors will not use the non-GAAP reports when issuing a final audit statement.

Tools for Analysis

One way to analyze financial information is through the use of ratios. There are four types:

1. *Liquidity ratio*—measures the organization's ability to pay its short-term obligations.

2. *Profitability ratio*—measures the profits (losses) over a specified period of time. The use of this ratio in evaluating nonprofit organizations is often questioned; however, profitability is just as important to nonprofits as it is to for-profit enterprises.

3. *Coverage ratio*—measures the projections for the interest and principal payments to long-term creditors and investors.

4. *Activity ratios*—measures how efficiently the organization is employing its assets.

Be mindful that ratios are only one of the tools you can use to evaluate past performance when attempting to predict the future. In addition, ratios may offer only the indicator or "red flag" to a bigger problem that should be addressed. Without an adequate feedback system by which management is promptly informed of a problem demanding attention or correction, ratio analysis is meaningless.

Another helpful technique is the use of horizontal and vertical analysis. In *horizontal analysis*, you compare similar figures from several years' financial statements. *Vertical analysis* is more specific: It compares parts of a total in a single statement.

For example, in a horizontal analysis, if sales of products in 1995 are approximately $100,000 and in 1996 are approximately $300,000, the association registered a 200 percent increase in sales ($200,000/100,000). Examining this type of directional magnitude within a financial statement can help determine if your organization is experiencing reasonable or even favorable trends.

Vertical analysis assumes that a financial statement item is used as a base value to which all other accounts can be compared. Under vertical analysis, statements showing percentages are referred to as "common size financial statements." Common size percentages can be compared from one period to another to identify areas needing attention. An illustration follows:

Net Sales	$300,000	100%
Less: Cost of Sales	- 60,000	20%
Gross Profit	$240,000	80%
Less: Operating Expenses	-150,000	50%
Net Income	$ 90,000	30%

Analysis is not just for the standard revenue-and-expense or income statement. The *balance sheet* also requires attention because it can point out potential problems long before they might arise. The balance sheet shows the relationship between assets and liabilities. It is important to note that there are no fixed rules concerning these relationships. What constitutes good financial shape for Association A may represent the brink of financial ruin for Association B.

Managing an organization's *cash flow* is a major factor in evaluating its ability to meet debt-retirement requirements and to finance new activities. The term commonly refers to funds derived from operations.

Cash flow is frequently regarded as the most meaningful way to assess an organization's ability to maintain operations without undue borrowing. This assessment can also be an important factor when deciding whether to buy or lease. Consistent positive cash flow can afford the organization latitude to venture into uncharted waters. On the other hand, negative cash flow—particularly in a consistent trend—can be lethal to an organization's health, well-being, and continued growth.

Audits

During the annual audit, internal controls, processes, and procedures are evaluated in detail—particularly when an association is working with a new auditing firm for the first time. Once the firm establishes a comfort level with internal operations and processes, the evaluation is not as difficult.

As a rule, audits occur in three phases:

1. **Audit planning.** At this point, key members of the association's financial management team meet with senior members of the audit firm's staff. The purpose of this meeting is to confirm what will be done during the audit and establish time lines in which the other phases will be completed.

2. **Document review.** This is a detailed look at specific financial documents, which auditors do to ensure that documents are being reviewed and managed in compliance with established internal procedures and controls.

3. **Financial statement reconciliation and analysis.** Once the auditors are satisfied with the information they have received in one-on-one meetings with association management and have established the time lines for the audit, they begin looking at financial reports for errors in accuracy or omissions.

At each phase of the process, management and the audit firm should be in regular communication to address any questions as they arise. As management, ensure that the auditors thoroughly understand your operations. That knowledge enables them to make recommendations that will streamline processes and help you to develop procedures that protect staff and the association.

Big or Little?

Should you use a big-name accounting firm or a smaller one? Large firms have national name recognition, along with strong credentials and numerous references. In addition, they have the resources to quickly provide their clients with specialized information and even consulting services as needed. The price tag for this type of service is usually not cheap and may be passed through to the client in higher fees. However, there is something to be said for having a big firm audit your books: In many cases, their name carries an implied value-added service.

Small firms typically charge less because they don't carry as much overhead. A smaller firm may not have the specialized expertise of a large firm—but it might have a better customer service ethic. For example, a small firm might be willing to answer questions without billing you for every call.

Some of your board members may raise the question, "Is an external audit necessary?" The answer is *absolutely*. An external audit—one performed by someone not affiliated with your organization—is the best way to doublecheck your internal financial processes, procedures, and controls. Outside auditors will identify weaknesses or systems that are no longer in compliance with GAAP.

The Management Letter

The annual audit process includes the completion and presentation of the management letter, which has a two-fold purpose. First, it is the way in which the audit firm formally reports any material weaknesses found to the fiduciaries of the organization (usually the executive board or finance committee). Second, the management letter contains recommendations made by the audit firm on how to improve financial processes. In addition, it can be a vehicle for staff to communicate concerns or point out needed changes in internal operations.

The process by which the management letter is prepared varies from one organization to the next. In general, the audit firm reviews the first draft of its management letter with key members of the staff. The group discusses the appropriateness of certain comments and how to best present the items that are mutually agreed upon for inclusion in the management letter. The revised management letter is then reviewed to make sure that it accurately reflects the discussion.

Audit firms often have several levels of firm management review the letter and corresponding financial statements before releasing them. Many times, the organization being audited will exercise the option to prepare a written response to address or clarify the items pointed out in the management letter; this response is presented to the board at the same time as the management letter.

The final step, the presentation, is given by the audit firm to the fiduciaries. If the process works well, all parties come away with a clear understanding of material weaknesses and how to correct them. In addition, the group will have several recommendations to improve operations.

Investment Management

The duties of a fiduciary—a person, such as a board member or director, who has a special position of trust in the association and obligations related to that position—do not end with the development of an investment policy statement and the selection of appropriate money managers to implement the policy. The fiduciary must ensure that the people charged with investment responsibility comply with the provisions of the plan's investment policy statement.

Most court cases arising out of the failure of a fiduciary to supervise properly indicate that it is not sufficient for the fiduciary to review an investment report from the money manager. The analysis should go much deeper. One should evaluate:

- **Whether the plan achieved its expected return and investment objectives.** This is the most significant question to answer. The fiduciary should determine whether the shortfall was a result of underexposure of assets classes offering greater returns, market upheaval, manager performance, high administrative or investment expenses, or a combination of these factors.
- **Whether the manager is abiding by the plan's investment policy statement.** Determine whether restrictions or constraints for different asset classes are being adhered to. This is one point in the supervisory process where the fiduciary should review whether the portfolio should be rebalanced to remain

aligned with the allocation agreed upon in the investment policy statement.

- **What contributed to the total return of the portfolio.** A number of components make up total return, but each should be analyzed in isolation.

Monitoring your association's money manager goes beyond simply reviewing figures provided by him or her. Changes in a manager's style, in staff, or in the plan objectives may necessitate the replacement of a manager. For instance, no fiduciary should entrust assets to an untested investment strategy. Also, be alert to a manager who initiates changes to increase returns by investing in the latest Wall Street trend; this adds undue risk to a portfolio. An inexperienced manager suffering from poor performance may try to redeem his or her record by taking inordinate risks, which can compound investment errors and further degrade performance.

Hiring a money manager or investment broker should not be a quick decision nor based solely on the recommendation of a colleague. You must do your homework and evaluate performance data of the firm as well as the type of personal attention your account will receive. Request for Proposals (RFPs) should not only outline the type of management you expect but also include questions on the type of support you can expect to receive. Face-to-face interviews and thorough reference checks should be done and consolidated into a formal report for presentation to the final decision makers.

Nothing in this process should be taken for granted. In most cases

Policy Guidelines

Investment policies should be clear and concise and give limitations on what, when, and where it is appropriate to invest the organization's funds. The main components of a good investment policy are:

- **Statement of purpose**—a clear statement of the fund's objective and the primary principles that will be followed.

- **Investment objectives**—the measure by which the fund will be gauged. This section should contain investment mix and return directives aimed at the investment manager.

- **Investment goals**—what the association plans to use the funds for. This section can also contain specific targets and performance consistency directives.

- **Authority**—an outline of who is responsible for each level of management with the funds. This section should identify key staff, volunteers, and the investment broker's responsibilities that should be reviewed regularly.

- **Investment guidelines**—any specific limits that the investment broker must follow in the investment of the association's funds. This section should address risk issues.

The policies might also address how often the fund manager must provide a formal report to the fiduciaries. Keep in mind that volunteer leaders—that is, the board or finance committee—are the true fiduciaries of invested funds and should feel comfortable in how they are managed. While the fiduciaries can delegate day-to-day oversight of investment management, they can not delegate their responsibility.

you will be entrusting large sums of your association's cash to this person or firm. Also remember that the investment policy statement is not a static document. As circumstances change, you will need to be flexible enough to change with them by revising the association's investment philosophy.

References

American Society of Association Executives, *ASAE Operating Ratio Report*, 9th ed., Washington, D.C.

Siege, Joel G., and Jab K. Shim, *Accounting Handbook*, 2nd ed., Barrons Educational Series, Inc.

Velma R. Hart, CAE, is the immediate past chair of the American Society of Association Executive's Finance and Administration Section Council. Hart is the director of financial management at the American Occupational Therapy Association, Inc., in Bethesda, Maryland. She has more than 14 years' experience in association management.

CHAPTER 13

FUND RAISING

WENDY MANN, CAE

From funding a public relations campaign, to attracting contributions for a political action committee (PAC), to raising revenues through affinity programs, fund raising is an integral part of every association's efforts to finance its activities. Understanding the factors that motivate members, suppliers, and even the public to give is key to the success of fund-raising efforts.

In his book, *Achieving Excellence in Fund Raising*, Henry Rosso notes repeatedly that people give to people—they don't give to strangers or to nameless, faceless groups. Beyond that, they give for a variety of reasons. For example, ego often motivates individuals competing for recognition in a specific industry or profession; of course, they may also support the organization's cause.

Organizations that raise funds for a specific cause may attract contributors who have been directly affected. For example, people who have a family member afflicted with arthritis, cancer, or alcoholism often make significant contributions to organizations that support research and education efforts in those areas.

Community-based organizations—such as homeless shelters, food banks, and children's outreach programs—touch other people who believe in making society a better place.

The desire to give back to their profession or industry may motivate still others: A member who has achieved success may feel compelled to support the new generation of professionals rising through the ranks by financially assisting his or her professional society. Or people who have received a scholarship from their professional society or a service award from their trade association may contribute as a way to show appreciation.

In terms of PAC contributions, the possibility of being adversely affected by pending legislation or stifled under stringent regulatory rules typically prompts people to contribute. Contributors view giving to PACs as a way of participating collectively and more effectively in government relations activities.

Scanning the Horizon

Organizations embarking on a fund-raising effort must begin with an environmental scan—an exploration of the external forces at work. Is the profession or industry booming or in decline? Is the industry in a downsizing mode or prone to mergers? Do potential donors feel good about the cause? What societal changes have affected the willingness of individuals to give at the grassroots level?

The environmental scan identifies societal, governmental, or organizational issues that may affect the association's fund-raising abilities. For example, the banking industry experienced a plethora of mergers during the mid-1990s, which decreased the number of corporate donors and their ability to give.

In terms of the membership and the industry or profession represented, the association needs to identify any declines in employment in the profession, public image, and legislative initiatives that adversely affect the giving potential of members.

Another factor to consider is the giving culture within the profession or industry: Do the organization's members support professional development? Do members feel a commitment to obtain training from the organization? Is there a professional tie to the organization? Do members financially support the organization in ways other than dues and training? If members are not prone to making financial contributions, the organization must begin an educational process to shift the culture to one that is more giving in nature.

Some economic factors contribute adversely to giving patterns. These include recession, populations shifts, changes in government (political, legislative, and regulatory), and inflation. According to the Independent Sector's *Giving and Volunteering in the United States 1994, Volume II*, "Between 1989 and 1991, the year in which the recession bottomed out, average household contributions dropped sharply by 15 percent, while average household income continued to rise from $35,972 in 1989 to $36,797 in 1991, a three percent increase." These statistics demonstrate that the decrease in giving can be traced directly to the recession, which is a leading economic factor. While household income increased during this period, giving declined—which is attributed to the recession.

As the baby boomers age and Generation X moves to the forefront, associations must revise their fund-raising initiatives to appeal to a different group of prospects. Societal trends that affect fund raising also include geographic shifts, divorce, child care, and the public's perception of the immediate problems within the society. For example, organizations that deal with children's issues and education may attract more visibility and media attention at certain times; they must be ready to capitalize on any wave of public support for dealing with children's needs.

Of course, thousands of organizations nationwide ask for contributions; the competition for charitable dollars is keen. That's why you also need to examine the marketplace to determine if other organizations are seeking funds from the same constituency pool and develop initiatives that set your association apart from competitors.

Prospecting for Gold

The L-A-I principle usually proves helpful when researching and identifying true prospects. The acronym stands for:

- **L — Linkage.** Any link, contact, bridge, or access through a peer to a potential donor.

- **A — Ability.** Whether the potential donor has the ability—sufficient financial holdings—to make a contribution.

- **I — Interest.** The potential donor's interest in the organization's cause, mission, or accomplishments.

Zeroing in on Donors

Next, the association must examine its base of potential donors to ascertain their attitudes, ability to give, willingness to give, and knowledge of the organization.

The interview process entails arranging personal meetings with potential donors or prospects—usually those likely to make large gifts. An interview will yield information such as a person's interest in specific types of programs and his or her personal perspective about the association's cause. The information obtained from the interview enables the association to tailor its fund-raising program and presentations to meet the needs of key constituencies.

Based on the identified factors for giving, plus willingness and ability to give, donor prospects are grouped into segments. A tailor-made giving program, which matches the motivating factors, is developed for each key segment. In other words, each constituency will have different "opportunities for giving." This concept of segmentation incorporates those who have a high level of knowledge and involvement with the organization as well as secondary constituencies that may have little or no knowledge or involvement.

For example, a volunteer with the organization who has given in the past may be approached for an special gift. Someone who hasn't been involved with the organization but has been identified as a prospect because of interest in the cause, profession, or industry, may be approached through a direct mail campaign designed to prospect donors.

As another example, someone who makes contributions based on the need for personal recognition may be approached about making a special gift for a newly instituted project. He or she is offered two or three ways to make the contribution and provided with the visibility and recognition among peers through publicity, an awards program, and a "top donors" VIP event.

Making the Case

A case statement explains to potential donors why they should support an organization. Board members, volunteers, current donors, and staff should all participate in developing this document, which typically does the following:

- **Identifies and validates the need.** Discuss the human or societal needs reflected in the organization's mission, incorporating statistics and information from external sources.
- **Documents the need.** Provide documentation from other agencies, organizations, or research bodies.
- **Identifies programs and strategies designed to address the needs.** Explain how the organization's programs can respond to the human or societal condition identified by the needs.
- **Establishes the competence of the organization and its staff.** Through testimonials, references, and service records, demonstrate that staff will be proper stewards of funds.

- **Explains who will benefit.** Identify not only the person on the receiving end of the organization's service but also the broader community that will benefit—the family, neighborhood, the community, or society at large. Each donation touches many lives.

- **Identifies the resources required to fund the programs.** Clearly and concisely outline the financial support needed to carry out the program. Make the case for why a potential contributor should give, then ask for the support.

- **Explains why the prospect should give.** Help the prospect understand the validity of the need, the importance of the gift, and the justification for your solicitation. Ensure that the solicitor takes enough time for making the case.

- **Tells the prospective donor how to give.** Include a variety of ways for donors to give, so they can select the method that best fits their interests and financial situation.

- **Responds to the prospect's unasked question.** Donors want to know, "What's in it for me?" It is natural for them to wonder what return they will receive on their investment. Solicitors should be sensitive to offering potential donors some type of "psychic paycheck" for their contribution.

Categories of Gifts and Donors

In general, organizations raise funds in four ways:

1. **Annual Fund.** The cornerstone of many fund-raising programs, the annual fund generates money for ongoing support and seeks to enroll new donors, renew donations, and upgrade the level of donation. Individuals are the primary contributors to the annual fund. Contributors to the annual fund typically support current programs by making unrestricted gifts—funds the organization can allocate at its discretion. The process of solicitation for a gift to the annual fund can also be a tool for educating potential contributors about the organization, which leads to a better understanding and possibly a donation.

   University alumni associations are an excellent example of organizations that operate successful annual fund programs. Universities contact alumni annually to make a gift to the fund. Each year, donors are asked to renew and upgrade their gifts. This method can be transferred directly to associations and association-related foundations, using the membership base as the key constituency for the annual gift.

2. **Capital Campaign.** These large gifts are typically sought as part of an intensive and carefully orchestrated effort aimed at constructing or renovating a building or purchasing equipment. Typically referred to as a "bricks and mortar" campaign, this fund-raising appeal runs for a scheduled period of time and encourages gifts in the form of multi-year pledges. The campaign may last five or six years, with the organization accepting commitments in the first year that will be fulfilled during the succeeding years.

3. **Planned Gifts.** Planned giving refers to the solicitation of gifts from current asset holdings or a person's estate. The planned gift can be cash or assets, such as stock certificates, real or personal property, or insurance bequests. The contributor makes the gift as a trust, contract, or gift. The principal benefit of the gift is not available to the organization until some future date when the gift matures.

4. **Endowment.** With endowments, the principal is invested for the long term, and the interest earned is used to support a specific cause or program; funds from an endowment may be restricted or unrestricted. While a capital campaign is intensive and short-term, an endowment campaign can be slow-paced to permit time for cultivation of planned gifts and big-gift prospects.

An endowment campaign can be built around a specific issue or a theme that the constituency is willing to support (based on prior research). Funds are available from four main groups:

- **Individuals.** The bulk of money given in the United States—as much as 80 or 90 percent—comes from individuals. The goal is to identify those individuals through meticulous research. Once you have identified them and educated them about the organization, you establish an exchange relationship.

  According to Henry Rosso in *Achieving Excellence in Fund Raising*, an exchange relationship exists when the individual donor brings his or her largess to the program or project, thereby enhancing the community well-being. The organization provides the donor with a sense of worth, value, belonging, and making a difference.

  This aspect of fund raising requires the collection of accurate data about potential donors. Profiles can be built through the individuals themselves or through public resources. The key is to collect information that provides a link to the fund-raising organization, the prospect's ability to give, and his or her areas of interest.

  An organization's "family" represents the key constituents for individual gifts. Family members include board members, alumni, volunteers, staff leaders, professional affiliates, former donors, gift-club members, and those known to believe in the organization's work. Ideally, develop profiles on individuals in each of these categories and break them into groups according to potential to give (from high to low).

  Following the collection of data, evaluate each prospect in terms of motivation for giving, link to the organization, and ability and interest in giving. Develop a plan identifying who will ask for the contribution, how they will ask, and the follow-up that will occur.

- **Corporations.** Corporations typically comprise only 5 percent of aggregate giving. They tend to give (in order of total contributions) to educational efforts, health and human services, and environmental causes. They also tend to support causes located in specific geographical areas, typically where they have operations and employees. Corporations give for a variety of reasons, including good citizenship, enlightened self-interest, individual leadership initiative, and location.

Cash contributions may come from corporate foundations, direct-giving programs, executive discretionary funds, subsidiary or individual plant budget, marketing budgets, or research and development budgets. Corporations may also provide non-cash gifts such as product donations, services, loaned executives, and support of events.

When soliciting a corporate contribution, it is important to know the giving philosophy of the company and the variety of ways the corporation can give to an organization. It is also imperative to identify an exchange relationship with the company.

- **Foundations.** Independent (private) foundations, company foundations, community foundations, and operating foundations represent 57 percent of giving. Charitable foundations, by law, must annually distribute grants of at least 5 percent of their portfolio assets.

Many foundations require the submission of proposals that meet specific

---

Corporate Strategies

The following are steps for effective corporate solicitation:

1. Create a clear, concise, and persuasive case for support. Potential corporate donors need to see clearly that an association has a specific mission, programs are in place that benefit the organization's constituency and the community, and how the contribution will be used. The corporate entity will also want to know how it will benefit from becoming involved.

2. Identify companies that have an interest in supporting your specific cause. The research process enables you to develop a list of high potential targets and provide higher yield during the solicitation process.

3. Design and implement a cultivation process that will attract the interest of potential corporate donors. Through cultivation, an association increases its visibility with a potential corporate contributor while educating the corporation about its mission, projects, and programs.

   Cultivation techniques—used before an actual request for funds—include sending the association's newsletter, program information, or updates on a fund-raising campaign. You may also gain access to the corporation by inviting one of its employees to become a volunteer.

4. Implement a solicitation strategy at the appropriate time. The basic premise of all fund raising is asking the right person, in the right way, at the right time, for the right amount of money.

   The face-to-face request for funds is the most effective form of solicitation. Most corporations have policies in place for accepting grant proposals. With personal solicitations, some type of link to the corporation is essential.

5. Follow up and provide additional cultivation. Once corporate support has been secured, continually provide information and updates to the corporate donor. In this way, you can continue the cultivation process and perhaps receive additional funds in the future.

---

guidelines and time lines. While foundation policies for reviewing requests are quite stringent, grants from foundations are typically large and can go a long way toward meeting a program or project need.

- **Government.** Federal monies are available for organizations to conduct research, meet human and societal needs, implement training programs, and implement a myriad other projects. There are specific guidelines and proposal forms for requesting federal funds; federal agencies often require highly detailed paperwork. This type of grant also comes with federal oversight and financial reporting requirements.

Fund-Raising Vehicles

An integrated development plan incorporates a variety of fund-raising methods aimed at meeting both long- and short-term needs. Based on the association's strategic plan, program development, and financial needs, an integrated plan may include initiatives for obtaining small and large gifts.

An integrated development plan may include the following:

- **Direct Mail.** With today's technology for targeting individuals and customizing appeals, a direct mail campaign can be highly successful. While the contributions are smaller (usually less than $500), direct mail enables organizations to discover new prospects for special and major gifts, educate its constituency, and convert peripheral constituencies into contributors. Direct mail solicitation requires researching and identifying prospects, culling market segments and mailing lists, and developing a campaign built around the donors' interests and ability to give as well as the organization's needs.

  Direct mail campaigns may be used to prospect as well as to raise funds. When an organization uses direct mail to prospect, the goal is to acquire contributors, not dollars. A direct mail prospecting campaign should operate to break even, not make money. The prospects identified then become part of the organization's house file—the database for donor development.

  Direct mail is also used to resolicit and upgrade past donors. An effective donor-development campaign using a house file should produce a response rate of 6 to 15 percent.

- **Telemarketing.** Phoning donors in combination with personal letters or appeals can increase the likelihood of securing a gift. By itself, telemarketing is less effective, particularly if the calls are made to purchased lists.

- **Individual Solicitation.** Having an association representative—or a team of solicitors—make personal visits is usually reserved for the people likely to make special gifts—large contributions that tend to be earmarked for a special purpose or project. Donors of large special gifts look to support well-managed organizations that exude confidence and meet a need. As a result, be prepared to answer questions about the composition of the board, preparation of responsible budgets, debt-free audits, gift and grant policies, and investment policies.

Planned gifts also require individual solicitation; in fact, an association volunteer or staff member may make several visits over a period of years before the gift is finalized.

- **Special Events.** These events may take the form of a theme party, award presentation, silent auction, fashion show, or sporting event, with the income after expenses benefitting the fund-raising cause. Special events can consume vast amounts of staff time and overhead to implement. However, in addition to raising funds, they can offer increased visibility and educate constituents about your association. This will pay off in future contributions.

Special-event fund raising requires the sponsoring organization to use many volunteers, develop a clear consensus on the type of event that the constituency will support, and mount a massive communications program to promote the event. Corporate sponsors are often asked to underwrite the costs of the event so that the funds raised will directly support the organization's projects and programs.

Direct Appeals

Components of a direct mail solicitation package include:

- **Messages.** Make the message clear and personal; relate it to the donor.

- **Envelope.** Size, shape, color, and contents are all important. Consider including "teaser copy" to boost readership.

- **Letter.** The copy should get right to the point, recognize the reader, state what the organization wants, state the problem by asking specific examples, restate the problem and its solution, ask for the money, ask again, and be timely.

- **Inserts.** Use these to reinforce and add credibility to the entire package.

- **Response forms.** The form should resell the reader, involve the reader, ask for action, and be specific. It should tell the person exactly what action to take.

- **Return envelopes.** To encourage the recipient to take immediate action, use copy on the envelope or a calendar with a due date for the contribution. Providing the return address of the potential donor provides a personal touch.

Managing the Development Process

Successful fund raising requires the support and determination of the entire staff and volunteer structure. The program staff and the fund-raising staff need to work with one another and support one another. In addition, the staff must offer complete support to the volunteer structure.

Volunteers play a key role in any fund-raising effort. They can provide the "linkage" to specific donors, create interest in previously uncultivated constituencies, and share their enthusiasm and commitment to the organization with others.

An effective volunteer structure begins with the governing board, which is responsible for the organization's financial health and stability. The board members set the climate for all volunteers involved in the organization. But before requesting funds from someone else, a board member must be a giver. When the board operates with enthusiasm and in a hands-on manner—by bringing in contributions and sharing the vision of the organization—other volunteers will take their cue accordingly.

The board, in tandem with an organization's staff, must carefully select a cadre of volunteers to participate in fund-raising efforts. The volunteers may participate in solicitation directly (face-to-face), via telephone, or via direct mail. Much of their success will depend upon the results of fund-raising research.

The chief executive officer (CEO) ensures that all the key components are in place for the board and volunteers to conduct fund-raising efforts. He or she also leads the staff in terms of vision and strategy, as well as program development and implementation. The development director creates specific strategies and action plans to meet fund-raising goals. His or her role is two-fold: Create materials and cultivate donors.

Materials include research, proposals, the case statement, operating plans, and publications. The cultivation aspect of the director's work is to build and maintain relationships with key constituencies. The development director also advances the board's and CEO's participation in fund-raising efforts.

Methods of Solicitation

Several methods of solicitation can be incorporated into your fund-raising plan. Consideration should be given to the comfort level of the solicitor and the amount of gift to be requested. Listed below are the methods in order from most effective to least effective:

1. Personal visit by a team (generally used only for solicitation of large or planned gifts).

2. Personal visit by one person.

3. Solicitation by personal letter with a follow-up telephone call.

4. Solicitation by personal letter without follow-up telephone call.

5. Personal telephone call by a peer with a follow-up letter.

6. Personal telephone call without a follow-up letter.

Costs and Risks

It takes money to raise money. Fund-raising endeavors must be assessed in terms of financial and resource risk versus possible return for dollars, staff time, and volunteer time expended. In general, fund raising through printed materials (letters, brochures, ads, and direct mail) is lower risk but has higher costs for lesser returns. People-to-people solicitations are at higher personal risk but tend to achieve the highest return on dollars and time.

Recognition

Thank everyone who makes a contribution to your organization. Sending a thank-you letter is good; creating a recognition program is even better. Your overall fund-raising plan should incorporate a formal recognition program for anyone who makes a contribution. For major contributors, consider creating special recognition clubs. Many alumni organizations, for example, have giving clubs for donors at certain levels. In addition, members of these giving clubs may receive special benefits, which increase with the level of contribution.

Once the recognition club or program has been approved by staff, the development committee, and the board, staff should prepare a brochure that explains each of the giving clubs, the organization's mission, the purpose of the fund-raising effort, how individuals can become part of the club, and a request for action. It is also important to list the names of board and development committee members, as well as any people who have already qualified for club recognition.

Active donors are among the first to be invited to participate in the recognition club program. The organization may also want to conduct a special event to honor individuals who make the initial commitments to the club. Through this special event, the organization increases its visibility and provides a forum for recognizing leading contributors.

Communication

Communicating the mission and programs of the organization is a fundamental responsibility of staff and volunteers. When undertaking a fund-raising program, the organization should continually create awareness about its mission and goals, foster an understanding of services that meet the mission, and invite constituents to make a commitment to the organization.

The goal of your communication plan should be to create awareness and educate potential donors about the work of the organization. A comprehensive communication plan will incorporate a newsletter, along with press releases, placement of articles in other publications, advertising, marketing promotions, and special events.

Policies and Guidelines

In *Achieving Excellence in Fund Raising,* Henry Rosso encourages organizations to develop donor guidelines to engender trust and to set standards for staff members. Examples of policies to consider include:

- The organization will not enter into an agreement, contract, or commitment with a donor when a conflict of interest is apparent.

- The association will retain legal counsel to review fund-raising materials and draft specific policies for negotiating trusts, determining the interval of payments, and making the final distribution of planned giving funds. Likewise, donors should retain legal counsel to assist them in major philanthropic contributions.

- The association and staff must keep all information pertaining to a contribution strictly confidential.

The federal government has established laws regarding the disclosure of contribution information and the exchange of tangible gifts for contributions. Organizations are required to supply donors with a letter or form confirming their contribution and specifically stating the amount that is deductible.

Additionally, when a donor receives a gift in return for the contribution, the value of the gift must be subtracted from the donation to determine the deductible amount. For example, if a donor gives your association a $500 contribution and receives in return a $50 gift pack of publications, the total deductible contribution is $450.

Establishing a Foundation

Many 501(c)(6) organizations have initiated 501(c)(3) subsidiary or "sister" organizations (foundations) to fulfill a special educational or charitable need. People may be motivated to give to a (c)(3) organization because their contributions will be tax-deductible. As an added bonus, 501(c)(3) organizations can take advantage of tax and postal-rate benefits.

When considering whether to initiate a charitable foundation, answer these questions:

FINANCIAL/FUNDING ISSUES

1. Will the association support the foundation? How much in cash contributions and how much in-kind? How long will the association provide this support?
2. What are the key sources of funding for the foundation? Will the association's members be a key constituency? Will they support the association through membership and the foundation through contributions? What are the other possible funding sources—suppliers, foundations, government, corporate?
3. What types of programs will be supported by key constituencies? Have you identified the types of products and services the foundation will offer and matched them with key donor constituencies?
4. Who will staff the foundation? Will you need a full-time fund raiser?

FUND-RAISING TECHNIQUES

1. How will you solicit regular members and suppliers: Direct mail? Personal visits? Telephone solicitations?
2. Will you hold special events to raise funds or for image building?
3. Will you accept in-kind contributions?
4. Will members be asked for an annual gift?
5. How can corporate members contribute? What are the benefits to them?
6. Based on the giving culture of your association's key constituencies and the external factors, what type of giving programs are possible?

GOVERNANCE

1. How will the governing board of the foundation be structured? Will the board be completely separate from the association? Will some association board members participate on the foundation board?

2. What type of stature and leadership skills will the foundation need to raise funds? The board should comprise individuals who can command respect and solicit contributions.

3. Will the association and foundation operate independently or as "sister" organizations? Will the foundation be required to obtain approval from the association for programs and projects? Will the foundation act in a complementary manner to the association—offering services that complement programs currently operated by the association?

4. What type of volunteer committees will the foundation need?

5. What type of structure will be developed for board members' fund-raising activities?

6. How will board members be selected? How many will the foundation need? How will the foundation board interact with the association board? (For example, will the foundation chairman provide monthly or quarterly reports to the association board?)

7. Will a staff person participate on the board in an *ex officio* capacity?

8. Who will develop the foundation bylaws? What type of policy manual will be needed? Who will develop the policy manual?

INCORPORATION

1. What is the purpose of the organization?

2. Who will write the articles of incorporation?

3. Who will file the legal documentation?

4. Who will monitor and obtain appropriate (c)(3) exemptions (federal and state)?

5. Who will file tax forms?

6. Who will be responsible for legal documentation and record keeping?

PROGRAMMING

1. Will the programs the foundation implements be community-based? Profession- or industry-based? Will the programs meet requirements for government and foundation grants?

2. Will the foundation publish educational material? Will the material be published in-house or outsourced? Will the material meet the needs of key constituencies?

3. Will the foundation offer scholarship grants, program grants, or research grants?

4. Will the foundation offer educational or training programs? Will the programs compete with or complement the association's programs? What type of topics will meet the needs of key constituencies?

5. Are some programs currently conducted by the association more appropriate for the foundation to carry out?

PUBLIC RELATIONS/MARKETING

1. What types of vehicles will be used to communicate the information, resources, and fund-raising efforts of the foundation? Newsletters, press releases, brochures, or annual reports?

2. How will the foundation market its products, programs, and services? What are the key market segments in relation to key fund-raising constituencies?

3. Which methods of donor recognition will be implemented to raise the visibility of donors and the organization—a special awards program for key donors or a donors club? What type of recognition do contributors expect?

PLANNING

1. Who will write the strategic plan?
2. What type of future efforts will the foundation work toward?
3. Who will monitor the strategic plan?
4. How will annual program, fund-raising, and marketing planning be conducted?

The decision to establish a charitable foundation incorporates a variety of planning and legal issues. Prior to moving forward, conduct planning sessions to formulate the goals and mission of such an organization. The planning process should include legal counsel to assist with all legal aspects of incorporation and documentation.

References and Recommended Reading

American Society of Association Executives, *How to Establish and Fund an Association Foundation*, Washington, D.C., 1985.

Carver, John, *Boards That Make a Difference*, Jossey-Bass, Inc., San Francisco, 1990.

Independent Sector, *Giving & Volunteering in the United States, 1994, Volume II*, Washington, D.C., 1995.

Jacobs, Jerald A., *Association Law Handbook*, 3rd ed., American Society of Association Executives, Washington, D.C., 1996.

Kotler, Philip, and Alan R. Andreasen, *Strategic Marketing for Nonprofit Organizations*, 3rd ed., Prentice-Hall, Inc., Englewood Cliffs, New Jersey, 1987.

Lindahl, Wesley E., *Strategic Planning for Fund Raising*, Jossey-Bass, San Francisco, 1992.

O'Connell, Brian, *The Board Members Book,* 2nd ed., Independent Sector, Washington, D.C., 1995.

Rosso, Henry A. *Achieving Excellence in Fund Raising,* Jossey-Bass, San Francisco, 1991.

Worth, Michael J., *Educational Fund Raising,* American Council on Education and The Oryx Press, Phoenix, Arizona, 1993.

Wendy Mann, CAE, has 12 years of professional experience in association management. She is an independent contractor working with associations in a variety of capacities, including communications, management, and product development. Previously, she served as executive director of the Greater Washington Society of Association Executives Foundation and vice president of Government and Public Relations.

CHAPTER 14

HUMAN RESOURCE MANAGEMENT

MICHAEL R. LOSEY, SPHR

For-profit corporations may have a competitive advantage because of their technology, a superior manufacturing process, or unique products and services protected by patents and trademarks. In trade and professional associations, however, success is primarily determined by how well members' needs and interests are met. Given the decreasing availability of volunteers and the increasing demands on their time, it often falls to association staff to identify and fulfill needs.

Such an organizational setting requires not only effective governance but also efficient, knowledgeable, and motivated staff who are involved in the administration and maintenance of member programs and services. The idea that employees are an association's most important resource is not mere rhetoric: The more efficient its ability to manage human resources, the more competitive and successful an association can be in meeting members' needs.

Larger organizations usually dedicate a separate department to managing human resources. This luxury, however, isn't enjoyed by most associations, according to *Policies and Procedures in Association Management 1996*, a study conducted by the American Society of Association Executives. In fact, the average association employs 23 full-time staff members, and only 12 percent of survey respondents have a full-time human resource or personnel director. Instead, as in any small business, the chief executive officer (CEO), office manager, or finance director typically has the responsibility for human resource management.

Few things will derail the career of a CEO or other senior manager faster than failing to create a work environment that fosters employee understanding of the association's mission and promotes teamwork, communication, and effective use of staff resources. Here are the key elements of a human resources program that contribute to a favorable and productive work environment.

Recruitment

Effective human resource management begins with recruiting the right people. And recruitment actually begins by defining the duties and requirements of the position needing to be filled and making sure that interviewers can answer general questions about the association and employment conditions. A standard approach to employee recruitment is recommended to help ensure consistency in the evaluation of candidates. The people who will be interviewing candidates should formulate questions that focus on job-related requirements, determine the order in which they'll ask the questions, and review the candidate's resume or application for employment before the interview begins.

Most organizations have a formal employment application that collects consistent data from all candidates; a person's resume can be attached as a supplement to—rather than a substitute for—the employment application. Most employment applications ask for the following information:

- Personal data (name, address, telephone numbers)
- Education and training
- Special skills the applicant possesses
- Work history (in order of latest to first)
- Authorization to check references
- Employment and other waivers
- Equal employment and affirmative action statements
- Applicant's signature

Before turning to outside sources to fill vacancies, determine who on your current staff may be interested and qualified. Employees who aspire to internal promotions and lateral moves as part of their career development process can acquire the necessary knowledge and skills to step in when an appropriate position becomes available.

Recruiting outside the association can be done by:

- Alerting your current employees in the event they know and can recommend others who may have an interest in the position.
- Running advertisements in the newspapers, association journals, or magazines.
- Reviewing resumes of individuals, including those who may have applied previously when the position was not available.
- Retaining an executive search firm for senior positions.

Most organizations want to ensure their recruitment efforts reach candidates who reflect the diversity inherent in the workforce and community. Aside from the legal aspects of equal employment opportunity, experience has shown that the more diverse the organization, the better its opportunities for excellence.

Efforts to achieve diversity may be disadvantaged and legal risks incurred unintentionally. For instance, alerting current employees to a vacancy in an attempt to solicit referrals could be discriminatory if all or most of your employees are white and might be expected to refer mostly white acquaintances or family members. In such cases, special affirmative efforts must be taken to attract applicants from minorities, older workers, disabled workers, veterans, women, and other protected classes.

Interviewing

Once you've obtained as many candidates as possible, you'll need to narrow the field from which to make your final selection. The first step is reviewing all employment applications or resumes. Those who appear to have the necessary qualifications must be screened and reduced to an even smaller number of candidates who can be interviewed. Through telephone screening—talking to the people who appear to have the necessary qualifications and experience—you can ensure they are still available, are willing to relocate (if necessary), understand the nature of the position, and have a reasonable level of interest.

The actual interview represents the candidate's introduction to the association. Depending on how the interview goes, it may affect the candidate's willingness to continue discussions or accept employment, if offered. Too, applicants might be current or potential members or people who are otherwise influential within the association and other industries. To maintain your association's professional standing, follow these interviewing guidelines:

- **Create a list of job-related interview questions.** By ensuring that all applicants for the same position are asked the same basic questions, you'll bring consistency to the interview process, which is practically and legally desirable.
- **Ask open-ended questions,** which prompt behavioral descriptions rather than a simple yes or no answer. For example, rather than asking, "Did you like your last job?" say, "Tell me what you liked about your last job."
- **Let the interviewee do most of the talking.** After an appropriate welcome and introduction to put the candidate at ease, move to questions you need answered. Listen carefully to the responses, take notes when appropriate, and provide verbal ("Yes, I understand" or "Good") and nonverbal reinforcement (such as nodding the head) to encourage the person to continue.
- **Avoid questions that might suggest discrimination.** Under Equal Employment Opportunity Commission (EEOC) and other guidelines, certain questions should not be asked. Also, under the Americans with Disabilities Act (ADA), employers with 15 or more employees must ensure that employment-related actions, terms, and conditions do not discriminate against any individual who has or could be perceived as having a disability.
- **Stay focused on the job and its requirements,** not preconceived assumptions about what an applicant can or cannot do. For instance, someone who comes across well may have had many jobs and a lot of practice interviewing but isn't necessarily the best person for the job.
- **Balance "selling" the organization with keeping expectations realistic.** Although you want to position the association in the best possible light, avoid making promises that, if unfulfilled, may lead to employee dissatisfaction and turnover.
- **Obtain background information** to use during the reference checking process. Ask, for example, if the applicant had full accountability for developing a new membership development program or if he or she had only a contributory role. Have the applicant complete a reference checking authorization, if one doesn't appear on the employment application. Specifically, verify educational credentials required for the position (the most frequent applicant misrepresentation).
- **End on a cordial note.** If possible, inform the candidate of the next step and the expected timing. While the interview is still fresh in your mind, complete an evaluation form on the candidate.

Interview Questions

CATEGORY	MAY ASK	MAY DISCRIMINATE BY ASKING
Sex and family arrangements	• If applicant has relatives already employed by the organization	• Sex of applicant • Number of children • Marital status • Spouse's occupation • Child care arrangements • Health care coverage through spouse
Race		• Applicant's race or color of skin • Photo to be affixed to application form
National origin or ancestry	• Whether applicant has a legal right to be employed in the U.S. • Ability to speak/write English fluently (if job related) • Other languages spoken (if job-related)	• Ethnic association of a surname • Birthplace of applicant or applicant's parents • Nationality, lineage, national origin • Nationality of applicant's spouse • Whether applicant is citizen of another country • Applicant's native tongue/English proficiency • Maiden name (of married woman)
Religion		• Religious affiliation/Availability for weekend work • Religious holidays observed
Age	• If applicant is over age 18 • If applicant is over age 21 if job-related (i.e., bartender)	• Date of birth • Date of high school graduation • Age
Disability	• Whether applicant can perform the essential job-related functions	• If applicant has a disability • Nature or severity of a disability • Whether applicant has ever filed a workers' compensation claim • Recent or past surgeries and dates • Past medical problems
Other	• Convictions if job-related • Academic, vocational, or professional schooling • Training received in the military • Membership in any union, trade, or professional association • Job references	• Number and kinds of arrests • Height or weight except if a bona fide occupational qualification • Veteran status, discharge status, branch of service • Contact in case of an emergency (at application or interview stage)

Source: Society for Human Resource Management, 1996.

Summary for Interviewing Persons with Disabilities

DO	DON'T
Do ensure that the interview facility is accessible to people with disabilities.	Don't assume the person is able to shake your hand in greeting.
Do inform the applicant of any special parking available.	Don't lean on an applicant's wheelchair.
Do allow the applicant at least a full day to prepare for your interview.	Don't shout or raise your voice to a person who is hearing impaired.
Do identify the essential functions of the job.	Don't touch or talk to a seeing-eyed dog.
Do make eye contact with the person.	Don't ask about a person's disability history.
Do talk directly to the person with the disability—not to an interpreter.	Don't ask about prior workers' compensation claims.
Do, after the initial greeting, sit down so that a person who uses a wheelchair can easily make eye contact.	Don't ask how the person became disabled.
Do ask about the person's ability to perform the job.	Don't ask how a person is going to get to work.

Source: Society for Human Resource Management, 1996

Checking References

Again, the most common error made in the employment decision is hiring people based on what you "think" they can do versus what they have proven they can do. Unfortunately, some employers hesitate to provide references or limit their comments to verification of employment dates. Reference checking, however, is receiving renewed attention given concerns about possible negligent hiring claims and the higher investment involved in recruiting professional and managerial talent. Many states, for instance, have passed laws to protect employers from legal action if they give a truthful reference.

When giving references on former employees, "truth" is an absolute defense. Specify who and how references will be provided in order to promote consistent and balanced treatment. (Note: If a candidate is not provided employment because of a purchased reference or credit report, consistent with the Fair Credit

Reporting Act, you must give the applicant notice of such a determination and the opportunity to review the report.)

Making the Offer

Thorough interviewing and reference checking assist in making a fair and unbiased employment decision. To reinforce a sincere interest in the candidate, make the job offer in person and follow up with a confirmation letter that includes "employment at will" rights.

An employment-at-will statement tells the candidate that his or her employment may be terminated at any time, by either party, for any reason. The notice might read as follows: "Just as you retain the right to resign from your employment with XYZ Association without notice or cause, XYZ Association may elect to terminate your employment without notice or cause. Your employment is for no definite term, regardless of any other oral or written statement by any XYZ Association officer or representative, with the exception of an express written employment contract signed by the President."

Once you've welcomed the new employee, provide an orientation to the association that emphasizes his or her employment accountability. Often overlooked or performed marginally, the orientation process should consist of two steps:

1. A *general orientation* provided by the human resource department or the manager who maintains employment records.

2. An *orientation checklist* used by supervisors to welcome the employee into the department and explain relationships to other departments, work hours, breaks, meal times, equipment, job description, safety and emergency procedures, and so forth.

Employee Performance

An employee's worst nightmare—and a major contributor to an association's lack of full employee utilization—is the lack of clearly identified performance expectations. Factors typically included are expectations of quality and quantity of work, interpersonal skills, reliability, and other performance issues.

The job description can provide a good starting point for establishing job requirements. However, based on current operational plans or initiatives, more specific requirements may be identified for a particular year. Assuming your association has a strategic or operational plan, it is usually best to discuss department or division goals with the employee and then establish individual goals that support the larger departmental and organizational goals.

It is important to identify such items at the beginning of a performance year so they can serve as a basis of evaluation throughout the year. In addition, provide continuous feedback as opposed to evaluating an employee's performance only during his or her annual review. Supervisors can do this by regularly noting specific job-related behaviors (both positive and negative), providing reinforcement immediately, and making note of major instances for future reference.

Performance Appraisals

Most organizations maintain a formal performance appraisal process. Almost universally, such reviews are conducted annually (on a 12-month basis). Some associations base formal reviews on the employee's anniversary date; this makes it difficult to relate reviews to annual departmental or organizational objectives. Others schedule the performance review 12 months from the date of the last salary increase; this has the same disadvantage as the first method, plus it may also suggest all compensation adjustments will be on a 12-month basis when a shorter or longer interval may be justified.

Another option is to conduct all performance reviews after the close of the organization's fiscal or program year. This approach requires that all reviews be done during the same period. Although time-intensive, it offers the advantage of consistency in establishing the relative rankings of employees and permits better linking of performance to specific departmental and organizational goals.

Regardless of when the review is conducted, the important point is that it *is* conducted. Failure to conduct a performance review after making a commitment to do so is one of the most significant sources of employee dissatisfaction. Simply stated, most employees do a good job and appreciate being told so. If you don't provide appropriate and timely performance reinforcement, employees may assume that future compensation adjustments will be delayed or otherwise affected.

Here are the critical steps in conducting an effective performance appraisal:

- Be prepared. Know the objectives and goals of the meeting.
- Have records of instances demonstrating both high and low performance.
- Pick an appropriate time and place—preferably a quiet, private spot.
- Make the employee feel at ease, and create a positive environment.
- Give balanced feedback, both positive and negative—but start with the positive.
- Ask questions and allow the employee to provide feedback.
- When discussing areas for improvement, talk about specific methods and objectives.
- Discuss the employee's aspirations regarding future employment opportunities within the organization and, if possible, necessary actions that might be taken to help prepare him or her for such opportunities.
- After the performance appraisal, follow up with the employee to see how plans are proceeding within the given time frame.

Accurate performance appraisals are the cornerstone to the establishment of the relative ranking of employee performance; they assist in determining how employees are paid.

Determining a Compensation Policy

It's key to link employee contribution and performance to compensation. Compensation differences among employees that are not supported by performance can be a greater source of dissatisfaction than an individual's perception that his or her compensation is not competitive when compared to the market.

Most organizations are prepared to pay employees competitively, that is, close to the *market value* for similar positions. Accurate compensation and benefits information for the market also helps explain the association's compensation plan to the board of directors, especially when the association market differs from the trade or profession represented.

As reported in *Policies and Procedures in Association Management,* 37 percent of associations have a formal salary administration plan. Formal plans are more common in larger associations—nearly nine out of 10 associations (89 percent) with a staff of 50 or more have a formal salary administration plan compared to only 18 percent of associations with a staff of five or fewer.

When defining a compensation policy, start with the description of each position. An accurate position description ensures that there is an understanding of the educational background, work experience, special skills, and other requirements related to the position. Such a description is not only helpful in recruitment but also helps to determine the relative worth of each position compared to all other positions within the association. Individual positions are then placed in different salary grades: A position in a higher-ranking grade has a higher relative value to the organization and the market than lower-rated positions. Positions within that same level or grade have the same relative value.

Within a particular grade there is customarily a range of salary rates (thus the name "rate range"). The mid-point of each range is usually the *market* rate. To establish the minimum or starting point of the range for employees meeting the minimum requirements of the position, the market rate is usually reduced by 20 percent. The maximum is 20 percent greater than the mid-point. The range, therefore, can have as much as a 50 percent difference between the minimum and the maximum ($120 - 80 \div 80 = 50\%$). This provides for appropriate salary positioning in the range for the newly hired employee, the progressing employee, the fully qualified employee, and the employee who consistently performs above the requirements of the position.

Once positions are grouped into the necessary grades, representative *benchmark* positions are selected to determine their actual competitive relationship to the market. Benchmark positions are those that, for purposes of comparison in salary surveys, can also be found in other organizations. Examples might be receptionist, secretary, meetings and conference manager, publications director, financial director, and executive director. It is important, however, not to rely simply on titles. Instead, ensure comparability of these positions in terms of such organizational issues as size of budget, number of members and employees, and other factors reflecting overall accountability.

Determining the market to be surveyed depends on where your association would normally recruit for such a position. For instance, secretarial, administrative, and lower level exempt positions would be found in a local market—so that market is surveyed to create the salary range. Since the local market customarily supplies not-for-profit as well as for-profit organizations, candidates for such positions in for-profit organizations should also be included in the survey. Higher level management positions would usually be recruited from a national market;

therefore, national market data should be used.

Rather than burdening themselves with establishing such position relationships and conducting their own surveys, many associations use a consulting firm that has already invested in a job-evaluation process and perhaps conducted association-related compensation surveys. A consultant may be able to more cost effectively benchmark the association's positions with jobs in an existing survey, plus provide credibility to employees, management, and the board of directors.

Consultants can also provide guidance on compensation policy. For instance, if the survey of the market indicates that the association pays 5 percent below the market in relation to similar positions in other associations, the consultant would need to determine if that positioning is appropriate or should be adjusted. Some organizations, either because of their inability to pay or a stated compensation policy, intentionally operate at a level below the established market. Others may establish a compensation policy to pay 5 percent or 10 percent above the market in order to assist in employee recruitment and retention. When appropriately administered, a compensation policy indicates to employees that they have approximately the same compensation opportunity within their current association as they could reasonably expect to find in other associations or firms in their market (local or national).

When the *pay practice* (the amount employees are actually paid) materially exceeds the policy (the amount the association wants to pay) corrective action may be required. The remedy is usually reducing future merit increase budgets until the proper position is re-established. If the pay practice is less than the compensation policy, the customary remedy is to petition the organization's board of directors for an *equity increase*—a one-time adjustment to make up for the differences between the stated policy and actual compensation practices. Such adjustments require a specific and continuing cost increase without assurances of improved or sustained association performance. Some organizations may, therefore, provide a necessary equity increase but not all at once, instead spreading the adjustment(s) over several years or making them contingent upon the association's meeting selected operating objectives.

Salary Planning

Once you've determined your association's compensation policy and compared it to actual practices, you're in a position to establish an annual compensation plan. Customarily, salary planning occurs along with or just before the annual budget process. In this way, the projected increase in salaries can be incorporated into the next year's overall operating plan. The rate ranges must also be adjusted depending on how the association's current compensation policy relates to the current market. In other words, if the current policy is to be equal to the current market and the market is anticipated to move 4.5 percent, then your association's policy line (rate ranges) would also move 4.5 percent. If, however, your policy line was already 3 percent greater than the market and the market was anticipated to

Writing Job Descriptions

Although the formats of job descriptions vary, they typically include the following components:

- **Summary**— a brief description that summarizes the overall purpose and objectives of the position, the results the worker is expected to accomplish, and the degree of freedom to act.

- **Essential functions**— the tasks, duties, and responsibilities of the position that are most important to get the job done.

- **Nonessential functions**— the desirable, but not necessary, aspects of the job.

- **Knowledge, skills, and abilities**— the specific minimum competencies required for job performance.

- **Supervisory responsibilities**— the scope of the person's authority, including a list of jobs that report to the incumbent.

- **Working conditions**— the environment in which the job is performed, especially any unique conditions outside a normal office environment.

- **Minimum qualifications**— the least amount of education and experience required to perform the job.

- **Success factors**— personal characteristics that contribute to an individual's ability to excel on the job.

Source: Society for Human Resource Management, 1996.

move 4.5 percent, the rate ranges would be increased only 1.5 percent (4.5% minus 3%) so they would more closely approximate the market.

The overall salary allocation is subsequently distributed to departments and individuals based on their relative positioning within their rate range. A merit type of compensation program typically exists, under which an employee may receive more or less than other employees based on his or her position in the range and level of performance. A good practice is to allocate available monies by department, then by supervisor, and ultimately to individual employees, making certain that performance differences are recognized and the supervisor stays within the budgetary guidelines.

The actual increase will be scheduled for a subsequent date during the actual budget year based on the time since the last increase, employee performance, and relative positioning in the rate range. For instance, if an employee is at or below the minimum in a range, accelerated increases may be justified after nine months. Normal increases would be at a 12-month interval. Employees who might be paid above the mid-point but are contributing only at the mid-point in terms of performance may exceed 12 months in order to correct pay relationships over a reasonable period of time.

Incentive Compensation

According to *Policies and Procedures in Association Management,* approximately 18 percent of associations have a cash bonus system and 66 percent apply the program to all staff. Part of the justification for the growth of association incentive systems is the desire to link key staff's compensation to association performance. In addition, the board of directors may want to adopt a "corporate model" for association management or may be more accustomed to incentive-compensation programs linked to organizational performance.

Nonprofit organizations do not offer long-term incentive-compensation programs such as stock options. The all-cash orientation for nonprofits is another justification for some organizations to seriously consider bonus incentive compensation opportunities for at least key employees.

Incentive opportunities can be effectively used instead of an equity increase when the organization's compensation practice lags behind its compensation policy. In this way, the association can commit to increased compensation opportunities but link them to specific performance objectives. For instance, if the executive compensation of key managers lags the market by 10 percent, that amount could be established as the *incentive target,* with more or less being paid based on specific performance criteria. If, however, the compensation practice is already close to or exceeds the market, an association wishing to establish an incentive program would need to decrease future base compensation increases in order to create a pool from which to generate the incentive compensation.

Executive Compensation Issues

Nonprofit organizations are subject to special regulations that, for instance, do not make available the customary nonqualified retirement options that exist in the private sector. Under the current tax code there is a limitation of $150,000 in program compensation that can be used for the determination of any pension. Executives and other members of management who earn more than $150,000—or are projected to earn that much by retirement age—may therefore be disadvantaged in terms of protecting a targeted income replacement ratio unless other arrangements are created. The terms are typically spelled out in an employment contract.

Key elements of employment contracts include:

- Term of employment (beginning and ending contract dates, renewal provisions).
- Salary, incentive compensation, benefits, special conditions, "perks."
- Duties of the position.
- Executive to devote full time to organization; any noted exceptions.
- Confidentiality of proprietary information.
- Reimbursement of expenses, memberships, and so forth.
- Termination of agreement (for cause, without cause, indemnities, notice, and so forth).
- Executive not to engage in specified competitive activities.

Employee Benefits

The average cost of employee benefits in most organizations can easily exceed 30 percent of payroll. This, of course, is not an insignificant cost and must be effectively managed.

Effective benefit management begins with reviewing all benefits provided employees to determine their competitive positioning. In other words, is the association policy to position its benefit program approximately at, above, or lower than other associations? In addition, accurate cost accounting must be accomplished to fully appreciate the cost of the various benefits (retirement, health insurance, dental, life insurance, time off, and so forth).

As in compensation planning, many associations lack the professional expertise to address such issues. For instance, an association's policy to provide fully paid health insurance for employees' dependents may put the association at a disadvantage compared to another employer that requires a premium contribution from the employee. Where the association requires no premium, and a spouse's plan requires a premium contribution, it invites the employee's spouse and dependents to elect the association plan, potentially costing the association more money.

One popular benefit that even small associations can offer is a 401(k) plan. This retirement savings vehicle is a "defined contribution plan"—employees decide what percentage of their salary goes into the plan (up to a maximum set by the IRS). Their eventual benefit depends on how their investments perform.

Legislation passed in August 1996 (effective for plan years beginning after December 31, 1996) allows employers to set up "Savings Incentive Match Plans for Employees" (SIMPLE plans), including 401(k) plans. Under the "simple" plan, employers are required to match employee contributions on a dollar-for-dollar basis for the first 3 percent of an employee's compensation.

Because of the complex administrative requirements, including determining what investment options will be offered, transfers between funds, regular reporting, discrimination testing, and fiduciary requirements, most associations choose to have 401(k) plans administered by an outside consultant.

HR Policy

Every association should take time to articulate its HR policy—not necessarily a manual of policies and procedures but rather the overall approach to employee relations. At a minimum, HR policy should represent a sincere definition of how management intends to define employee relationships and their role in advancing the interest of the association. This can range from broad policies that establish a supportive employee culture to specific policies or procedures where supervisory guidance is necessary to promote consistency of application, fair treatment, and, in some cases, compliance.

Customarily, specific policies exist for such areas as working hours and attendance, paid and unpaid time off, corrective disciplinary procedures, employee's rights of appeal, and health and safety regulations. Sample policies are available from a number of sources. Also, some software programs permit sample policies to be modified to suit an organization's particular requirements.

Corrective Discipline

The word *discipline* actually comes from the root word "disciple," which means "to teach." Discipline, therefore, is a "teaching and counseling" attempt to correct inappropriate behavior or job performance. Most situations can be corrected by promptly bringing the issue to the employee's attention.

Lack of improvement generally results in the escalation of disciplinary action, thus reinforcing the seriousness of the performance issue. Sanctions could include extending initial verbal counseling or reprimands to a more formal level of documentation. If the employee cannot make the necessary corrections or remains indifferent to the need for improvement, discharge is usually justified. Immediate discharge can also be justified if the employee commits a severe breach of association policy.

An employer should always protect the right to terminate an employee by establishing and maintaining an Employment At Will Policy. Use the following checklist to investigate situations before taking corrective disciplinary action:

- Thoroughly investigate and review the facts.
- Find and obtain statements from witnesses, if applicable.
- Talk with the employee to get his or her prospective on the situation.
- Obtain related, current, and prior documentation, if applicable.
- Summarize and outline the facts of the most recent situation.
- Examine the employee's previous disciplinary history and work record.
- Examine records of employees with similar infractions and compare the discipline imposed in those situations.
- Allow adequate time for all parties to review the details of the offense.
- Determine if the employee is in a protected class. If so, determine if disparate treatment or treatment that is the result of the disparate impact (not intentional but nevertheless discriminatory) has occurred.
- If appropriate, review the facts of the investigation with an objective third person.
- Pinpoint the basis for corrective action or termination.
- Determine if the discharge violates any federal or state laws: employment at will, unfair dismissal, equal employment opportunity, disabilities, and veteran's protection rights.
- Discuss your decision with an HR professional, employment attorney, corporate association counsel, or a professional society with human resource expertise before implementing the final decision.
- Determine the best time and place to conduct the disciplinary interview.
- Carry out the corrective discipline or discharge in a calm but direct and compassionate manner. Consider including a witness in this meeting, if appropriate.
- Document what was said and actions taken during the disciplinary interview.

- If the employee was terminated, arrange for the employee to obtain personal belongings, return company property, and leave the property promptly, without creating an awkward and embarrassing situation.

Employee Development

Employees' ultimate opinion of their association as a good and productive place to work rests with how they are treated daily and whether their employer demonstrates a sincere interest in their continued training and development. The best way to accomplish this is to train employees to not only do their current job but also meet the future requirements of positions for which they may be considered. Training of employees should normally be done on an individual basis, recognizing the wide range of development needs. When an association-wide developmental need exists, however, training can be delivered cost effectively. Examples of training topics include effective report writing, giving presentations, or understanding the association finances.

Managerial training is especially critical because employees' satisfaction with their job frequently reflects little more than the treatment they receive from their immediate supervisor. Such training includes a complete understanding of the association's policies and procedures, especially as they relate to its human resource management policies. Emphasis should also be given to consistency of treatment, recognizing that frequently it is not how generous a policy is but how fairly it is applied that determines employee satisfaction. Effective communication and interpersonal skills are also important characteristics that contribute to effective leadership.

Most supervisory and employee development, however, occurs on the job, not in the classroom. Therefore, managers should learn to carefully identify the individual development needs of each subordinate and tailor a plan to meet those needs. The most effective development need is to identify on-the-job projects and accountabilities through which the employee can develop new skills and gain important experience.

Feedback Mechanisms

Providing association members with good customer service requires a total team effort to ensure that departments are not operating independently. In turn, each member of the team must understand how his or her work fits into the total package of products and services offered to the membership.

Employee feedback can enhance individual contributions and foster teamwork. It's best obtained through *effective supervision*—especially when the supervisor has a good appreciation of how employees feel about their work and the association. A more formalized approach to feedback uses an *employee attitude survey*, particularly effective when the association can benchmark its results against those obtained by similar organizations. In addition, when done at regular intervals, surveys can be benchmarked against the association's employee responses as gathered over time. A note of caution: Attitude surveys require substantial follow-up and should not be attempted unless top management has a sincere commitment to pursue the issues that employees indicate need attention.

State of the society (or association) meetings, if conducted regularly, can help employees deepen their understanding of their employer's activities and operations. For example, employees may have a poor understanding of the interests and nature of the membership, the association's revenue and expenses, or the role of unrelated business income. One large association typically holds such meetings immediately after its board of directors meetings—the agenda includes not only promptly updating employees on the status of major organizational objectives but also summarizing actions taken by the board.

Another mechanism is for the CEO to regularly conduct informal *koffee klatch* meetings with selected employees. Such meetings typically include a brief update by the CEO, followed by an opportunity to actively solicit employee questions and suggestions. Over time, such informal meetings build the expectation that the association is willing to share information and structure a situation for direct employee input and feedback.

Similarly, in *skip level interviews,* managers meet with subordinates two levels below their direct level of supervision to solicit direct feedback.

Emerging Trends

The following trends have recently emerged in human resource management and bear watching:

- **Workplace Diversity.** As more women and people of many ethnic groups enter the workforce, employers are making an effort to value the unique contributions that diverse individuals and groups have to offer. Respect for individual differences enriches the work environment and brings with it new ideas and ways of working.

  Employers who focus on diversity believe that differences among people can contribute to the success of the business and that all employees, regardless of their differences, have the same opportunities to contribute. Employers who are cognizant of the changing workforce take steps to not only ensure diversity as an objective in recruitment and promotion but also to build an awareness of diversity issues into their workplaces. This includes offering diversity training programs that promote respect and teamwork among staff members.

- **Telecommuting.** As the range of computer and communications options grows, employers find that some employees can accomplish their tasks away from the traditional workplace. Using a personal computer and modem, fax machines, and multiple phone lines, employees can access files remotely and assist members and customers from a home or satellite office. Many of these employees, for various family and personal reasons, prefer to work from home, at least part of the time.

  Disadvantages to telecommuting include the costs of setting up equipment in employees' homes; difficulty in assessing employee performance when managers do not see day-to-day operations; and difficulty in determining the hours actually worked by an employee. Too, if an employee is injured while working at home, it may be difficult to ascertain whether the employee is entitled to workers' compensation. Employees may feel neglected and "out of the loop" and find it difficult to establish boundaries between working and other tasks at home.

Still, telecommuting employees can save on transportation, parking, and clothing costs; decrease their stress levels; and assist with family care needs. Telecommuting may allow employees more flexibility and control over their work and lives. For employers, it can help retain talented employees while reducing expenses for office space and parking.

- **Flextime.** This practice allows employees to vary their schedules within limits established by the association. Most employers set a "core" time when all employees must be at work, for example, between 10 a.m. and 3 p.m. Outside the core hours, employees may choose to work from 7 a.m. to 4 p.m., or from 9 a.m. to 6 p.m. Usually employers ask staff to set a definite schedule but allow occasional changes.

  Some employers allow employees to work four 10-hour days, and have one day off each week—or work nine days for 80 hours in a two-week period, with a day off every two weeks. This variation on flextime is usually called a *compressed work week.*

  Flextime, if matched to the association's culture and business needs and managed well, can give employees more scheduling freedom and allow employers to experience increased productivity and coverage without increased costs.

- **Employee Privacy.** Employees have become increasingly concerned about their right to privacy as employers have developed the means to collect more information. Electronic mail messages, for example, may appear to be private correspondence between employees yet are often read by management or MIS employees in the course of their duties. Such messages can also be retrieved even after being deleted and have been used as evidence in court.

  Employees should not expect privacy in the normal course of business. E-mail, voice mail, desk space, locker space, and the like, are property of the organization, not of the individual. Special efforts, however, should be taken to keep personnel records private, available only to management on a need-to-know basis and available for review by employees on request. Medical records should always be kept private—and separate—from other files.

- **Independent Contractors.** An independent contractor is someone hired to do a particular task, according to his or her own methods, and not subject to employer control except for the result. Employers do not pay Social Security taxes, unemployment taxes, health benefits, and so forth, for independent contractors.

  Determining whether an individual is an employee or an independent contractor is critical for an employer's tax reporting and withholding obligations.

The Internal Revenue Service makes specific distinctions between employees and independent contractors. Factors to consider when testing whether a person is an independent contractor are: extent of control of employer over the details of the work; whether the person is engaged in a distinct occupation or business; the kind of work to be performed; the skill required for the work; whether the employer supplies the tools and location; the length of time the person is employed; the method of payment (hourly or by the job); whether the work is a regular part of the employer's business; the intent of the parties; the opportunity for profit or loss; and whether the employer is in a distinct business. By classifying individuals correctly, you can avoid fines, penalties, and additional taxes.

Federal Labor Laws

All organizations are expected to operate within the law. The breadth and scope of employment-related legislation may create a situation where organizations, especially small ones, find it difficult to fully understand and comply with current laws. Outlined below are the basic requirements of the laws that affect an overwhelming majority of small businesses and associations. (Please recognize that organizations must also be aware of municipal and state laws that may regulate terms and conditions of employment, discrimination, workers' compensation, family medical leave provisions, and so forth.)

Consumer Credit Protection Act
(1 or more employees)

The Consumer Credit Protection Act prohibits employees from being terminated for garnishments for any one indebtedness. Although two or more garnishments from separate organizations allow an employer to terminate, exercise care to prevent disparate impact if the employees being terminated are mostly women and minorities.

Penalties for non-compliance: fine of up to $1,000, one-year imprisonment, or both.

Employers who have a legitimate business need to evaluate and monitor employee credit problems, and who use credit reports to do so, should also be aware of the Fair Credit Reporting Act. The FCRA requires employers who deny employment on the basis of a credit report to so notify the applicant and to provide the name and address of the consumer reporting agency used. *Penalties for non-compliance:* actual damages, punitive damages, attorneys' fees.

Americans with Disabilities Act
(15 or more employees)

ADA is a federal anti-discrimination law that prohibits private employers, state and local governments, employment agencies, and labor unions from discriminating against qualified individuals with disabilities in job application proce-

FEDERAL LABOR LAWS BY NUMBER OF EMPLOYEES

1 or more	11 or more	15 or more	20 or more	50 or more	99 or more
Fair Labor Standards Act (FLSA) (1938)	Occupational Safety & Health Act (OSHA) (1970)	Civil Rights Act of 1964 Title VII, Civil Rights Act of 1991	Age Discrimination in Employment Act (1967) (ADEA)	Family and Medical Leave Act of 1993 (FMLA)	Worker Adjustment & Retraining Notification Act of 1989 (WARN)
Immigration Reform & Control Act (IRCA) (1986)		Title I, Americans with Disabilities Act of 1990, (ADA)	Consolidated Omnibus Budget Reconciliation Act of 1985 (COBRA)	EEO-1 Report filed annually w/EEOC if Organization is a Federal Contractor	EEO-1 Report filed annually w/ EEOC if Organization is not a Federal Contractor
Uniformed Services Employment & Re-employment Rights Act of 1994		Pregnancy Discrimination Act of 1978			
Equal Pay Act of 1963					
Consumer Credit Protection Act of 1968					
National Labor Relations Act (NLRA) 1935, including Labor-Management Relations Act (Taft-Hartley) 1947					
Employee Retirement Income Security Act (ERISA) 1974 (if Co. offers benefits)					
Uniform Guidelines of Employee Selection Procedure (1978)					
Federal Insurance Contribution's Act of 1935 (FICA) (Social Security)					

Source: Society for Human Resource Management, 1996

dures, hiring, firing, advancement, compensation, job training, and other terms, conditions, and privileges of employment.

This law is designed to remove barriers that prevent qualified individuals with disabilities from enjoying the same employment opportunities available to people without disabilities. When a qualified applicant's disability creates a barrier to employment opportunities, the ADA requires employers to consider whether a "reasonable accommodation" could remove the barrier.

An individual has a disability under ADA when he or she:

- Has a physical or mental impairment that substantially limits one or more major life activities.
- Has a record of such an impairment or is regarded as having such an impairment.

Someone who currently uses illegal drugs does *not* have a disability under the ADA. Tests for drug screening are the only pre-employment medical tests allowed under the ADA. Addiction to illegal substances *in the past* is a covered disability as long as the person is not a current illegal drug user.

A qualified individual is one who, with or without a reasonable accommodation, can perform the essential functions of a job. A reasonable accommodation is a modification that will allow a person with a disability to perform the job's essential functions. A reasonable accommodation may include but is not limited to:

- Making facilities used by employees readily accessible and usable by persons with disabilities
- Job restructuring
- Modifying work schedules
- Reassignment to a vacant position
- Acquiring or modifying equipment or devices
- Adjusting or modifying examinations, training materials, or policies
- Providing qualified sign language interpreters

A reasonable accommodation does *not* include lower production or quality standards. Also, the employer need not provide an accommodation that would impose an "undue hardship" upon it.

Penalties for non-compliance: The Equal Employment Opportunity Commission enforces ADA, and the penalties are the same as for violations of Title VII of the Civil Rights Act, with maximum amounts for intentional discrimination mandated by the Civil Rights Act of 1991.

For more information: Call the Job Accommodation Network at (800) 526-7234.

Federal Insurance Contributions Act of 1935 (1 or more employees)

Virtually all employers and employees are covered by FICA—otherwise known as Social Security. It provides employees with retirement income, as well as income security in the event of disability for surviving members of deceased workers and hospital insurance for disabled and retired persons (age 65 or over).

It is financed by employee and employer contributions made at rates set by the IRS and the Social Security Administration. Mandatory employee contributions are withheld from wages; employer contributions are deposited on a regular schedule of payments. All monies deposited with the IRS are held in a Social Security Administrative Trust Fund from which all benefit payments to eligible retirees and others are drawn. All wages up to the "taxable wage base" (set each year) are subject to withholding.

For more information: Call the IRS at (800) TAX-FORM or the Social Security Administration at (800) 772-1213.

Fair Labor Standards Act (1938)
(1 or more employees)

Most employers are covered by the Fair Labor Standards Act (FLSA), which applies to public agencies and businesses engaging in interstate commerce or providing goods and services for commerce. The FLSA provides guidelines on employment status, child labor, minimum wage, overtime pay, and record-keeping requirements. It determines which employees are exempt from the act (not covered by it) and which are *non-exempt* (covered by the act).

Penalties for non-compliance: The U.S. Department of Labor administers FLSA. Employers who willfully or repeatedly violate the act may be penalized up to $1,000 per violation. Plaintiffs can recover back pay and liquidated damages if the violation was willful. The Secretary of Labor may sue to enjoin the interstate shipment of goods of an employer who violates the act. Penalties are higher for child labor violations.

Specific provisions include the following:

- **The Minimum Wage.** Raised to $4.75 per hour, effective October 1, 1996, it will increase to $5.15 per hour as of September 1, 1997. The minimum wage is subject to review by Congress and may change from time to time. (Note: Many states have higher minimum wage provisions that supersede the FLSA.)

- **Overtime.** Employees covered by the Fair Labor Standards Act must be paid at least one-and-one-half times their regular rate for all hours worked in excess of 40 in a week (seven consecutive days). The regular rate of pay must be determined to calculate overtime pay; it includes the base rate, bonuses, commissions, piece rates, incentives, shift differentials, and training pay.

  The regular rate of pay excludes: premium pay under a union contract for Saturdays, Sundays, and holidays; pay for time not worked (vacation, sick time, holidays); contributions to pension and insurance plans; gifts or employer discretionary bonuses; distributions from profit-sharing plans that meet Wage and Hour regulations; contributions to bona fide thrift and savings plans; and longevity pay. Tests for Exemption from the overtime provisions of the FLSA follow. *(Note: The following Department of Labor guidelines are substantially out of date and inconsistent with current minimum wage provisions. Nevertheless, they remain the applicable salary test.)*

Executives are Exempt from the Act:

1. Whose primary duty is managing an enterprise or customarily recognized department or subdivision.
2. Who customarily and regularly direct the work of two or more employees.
3. Who has the authority to hire or fire other employees.
4. Who customarily and regularly exercises discretionary powers.
5. Who does not devote more than 20 percent of work time to non-exempt work.
6. Who is compensated for services on a salary basis at a rate of not less than $155 per week.

Administrative Personnel are Exempt from the Act:

1. Whose primary duty consists of either
   a) performance of office or non-manual work directly related to management policies or general business operations
   b) Administration of a school system
2. Who customarily and regularly exercises discretion and independent judgment.
3. Who regularly and directly assists a proprietor, a bona fide executive, or administrative employee.
4. Who performs work under only general supervision along specialized or technical lines.
5. Who does not devote more than 20 percent of work time to non-exempt work.
6. Who is compensated for services on a salary or fee basis of not less than $155 per week.

Professionals are Exempt from the Act:

1. Whose primary duties consist of the performance of either
   a) work requiring knowledge of an advanced type in a field of science or learning
   b) work that is original and creative in character
   c) teaching, tutoring, or instructing
2. Whose work requires consistent exercise of discretion and judgment in its performance.
3. Whose work is predominantly intellectual and varied in character.
4. Who does not devote more than 20 percent of work time to non-exempt work.
5. Who is compensated for services on a salary or fee basis at a rate of not less than $170 per week.

OUTSIDE SALESPEOPLE ARE EXEMPT FROM THE ACT:

1. Who customarily and regularly work away from the employer's premises in making sales or obtaining orders or contracts.

2. Whose work other than making outside sales or obtaining orders or contracts for service cannot exceed 20 percent of the hours worked in a work week by non-exempt employees.

COMPUTER-RELATED OCCUPATIONS ARE EXEMPT FROM THE ACT:

1. Whose primary duties consist of either

   a) The application of systems and analysis skills to determine hardware, software, or system function specifications.

   b) The design, analysis, testing, or remodification of computer systems or programs based on and related to systems design specifications.

   c) The design, testing, or modification of computer programs related to machine operating systems.

   d) A combination of the above.

2. Who is compensated on a salary or fee basis at the rate of $250 per week or any other basis as long as the hourly rate is not less than $27.63 (6.5 times the minimum wage before it was raised as of October 1, 1996) for all hours worked in the week.

FLSA requires employers to maintain the following employee records *(Note: State requirements may be more strict):*

- Name, address, date of birth if under 19
- Day and hour on which the work week begins
- Number of hours worked each day and total number of hours worked each week
- Inclusions and exclusions from regular rate of pay
- Total daily or weekly straight time earnings
- Total overtime earnings
- Total deductions from earnings
- Total wage each period
- Date of payment, amount, and period included in payment
- **Hours of Work:** All time spent in an employee's principal duties and all essential ancillary activities must be counted as work time. Principal duties include productive tasks. Work time is compensable if expended for the employer's benefit, if controlled by the employer, or if allowed by the employer. Activities that occur before or after an employee's principal duties need not be counted as work time. Some examples:

  — **Clothes changing and washing:** Not compensated unless done at the workplace at the employer's request or because of the nature of the principal duties, such as handling toxic chemicals.

— **Travel time:** Travel to and from work is not generally compensable. Travel in the course of the day, such as from one job site to another, is compensable work time. Travel out of town may be compensable, depending on when it occurs and whether the trip is overnight.

— **Meal periods and breaks:** Meal periods are not compensable if they last for more than half an hour; if the employee is relieved of all duties; and if the employee is free to leave the work station. Breaks of 15 minutes or less are considered work time and are compensable.

— **Training time:** Training is not considered work time if all these conditions are met: It is outside of regular work hours; attendance is voluntary; no productive work is performed there; and the training is not directed toward making the employee more proficient in his or her current job.

- **Child Labor:** The FLSA prohibits the employment of oppressive child labor and regulates the hours that children may permissibly work. The requirements become more strict as the age decreases. Children are divided into three groups for regulatory purposes: 16- and 17-year-olds, 14- and 15-year-olds, and all younger children. The hours that they may work and the occupations at which they may work vary from group to group.

Anyone under the age of 18 is considered a child. States frequently regulate the employment of minors; the requirements vary.

Consolidated Omnibus Budget Reconciliation Act of 1985 (20 or more employees)

COBRA mandates that employers (with more than 20 employees on 50 percent of the business days of the previous year) continue healthcare coverage for employees enrolled in their healthcare plan for a certain number of months (usually 18) after the employees have lost healthcare benefits—usually through termination of employment, a reduction in hours, or a life event (such as a divorce) that makes an employee or dependent ineligible for the benefit plan.

All people covered by a plan, including spouses and children, are eligible for COBRA. Healthcare continuation coverage premiums are paid in full by the employee, and the employer may charge the employee 2 percent of the premium for administrative costs. The act mandates the length of time employees have to elect COBRA benefits, response time for employers, and what notices must be provided.

Penalties for non-compliance: Under ERISA, for failure to provide notice, the penalty is $100 per day per violation until notice is provided to employees or beneficiaries. Under the Internal Revenue Code, excise tax of $100 is charged per day per violation for each qualified beneficiary during the non-compliance period. A qualified beneficiary who did not receive coverage can bring a lawsuit against the employer.

Equal Pay Act (1 or more employees)

This amendment to the Fair Labor Standards Act prohibits employers from discriminating between men and women by paying one gender more than the other "for equal work on jobs the performance of which requires equal skill, effort, and responsibility, and which are performed under similar working conditions."

Penalties for non-compliance: Back pay for up to two years (or three years if the violation was willful) and liquidated damages in an amount equal to back pay.

Employee Retirement Income Security Act of 1974 (1 or more employees)

ERISA sets requirements for the provision and administration of employee benefit plans such as healthcare, profit sharing, and pension plans. ERISA was passed to protect the interests of participants and their beneficiaries in employee benefit plans by establishing standards of conduct, responsibility, and obligations for plan fiduciaries.

ERISA does not force employers to create employee benefit plans. It does set standards in the areas of participation, vesting of benefits, and funding for existing and new plans. ERISA requires companies that meet certain criteria to file a form (Form 5500) annually with the Internal Revenue Service that discloses basic information about each benefit plan, such as expenses, income, assets, and liabilities. ERISA also requires employers to submit a Summary Annual Report to plan participants and beneficiaries.

Penalties for non-compliance: The IRS and the Department of Labor jointly enforce ERISA requirements. Willful violations result in criminal and civil penalties.

Age Discrimination in Employment Act (20 or more employees)

The Age Discrimination in Employment Act of 1967 (ADEA) prohibits discrimination against workers aged 40 and over in any employment or employment-related decision. One of the act's main provisions is that employers, with few exceptions, cannot force an employee to retire. Voluntary retirements are allowed; however, specific conditions must be met to avoid violation of the act.

Penalties for non-compliance: Employees may be awarded back pay, reinstatement, retroactive seniority, and attorney's fees. Liquidated damages equal to the amount of back pay may be awarded if the violation is willful.

Family and Medical Leave Act (50 or more employees)

FMLA allows employees who have met minimum service requirements (12 months employed by the company with 1,250 hours of service in the preceding 12 months) to take up to 12 weeks of unpaid leave for either:
- A serious health condition

- To care for a family member with a serious health condition
- The birth of a child
- The placement of a child for adoption or foster care

Although there is no complete list of serious health conditions, six categories must be evaluated to determine if an employee (or their family member) has such a condition. The determination is made by the employee's (or family member's) doctor on the "Certification of Health Care Provider" form. Those categories are: hospital care, absence plus treatment, pregnancy, chronic conditions requiring treatments, permanent or long-term conditions requiring supervision, and multiple treatments (non-chronic conditions).

FMLA requires employers to allow their eligible employees to take up to 12 weeks of unpaid leave for the above circumstances; provide continued health benefits during leave on the same basis the individual enjoyed while actively employed; restore employees to the same position upon return from leave (or to a position with the same pay, benefits, and terms and conditions of employment); and appropriately notify employees of their rights and responsibilities under the act.

Scheduling: Employees can take 12 weeks of leave in one block of time, in smaller blocks as needed (intermittent leave), or on a reduced work schedule (for example, part time for 24 weeks). Managers may need to rearrange the duties of other workers or hire a temporary to cover the responsibilities of a worker on FMLA leave. With few exceptions, it is important not to interfere with an employee's right to use FMLA leave and be reinstated upon its completion. The employer, however, can expect reasonable notice and may exercise some control in cases of intermittent or reduced work schedule leave.

Recording FMLA Leave: It is the employer's responsibility to designate leave as FMLA leave, whether the employee mentions FMLA or not. The employee must be promptly notified that leave will be counted as FMLA leave in order to limit the total amount of time the employee can be away from work. The employee has the responsibility to notify the employer of the need for leave and to provide enough information so the employer can determine if the leave qualifies under FMLA.

Penalties for non-compliance: Employees may recover back pay and benefits with interest, as well as reinstatement or promotion. Attorney's fees and costs may also be awarded. Where FMLA, state family and medical leave laws, and state temporary disability requirements do not apply, small organizations have several options. They can provide no paid leave or guarantee of reinstatement following absence for family or medical reasons; provide paid leave for medically necessary absences only (pregnancy must be treated like any other medical absence); or provide some combination of the above.

Immigration Reform and Control Act (1 or more employees)

IRCA prohibits the employment of individuals who are not legally authorized to work in the United States or in an employment classification that they are not authorized to fill. The act requires employers to certify (using the I-9 form) within three days of employment the identity and eligibility to work of all employees hired. I-9 forms must be retained for three years following employment or one year following termination. Acceptable proof of the eligibility to work is one of these documents:

- An original Social Security Number Card
- A birth certificate issued by a state, county, or municipality
- An unexpired INS Employment Authorization Specify form

This act also prohibits discrimination in employment-related matters on the basis of national origin or citizenship. Discriminatory actions include, but are not limited to, requesting additional documents beyond those required, refusing to accept valid documents or consider an applicant who is suspected of being an illegal alien, and harassing or retaliating against employees for exercising their rights under the law.

Penalties for non-compliance: Civil fines of $100 to $10,000 per violation for record-keeping and employment violations. Back pay/front pay and attorneys' fees for discriminatory actions. Criminal penalties may be imposed for repeated violations.

National Labor Relations Act (1 or more employees)

The National Labor Relations Act (NLRA), passed in 1935, provides that all employees have the right to form, join, and assist labor organizations and to bargain collectively with their employers. The National Labor Relations Board enforces the act, and the body of decisions and regulations from the NLRB forms an extensive set of standards for electing and decertifying unions, for negotiating bargaining agreements, and for defining activities as fair or unfair labor practices.

Penalties for non-compliance: Violations of the act are addressed by the National Labor Relations Board. A wide variety of penalties may be applied, depending on the type of violation.

Occupational Safety and Health Act (11 or more employees)

The Occupational Safety and Health Act of 1970 (OSHA) includes a "general duty clause," which requires employers to maintain a workplace free from recognized hazards that would cause injury or death to employees. Most employers must comply with OSHA safety and health standards that apply to their workplaces. OSHA requires employers to maintain a log of certain injuries and illnesses (Form 200), report certain deaths and multiple hospitalizations, and post supplementary records on an annual basis.

Employers may not discharge employees who refuse to do a job that, by their reasonable apprehension, places them at risk of injury or exposes them to a hazardous workplace condition. The standards are voluminous and may be obtained from the Government Printing Office.

Penalties for non-compliance: Civil penalties up to $1,000 for individual violations; up to $10,000 for repeated and willful violations; back pay and reinstatement for employees who suffered discrimination.

Title VII (15 or more employees)

Title VII is a provision of the Civil Rights Act of 1964 that prohibits discrimination in virtually every employment circumstance on the basis of race, color, religion, gender, pregnancy, or national origin. The purpose of Title VII's protections is to "level the playing field" by forcing employers to consider only objective, job-related criteria in making employment decisions.

The above classes of individuals are considered "protected" under Title VII because of the history of unequal treatment identified in each class. Title VII must be considered when reviewing applications or resumes (for example, by not eliminating candidates on the basis of a "foreign" last name), when interviewing candidates (by not eliminating candidates on the basis of sex or race), when testing job applicants (by treating all candidates the same and ensuring that tests are not unfairly weighted against any group of people), and when considering employees for promotions, transfers, or any other employment-related benefit or condition.

The Pregnancy Discrimination Act of 1978 amended Title VII to provide that pregnant women are treated the same as other employees who are disabled. The employer's policies for taking leave, health benefits during leaves, and reinstatement after leave apply equally to pregnant women and other employees. (See also the Family and Medical Leave Act.)

Penalties for non-compliance: For intentional discrimination, employees may seek a jury trial, with compensatory and punitive damages up to the maximum limitations established by the Civil Rights Act of 1991 according to the employer's number of employees:
- 15-100 employees, a maximum of $50,000
- 101-200 employees, a maximum of $100,000
- 201-500 employees, a maximum of $200,000
- More than 500 employees, a maximum of $300,000

Remedies of back pay, reinstatement, and retroactive seniority are available for all types of discrimination, whether intentional or disparate impact.

Sexual Harassment (15 or more employees)

Since 1980 Title VII of the Civil Rights Act has prohibited sexual harassment. Unwelcome sexual advances, requests for sexual favors, and other verbal or physical conduct of a sexual nature constitute sexual harassment when either of these applies:
- Submission to such conduct is made either explicitly or implicitly a term or condition of an individual's employment.
- Submission to or rejection of such conduct by an individual is used as the basis for employment decisions affecting an individual.

• Such conduct has the purpose or effect of unreasonably interfering with an individual's work performance or creating an intimidating, hostile, or offensive work environment.

Whenever sexual harassment is claimed or suspected in the workplace, it should be promptly and thoroughly investigated. Ignorance of its occurrence within the workplace only serves to increase the organization's possible liability. Sexual harassment has the same penalties for non-compliance as the Civil Rights Act.

Uniform Guidelines on Employee Selection Procedures (1 or more employees)

These address the use of interviewing, testing, training, and other employee selection tools and their effect on discrimination based on race, color, religion, sex, or national origin. Specifically addressed is "adverse impact," measured by the 80 percent test—if a selection practice yields less than 80 percent of a protected group as compared to the most frequently selected group, there may be evidence of discrimination.

The guidelines also require employers to maintain records, for an unspecified period of time, on their selection procedures and any adverse impact noted, as well as records of the employer's workforce broken down by race and ethnic groups.

Uniformed Services Employment and Reemployment Rights Act (1 or more employees)

The Uniformed Services Employment and Reemployment Rights Act (USERRA), which replaced the Veterans' Reemployment Rights Act, broadly prohibits employers from discriminating against individuals because of past, present, or future membership in a uniformed service (including periods of voluntary training and service). The act:

1. Prohibits discrimination in employment, job retention, and advancement.
2. Requires employers to provide retraining opportunities.
3. Requires healthcare and pension benefits to continue during leave.
4. Allows an employee to take military leave up to five years.
5. Provides additional protection for disabled veterans.
6. Requires employees to provide notice of their need for leave.
7. Requires service members to notify their employers of their intention to return to work.

Individuals reemployed after a period of military service are generally required to be allowed to return to work and receive all the benefits and seniority they would have, had they remained continuously employed.

Penalties for non-compliance: Back pay and benefits and liquidated damages (if conduct was willful).

FEDERAL REPORTING REQUIREMENTS

The following summarizes the general requirements for employers to file reports with various government agencies.

Function	Reporting Requirements	Forms
Payroll	Income Taxes, Federal Unemployment Taxes, Social Security Taxes	Forms 940, 941, 942, 943, 1099, W-2, W-4
Benefits	Employee Retirement Income Security Act (ERISA) requires employers to file summary plan descriptions and annual reports on employee benefits offered	Form 5500 Series, 990 series, PBGC forms and others
EEO	Under Title VII, employers must file the appropriate EEO form indicating employment by covered categories; federal contractors have similar requirements	EEO-1 or similar form based on type of organization covered; also VETS-100 for federal contractor
Health & Safety	Occupational Safety and Health Act (OSHA) requires employers to verbally report incidents of death or multiple-employee hospitalization. Selected employers must complete and file an annual survey of occupational injuries and illnesses	BLS-9300
Labor Relations	The Landrum-Griffin Labor Management Reporting and Disclosure Act (LMRDA) requires unions to file reports on the union's constitution, bylaws, status and finances. Union officials have additional reporting requirements	LM-1, LM-1A, LM-2, LM, 3, LM-4, LM-10, LM - 15 and others

Source: Society for Human Resource Management, 1996.

COMPLIANCE CALENDAR

Use this chart to prepare for upcoming deadlines.

Pension Plan Documents:

Summary Plan Description (SPD)	Provide to new participants no later than 90 days after the person first becomes covered
	Provide to participant within 30 days of request for copy
	File with DOL and provide to participants SPD's for a new plan within 120 days after it is adopted
Summary of Material Modifications (SMM)	Provide copy within 210 days after end of plan year in which amendments are adopted
	Provide at least every 5 years to plan participants when plan has been updated
Summary Annual Report (SAR)	Provide within 9 months after close of plan year (additional 2 months if extension is granted)
Form 5500	Annually. File by the last day of the 7th month following the end of the plan year (July 31st for calendar year plans). One-time extension of 2 ½ months may be granted upon submission of extension request form.

Federal Contractor Requirements:

VETS-100 Form	March 31st

Payroll/Taxes:

Federal Unemployment Tax Return	January 31st for previous year. Additionally, if state contribution is paid in full by that date, employer can take a credit of 5.4% of the unemployment taxes paid. If paid after that date, credit is 90% of regular credit

Equal Employment:

EEO-1 Report	September 30th for the previous year

Source: Society for Human Resource Management, 1996.

References

Allison, Loren K., *Employee Selection: A Legal Perspective,* Society for Human Resource Management, Alexandria, Virginia, 1996.

American Compensation Association, *Building Blocks in Compensation* (series), Scottsdale, Arizona.

Bacarro, Joseph P., *Getting Started in Human Resource Management,* Society for Human Resource Management, Alexandria, Virginia, 1996.

Beam, Burton T., and John J. McFadden, *Employee Benefits,* 3rd ed., Dearborn Financial Publishing, Dearborn, 1992.

Dixon, R. Brian, *The Federal Wage and Hour Laws,* Society for Human Resource Management, Alexandria, Virginia, 1994.

Johnson, Richard E., *Flexible Benefits: A How-To Guide,* International Foundation of Employee Benefit Plans, Brookfield, Wisconsin, 1992.

Mathis, Robert L., and John H. Jackson, *Human Resource Management,* 8th ed., West Publishing, St. Paul, Minnesota, 1997.

Nelson, Bob, *1001 Ways to Reward Employees,* Workman Publishing, New York, 1993.

Rock, Milton L., and Lance A. Berger, eds., *The Compensation Handbook: A State-of-the-Art Guide to Compensation Strategy and Design,* McGraw-Hill, New York, 1991.

Michael R. Losey, SPHR, is president and chief executive officer of the Society for Human Resource Management, in Alexandria, Virginia.

CANDIDATE EVALUATION FORM

Name of Applicant _____

Position _____ Department_____

Answer the following questions as they pertain to the requirements of the job:

Education
- ❑ excellent/more than required
- ❑ does not meet job requirements
- ❑ meets job requirements
- ❑ not applicable for this position

Comments _____
_____

Relevant Job Experience
- ❑ excellent/more than required
- ❑ does not meet job requirements
- ❑ meets job requirements
- ❑ not applicable for this position

Comments _____
_____

Supervisory Experience
- ❑ excellent/more than required
- ❑ does not meet job requirements
- ❑ meets job requirements
- ❑ not applicable for this position

Comments _____
_____

Technical Skills
- ❑ excellent/more than required
- ❑ does not meet job requirements
- ❑ meets job requirements
- ❑ not applicable for this position

Comments _____
_____

Interpersonal Skills
- ❑ excellent
- ❑ does not meet job requirements
- ❑ meets job requirements
- ❑ not applicable for this position

Comments _____
_____

Motivation
- ❑ excellent
- ❑ meets job requirements
- ❑ does not meet job requirements
- ❑ not applicable for this position

Comments _____
_____

Strengths_____
Comments _____

Weaknesses _____
Comments _____

Overall ranking
- ❑ excellent
- ❑ meets job requirements
- ❑ does not meet job requirements
- ❑ not applicable for this position

Comments _____
_____

Salary Expectations: _____Date Candidate Available to Begin Work _____

Interviewer _____Date of Interview _____

Source: Society for Human Resource Management, 1996.

REFERENCE CHECKING FORM

(Verify that the applicant has provided permission before conducting reference checks)

Candidate Name _____

Reference Name _____

Company Name _____

Dates of Employment: From: _____   To: _____

Position(s) Held _____

Salary History _____

Reason for Leaving _____

Explain the reason for your call and verify the above information with the supervisor (including the reason for leaving):

1. Please describe the type of work for which the candidate was responsible.

_____
_____

2. How would you describe the applicant's relationships with co-workers, subordinates (if applicable), and with superiors?

_____
_____

3. Did the candidate have a positive or negative work attitude? Please elaborate.

_____
_____

4. How would you describe the quantity and quality of output generated by the former employee?

_____
_____

5. What were his/her strengths on the job?

_____
_____

6. What were his/her weaknesses on the job?

_____
_____

7. What is your overall assessment of the candidate?

_____
_____

8. Would you recommend him/her for this position? Why or why not?

_____
_____

9. Would this individual be eligible for rehire? Why or why not?

_____
_____

Other comments?

_____
_____

Source: Society for Human Resource Management, 1996.

SAMPLE JOB OFFER LETTER

August 12, 1997
XXXXXXX
XXXXXXX
XXXXXXX

Dear XXXXX:

The (Organization Name) is very pleased to extend to you an offer of employment as (position title) in the (department name) at a biweekly rate of XXXXX (which is XXXX per year on an annualized basis) beginning Monday, September 10, 1997. Your employment is contingent upon receipt of proof of eligibility to work in the United States (see attached form) and completion of a satisfactory reference check.

Just as you retain the right to resign, without notice or cause, (organization name) has the same right with respect to termination. Your employment is for no definite term, regardless of any other oral or written statement by any (organization name) officer or representative, with the exception of an express written employment contract signed by the President. If you understand and accept these terms, please sign and return one copy of this letter to our Human Resource Department in the attached envelope.

We believe (organization name) is an outstanding organization with a capable, dedicated staff. We believe you will become a valuable, enthusiastic member of our team. Welcome to (organization name)!

Sincerely,

XXXXXXX
XXXXXXX

_____   _____
Accepting Signature   Date

_____
Source: Society for Human Resource Management, 1996.

HUMAN RESOURCES—ORIENTATION CHECKLIST

Name _____

Department _____

Hire Date: _____

Introduction to the Association
- ❏ Organization and Its Function
- ❏ Corporate Culture
- ❏ Association Mission
- ❏ Association Literature/Video

New Employee Paperwork
- ❏ W-4 and State Tax Forms
- ❏ I-9
- ❏ Health, Life & Disability Insurance Enrollment Forms
- ❏ Copy of Employee Handbook

Benefits and Compensation
- ❏ Health, Life, Disability Insurance
- ❏ Retirement Benefits
- ❏ Educational Assistance
- ❏ Employee Assistance Program
- ❏ Child Care
- ❏ Pay Procedures
- ❏ Salary Increase/Performance Review Process
- ❏ Incentive/Bonus Programs
- ❏ Paid and Unpaid Leave

Training Scheduled or Completed
- ❏ Computer System
- ❏ Log on
- ❏ E-mail
- ❏ Software
- ❏ Telephone System
- ❏ Voice Mail
- ❏ Long-Distance Calls

Other Items
- ❏ _____
- ❏ _____
- ❏ _____
- ❏ _____

Date Completed:_____ By: _____

To be filed in employee's personnel file upon completion.

Source: Society for Human Resource Management, 1996.

ORIENTATION CHECKLIST FOR SUPERVISORS

❏ **Welcome New Employee**
- ❏ Introduction to Work Group
- ❏ Tour Department and Important Places: Restrooms, Coffee Area, Kitchen, Coat Area

❏ **Introduction to the Organization (may be handled on a separate day)**
- ❏ History
- ❏ Products and Services
- ❏ Resources for Association Information
- ❏ Tour of Association

❏ **Introduction to the Department**
- ❏ Purpose
- ❏ Relation to Other Departments
- ❏ Organization of Department
- ❏ Procedures for Leave, Overtime, etc.

❏ **Introduction to the Job**
- ❏ Work Space
- ❏ Work Hours, Breaks, Meal Times and Other Rules
- ❏ Equipment
- ❏ Telephone Number
- ❏ Copier
- ❏ Mail
- ❏ Fax Machine
- ❏ Tools
- ❏ Job Description
- ❏ Duties, Responsibilities, Purpose
- ❏ Handling Confidential Information
- ❏ Performance Expectations/Goals
- ❏ Promotions/Transfers
- ❏ Safety/Emergency Procedures
- ❏ Emergency Exits
- ❏ Injury Prevention
- ❏ Reporting Injuries

❏ **Introduction to Mentor, Coach, or Buddy**

❏ **Performance Objectives/Expectations**

Source: Society for Human Resource Management, 1996.

JOB DESCRIPTION WORKSHEET

Job Title: _____ Salary Range: _____

Department: _____ Reports to: _____

Position Summary: _____

_____

_____

Essential Functions/Percentage of Time Spent on Each:

Percentage

1._____ _____

_____

2._____ _____

_____

3._____ _____

_____

4._____ _____

_____

Other Functions:

1. _____

_____

2. _____

_____

3. _____

_____

Minimum Job Requirements:

Education: _____

Experience: _____

Specific Skills: _____

Specialized Knowledge, Licenses, etc. _____

Supervisory Responsibility, if any: _____

_____

_____

_____

Source: Society for Human Resource Management, 1996.

MONTHLY ABSENTEEISM TRACKING FORM

Record staff absences/reasons as follows:

V=vacation   S=sick   B=bereavement   P=personal   M=military   J=jury   F=FMLA   H=holiday

MONTH: _____

EMPLOYEE	1	2	3	4	5	6	7	8	9	10	11	12	13	14	15	16	17	18	19	20	21	22	23	24	25	26	27	28	29	30	31

Source: Society for Human Resource Management, 1996.

CHAPTER 15

RESEARCH AND STATISTICS

MICHAEL SHERMAN, CAE

Often, a major benefit of membership in an association is the information collected by the organization for the mutual benefit of all members. An association provides a legal way for competitors to share information that helps them compete more effectively and efficiently. Unlike government statistics, which usually provide a breadth of coverage because they must meet the needs of many audiences, information gathered by an association can be as detailed and targeted as the industry or profession requires. Associations can change data-reporting systems much faster than government agencies; this is especially important in high-tech industries or emerging professional specialties in which information needs are dynamic.

Individual membership organizations offer a variety of surveys and research products, including:

* Individual salary and compensation
* Member demographics
* Individual fringe benefits
* Education and training requirements of the profession
* Trends in the profession (careers, education, and so forth)
* Cost of doing business for a professional office
* Public opinion polls of the profession

In their surveys, trade associations generally emphasize business statistics or information about markets, employees, and products. Typical areas include:

* Salary and executive compensation
* Wages
* Fringe benefits
* Business conditions (monthly, quarterly, annually)
* Business trends and forecasts
* Cost of doing business (operating ratios)
* Industry demographics
* Industry practices (related to advertising, use of technology, and so forth)
* Factory safety analyses

Regulatory hearings and legal proceedings often require supporting documentation that associations can gather by sponsoring surveys related to product safety, measurements of compliance with regulations (for example, EPA and

OSHA), background and education of professionals, economic damages suffered by an industry or profession, and measurement of participation in voluntary programs (such as standards-setting and credentialing programs).

External and Internal Research

All these types of surveys and studies, conducted to gather data that members can use to make business or professional decisions, are considered *external research*. In other words, members and others outside the association use the information and statistics for their own benefit. On the other hand, *internal research* is used by staff and leaders for making decisions about the association itself. The results of internal research are not necessarily distributed to members or other constituencies.

Internal research gathers data about members, nonmembers, and related industries or professions. Armed with this information, you can segment markets by individual characteristics such as age, gender, length of experience, and education, and business characteristics such as size, location, type of business, and years in operation. This type of information proves helpful in identifying markets and their need for specific products or services.

For instance, a common type of internal research conducted by associations is the *needs assessment* or *general membership survey*. Its primary objectives are to determine the characteristics or background of members and discover members' familiarity with and evaluation of association services and programs. Another objective might be to solicit members' opinions about existing and anticipated problems or opportunities, along with their priorities for new products and services needed to cope with changes in the industry or profession.

Internal research also plays a role in:

- **Issues management.** To effectively represent members, the association must determine the governmental, environmental, and economic issues that will have the greatest effect on the industry or profession. Asking members what is important to them will identify the legislative and regulatory priorities that, in turn, will shape the government relations program.

- **Strategic planning.** A key component of the planning process is determining members' needs and interests, as well as their feelings and perceptions about the future of the industry or profession.

- **Meetings and trade shows.** Many organizations survey attendees and exhibitors and use the evaluations to ensure these events meet the needs and expectations of all parties.

- **Member satisfaction.** A diagnostic tool known as the member satisfaction survey, patterned after the customer satisfaction models used by many corporations, monitors how members feel about the association in a general or overall sense. By determining the mood of members, such surveys can help associations pinpoint and correct problems before they negatively affect retention.

Primary and Secondary Research

Research can be either primary or secondary. In spite of its name, *secondary research* should be considered the first step in any research project because it refers to information that already exists. As a result, you spend far less time and money locating it than initiating research to gather new data.

A good source of secondary research is your association's archives. You may have research already on the shelf, plus a large amount of data about your members just sitting in the membership database. Another source is related associations that may have conducted research on your primary or associate members.

Trade publications offer a wealth of information about a profession or industry, ranging from subscriber demographics to specialized studies. Too, many U.S. government agencies gather information or fund outside research. The Bureau of Health Professions in the Department of Health and Human Services, for example, tracks education and human resource levels in many health-related professions. The U.S. Bureau of the Census provides statistics about industries and retail and wholesale markets, while the Bureau of Labor Statistics covers not only labor markets but also regional and local inflation rates.

Colleges and universities also are excellent sources of research—especially schools that concentrate on a particular industry or profession—as are commercial enterprises that develop and sell research products and services.

If you cannot locate the desired information from existing sources, the association must establish a process for gathering and analyzing data. This is known as *primary research*. Careful planning will yield the specific information you need—but it will cost more and take longer to complete than relying on secondary research. Most external research, for example, is primary and usually involves collecting data from members and nonmembers alike.

Planning Research

Whether for internal or external use, all research projects must be well-planned and focused. If they aren't, you run the risk of annoying members who may feel that surveys are an intrusion.

Several considerations underlie a good research plan. First, why is the research being done? Is it a management decision to learn about specific products or markets, or is it a reaction to a committee or board request to "see if we're doing a good job" or to "find out what the members want"? In both cases, you must be able to visualize the desired product—the statistical tables or data—as they will appear after the project is completed. During the planning stage, emphasize the "answers" you need more than the "questions" that will be designed to get them.

Your research plan should describe sampling methodology (who should be surveyed), questionnaire development, timetables, and who will approve the research program. Approval and buy-in by a committee or the board at the early stages will help you develop a realistic timetable; asking an entire committee to approve a survey instrument, for example, can add many weeks to a project. Also include a comprehensive budget: Your financial and staff resources will affect what information you are able to gather and how you accomplish the task.

Having specific objectives keeps the research focused and manageable. It is hard to resist the temptation of asking members for additional information when they already have a questionnaire in front of them. For example, some associations request salary information in the middle of an opinion survey. This mixes confidential data—personal compensation, which many members don't wish to share with association staff—with general opinions that they don't mind sharing. Asking for information that is not targeted to your overall purpose or that is highly sensitive can lower your overall response rate.

Adding questions designed to educate or inform rather than elicit information also dilutes a survey's effectiveness. Take, for example, this question: "Did you know that new IRS regulations will increase the likelihood that individuals in our profession will be audited next year?" Avoid this type of question as it is not consistent with research objectives. Communicate and educate in other, more effective ways.

When planning external research, determine whether your members have access to the data you're requesting; if they do, will they share it with the association? Some data are proprietary and highly confidential. And, in some cases, data such as price levels should not be collected or distributed due to antitrust laws and other legal considerations.

Survey Research Methods

The four basic techniques used to collect data are:

1. **Mail surveys.** One of the least expensive ways to gather objective data from a large group of people is with a written questionnaire. This format accommodates complex questions and is especially useful when asking respondents to compare options. Also, a written survey gives respondents a high level of anonymity, which is especially important when encouraging frank opinions that might be critical of the association, its products, or its policies. Nonmembers also appreciate the anonymity of mail surveys, so they are more inclined to respond.

   A primary disadvantage of mail surveys is the length of time required to complete the entire research project—usually four to six months. Another drawback is the low response rate usually achieved. When surveying members, response rates can vary from 25 percent to more than 50 percent; for nonmembers, response rates are typically half that of members.

   If the instrument appears complicated or time-consuming, you risk losing the respondent's interest. The best "hook" is a cover letter that discusses the overall objectives of the survey and why participation is important to the respondent and the association. Emphasize the member's involvement and commitment.

   For the survey itself, start with questions that are easy to read and answer, such as background demographics (respondent's location, age, gender, education, and so forth). Questions should graduate from simple to more complex, and from general to specific. Objective response mechanisms—check boxes, yes/no questions, and rating scales—further ease the burden on the respondent and simplify data entry. Conversely, open-ended questions require more of the respondent's time and are hard to code and analyze. One option is to anticipate possible answers to an open-ended question and provide respondents with a list; they'll have an idea of what type of information you're looking for and will spend less time contemplating each question.

Incentives may improve the response rate—but be careful about the impression you create. For instance, including a dollar bill might be viewed as wasteful for a nonprofit organization; a discount on association publications or an optional check box of charities to which a small amount will be donated may accomplish more.

It's preferable to spend the extra money to mail the survey first class versus bulk rate. First-class mail is delivered much faster and is less likely to get lost in the system. Plus, some organizations routinely discard, unopened, any mail that is not first class. As for mailing considerations, an ideal size for a survey instrument is four 8 1/2" x 11" pages of copy (two-sided). The instrument, a cover letter, a #9 business reply envelope, and the #10 envelope used for the mailing can be produced to weigh less than one ounce, to keep postage costs to a minimum.

2. **Telephone surveys.** When based on carefully scripted questions and handled by experienced interviewers, telephone surveys can be completed quickly and, with appropriate call-backs, achieve a high response rate. They are the fastest way to obtain quantitative data. On a per-respondent basis, however, telephone surveys cost more than written surveys.

   Such surveys require a high level of training and supervision, and sometimes interviewer "bias," which can come from interpretation, can be a problem. Associations sometimes propose using staff members to conduct a telephone survey and thereby save money. A poorly designed and inadequately executed telephone survey, however, will not produce reliable, accurate, or representative data.

3. **Individual interviews.** Person-to-person surveys accommodate the most complex of questions and allow the interviewer to ensure that the respondent understands the question and gives a reasonable response—something that is difficult to do with a written survey. The interviewer can also ask for clarification or refinement of a respondent's opinions or beliefs.

   Interviewing requires a lot of time to cover a truly representative group of respondents. It is also expensive because of the time needed to acquire the data and analyze the transcripts. Of all the survey techniques, interviews are most likely to be affected by interviewer bias and subjectivity.

4. **Focus groups.** Focus groups are best-suited for brainstorming sessions or where interaction among respondents is desired. This type of qualitative research is especially useful when asking simple questions, such as, "What do you, as a member, want from our association?" Most people tend to limit their

thinking to what is already available, but they typically go beyond that barrier when discussing ideas with peers.

Focus groups are moderately expensive and require more logistical support than other survey techniques. To properly conduct a focus group you should have a trained moderator and a research plan known as a moderator's guide. Also, facilities are required that are centrally located and conducive to discussion. Depending on the type of respondents desired, you might need some assistance in recruiting a representative group of people.

No matter how representative a focus group is, a sample of just eight to ten people—or even samples from six different groups—is far too small to project onto a large or even moderate-sized group. A focus group can provide invaluable insights, but the results must be quantified by some other research technique in order to draw reliable inferences about the entire membership.

COMPARISON OF RESEARCH TECHNIQUES

Survey Techniques

	Mail	Telephone	Individual Interviews	Focus Groups
Relative Cost	Low	Moderate	High	Moderate
Length of Time	Long	Short	Long	Short
Response Rate	Low	High	Moderate	High
Respondent Confidentiality	High	Low	None	None
Complexity of Questions	Moderate	Low	High	High
Potential for Interviewer Bias	Low	Moderate	High	Moderate

The four traditional methods of data collection remain the workhorses of survey research. Advances in communications technology, however, are providing researchers with new tools for data collection, such as the following:

- **Fax surveys.** If a written survey is faxed to a carefully designed sample, it has the same characteristics as a mail survey—plus a few advantages. Distribution of the questionnaire is faster, and a fax may draw more notice from the respondent. Surveys that are either mailed or faxed can both be faxed back by the respondent.

Be wary of the "fax back" survey that is dropped into the middle of a publication. Although inexpensive, this approach does not have a designed sample and it presumes—erroneously—that everyone reads the magazine or all parts of it. Therefore, the results can easily be biased.

- **E-mail (Internet) polling.** As more members move online, associations will have excellent opportunities to distribute questionnaires by e-mail. Sampling techniques, of course, should be used to ensure valid and reliable responses. This method will hasten turnaround time and, due to its novelty, should pump up response rates. However, once responding to e-mail takes as much time as hard copy does right now, there is no way to predict the effect on response rates.

- **Web-site surveys.** Although this is a convenient way to distribute a questionnaire, you must deal with a self-selected and perhaps non-representative sample. If you want to survey regular users of your association's home page, this is an appropriate forum. If you want to know about all members, however, a web survey is not appropriate unless all members have access to the site.

- **Interactive surveys.** Computer-assisted surveys (distributed on diskette or via the Internet) tailor questions to the initial responses. For example, a regular member might see certain questions while an associate member might see others. As a further refinement, a large company might be asked about different issues than a smaller one.

- **Instant-response units.** Freestanding boxes or kiosks represent another means of computer-assisted data collection. They can be used at a meeting or trade show to gather on-the-spot evaluations and information. The major drawback of such devices is that respondents are self-selected and might not necessarily be representative of all meeting attendees.

Some of the new approaches offer convenience or cost savings to the association, some purportedly lower the burden on respondents, and almost all promise expediency. The overriding question to answer is whether the data collection method will help your association reach its research objectives within a given budget.

Survey Sampling

After you have established a research plan, you must address how many people to survey. In many associations, the first inclination is to survey all of the members. Depending on the size of the organization, however, doing so could prove very expensive and time consuming.

It's usually appropriate and more efficient to survey a specially selected subgroup of members. There is a scientific basis for determining how large a sample is required to provide a statistically significant representation of the entire group. If you have a large membership or list of names, a probability sample can be constructed that will produce statistically reliable estimates of the attitudes and opinions of the entire association. For example, 400 randomly selected responses from an association with 10,000 members will produce statistics that are within 5 percentage points of the statistics for the entire group, 95 percent of the time. This is a standard of reliability that is customarily expected of association surveys.

Using a sample enables you to save on printing and postage (for a written survey) and on data entry and tabulation fees. A smaller sample is easier to manage and follow up, especially if a telephone survey is being conducted. By using sampling procedures, you can determine the precision of the statistical estimates derived from the sample—the level of confidence and level of sampling error.

In general, the total number of questionnaires received is less important than the percentage of people who responded. Consider a trade association with 2,000 corporate members. If you mailed a questionnaire to all members and 500 of them returned it, you would have a reasonably large database on which to conduct statistical analysis. However, 500 out of 2,000 is only a 25 percent response rate; you have *not* heard from 75 percent of your members, after giving everyone a chance to respond.

For comparison, suppose you sent a questionnaire to every other member, a sample of 1,000. Furthermore, you send a follow-up mailing of the questionnaire to the same group—your total out-of-pocket costs are the same as the first example, a mailing of 2,000. If you again receive 500 responses, your response rate is 50 percent (500 out of 1,000 names) and your statistics are based on one-half rather than one-fourth of all members. There is a greater likelihood that the second group of respondents (based on a 50-percent return) is more representative than the first scenario in which the response rate was only 25 percent.

The science of sampling is well-established, and much of the information we are exposed to every day is based on sampling. Political polls, for example, are based on relatively small samples of voters (less than 2,000) and usually provide accurate estimates of how the larger group will vote. Government and businesses frequently use sampling techniques to provide information for decision making while minimizing the cost of research and reducing the time it takes to collect data.

Sampling Terminology

The total group you would like to gather information about is referred to as the *population*. This could be all of your members or, more likely, everyone in your profession or industry—both members and nonmembers. The *sampling frame* is the actual source of names used to select the sample. While the *universe* (another term for population) might be all people in your profession, your only source of nonmembers might be the subscription list of a professional journal. This list, therefore, becomes the sampling frame.

A *probability sample* is a group of people selected or drawn so that everyone in the population has a known probability of being included. Combining the probability of being selected with known characteristics of the population—such as age, location, and gender—allows you to develop a sample that, in fact, represents the population. The reliability of information obtained from a probability sample can be computed with the help of statistical theory.

A sample in which each person in the population has an equal chance of being selected is known as a *simple random sample*. Statistical measures exist to indicate how reliable the data from a random sample will be. Many associations have sophisticated membership databases that can select a random sample of any given size. (Remember to print or make additional copies of the list for reference because you usually cannot reproduce a random sample at a later date.)

A practical approach to obtaining a probability sample is the *systematic* or *nth name* sample. This is useful if you don't have the capability of drawing a random sample or if the sampling frame is only available as hard copy, such as membership directories or mailing labels. To obtain a systematic sample, first determine the size sample you need. (Remember, if you want opinions from 400 respondents but you expect a 50 percent response rate, you need to include 800 people in your sample. When half of the 800 respond, you will have sufficient data for your analysis.)

The proportion of the sample size to the sample frame is expressed as a fraction, such as "one-fourth" or "one twenty-fifth" or "one nth." Finally, sample units are chosen by determining a random statistical starting point and then choosing every "nth" name from the sampling frame. For example, if you need 800 names from a mailing list of 3,200, you would determine a random starting point between 1 and 2,400 (using a random number table, computer programs, or even a calculator), and select every fourth name thereafter (800 divided by 3,200 = one fourth). If you want the sample to be representative geographically, use a mailing list in zip code order.

Associations often want to make sure their sample is representative of various subgroups or "strata." *Stratified sampling* requires you to divide the population into smaller groups of people with similar characteristics—strata—and draw a separate sample from each group.

For example, if 20 percent of your membership is female, a random sample of the entire membership might not generate enough questionnaires from females to do any reasonable analysis. You can obtain a larger number of females with a stratified random sample. First, treat male members as one strata or group, and select a random sample of all males; next, select a separate random sample of females. The size of each sample can be adjusted or weighted so that you end up with a total group of respondents that is representative of the entire sampling universe.

A *non-probability sample* simply means everyone in the group does not have an equal chance of being selected. A frequently used non-probability sample is the *convenience sample*, which includes people who can be contacted easily—such as those attending a convention or members of a committee. Frequently, however, those groups are not representative of the entire association membership.

An inexpensive means of sampling, especially for personal interviews or telephone calls, is *quota sampling*. With this technique, the interviewer selects people until a predetermined quota is reached. For example, a personal interview (intercept) at a trade show might require the interviewer to talk to the first 20 men and the first 35 women he or she encounters, then stop after each quota is reached. Here again, you have no way of ensuring that these interviewees are representative of the larger universe of trade show attendees.

Accuracy and Precision of Results

There is no guarantee that the sample used for a survey is actually representative of the entire population. You can, however, measure the *sampling error* associated with the results to determine the precision of the survey's findings. Precision is measured by two values: the confidence level and the level of error.

The *confidence level* is a measure of how representative the sample is of the total population. There is a large number of random samples that can be drawn, but since you will only conduct the survey once, you use the first random sample drawn. The question then arises whether the first sample drawn is, in fact, representative of the entire population. You can design a sample—determine how large it should be relative to the population—so that if you drew 100 different random samples, 95 of them would be very representative of the population. The other five samples might be a little biased. This is an example of a 95 percent confidence level.

The other ingredient in the precision of survey results, the *level of error*, refers to the variation in responses between the sample and the entire population. Expressed as a plus-or-minus figure (+/- 5 percent is typical for association membership surveys), it gives you the projected range of responses had you surveyed the entire population. With a +/- 5 percent level of error, for example, if 75 percent of respondents answered "Yes" to a certain question, you could assume that between 70 and 80 percent of the entire population would answer the same way.

Usually, you first decide the acceptable level of error for your survey. Then, by referring to the statistical table, you can determine how large a sample you need (number of questionnaires returned, not mailed out) for any given population. The table contains sample sizes required for finite populations, given a 95 percent confidence level, for a given maximum sampling error. It gives the highest sampling error and, consequently, the most conservative estimate of the sample size needed to obtain the desired sampling error.

To use the table, look up the size of the population you want to survey—say, 4,800 members—and the sampling error you are willing to accept (5 percent). The value at the intersection in the table (rounding off the size of the population to 5,000) is 357 individuals. The survey results estimated in a sample of 357 will be within 5 percentage points of the actual value of the entire membership of 4,800. Remember, to get 357 responses, you will have to sample a larger group since it's unlikely you will achieve a 100 percent response rate. For most associations, a random sample of 1,000 members would produce a response of at least 350, a 35 percent response rate.

Special Considerations

Association surveys are voluntary—you can't force members to participate. You can, however, restrict the results of a survey to participants, thereby providing a tangible incentive for members to submit data.

With a large membership, the same sampling considerations apply to external research surveys as to internal ones. This is appropriate when you are estimat-

SAMPLE SIZES REQUIRED FOR FINITE POPULATIONS

95% Confidence Level
Percent in population assumed to be 50%*

Size of Population	± 3%	± 4%	± 5%
1,000	**	375	278
2,000	696	462	322
3,000	787	500	341
4,000	842	522	350
5,000	879	536	357
10,000	964	566	370
20,000	1,013	583	377
50,000	1,045	593	381
100,000	1,056	597	383
>500,000	1,065	600	384

* Use this table when unable or unwilling to estimate a maximum or minimum percentage value to be expected. Using 50 percent, while conservative, will result in a larger sample size than if an estimate other than 50 percent is used.

** In these cases, more than 50 percent of the population is required in the sample.

Source: Adapted from tables in H.P. Hill, J.L. Roth, and H. Akin, *Sampling in Auditing,* The Ronald Press, New York, 1962.

ing values that are typical of a whole class of individuals or organizations, such as salaries, operating ratios, and so forth. If the objective of the survey is to project a total value for a group, such as industry shipments or the aggregate revenue of a group of professionals, other sampling approaches are appropriate.

The U.S. Bureau of the Census uses special sampling methodologies, such as trying to achieve very high participation rates for the largest companies but accepting lower participation rates for smaller companies. This is the well-known 80-20 rule or Pareto's Law: You obtain about 80 percent of the total units from about 20 percent of the companies (the largest ones). Also, if you must make estimates for some missing companies, those for smaller companies will have a much smaller effect on the overall value you wish to quantify.

Some trade association research programs aim to estimate the total size of the industry. Since participation is voluntary and nonmembers might be excluded, there are always some companies that do not submit shipments or sales data. The data from the association's sample of participants can be extrapolated or projected up to an industry total by two methods.

The first method uses association data to estimate periodic changes, such as month to month, which are benchmarked to independent estimates of the industry total. This is known as the *link-relative method*—literally linking one period of time with a previous period. You can obtain the independent estimate from government reports, such as the Annual Survey of Manufacturers published by the Bureau of the Census. Some associations even hire consultants to conduct their own annual census of all known companies, using the resulting information to benchmark periodic surveys.

The second technique used to generate an industry estimate is known as *load factoring*. This procedure requires you to identify all companies in the industry that do not participate in the association survey. Members who participate in the association's program are then asked to estimate the size of each non-participating company. These independent estimates are analyzed, and a composite estimate of each non-participant is factored into the association's periodic survey to produce an estimate for the entire industry.

Survey Logistics

Some associations with comprehensive statistical research programs rely on full-time specialists or a department to handle all aspects of a project internally. Staff responsibilities will vary from association to association, but may include committee liaison, data collection, statistical tabulations, and report preparation and distribution.

The scope of in-house research activities can be broad, ranging from surveys of members and nonmembers to surveys of constituents such as the general public, industry customers, or industry suppliers. Some associations allow their research departments to sell reports and conduct custom research for outside organizations.

Another alternative is to outsource the entire research function to an outside vendor or consultant. Vendors can serve as an extension of the association's staff, not only collecting and tabulating data but also communicating directly with members and even serving on the research committee. It's also possible to combine the two approaches, so that the association's staff collaborates with a vendor —each performs some elements of the research function.

Associations with formal research programs usually rely on a committee for guidance and policy setting, with implementation handled by staff or consultants. The statistics or research committee is typically charged with defining the products, services, job descriptions, and so forth, that are measured by the research program. It also monitors the accuracy and reliability of the data being generated. Committees can be standing or ad hoc and may have budget authority. However configured, the statistics or research committee is the members' voice in gathering useful and valuable information.

Legal Issues

Although associations can gather and disseminate data, even from and to competitors, they must not run afoul of antitrust laws in the process. The association may not use its research to fix prices, allocate markets, or reduce competition in general.

Based on legal opinions and interpretations of federal guidelines issued by the Federal Trade Commission and the U.S. Department of Justice, observe the following guidelines when conducting association research:

1. Participation in the program must be voluntary.
2. Clarify that the program's intent is to collect and furnish useful business information and not to affect any agreement or understanding between competitors with respect to business activities.
3. Data received should involve historical or past transactions.
4. Preserve the confidentiality of an individual participant's data.
5. Present information in a composite or summarized form.
6. Do not show data supplied by one participant to any other participant.
7. Ensure that published reports do not contain comments that may be interpreted as advising or recommending to participants that they take any sort of joint or concerted actions.
8. Make results of association statistical programs available to nonmembers, including customers and suppliers of members, if they have a legitimate business need for such information.
9. You may charge nonmembers a higher price for the results than members— but the price charged may not be so high as to compel membership.
10. The results of a survey may be restricted to participants, but neither nonparticipating members nor nonmembers may have access to the results.

References

American Society of Association Executives, *Attracting, Organizing & Keeping Members,* Washington, D.C., 1989.

American Society of Association Executives, *Principles of Association Management,* 3rd ed., Washington, D.C., 1996.

Carey, Stephen, ed., *Marketing the Nonprofit Association,* The Greater Washington Society of Association Executives Foundation, Washington, D.C., 1991.

Foundation of the American Society of Association Executives, *How to Conduct Association Surveys,* Washington, D.C., 1976.

Jacobs, Jerald A., *Association Law Handbook,* 3rd ed., American Society of Association Executives, Washington, D.C., 1996.

Kotler, Philip, *Strategic Marketing for Nonprofit Organizations,* 5th ed., Prentice-Hall, Englewood Cliffs, New Jersey, 1996.

Webster, George D., *The Law of Associations,* Mathew Bender, New York, 1975.

Michael Sherman, CAE, is president of Association Research, Inc., an independent research firm that specializes in conducting surveys for associations. Before founding ARI in 1984, Sherman served on the staff of the National Association of Furniture Movers for 10 years, the last 3 as executive vice-president.

CHAPTER 16

MANAGING INFORMATION TECHNOLOGY

MAYNARD H. BENJAMIN, CAE

A truism regarding association management states that an association is about the management and sale of information. Everything association executives do concerns gathering, processing, and presenting information to members. For example, the meetings and education function concerns the exchange of information as much as the research function does. Yet how to effectively use technology to manage information frequently eludes associations. The challenge is to match the technology employed with the information to be managed.

Understanding the Technology

Many association executives operate within limited frames of reference about what information technology can and cannot do. They may shy away from computers and computer consultants as being too technical. Yet advances in personal computers and software, increased media coverage of technological issues and developments, and educational opportunities available through professional organizations enable association executives to fully understand technology and make intelligent purchasing decisions.

Following several steps will help you better understand the technology you could potentially use to manage association-related information:

- **Scan the literature.** What do information technology experts in the field of association management read regularly? Ask them and you may hear titles such as *Byte Magazine, Computer Shopper, New Media, Windows Magazine,* and *Wired* (an online publication).

There may be much in these magazines that you don't understand. Still, scan each issue, look for key words, and tear out or download (copy a file onto your system) articles you'd like to read more completely. In addition, look through the new products and press releases sections for the latest in hardware, software, or services. A number of the publications listed above can be found on commercial services such as America Online or CompuServe, which make it easy to conduct a key-word search and download articles for later reading.

- **Build a glossary.** Understanding the terminology is critical to understanding the technology. Yet you may not understand many of the terms you encounter when scanning technology publications. Many articles will define the terminology used at the beginning of the article; use the definitions to build a glossary that you keep on your word processor for easy reference. Other association executives may be willing to share their glossaries with you, too.

- **Take notes.** If you clip articles for future reference, consider cross-referencing them through notes on your word processor. Then, if you're looking for something in your files on a particular subject, you can begin with the computerized notes, which are cross-referenced to the physical files. Many technology magazines publish cross-references or indexes that will help you if you do not want to go through the laborious note-taking process.

- **Keep members updated.** Let your members know you are thinking about how to employ technology to improve association services or products and tell them about technologies that may affect their profession or business. This technology coverage can range from a few paragraphs or a column in your monthly magazine to a full-blown study on a technology subject. You might decide to delegate these four steps to someone on your staff, who will provide you with a monthly summary. However you accomplish this task, be sure to set up a scanning function within your association so that you're always looking for new ideas, tools, and concepts related to information management.

Implementing the Process

The effect of technology management on association management and governance is just beginning to be understood. A few associations link technology expenditures to the capital budgeting process; fewer still link technology acquisition with strategic objectives. Change in the composition of membership for most associations is so continuous that technology is difficult to plan for, much less keep up with. Yet that is exactly the discipline required of technology management.

The technology management process involves these four steps:

1. **Understanding.** Associations gather, repackage, and sell information. That is the "heart and soul" of what associations do for their members. The only way to understand how an association functions and meets the service and product requirements placed against it is to understand the information flow within the association.

A needs analysis is a normal part of the process of documenting information requirements of association staff. An auditor, consultant, or other independent source is best-suited to conduct this analysis; staff members tend not to look at the association as a whole and thus provide an incomplete analysis.

Every time the association considers acquiring a new technology, a needs or requirements study should be made; requirements statements can be as simple as several paragraphs or as complex as a multi-chapter document. The study has three distinct sets of information:

- *Reports that are received.* For each report a staff member receives, list the information contained in the report and describe where that information is created. Also include the frequency of the report and how the staff member uses the information. Ask the person receiving it to comment on how the information could be improved in content and form.

ABC Association Reports Received Survey

Name	Information	How Created	Frequency	Staff
Membership Report	— Member name — Member address — Member phone — Dues paid date — Member type code — Member since	Member management Module	Monthly	Tim S.
Registrar's List	— Registrant name — Registrant address — Registrant company — Registration date — Registration events — Fees due — Fees paid	Meeting management module	Weekly (During meetings)	Susan M.

- *Reports that are generated.* For each report a staff member generates, list the information contained in the report and describe where that information is created. Include the frequency of the report and the people who use the information it contains. Ask users for suggestions on improving each report's content and form.

XYZ Association Reports Generated Report

Report	Information Contained	Where Created	Frequency	Use
Master List	— Member name — Member title — Member company — Member address — Member phone — Member type — Reporting codes	Member master File	Monthly	All Staff
		Reporting master File		Tom S.

- *Information requirements neither generated or received.* For each staff member, list each information requirement that currently is not being met via a report. These are the "blue sky" requirements staff members may have for information to support a new program or activity. Have the staff member define the requirement and explain why a report should be generated, how often it is needed, and in what form.

For example, a staff member might say, "I need to know rooms occupied by type of member by hotel for the annual meeting." Where is this information? How can it be acquired? How often is it needed? In what form? What is the cost of acquisition? Why is it needed? What part of the staff member's job will it enhance if it is available?

2. **Analyzing.** Next, look at your association's technology system from three perspectives:

- What are the problems of the current information system? Each component of an information system—whether photocopier, telephone, computer network, fax machine, or stand-alone computer system—has performance objectives defined by either the manufacturer or association staff. Those who use the components also have performance objectives. Are these objectives being met? Why or why not?

Wherever the technology fails to meet performance objectives, it probably also fails to meet information needs. The failed performance objectives point to technology solutions that may bring the system into compliance with performance objectives.

- Is the current technology system meeting the goals and objectives the association has for it? Remember, goals and objectives also can be financial. Is it costing too much (that is, beyond the expectations of the organization when the technology was acquired) to operate a particular piece of equipment or software? Does the technology hinder or support the accomplishment of the association's mission?

Document not only where the technology doesn't support the association's goals and objectives but also where it does. Also record where you feel change to the current system is necessary to meet the goals and objectives. You don't need to know the exact form of the technology needed, just the type. For example, if the office fax machine isn't keeping up with the number of outgoing faxes, your proposed solution might be a fax server. The type, capabilities, costs, and other details can be determined later—or as an addendum to the evaluation phase.

- What is the association's information blueprint? Thanks to the requirements analysis you accomplished earlier, you have a "map" of how and where information flows within the association. Overlay that map on the information system you currently have in place. By comparing information requirements to the current system's components, in view of the support/equipment issues, you can develop a fairly extensive picture of how well (or whether) needs are being met.

Even if needs are being met, do they fulfill the association's long-term objectives? If not, do processes and equipment need to change? Do people need different skills? Or is new equipment needed to better support current and future needs?

3. **Linking.** At this point, you bring together the need for information and the process, software, or hardware necessary to provide that information. This step links the analysis that was conducted in Step 2 with the technology that would be needed to satisfy the needs and objectives you've identified.

Linking needs with technology requires you to go through an organized thought process that justifies why the technology selected will satisfy the need, meet the objective or goal, and be affordable. In essence, every piece of technology—be it hardware or software—has a mission and objective it must perform. These are its performance objectives, the staff needs it will meet, and the benefits the association will receive from using the proposed technology.

You can now consolidate the changes that need to be made to your system, calculate the approximate costs of these changes, and draft a recommendation and action plan. More specifically, the linking step requires you to document the following:

- Current association environment

- Association objectives
- Major processes reviewed
- Major problems identified
- Current technology supporting processes reviewed
- Information requirements met or not met by the processes and technology reviewed
- Findings and conclusions
- Recommendations

For this step, it's often helpful to call in a technology professional to provide equipment details such as the make, model, performance expectations, costs, and other technical information.

4. **Implementation and evaluation.** This involves successfully installing the technology—and ensuring that requirements are met *during* the installation. The new technology should make a difference immediately—or it may be the wrong choice. Before installation is complete, the association should make a final check to ensure that it has either satisfied all the objectives it had in acquiring the technology or understand which objectives aren't being met. For instance, if you are repairing or upgrading a system, ensure that the "new part" is the right part for the system.

Frequently, implementation and evaluation are accomplished by benchmarking the old technology against the newly acquired technology. You already have most of the information needed for the benchmark. For the existing technology you will need: a description of the reason for the change, a description of the technology, the operating costs of the technology, a documentation of one or two selected processes supported by the existing technology you wish to benchmark, and a baseline performance in both qualitative and quantitative terms. For example, if the technology was a copier, how many copies per hour, at what cost, at what print quality?

For the new technology, you need: a brief description, the justification for the technology, the purchase and lifetime costs of the technology, the processes benchmarked with the new technology, the difference between the existing and new technology, and the savings to be achieved or new services to be offered.

It's best to wait until a new technology has been appropriately seasoned in the association's environment before beginning the benchmarks. In other words, wait until you've gotten the kinks worked out of the new technology.

Information management technology is a tremendous tool that associations can use to better serve members and to more effectively use organizational resources. Associations should take the lead in using information management technology rather than reacting to the technology already in place in members' organizations or offices.

References

Anderson, R.H., T.K. Bikson, S.A. Law, and B.M. Mitchell, *Universal Access to E-Mail: Feasibility and Societal Implications,* RAND Corporation, Santa Monica, California, 1995.

Carlsen, Robert D., and J. A. Lewis, *The Systems Analysis Workbook,* Prentice-Hall, Inc., Englewood Cliffs, New Jersey, 1979.

Cusumano, Michael A., and R. W. Selby, *Microsoft Secrets,* The Free Press, New York, 1995.

Gates, Bill, *The Road Ahead,* Penguin Books, New York, 1995.

IBM Corporation, *Business Systems Planning,* White Plains, New York, 1978.

Negroponte, Nicholas, *Being Digital,* Alfred A. Knopf, Inc., New York, 1995.

Maynard H. Benjamin, CAE, is president of the Envelope Manufacturers Association, Alexandria, Virginia, and a technology columnist for ASAE's Association Management *magazine.*

CHAPTER 17

FACILITIES MANAGEMENT

WAYNE E. LEROY, CAE

How an association designs, furnishes, and equips its offices can greatly affect staff productivity and satisfaction. In addition, the association's physical environment contributes to the perception members have of the overall organization.

Association office space is usually obtained in one of three ways:

- *Renting* is primarily for temporary or short-term arrangements, approximately two years or less. Associations often rent space during a transitional phase—such as when preparing to relocate or searching for different space requirements—or when they have a small staff and little capital to invest in property. In general, renting is the most expensive of the three options.

- *Leasing* is the method used by most associations. Lease arrangements usually are negotiated for three, five, or even ten years. Unlike renting, leasing gives the association greater control of occupancy expenses and the ability to negotiate leaseholder improvements to the space.

- *Owning* space or an entire building is the choice of associations that want permanency in a particular area or location. Like all forms of space occupancy, ownership has its pros and cons. Some of the positive aspects include the ability to budget for long-term expenditures, tax advantages (primarily in the area of depreciation), and more flexibility and control of space. On the downside are the responsibilities of maintaining and operating the facility.

No matter how space is obtained, consult experts in the fields of real estate, contracts, and property management before making your decision.

Occupancy Satisfaction

The people who use and visit the office space ultimately determine its efficiency, effectiveness, and appropriateness. Their satisfaction will depend upon how well the space and facilities perform in these four categories:

1. **Heating, Ventilating, and Air Conditioning (HVAC) Systems.** Occupants expect heat when the outside temperature is cold, and cool air indoors when the outside temperature is hot. A well-designed system will perform these functions satisfactorily, while at the same time providing an appropriate mix of fresh outside air in exchange for exhausting inside air.

2. **Lighting.** Adequate, non-glare lighting is important for all employees, particularly those who spend much of their time in front of computer screens. Most office environments now use energy-efficient fluorescent lights with electronic ballasts. When designing appropriate lighting configurations, it is recommended that a minimum of 75 foot candles be provided in all work areas.

3. **Facilities Services.** These are the "little things" that go far in determining satisfaction or dissatisfaction with the space. They include custodial services (people expect their trash baskets to be emptied along with an occasional dusting of the furniture and vacuuming of the carpet) and parking (in reasonable proximity to the office and elevators). Other amenities that might be important to staff are eating areas for breaks and lunch and the availability of coffee, soft drinks, or snack items.

   Many cities and municipalities mandate recycling for certain items, such as office/white paper, glass, plastic, aluminum cans, newsprint, and cardboard. Recycling efforts are usually accomplished with the cooperation of the facility's custodial or housekeeping services; this may include providing specially designated containers in the office environment to encourage recycling initiatives.

4. **Aesthetics.** This is the intangible "feel" an office evokes—possibly through plants or greenery in the lobby, through framed photographs depicting the trade or profession the association represents, or through a display of the association's award-winning magazines and books. Whatever the furnishings chosen, they should reflect that people enjoy working in the environment and prompt visiting members to say, "I belong to a first-class association."

Health and Safety

Many factors control the health, safety, and well-being of association staff and visitors. Three areas require special attention:

- **Environmental health and safety**—The Environmental Protection Agency (EPA) and the U.S. Department of Labor, which oversees the Occupational Health and Safety Act (OSHA), can provide volumes of materials on safeguarding the well-being of office occupants. Because this area is the responsibility of managers and supervisors, it should appear in their job descriptions. Supervisors and managers are then more likely to treat the subject seriously by periodically holding safety discussions. During a staff meeting, for example, employees might talk about burn prevention in the kitchen or the use of handrails when going up and down stairs.

  Although common sense, along with wise and prudent judgment, will go a long way toward preventing office accidents, it's still helpful to provide health and safety training to employees. Appropriate training may be as simple as reviewing instructions for properly lifting or moving heavy items, such as boxes of materials being prepared for shipment to the annual meeting.

- **Building security**—The goal is to protect the occupants of an office as well as

A Checklist for Productivity

Office space should be designed to allow optimum use and efficiency. Here are some general guidelines for office layout and furniture arrangement:

1. Plan each room with a purpose. Decide what the room will be used for and by whom.

2. Keep furniture within the scale of the room.

3. Provide space for traffic by keeping doorways and major traffic lanes unobstructed. To redirect traffic, turn a sofa, a desk, or chairs toward the room and at right angles to the door, leaving a passageway.

4. Arrange furnishings to give the room a sense of equilibrium. For instance, balance high and low, angular and rounded furniture. If all furniture is low, create a feeling of height by incorporating shelves, mirrors, or pictures in a grouping.

5. Consider architectural and mechanical features. Nothing should interfere with the opening of windows or doors or with the operation of heating or air conditioning devices.

6. Don't overcrowd a room. It is always better to underfurnish than overfurnish.

7. In general, place large pieces of furniture parallel to the walls.

8. Avoid pushing large pieces tightly into a corner or close against floor-to-ceiling windows where a passageway should be allowed.

9. In rooms with slanted ceilings, arrange the heaviest furniture grouping along the highest wall.

10. For each employee—including his or her desk, chair space, and share of the aisle—calculate 50 to 75 square feet of working space.

11. A minimum of 9 feet by 12 feet is a standard size for small private offices.

12. Standard widths for main circulating aisles vary from 5 feet to 8 feet. Less important aisles vary from 3 feet to 5 feet.

13. Allow for at least two phone jacks in every office, to accommodate a telephone and a computer modem. Also consider the addition of high-speed electronic connections such as ISDN, ADSL, and T-1 lines.

its contents. For optimum security, only staff or other designated personnel typically have entry access to office space. Visitors' access may be controlled by staff at a receptionist area or some other type of security system (sign-in sheet, visitors' badges, employee escort, and so forth).

Other security concerns include adequate lighting in outside areas such as parking areas and courtyards.

• **Emergency preparedness and fire protection**—The local jurisdiction in which the office is located will determine emergency requirements, which vary from one area to the next. Four common building requirements are:

1. Fire alarms and smoke detectors.

ADA Compliance

The Americans with Disabilities Act (ADA) became effective in the early 1990s. The original ADA regulations were divided into two categories:

1. Existing facilities. The basic provisions in the regulations indicated that existing buildings had to be made accessible to people with disabilities as long as making the required modifications did not constitute an undue financial burden on the facility owner.

2. New construction. New facilities were required to meet more extensive specifications for ensuring accessibility, which are contained in a document known as the ADA Accessibility Guidelines (ADAAG).

Two federal agencies administer the provisions of the ADA. The Department of Justice (Civil Rights Division) is responsible for the public accommodations regulations, while the Architectural and Transportation Barriers Board (Access Board) has responsibility for reviewing accessibility guidelines for both existing and new facilities.

ADA has multiple areas of compliance. The ones having the greatest effect on association facilities can be grouped into these four areas:

- **Detectable warnings.** This category includes warnings for such areas as curb ramps, hazardous vehicular areas, reflecting pools, platform edges, and so forth.

- **Employee work areas.** Current regulations for employee-only work areas require that a person be able to "approach, enter, and exit" the area.

- **Toilet rooms.** Toilet rooms must be accessible with appropriate door widths, wall clearance, handrails, and fixture heights.

- **Elevators.** Elevators should be equipped with audible systems, reachable control pads, touch identification, and an emergency telephone.

Regulations are constantly being reviewed and updated. For the most up-to-date information regarding the facilities component of the ADA, contact the Architectural and Transportation Barriers Compliance Board, 1111 18th St., NW, Suite 501, Washington, DC 20036-3894; (202) 653-7834.

---

2. Sprinkler systems. All facilities require some type of fire-suppressant device—if not a full-fledged sprinkler system, then at least numerous fire extinguishers. Note that fire extinguishers require periodic inspection to ensure they will function when needed.

3. Emergency lighting. If the building's electrical systems are designed to automatically shut off when an emergency system is activated, emergency lighting is necessary to guide office occupants to the nearest exits.

4. An emergency plan. In addition to discussing emergency operations for office evacuations at staff meetings, an association should develop an emergency plan and distribute it to all staff members.

In an Emergency

To ensure the health and safety of staff, your association should have an emergency plan. Although the details will vary depending on the type of facility, a plan should address these four types of emergencies:

- Natural element—any unusual natural occurrence that has the potential to disrupt normal activities. Examples include earthquakes, floods, high winds, snow, and tornadoes.

- Civil disorder—actions by a person or people that have the potential to cause bodily harm. Examples are demonstrations, domestic disturbances, looting/robbery, and suicide.

- Structural—any emergency related to the building or facility, such as a bomb threat, fire, explosion, or other structural failure.

- Utility—problems associated with operation and functioning of the building. Examples include loss of electricity, loss of water, natural gas or steam leaks, and general loss of communications equipment (telephones and computers).

Emergency plans should be included as part of new staff orientation as well as periodically reinforced during staff meetings. In addition, post the telephone numbers of emergency agencies and emphasize the calling of 911 for emergency situations.

Facilities Resources

If you are looking for office space, furnishings, layout ideas, and so forth, here are just a few of the associations that can provide assistance.

American Institute of Architects, 1735 New York Ave., NW, Washington, DC 20006-5292; (202) 626-7300

American Society of Heating, Refrigerating, and Air Conditioning Engineers, 1791 Tullie Circle, NE, Atlanta, GA 30329-2305; (404) 636-8400 or (800) 527-4723, http://www.ashrae.org

APPA: The Association of Higher Education Facilities Officers, 1643 Prince St., Alexandria, VA 22314; (703) 684-1446, http://www.appa.org

Association of Energy Engineers, 4025 Pleasantdale Rd., Suite 420, Atlanta, GA 30340-4264; (770) 447-5083

Association for Computer Operations Management, 742 E. Chapman Ave., Orange, CA 92866; (714) 997-7966

Association for Facilities Engineering, 8180 Corporate Park Dr., Suite 305, Cincinnati, OH 45242; (513) 489-2473, aipe@ix.netcom.com

Building Owners and Managers Association, International, 1201 New York Ave., NW, Suite 300, Washington, DC 20005; (202) 408-2662, www.boma.org

Business and Institutional Furniture Manufacturers Association, International, 2680 Horizon Dr., SE, Suite A-1, Grand Rapids, MI 49546-7500; (616) 285-3963, www.bifma.com

Illuminating Engineering Society of North America, 120 Wall St., 17th Flr., New York, NY 10005-4001; (212) 248-5000, IESNA.org

International Facility Management Association, One E. Greenway Plaza, Suite 1100, Houston, TX 77046-0194; (713) 623-4362

Society for Occupational and Environmental Health, 6728 Old McLean Village Dr., McLean, VA 22101; (703) 556-9222

Wayne E. Leroy, CAE, is executive vice president of the Association of Higher Education Facilities Officers, Alexandria, Virginia.

CHAPTER 18

GOVERNMENT RELATIONS

JANIS L. TABOR, CAE

L
ike governments, associations form for the purpose of achieving common goals. Government relations activities conducted by associations give members a greater voice in government decisions: Collective action stands a better chance of getting results. In addition, the public benefits from sound laws and regulations.

Although some associations are formed primarily to advocate for their members in the government arena, more have added a government relations function as laws and regulations increasingly affect individual, professional, and business interests. For associations whose members are highly regulated, a government relations program is likely to be a necessity, not an option.

Increased Activity

Associations interact with government at the federal, state, county, city, and international levels. Government relations at the federal level has steadily increased since the mid-1970s, when regulatory growth and reach began to accelerate and widespread reforms were initiated in response to the Watergate scandal. Congress opened committee processes for public information and involvement. Formation of the Federal Election Commission opened the door for political action committees (PACs). The Freedom of Information Act provided the option of accessing executive branch information, and the Office of Management and Budget assumed an expanded role in regulatory matters.

Increased opportunities for public interaction with government led to a proliferation of interest groups on all sides of the issues. Collectively, government relations professionals became known as "the third house" of the legislature or "the fourth branch of government." Eventually, the opinion pendulum swung back; terms such as "special interest groups" and "lobbyists" developed less positive connotations and presaged a new round of reforms.

In the mid-1990s, for instance, Congress tightened rules for lobbyists, eliminated the tax deductibility of association dues applied to lobbying activities for some tax-exempt categories, and proposed campaign-finance reforms. Although most organizations believe public disclosure is appropriate, the association community expressed concern about being unduly singled out and put at a disadvantage for working with government. Still, the trend of associations participating in government relations continues.

In the states, government relations activities have increased under "new federalism"—shifting power from the federal to the state and local levels. And as business and professional practices have become more global, many associations have done likewise by becoming involved in international government relations activities. These associations may form alliances with international counterpart organizations to develop a presence before multi-national or regional government entities and to become involved in matters associated with government-to-government policy making.

Each locale and level of government has certain rules and requirements. Although the details may differ, the basic principles apply to all levels. For the sake of simplicity, the discussion below focuses on domestic federal government relations.

Associations' Role

Few government officials have a working knowledge of the activities in which association members are involved. Associations are especially well-equipped to provide accurate, timely information about their areas of interest. The most successful government relations programs couch issues in the context of the overall business and professional community and society in general—the framework in which government decisions are made. When laws and regulations are well-thought out and properly applied, they can stimulate growth and improve services to the public. Conversely, the actions of uninformed lawmakers and regulators can demoralize or even destroy an industry or profession, thus denying services to society.

The role of associations in government relations is to communicate the perspectives and views of members to officials in the legislative and executive branches of government. These views should be based on the members' technical or professional knowledge.

Associations have a right and a responsibility to educate legislators and other government officials about issues affecting members' businesses and professions. When properly managed and conducted, a government relations program benefits both association members and the public at large. Its goal may be simply to make information available; in other instances, the goal may be to achieve a specific outcome on a bill or regulation.

Legal Issues

An association's tax-exempt category provides the legal parameters for its government relations activities. Key issues include the amount of lobbying and political activity allowed (as defined by the Internal Revenue Service). The following chart outlines in general terms the nature and extent of lobbying and political activity currently allowed for charitable, social welfare, and trade associations.

Tax Status/ Description	Lobbying	Political Activity	Qualifiers
501(c)(3) **charitable** scientific, educational, religious	Limited*	Prohibited	• (c)(3) criterion: "exclusively" devoted to public benefit activities * "Insubstantial" lobbying only
501(c)(4) **social welfare**	Unlimited (if for social welfare)	Limited*	• (c)(4) criterion: "primarily" devoted to social welfare * Political activity must be less than half of total activity
501(c)(6) **business league** trade	Unlimited	Yes*	• (c)(6) criterion: "primarily" devoted to common business interests of members * Political activities not restricted by IRS, but may be subject to other laws (e.g., FEC)

Most associations rely on legal counsel to ensure their government relations activities comply with tax, lobbying disclosure, and government ethics laws. Legal experts can also explain current interpretations of terms such as "exclusively," "primarily," and "insubstantial."

Many charitable associations erroneously believe their tax status prevents them from conducting a government relations program. Although it is true that 501(c)(3) organizations must limit and control the nature and extent of their government relations activities, they are not precluded from lobbying as an "insubstantial" portion of their overall activities. However, exceeding the "insubstantial" limit or participating in political activities puts the charitable association at risk of losing its exemption from federal income taxation.

Issues associated with the association's tax status and its ability to lobby should not be confused with registration requirements for lobbyists.

Showing Value to the Board

Despite the benefits of a government relations program for many associations—and for society as a whole—selling the board of directors on the activity can be difficult. Many people are uncomfortable with government interaction and reticent to get involved unless a clear and imminent threat is evident. Others find the concept of lobbying unappealing and believe it to be the main form of government relations.

Boards should understand the concept of the association as a good citizen with useful knowledge to share, the educational nature of government relations, the acceptability of association lobbying under the law, and the need to develop relationships with policy makers *before* a crisis occurs.

The first step in establishing the value of government relations to the association is to engage the board in assessing the public policy priorities of the business or profession. Once a government relations program is underway, the board should be kept informed of progress on those priorities and ask for feedback on how the effort is proceeding.

Board members need to be instructed that clear-cut victories are the exception rather than the rule in government relations. Successes on issues are most often characterized by slow and incremental progress. Achievements are best couched in terms of how the association is participating in shaping the issues and how the issues are evolving. Often, a government action not taken is a victory.

Quantitative metrics are not useful in government relations—the number of meetings held or statements issued does not show that objectives are being met. What is meaningful is that the association helps members have a voice in shaping the outcome of selected issues.

Government relations activities are better understood by board members who have first-hand experience. It is good practice to give association leaders opportunities to interact with key government officials, and such "leader-to-leader" interactions can be an excellent way of advancing the association's values.

Plans and Procedures

Government relations involves placing the association's name and members in a potentially high-profile public arena. Consequently, high-level commitment to this activity is essential and is preferably articulated in the strategic plan.

Government relations goals—for programs as well as issues—need to be established and updated annually with broad-based input from association leaders and members. Some associations determine their goals by surveying association leaders. Others conduct focus groups or annual retreats to identify issues and evaluate ongoing efforts. Association staff play an important role in this process by educating leaders on the external environment, issues outlook, and potential effects on members, as well as by recommending strategies.

The association's public policy issue priorities should be concisely stated and approved by the association's board of directors. They must reflect the needs and interests of the association and its members and take into account government agendas. Because there are usually more issues than resources to address them, getting consensus on the issues of greatest importance to the association helps to focus efforts—and staff resources. Associations that do not establish agendas often find their efforts fragmented by individual member concerns that take a lot of time but yield little benefit for the association as a whole.

Each association also needs board-approved policies or procedures for conducting the government relations function. The culture of the organization will determine if a simple policy or a detailed set of procedures is needed. Key items to address are the review and approval process for position statements, who has the authority to speak for the organization, and how the board is to be kept informed of actions taken on behalf of the organization.

Such policies or procedures should clarify the respective roles of members and staff. In some organizations, for example, staff represent and speak for the organization both informally and formally. In others, staff serve more as government relations advisers and facilitators.

Once procedures are in place, the board of directors delegates responsibility for the government relations function to a separate standing committee. This committee should have a reporting path to the governing board as well as responsibility for recommending changes to the government relations policies and procedures, as needed. The role of the government relations committee varies widely, providing basic program oversight in some associations while preparing and presenting the organization's views in others. Some associations establish separate committees or subcommittees for federal, state and local, and international government relations activities. Criteria used in selecting government relations committee members might include links with other key programs of the association, geographic location, government affairs experience, and political contacts.

Types of Programs

Government relations programs can be informational, reactive, proactive, or a mix. Some associations do not take positions or make specific recommendations on legislation or regulations but do interact with policy makers and provide information about their members' profession or business. They also alert association members to relevant legislative and regulatory developments.

Because many associations become involved in government relations to respond to a threatening situation, government relations programs are frequently *reactive:* They respond to legislation that has already been introduced, mobilizing grassroots volunteers when a bill is approaching final action, or commenting on published regulations. Threatening situations often develop because government itself tends to operate in a crisis mode.

Reactive efforts do not necessarily mean the end of the line for an issue. Even after legislation has been introduced, an association may have opportunities to provide input to lawmakers, especially those on the committees or subcommittees that work on fine-tuning bills. In fact, some organizations intensively work issues at this stage, strategically involving association members from the districts of legislators who serve on the relevant committees. By the time a bill goes to the full legislative body for deliberation and voting, however, changes are hard to make. At this point many associations go for the numbers and mobilize their full membership or grassroots network.

With the collective views of their members—and a body of knowledge in the form of statistics, standards, and other information—associations are in a unique position to identify legislative and regulatory needs for industries or professions. They can take a *proactive* approach to government relations by initiating legislation and providing input for laws and regulations as they are written.

Proactive government relations requires internal collaboration between government relations and technical groups within the association to identify members' needs and concerns; it also requires external communications with decision makers, to help them understand and act on issues. These activities can be costly from the standpoint of staff and volunteer time, but the return on investment can be great in terms of the association's influence on the public policy process.

Program Components

All types of government relations programs have one vital component: ongoing education of government. Organizations may educate policy makers directly through written information and briefings or indirectly through publicity or public service activities that enhance understanding of the business, profession, or other interests represented by the association. Through these efforts the association gains a credibility and visibility that can increase its opportunities to participate in the public policy process.

Association government relations programs typically include some or all of these activities:

- *Issues identification and analysis.* Spotting issues of potential interest or concern—and providing expert analysis of their potential effect on the association and its members—is usually a reactive activity that involves monitoring hearings, bills, and proposed regulations. It can also mean working within the association to determine areas of need for legislative or regulatory action that the association might promote.

 In either case, the legislative calendar and regulatory process drive issues management. Most legislative initiatives are spawned early in the legislative session (and most sessions in the United States begin early in the calendar year). The regulatory process is year-round, with prescribed review steps and timetables.

- *Position statements.* The views conveyed to government on behalf of the association must be based on written position statements that have been approved for public release in accordance with the association's policies and procedures. Because government timetables are geared to internal schedules and priorities, the time frame for preparing position papers is often tight. As a result, association procedures need to have built-in flexibility to shorten the approval process in urgent circumstances.

Some associations empower their chief elected officer to approve statements in special circumstances. Others have two levels of statements with different approval chains: one for the organization as a whole and one for subordinate groups within the organization. Subordinate group statements are useful in larger organizations that have a diversity of expertise and interests. For example, technical divisions in a large professional society will have expert knowledge about specific topics that other divisions may not have. Rather than committing the whole organization to a position on a topic not all understand, authorship is attributed to the technical division that prepared the statement.

- *Government interaction.* Although most associations must work diligently to develop and maintain contacts, government decision makers do seek and are receptive to the views of associations. Successful programs recognize that government officials have many urgent and complex problems to address: They provide information that will help government officials solve these problems but do not expect the officials to become fully conversant with the members' business or profession.

Like most people, government decision makers endeavor to do well and appreciate support. The best rule for maintaining good relations with them is to observe the Golden Rule. Legislators and government officials are likely to respond favorably when approached positively and given due credit for their efforts. In addition, legislators and other government officials rely heavily on their staff for advice and counsel. Association members should recognize that these staff are often vital links in the decision-making process and should be treated accordingly.

Interactions with government officials must be thoughtful, brief, to the point, and technically accurate. Under no circumstances should the interaction become adversarial in tone. Interaction may be through letters (mailed, faxed, or e-mailed); telephone calls; face-to-face meetings with legislators, their staff, or executive branch officials; or formal testimony on legislative or regulatory proposals. A constructive, considerate approach and a reputation for reliability, follow-through, and a willingness to go the extra mile are the keys to successful relations with government officials.

- *Testimony.* Oral testimony is an important and formal method for communicating the association's views to government. It is usually based on an approved position statement, which can subsequently serve as the source document for an entire legislative campaign. Associations often have an edge in gaining the opportunity to present oral testimony because they represent constituencies of people who are knowledgeable about the issues.

A witness presents testimony at a hearing convened by a government entity, such as a congressional committee or a regulatory agency. The witness may be the chief elected officer; the chief staff executive (CSE); or an association member, staff person, or consultant who is particularly knowledgeable about the subject. Although most testimony is submitted in writing, the oral proceeding is usually recorded and transcribed for a written record of the hearing. That's why it is important for witnesses to possess excellent public speaking skills.

In addition, a witness should be thoroughly briefed on the issue, the purpose of the hearing, the presiding officer(s), and on practical matters (such as forms of address, where to sit, and the likely sequence of events). The opposition's case needs to be thoroughly studied so the witness can be prepared to fairly respond to the opponent's arguments. Even the most experienced witness is likely to benefit from rehearsing the testimony and question-and-answer period; using a videotape for rehearsal can greatly improve the witness' performance and comfort level.

Witnesses need to possess all the facts on the issue at hand and be prepared to answer difficult questions. They also should be instructed to acknowledge when they do not have the answers and to offer to gather the information requested. Finally, an association staff person should accompany the witness and provide assistance as needed.

- *Regulatory government relations.* Executive branch personnel—from City Hall to the White House—far outnumber those of the legislative branch. Their actions (or inactions), interpretations of the law, and rule making can greatly affect association members. Some association government relations programs deal primarily with the regulatory process and often provide input as regulations are being drafted.

  Associations also provide comments when a regulatory agency publishes proposed regulations and solicits public comments. These comments are themselves an association position statement and need to be approved in accordance with established procedures. Regulatory comments are submitted in writing and also may be presented orally at hearings.

- *Member involvement.* Although the collective voice of the association works most effectively for some government interactions, individual legislators want to hear from their own constituents. Members can benefit from and advance the association's government relations program by interacting with their own elected officials.

  Associations can facilitate this one-on-one interaction by establishing grass-roots networks of members. A network may be selective (for example, participants must have an existing relationship with legislators) but always is voluntary—some members don't have the time, don't want to interact with their legislators, or are limited by their employment in doing so. Member networks can provide a means for high-volume communications, which can be particularly effective when an issue is coming up for final consideration by Congress or the President.

  Ongoing communication with participants is essential to a network's success.

Some associations schedule contacts regularly throughout the year, in the form of suggestions for framing a clear and concise message, issue updates that call participants to action, requests for feedback on contacts with legislators, and reports about the outcome of issues addressed by the network.

Some associations encourage members to develop relationships with their elected representatives. A particularly good technique is the "site visit"—when a member invites government officials to tour a plant, laboratory, or other facility as a means of increasing understanding of the member's business, problems, and contributions to the well-being of the area. Inviting local media to these events provides both the association member and the legislator with publicity while advancing the public's understanding of the association's interests.

• *Coalitions.* Associations rarely stand alone before a legislature or government agency. Opponents of the association's views often are present, as are allies. The most effective government relations programs include networking with others on common issues for a variety of purposes, from information sharing to collaborative action.

Coalitions range from formal, dues-supported organizations with paid staff to ad hoc groups where one member organization serves as the volunteer secretariat. Associations that participate in coalitions need to specify the nature and extent to which their organization's name is used in coalition activities. (See Chapter 20.)

• *Public relations.* Communicating the association's views can be as simple as issuing a news release that announces a public policy position or action taken. Guest editorials and letters to the editor can educate the broader public about the association's perspective, while large advertisements—a costly option—can capture the attention of both the public at large and government officials.

The association's tax status may affect its choice of a communication vehicle (see the discussion of grassroots lobbying below). But whatever the vehicle selected, the content should be based on the association's approved position statements.

• *Informing members.* Information about laws, regulations, and legislation may be the most visible benefit of the government relations function for most association members. Government relations information typically includes updates on the status of legislative or regulatory issues, in-depth analyses of major issues, interviews with or articles by government officials, positions adopted by the association, and summaries of the actions taken to promote those positions.

In addition to providing timely information on pending and proposed actions, some associations distribute in-depth information on enacted laws and regulations along with instructions on how to comply with them. Although costly to compile in terms of staff time and legal services, such information may be a primary reason for belonging to the association.

Electronic options have greatly enhanced the timeliness and usefulness of government relations communications. Although weekly, biweekly, or monthly newsletters are a mainstay, updates via fax and e-mail are being used increasingly to supplement or replace print communications. Computer bulletin boards on government relations topics not only give members an opportunity to comment on or debate issues but also provide government relations committees and staff with insights into members' priorities and perspectives. Government relations-related archival and reference material can be made available through the association's home page on the World Wide Web.

- *Speakers, briefings, and trainings.* Associations provide information to their members via training in government relations techniques; seminars, conferences, or roundtables on specific issues; and presentations by high-level speakers.

  For example, many associations conduct annual or biennial government affairs conferences to help inform their members about current issues and, at the same time, help legislators better understand their concerns. Typically, such conferences assemble association members and involve people from the legislative and executive branches of government for speeches, question-and-answer sessions, and person-to-person contact. The conference may also feature mass visits by association members to legislative offices. Detailed planning and thorough preparation of members are essential to the success of these visits.

- *Candidate events.* All associations—even 501(c)(3)s—can interact with candidates and political parties, but IRS rules that apply to the association must be clearly understood. In addition, associations that can participate in political activities sometimes find it risky, in terms of internal politics, to take a position on a candidate. A safe option is to create forums or other mechanisms, such as questionnaires, to sound out the field of candidates on issues important to association members.

- *Political action committees (PACs).* These are vehicles that enable associations—except 501(c)(3)s—to participate in the election process. While associations are forbidden from contributing to candidates, they can establish PACs to raise and contribute funds to political campaigns. PACs must be registered with the Federal Election Commission and comply with applicable laws. Funds may be solicited only from association members and staff. Members who participate in a PAC typically increase their political awareness and interest in the issues.

  PACs are subject to stringent federal, state, and local regulations. Before establishing a PAC, an association should look at the legal issues, its objectives for the PAC, the funding expectations that legislators may have, and its ability to raise sufficient funds to meet those expectations.

Management and Administration

Because government relations is a representational function, the association's CSE usually has a role in the government relations program. When additional resources are needed, two options exist: hire in-house staff or contract with a consultant or outside lobbyist.

Contracting with a consultant or lobbyist may be the best option when association staff lack expertise in an area, when the issue is of limited duration and does not warrant internal staffing, or when additional help is needed on critical issues. If no conflict of interest exists, it may be feasible for associations with limited government relations needs to team up and jointly retain a government relations professional.

With regard to in-house staff, some associations combine government relations with another function, such as public relations. Others establish a separate government relations department with multiple staff members, whose responsibilities may be divided by federal, state and local, or international levels; by legislative or regulatory affairs; or by topic or issue.

Whether in-house staff or outside consultant, government relations professionals serve as representatives of the association. They must be familiar with the association's priorities and procedures, know legislative and regulatory processes and the primary "players" in the association's area of interest, be comfortable working with high-level officials, and have excellent oral and written communications skills. High ethical standards, honesty, integrity, and credibility are also essential traits in the sensitive world of government relations and advocacy. Any action that smacks of deception or manipulation can mortally wound relationships the association has spent years building.

Because so much is at stake, a high degree of trust in government relations professionals is required. For in-house staff, a close reporting relationship between the top government relations staff executive and the CSE helps build that trust. To help keep contractors and outside lobbyists in tune with the association's priorities, build checks and balances into the working relationship.

Additional Areas

Other areas that require attention include:

- *Lobbying rules and taxation.* Multiple definitions of lobbying and an array of record-keeping requirements for nonprofit organizations have emerged from changes in federal laws that govern the tax treatment of association dues applied to lobbying, the registration of lobbyists and disclosure of lobbying activities, and ethics rules for legislators and other government officials. It is imperative that an association know the current applicable laws and regulations and operate within their limits.

For example, lobbyist restrictions and reporting requirements vary from place to place and are subject to periodic review. And, although there is no limitation on grassroots activities within the association's membership, advocacy efforts that involve the public at large will have tax implications for some associations. Associations often use the term "grassroots" to refer to their own members, but the IRS defines "grassroots" as the broader public. Associations must find out what rules apply before they take action.

Information on lobbying rules is readily available from the IRS, Congress, the Office of Government Ethics, the Federal Election Commission, and state legislative services offices, as well as from the association management community.

* *Political activities.* In addition to PACs—which require separate governance, registration, record keeping, and reporting—associations must monitor and control all political-related activities to ensure they comply with the law. All members must be informed of the rules and restrictions that apply to the association. At the same time, they should be encouraged to fully exercise their rights and responsibilities as individual citizens.

* *Government ethics.* Ethics rules related to entertaining and gift-giving are common for legislative and executive branch officials and staff. For example, certain officials may not be able to accept a complimentary meal or to travel to an event under some circumstances. Being aware of the rules will ensure the association avoids embarrassment and rule violations.

Trends in Government Relations

Government relations will continue to be a dynamic and demanding area for associations. To survive and prosper, associations must exert leadership in developing and executing effective government relations and advocacy programs on behalf of their members at all levels of government.

Association member issues are not the only public policy concerns of associations, however. Government has increased its scrutiny of business and tax matters, including those pertaining to associations. The specific issues under discussion range from nonprofit postal rates to unrelated business income tax, from taxation of lobbying activities to tort law reform. Even when the association does not wish to undertake a government relations program to address member interests, the CEO must stay on top of issues that could affect the association's ability to fulfill its mission in the future.

References

Ernstthal, Henry, *Principles of Association Management,* 2d edition, American Society of Association Executives, Washington, D.C., 1988.

Jacobs, Jerald A., *Association Law Handbook,* Bureau of National Affairs, Washington, D.C., 1986.

Butler, Wilford A, ed., *Attracting, Organizing & Keeping Members,* American Society of Association Executives, Washington, D.C., 1989.

Expert editorial contributions to this chapter were provided by Timothy F. Burns of the Chemical Manufacturers Association, Washington, D.C., and Kathleen A. Ream of the American Chemical Society, Washington, D.C.

Janis L. Tabor, CAE, is the director, external relations, for the Council for Chemical Research. She has more than 25 years of experience in government relations, including 7 years on Capitol Hill, 7 years as president of a public policy consulting firm, and 11 years in association management.

CHAPTER 19

PUBLIC RELATIONS

WILLIAM J. WILSON, APR, CAE

A s a management function, public relations facilitates two-way communication between an organization and the groups it wants to influence. Public relations practitioners are not mere purveyors of information. Rather, their role is to discern what is happening in the external environment, communicate that to management in the internal environment, and counsel management how to respond.

In addition, public relations is a leadership function: It helps managers establish, regulate, and maintain satisfactory relationships between and among various groups. Public relations practitioners discover or initiate networks of people with common bonds, usually referred to as publics.

To accomplish its twin goals—to shape public opinion and to shape an organization's response to public opinion—public relations relies on persuasion. This communication process changes or neutralizes hostile opinions, crystallizes unformed or latent opinions, or reinforces favorable opinions. To change public opinion, public relations must influence the decisions of the power structure associated with a particular issue.

The Association Environment

An association's constituency or membership defines its issues, and the issues define its publics. The association's mission statement (which embodies its reason for being) and its strategic plan (which spells out what it hopes to achieve) drive its public relations strategies (the tactics used to recruit and positively influence its publics).

Whether they work in corporations, government agencies, associations, or other nonprofit organizations, professional communicators have similar responsibilities. As part of the senior management team, they help organizations define goals and objectives, develop messages, pinpoint target publics, and devise strategies to communicate those messages to selected publics.

However, a number of factors make association public relations a distinct subdiscipline within the overall profession. Those factors are:

- **Greater integration of responsibilities.** Small and mid-sized associations usually lack the staff and budgets to maintain specialized departments for handling media relations, publicity, special events, publications, and other related functions, which are frequently staffed separately in large agencies or corporations. Instead, these responsibilities are typically lumped together in the association's communication or human resources department.

- **Wider range of roles.** Given the lack of staff and centralized responsibility, practitioners in associations often are called on to be generalists and must exercise a greater diversity of skills than their corporate or agency peers.

- **More target publics.** Associations generally try to reach more target publics than a corporation or an agency client, including their members, the industry or profession, the media (trade and consumer), the government, and the general public.

- **Rule by committee.** Responsibility, accountability, and decision making are diffused among the board, committees, and executive staff in a way not found outside the association field. The association decision-making process often

---

Coming to Terms

Public relations is connected with a number of other organizational communication activities, especially those defined below:

Publicity is an uncontrollable part of public relations. It disseminates information through selected media based on the information's news value and without payment. In the extreme, publicity becomes press agentry, with the sole purpose of getting the client's name in the media.

Advertising is paid, one-directional communication, based largely on appeals to the emotions. Public relations uses both intellectual and emotional appeals. Advertising is totally controlled: The association selects the media, timing, placement, frequency of repetition, and so forth.

Marketing is also a one-way communication process. It motivates publics to purchase goods, services, or ideas, based on a *quid pro quo* exchange with the marketing organization (for example, I provide you with a car; you give me money or sign a financing agreement.)

Promotion includes special events and activities designed to create interest in a person, product, organization, or cause.

Public affairs is the government's name for public relations. When applied to corporations, it concerns corporate citizenship and public policy issues.

Government relations concerns dealings and communications with all three branches of government.

Community relations communicates with the citizens and groups within an organization's area of operation.

Media relations deals with the press. It involves obtaining media coverage for the association and its agenda and facilitating access of the press to the group's sources of information.

Industry relations focuses on communicating with other companies within the industrial sector of the organization.

Lobbying directly attempts to influence legislative and regulatory decisions of government.

---

baffles agency and corporate practitioners, who may mistake slowness for inaction and indecisiveness.

- **Scarcity of training.** Although colleges and universities offer courses in public relations and communications, these tend to be geared toward corporate or agency careers. No college-level offerings deal specifically with association public relations. Association public relations practitioners tend to acquire most of their knowledge through on-the-job training.

The Court of Public Opinion

A public is a group of people tied together by a common bond or interest who share a sense of their commonality. Some bonds—nationality, religion, profession—are relatively permanent and stable. Others are transitory, such as when groups focus on getting a specific candidate elected or a specific piece of legislation passed. Every specific issue, problem, or interest creates its own public. Thus we have "pro-life" and "pro-choice," timber interests and environmentalists, the gun lobby and the gun-control lobby.

Public relations targets those groups whose common interests are affected by the acts and policies of an organization—or whose acts and opinions affect that organization. To communicate effectively with individuals within a public, an association must make its appeals significant and relevant to the whole group's interest in a particular situation. A person's group relationships provide the context in which he or she formulates most of the communication received and transmitted.

Two basic kinds of groups exist. *Statistical groups* are bound together by sex, income, education, and occupation. Individual members tend to respond in the same general way. *Functional groups*—those bound by a common purpose—tend to conform to mutually accepted standards.

Furthermore, individuals within groups tend to conform to one of three basic types:

1. *Tradition-directed* individuals are marked by rigid adherence to the accustomed way of doing things.

2. *Inner-directed* people base their opinions on long-standing personal goals and values.

3. *Other-directed* individuals derive their opinions and values from the outside from peers, associates, friends, and the media.

An *attitude* is a mental position about an issue. An *opinion* is the expression of a belief, which is based on what the person perceives as the truth. Through public relations, an association can create, manage, or change the opinions and attitudes of publics, lead people to change their personal attitudes on an issue, and then encourage them to express those changed beliefs.

Before it can bring about any changes, however, an association must understand how people in groups form their opinions. There are five basic ways:

- **Cognitive dissonance.** People avoid information that is adverse to their views or situation; they seek information that is compatible with their view of how the world works. Because people tend to accept information that reinforces the values they already hold, changing their attitudes is difficult.

- **Spiral of silence.** When one member of a group speaks up, followed by others who espouse the same point of view, the rest of the group tends to remain silent rather than risk losing group membership by disagreeing with those who have already spoken up. This spiraling process increasingly establishes one opinion as prevailing within the group.

- **Predisposition.** Individuals in a group are already inclined to act in a certain way—or not act at all—when an issue arises. Public relations aims to strengthen favorable predispositions and alter unfavorable ones.

- **Perception.** What a person perceives or believes to be true is true for him or her. The same "perception is reality" phenomenon applies to groups.

The Nature of Public Opinion

Public relations programs shape and are shaped by public opinion, which operates in ways that can be anticipated. For example:

- Opinion is highly sensitive to important events.
- Events of unusual magnitude swing opinion temporarily from one extreme to another.
- Opinion is generally determined more by events than by words.
- Verbal statements and outlines for action count most before opinion has become focused and crystallized.
- Public opinion does not anticipate emergencies; it reacts to them.
- Psychologically, individual or group self-interest determines opinion.
- Opinion does not remain aroused long unless sustained by events or unless people feel strong involvement.
- Once self-interest is involved, opinions are not easily changed.
- When self-interest is involved, public opinion is likely to be ahead of official policy.
- If an initial opinion is lightly held or held by a few people, an accomplished fact tends to shift opinion toward acceptance of the new opinion.
- In crises, people become more sensitive to the adequacy of their leadership.
- People are willing to let leaders decide provided they feel that they are included in the decision.
- People form opinions more easily about goals than about the means to achieve those goals.
- Public opinion is colored by desires (the real motives and wants of the individuals in the group).
- Public opinion reveals a hard-headed common sense.

Public relations deals with perceptions, rather than the realities behind those perceptions.

- **Public opinion.** This refers to the sum of accumulated individual opinions on an issue in public debate. Public opinion includes both the attitudes and the supporting behavior that results from those attitudes.

What a person doesn't know can influence his or her opinions as much as what is known. Censorship is an effort to influence opinions by suppressing what people might otherwise see, read, or hear. Artificial censorship is a deliberate attempt to silence a source or lines of communication; natural censorship refers to the physical, psychological, and semantic barriers people erect themselves.

For instance, one form of natural censorship is selective attention: People tend to see, hear, and believe what they wish to see, hear, and believe. People also engage in selective retention. They easily remember the facts that enhance their views and suppress or forget information that contradicts their views. Such suppression flows from a person's mental set—his or her values as derived from heritage, previous experience, sentiments, likes and dislikes, sense of obligation to others, ideals, goals, and definition of self-interest.

A Step-by-Step Approach

This four-step model applies to any public relations program:

Step 1: Research. Where are we? What's going on in the external environment? Research answers such questions by systematically gathering information in order to identify target groups; monitor the opinions, attitudes, and behavior of those groups; and test effective message forms and media to effectively reach those publics.

Research can be categorized in a number of ways. *Primary research* is information gathering that the association conducts in-house or hires an outside firm to do. *Secondary research* is analysis based on others' primary research.

Informal research is exploratory. It is not gathered from scientifically representative samples but rather from sources such as databases, literature searches, personal contacts, informants, community forums, focus groups, advisory committees, field reports, and analyses of phone calls and mail.

Formal research refers to statistically valid studies. It includes surveys—mailed questionnaires, interviews by phone or in person, cross-section samples, and panel studies. Both informal and formal research can be *structured* (that is, rely on the use of a questionnaire) or *unstructured*. Structured research may be conducted via personal interview, telephone interview, intercept ("person on the street") interview, or a mail survey. (For more information on research and statistics, see Chapter 15.)

Step 2: Planning. At this point, the practitioner asks: Who do we want to reach (target publics)? What do we want them to do or not do (objectives)? Where do we want to go—and why?

This step takes the intelligence gathered during the research phase and translates it into policies and programs that further the association's agenda. The

Principles of Persuasion

In deciding to adopt and act on a matter of opinion, publics go through the following stages: awareness (learn about the new idea or practice), interest (get more information about the idea), evaluation (try out the idea mentally), trial (use or test the idea), and adoption (accept idea for continued and full-scale use).

The persuasiveness of a public relations message depends partly on where people are in the decision-making process. While they are still forming opinions, people generally don't avoid adverse information. But once they have made up their minds, persuading them to adopt a different point of view becomes a great challenge.

To successfully influence a public's opinions, public relations practitioners must focus on the factors that facilitate persuasion. They are:

- **Identification.** The message must be presented in terms of the audience's interests. If people don't understand how a message affects them, they will ignore it.

- **Action.** Unless a means of action is provided, people tend to shrug off appeals to act. The association must spell out what it wants people to do and make it easy for them to act on that information.

- **Familiarity and trust.** The listener is not likely to listen to or believe a speaker in whom he or she has no confidence. This is why selecting an appropriate, credible spokesperson is critical to the success of a public relations campaign.

- **Clarity.** The message must contain words, symbols, or stereotypes that the receiver comprehends and can respond to. The association must identify any action it is recommending in familiar and clear terms.

planning process typically includes these activities:

- State the goal, problem, or issue.
- Analyze the external and internal factors that affect the issue. For example, take an issue such as smoking. A public relations campaign favoring freedom of choice for smokers would face a much more receptive audience in a southern tobacco state than in one that does not have an economy dependent on tobacco growing.

   The external environment can facilitate or impede an issues-oriented public relations campaign. Or, an issue may be so inherently complex that communication becomes extremely challenging. Medical, engineering, and scientific associations, for example, often must work hard to communicate to the lay audience the important benefits that are being achieved by their members' accomplishments.

- State the public relations program's goals, including a broad program objective.
- List the significant publics. Limit the list to three. A public relations strategy

that tries to reach many publics can end up accomplishing little or nothing.

- Define quantifiable, measurable, and time-sensitive objectives for each public. For instance, it is not sufficient to say, "We are going to reach teenagers with a 'Just say no to drugs' message." A workable objective must be more precise, such as, "Next year we will create a 'Just say no' brochure and place it in the hands of every tenth-grade teacher in the 20 largest cities in the United States by the end of the fall semester."

- Develop communication and action strategies for each objective. Include message strategies (What do we want to say? What is the best way to say it?), media strategies (What media are most likely to reach our target publics?), and selection of a spokesperson (Who is the most suitable person to deliver the message?).

- Design implementation plans, including assignment of responsibilities, implementation schedule, and budgets.

- Test the program. Testing enables the organization to refine its objectives, strategies, messages, and media based on the results achieved in small trial runs and to establish benchmarks against which to measure the final results.

- Evaluate the test: Obtain feedback and adjust the program accordingly.

- Implement the program.

- Evaluate the program.

Step 3: Implementation. Here you answer the questions: What will we do to achieve our objectives? When will we do this? Implementation chooses and uses the tools that make public relations happen: publicity, special events, emergency plans, and so forth. It embraces a wide range of activities, including media campaigns, news conferences, publications, production of videos, special events, crisis management, coalition building, meetings, conventions, fund-raising drives, cause-related activities, and celebrations of anniversaries.

There is an inverse correlation between the amount of control an organization exercises over the media it uses and the credibility of the messages communi-

Recruiting Allies

At its most effective, public relations is proactive: It identifies potential issues, reads the climate of public opinion, and counsels management on which strategies will build a credible reputation with the target publics. Those strategies may include teaming up with like-minded organizations to promote common causes.

These questions can help you identify possible partners for building an alliance:

- What similar groups share our goals and objectives?

- What groups have goals or objectives that depend in part on whether our association achieves its objectives?

- What groups do we need to achieve our objectives?

- Who purchases the products that are ultimately made with what our members produce or manufacture? Who purchases the services that our members provide? What are those groups' major concerns?

cated. In other words, the less control the association has over a particular medium, the more apt the public is to believe what is said about the association. Conversely, the more control the organization has over the media, the more likely the public is to assume self-interest, "spin" control, or questionable accuracy in the messages it is asked to accept.

Controlled media include association house organs and possibly the trade press; films, videos, or CD-ROMs generated by the association or its members; computer bulletin boards and World Wide Web sites; billboards, posters, circulars, and brochures; advertising messages; and point-of-purchase advertising items.

At the other end of the spectrum, the least controlled media are general-interest newspapers, consumer magazines, and radio and television programs. Practitioners simply issue the message in the form of a media release, personal appearance, or media event. How, when, and even whether the target media carry the message is beyond the association's control. It is up to the media to decide whether the treatment is favorable or unfavorable to the association, how much space or time is devoted to the message, and whether the organization's message is incorporated into a larger story.

The onset of electronic technology has altered the forms and logistics of reaching a reporter or editor, but the basic strategy remains the same: An organization must package its message to break through the logjam of similar releases reaching the media on a given day. The classic vehicle for conveying a message to the media is the press release. Whether sent in the traditional format (double-spaced and printed), by e-mail, or by broadcast fax, a press release must meet the following tests of viability:

- Is this really news?
- Is the announcement properly identified, including the organization's correct name, address, contact person, and phone number? (Don't forget Internet or e-mail address if available.)
- Is the lead attention-getting and complete?
- Is the release formulated suitably for the target media?
- Is the information really of interest to and suitable for the target public?

Another classic tool of the public relations trade is the media kit. They must be designed to catch the interest of editors, assignment desks, and columnists. They should also supply all the basic information an editor, reporter, or newscaster would need.

A basic media or press kit includes a general fact sheet; a background fact sheet on the association and key issues; a program or schedule for a campaign or event; a news story about the event itself; lists of the participants or parties involved; biographies and photos of those who have key roles; visual materials (printed charts and graphs, video news releases, CD-ROMs); a longer, feature-type story supplying more background and sidebars (short, supplementary pieces) on related topics; a customized fact sheet listing features of particular interest to that publication's or radio/TV station's audience; and organizational brochures.

Another popular way to obtain visibility and media coverage is through a special event, including the press conference. Because newspapers and broadcast outlets have reduced the size of their reporting staffs, they do not routinely cover organizational meetings, conferences, conventions, or trade shows. Therefore, when calling a press conference, make sure that the announcement is truly news. The media will not assign scarce resources to cover what they consider a minor organizational event, even if the association president considers that event of utmost importance. Too, another event may totally overshadow your press conference—a major disaster or accident, outbreak of war, or late-breaking scandal involving a celebrity. It is possible to do everything right and still have an empty press room on the day of a carefully orchestrated media event.

Look for trade-outs—reasons why other groups might cosponsor your event in exchange for future sponsorship or partnering in theirs. And keep in mind that frequency counts. Consider staging a series of events related to a single theme. For example, a strategy might involve staging a walk-a-thon to call attention to an issue in cities across a state, followed by a march on the state capital or Washington, D.C.

Step 4: Evaluation. Evaluation answers these questions: Have we met our objectives? How can we improve our efforts? What did we learn?

Evaluation not only weighs the effectiveness of the program's final results but also examines the research and planning stages and the efficacy with which the various strategies and tactics were carried out. It should be performed at key stages during program implementation so that, if necessary, appropriate mid-course corrections can be made to ensure objectives are met.

Suppose, for example, that the ABC Association, a health-related organization, has launched a campaign to have men over 40 seek physical exams for prostate cancer. The messages are formulated for the male target audience, and media are chosen based on what the target public reads or watches.

Mid-course research discovers that men are tuning out the message because they find it too threatening. Women, however, who are only serendipitously receiving the message, are convincing their husbands and other men they know to seek exams. The campaign should then be refocused, with a modified message and new media designed to reach the female significant other. She is the key influencer in a man's decision to have the examination.

A properly implemented research phase includes the establishment of benchmark measurements against which the program's results can be compared. These may be published standards of performance for certain types of advertising or direct mail programs; attendance records; orders for program materials; number of names on petition; totals from sign-in sheets, evaluation forms, or exit polls; tallies of letters and phone calls received; or sales totals.

The measurability of public relations is the subject of perennial debate. Impressive media numbers are not enough. Public relations is about influencing attitudes and actions. True follow-up research will determine whether the attitudinal and action benchmarks embodied in the program's objectives have been achieved. For instance, if an association said it was going to raise awareness of an issue by 10 percent in a given market within six months, research will indicate whether it succeeded.

For measurements to have meaning after the fact, they must be compared with benchmark measurements taken *before* the public relations program was implemented. It is important to tally the negative outcomes as well as the positive ones. Also, if the program stretches out over time, include evaluation points at various stages to determine whether the trend line for results is moving in the expected direction.

Crisis Planning

A crisis can be anything from a terrorist bombing to the leaking of a toxic substance to a sexual-harassment charge against the chief executive officer. Crisis planning in public relations is like life insurance: Those who wait until they need it are too late. The association that plans for crises before they happen maximizes its chances of successfully weathering the storm.

Crises don't just go away, but they can be managed. Here's what to do:

1. **Name a team leader**— the point person for all inquiries and information flow during the crisis. The team leader is not the spokesperson but rather the person through whom all information and decision making are channeled.

2. **Establish communications procedures.** Have a list of all organizational personnel who must be involved in handling the crisis, along with daytime and evening phone and fax numbers. Maintain an up-to-date media list, with names and phone and fax numbers.

3. **Prepare a notification list.** In addition to the media, who must be notified? What government agencies are involved? Is there a need to contact any next of kin? What about other individuals or groups who may be affected by a disaster?

4. **Train the crisis team**—everyone who would be involved in dealing with the situation.

5. **Draft alternative scenarios** for the types of crises that could affect the organization. For each, develop message points to reply to anticipated media inquiries. Select and train spokespeople, including volunteer leaders and experts in specialized areas.

6. **Accept all media inquiries.** No one can successfully dodge a good reporter for very long.

7. **Establish a media command center.** Set up a chain of command for who will run it and who will speak to the media. On every communication include the center's phone and fax numbers, as well as the name and home phone number of the contact person and his or her backup.

8. **Do not stonewall, lie, or speculate.** If the association has no comment to make, say so.

9. **Be cautious in drawing conclusions.** However, when the crisis is clarified, give the media a complete report, while still respecting issues of client confidentiality, legal ramifications, and any unresolved matters.

Speaking Up

An important part of any communication with the media is the effectiveness of the spokesperson who represents the association. Usually the media will want to speak to a major player, such as the chief elected or chief executive officer. An expert spokesperson may be more appropriate, however, particularly if addressing manufacturing processes, legal matters, or industry statistics.

One look at TV news magazines is enough to show how vulnerable an organization's spokesperson can be when confronted by aggressive, well-briefed reporters. The following tips can help a spokesperson appear credible, expert, and articulate:

- **Prepare for the interview.** Find out who the reporter is, what publication or program the interview will appear on, the format the interview will take, and the target audience.

- **Draft message points.** The association must be clear on what it wants to achieve through the interview; translate these objectives into points that the spokesperson should be sure to cover. In addition, anticipate questions the reporter is apt to ask and prepare responses. The spokesperson should know message points so well that he or she can answer even the toughest questions promptly and calmly.

- **Speak the way old-time reporters write: in an inverted pyramid.** Start with a headline—in other words, the conclusions, stated briefly and directly. Then fill in facts, anecdotes, and statistics as time permits.

- **Don't say too much.** Short answers are better than long ones. A favorite tactic of interviewers is to say nothing, hoping the interviewee will become uncomfortable with the silence and start speaking to relieve his or her tension. Many a "scoop" has come from a spokesperson who didn't know when to stop talking. Don't answer hypothetical questions—label them as such—and admit if you don't know an answer. Offer to supply the information later, and make good on your promise. Or, refer the interviewer to another source of information.

- **Stay positive.** Always frame a reply in positive terms, no matter how negative the reporter's statement or question. Try to be likable and friendly, no matter how hostile the reporter appears.

- **Speak clearly.** Avoid jargon and bureaucratic language.

- **Know your rights.** If the interviewer is taping the session, your association can also record the interview, especially if the media's approach is likely to be negative or hostile.

- **Dress for success.** For a television interview, men should wear a dark suit, blue shirt, and a tie with a simple pattern (avoid stripes and paisley patterns). Women should wear a dark outfit in simple colors and avoid large, shiny, or noisy jewelry. Assume a relaxed, erect sitting posture; men may unbutton their suit jackets when seated.

For television interviews, look at and talk to the interviewer, not the camera. Speak and gesture naturally, and maintain a pleasant expression; smile, if appropriate—an expressionless face comes across as angry on camera. Keep the interview mind-set and posture until the camera and microphones are off. Even if the reporter continues chatting after the cameras are off, don't say anything you wouldn't have said with a "live" microphone. Always assume the microphones are on.

References

Cutlip, Scott M., *Public Relations History: From the 17th to the 20th Century,* Lawrence Erlbaum Associates, Mahwah, New Jersey, 1995.

———, Allen H. Center, and Glen M. Broom, *Effective Public Relations,* 6th ed., Prentice-Hall, Inc., Englewood Cliffs, New Jersey, 1995.

Dennis, Lloyd B., *Practical Public Affairs in an Era of Change: A Communications Guide for Business, Government, and College,* Public Relations Society of America and University Press of America, Lanham, Maryland, 1995.

Horton, James L., *Integrating Corporate Communications: The Cost-Effective Use of Message and Medium,* Quorum Books, Westport, Connecticut, 1995.

Newsom, Doug, and Bob Carrell, *Public Relations Writing, Form & Style,* Wadsworth Publishing Company, Belmont, California, 1995.

Young, Davis, *Building Your Company's Good Name: How to Create and Protect the Reputation of Your Organization,* Amacom, New York, 1996.

William J. Wilson, CAE, is director of public relations for the Vision Council of America, Rosslyn, Virginia. His 25-year career in communications includes journalism, book publishing, public relations, and publicity and promotion.

CHAPTER 20

COALITION BUILDING

JOHN J. MAHLMANN

Since the 1980s, associations with public policy goals have become increasingly vigorous in pursuing their agendas; they seek to head off or reinforce emerging trends—or to create new ones. Association staffers with "public affairs" duties in their job descriptions have become commonplace.

In policy-related areas, the usual approach to creating change is through lobbying—a focused effort that provides legislators and other decision makers with information and arguments aimed at persuading them to vote one way, while pointing out the consequences of voting the other way.

Lobbying efforts tend to be highly targeted and narrowly defined by the specific interests of the organization doing the lobbying. A lobbyist's goals are typically short term: *this* piece of legislation must be defeated, *that* vote must be speeded up, or *another* set of talking points must be delivered to a key legislator.

In the give-and-take of the policy-making process, an effective tool for advocacy is often overlooked—the coalition. The coalition strategy itself is certainly not new. Samuel Gompers employed it effectively early in the 20th century when he redefined the narrow interests of many craft and building trades (for example, plumbers, carpenters, and garment workers) to create the American Federation of Labor. He saw that these trade groups would each benefit more if they defined themselves as members of a single force—skilled workers—above and beyond their identity as practitioners of a specific craft.

The fundamental proposition undergirding all coalitions is simple: People who share a common purpose and perspective can accomplish more when they collaborate than when they pursue narrower interests on their own. Of course, associations themselves are coalitions—members joining together to do more than they can independently. Yet associations often neglect to take their "base coalition"—their members—to what can be a more productive level.

Associations that form coalitions commonly bring together people in the same business or profession. It is fairly easy to identify the common interest of different organizations in the various art forms, or even among some manufacturers in industries as divergent as medical equipment and machine tools. But the possibilities for leverage on issues—and more important, for developing new perspectives on issues that cut across constituencies—are necessarily limited.

A Shared Vision

Coalitions can broaden their self-definitions and their reach by including organizations with interests that run *parallel* with their own or that converge in some areas. That was the case with the formation of the National Coalition of Music Education (NCME), which includes three very different associations:

- Music Educators National Conference (MENC), Reston, Virginia, the *education* association for the nation's public school music teachers. Its mission is to achieve better music instruction in the schools.

- National Association of Music Merchants (NAMM), Carlsbad, California, a national *trade* association comprising local music store owners, music instrument manufacturers (including electronic music), and music publishers. NAMM focuses on helping its members operate successful and profitable businesses.

- National Academy of Recording Arts & Sciences, Inc. (NARAS), Santa Monica, California—the Grammy® Award people—an *industry* association made up of performing artists, music producers, and recording industry craftspersons. The mission of NARAS is to preserve the cultural and financial health of the American recording industry.

As different as their missions are, the three coalition partners agree on one simple point: The future of all three associations depends significantly on healthy and widespread programs of school music. Without those, music teachers would be out of work; band instrument rentals and instrument sales in local music stores would plummet, with a ripple effect on manufacturers, music publishers, and those who do instrument maintenance; and future audiences of recording artists (buyers of compact discs, videos, and concert tickets) would decrease.

A persistent, nationwide erosion of music education, characterized by cuts in both funding and instructional support for school music programs, provided the impetus for the coalition. Increasingly, arts programs operating in financially strapped districts were viewed as expensive "extras." NAMM spotted and identified this development as a future threat to its members and recognized the threat to others as well. Therefore, NAMM joined with the other two associations. Since its founding in 1990, the coalition has succeeded in getting its message before the public and attracting more support for its objectives.

Making It Work

These activities apply to associations that might be considering a coalition strategy:

- **Redefine core issues in terms that appeal to new (and perhaps unlikely) allies.** This is the organizational equivalent of "thinking outside the box." Instead of identifying allies from among fellow travelers on familiar paths, look off to the side of the road. In the music coalition, for example, NAMM members had never before viewed educators or entertainers as their natural allies; while NAMM focused on helping members in their businesses, music teachers were not businesspeople nor was their association profit-oriented. For its part, MENC's natural allies were other educators and their associations, who communicated well in "schoolspeak." They saw the decline in school music as a professional and cultural disaster, not an economic problem. As for NARAS, because of its constituency's strong concern about royalties, copyright issues, and the role of music in the entertainment business, it had more in common with people in book publishing and the movie industry than with educators, instrument manufacturers, or store owners.

Whatever the predictable interests of their constituencies, the three associations all had a vital stake in creating more music makers. This was the redefining proposition that made it possible to see many issues as part of the same issue. In other words, the redefinition created a new set of stakeholders.

Once MENC could see the future of music education in terms of creating music makers—not just espousing the importance of music education or the professional development of teachers—new advocacy possibilities opened up immediately. Once NARAS could see beyond promoting the recording industry and acknowledge that building and strengthening a musical infrastructure was necessary for tomorrow's audiences, it could envision a new role for many of its members—especially nationally known performers who could serve as spokespersons for music education. And once NAMM could think in terms of creating the next generation of its members' customers—not just selling to the current generation—local music store owners became catalysts for coalition building at the community and school levels.

- **Create an immediate focus.** Both to generate energy and sustain involvement, coalitions need an action focus. For NCME, that focus came in the form of a 60-member National Commission on Music Education. Its purpose was to define issues, make contact with decision makers, issue a national report, and attract public attention.

MENC recruited presidents and CEOs of about a dozen leading education associations, both within and outside the arts, to serve as commission mem-

Unique Contributions

Based on their members and missions, the three associations that form the National Coalition for Music Education each contribute something different to the joint effort.

MENC	NAMM	NARAS
• Strong content expertise in music education	• Business sense	• High public visibility
• Respect of educators' experience	• Strong focus on outcomes; bottom-line orientation	• National public relations capabilities
• Entree to other allies in education	• Involvement in music beyond the schools	• Market orientation

bers. NAMM brought in leading members (both individuals and companies) from the music products business, and NARAS persuaded more than a score of famous recording artists to join the commission and serve as advocates in a publicity campaign. Five members of Congress and a U.S. senator, all known for a personal commitment to the arts, signed on as well, as did a number of luminaries from the nation's cultural and higher education communities.

The commission sponsored regional meetings in Los Angeles, Chicago, and Nashville, with appropriate press coverage and local radio interviews, to hear testimony from parents, teachers, students, school administrators, music store owners, performers, university professors, and politicians on the state of music education and its prospects. The commission's final report, *Growing Up Complete: The Imperative for Music Education*, was released nationally and presented at a 1991 conference titled "America's Culture at Risk."

From that point forward, the commission's recommendations became the programmatic floor beneath the coalition's agenda, in the form of three broad goals:

1. Every child in every school should receive a balanced sequential, high-quality program of music, taught by certified music teachers.

2. Every school should receive what it is entitled to: The full support of local musicians, music organizations, indeed, the entire music community, in its efforts to provide high-quality music education.

3. Every community should have in place policies and strategies to ensure that music education in the schools is integrated with significant opportunities for music experiences, through such community resources as music groups, vocal and instrumental concerts, and theaters.

The motto devised for the report and later adopted by the coalition succinctly summed up the goals: "Just as there can be no music without education, no education is complete without music. Music makes the difference."

Of course, creating a "National Commission on Our Problem" is not a strategy open to all coalitions, nor is it necessarily the most effective in getting people's attention. Coalitions forming around different issues and goals might register equal success with a press campaign, a video campaign, the creative use of an Internet home page, or a well-orchestrated and publicized event.

Because what was happening to music education was part of the larger education-reform picture, the coalition next linked its efforts to the work of the arts education community across the United States. As for any coalition, the strategic concern was finding the right issue to hang the argument on. For NCME, that issue arose when the arts were omitted from the list of core academic subjects in the National Education Goals.

That omission became the coalition's "soapbox." An education in music and the other arts, the coalition insisted again and again, is not an "extra"; it is essential to what it means to be an educated human being. The skills that an education in the arts teaches directly—for example, problem-posing and problem-solving, self-discipline, and cooperation—are valuable workplace skills.

As the coalition built its own network of advocacy for music education around these points, it attracted new allies in its campaigns to have the arts included in the National Education Goals and, later, to develop the National Standards for Arts Education.

- **Build from the bottom up, not the top down.** For all its importance in initiating action, the national commission was short-lived: Its job was to make recommendations for other people to carry out, period. The real work was left to the coalition itself.

Even as the national commission was holding its hearings, NCME had begun building a network of state and local coalitions to focus on these five goals:

1. Rescuing music programs in trouble.

2. Building parent advocacy networks for school music programs.

3. Building pressure for including music and the other arts in the National Education Goals and the Goals 2000 legislation.

4. Creating a favorable climate for adoption of the National Standards for Arts Education.

5. Publicizing state and local efforts.

By the end of 1994, coalitions had been established in 40 states. Materials available to them included an Action Kit for Music Education; an organizing manual; three videos; a host of feature articles placed in local newspapers and magazines; brochures, fact sheets, and leaflets; a monthly national newsletter; and a speakers bureau featuring coalition leaders.

The most important resource in any local political campaign is shoe leather—people talking to people they know, telling others what's at stake, describing why it's in their interest to act, and enlisting their support. The grassroots efforts of coalition members rippled outward until the ripples intersected and created waves at the state and national levels.

- **Maintain visibility.** Although a "behind the scenes" strategy is sometimes called for, visibility is important when public pressure is a key to success. After its initial splash, a coalition has to stay visible if it is to remain effective. NCME accomplished this in a dramatic way on the night of the 1992 Grammy Awards, when the NARAS president gave the customary welcoming speech. With approximately 1 billion TV viewers tuned in, he reminded the audience of the importance of an education in music and the other arts. In part, he said, "If current trends persist, music will no longer be a universal entitlement, but one of the markers future historians point to as the beginning of a cultural caste system tied to personal and class economics.... [I]f a child has never been inspired by a poem, if a kid has never been moved to tears by a great symphonic work...why on earth should we believe that our future generations could even be bothered by the banning of records or the burning of books?"

A week later, the coalition's local organizing efforts paid off when a choral music teacher in Maryville, Tennessee, opened her students' spring concert with an empty stage. She commented to the audience and local newspapers that, "If the arts are not included as part of Goals 2000, then maybe by the year 2000, there will be no honors course in chorus"—and created an auditorium of concerned parents. Then-Secretary of Education Lamar Alexander (a Maryville native and piano player) immediately reopened the policy discussion about core subjects by launching a "National Arts Education Partnership." That eventually led, on Secretary Richard Riley's watch, to the addition of the arts to the list of core subject areas in the Clinton Administration's *Goals 2000: Educate America Act of 1994.*

Not every coalition will have access to a platform like the Grammy Awards for its message. But local venues of one kind or another are within every coalition's reach. The lesson of visibility applies at any organizational level.

- **Never stop organizing.** All planning and activity must be jointly executed, which requires some form of central coordination to keep everyone's efforts on point and moving toward the agreed-upon goals and objectives. Some sort of "coalition central" must be empowered to act on behalf of the partners in carrying out activities that advance the group's goals.

Associations unaccustomed to anything but "lone eagle" status may find this the most difficult part of coalition building. After all, most groups do not relish a process that may put their good name at risk or place their resources into the hands of people who have only recently been relative strangers.

NCME approached these issues from three directions. First, a great deal of time was spent up front in defining the nature of the associations' commitment, stating clear goals, and deciding who would be in charge of what. As discussions continued, the trust level rose, partly because the commitment level was so high. Each partner wanted to make the coalition work.

Second, the CEOs and boards of the three associations were all highly committed to the coalition. That commitment was strengthened as each CEO repeatedly defined the coalition effort for his own members through journal articles, letters to members, and speeches. Frequent strategy sessions, memos, and e-mail messages kept all decision makers current and served as an early-warning system about potential disagreements.

Third, the coalition was well-staffed. NAMM "loaned" its director of market development and an administrative assistant; they worked almost exclusively on coalition matters. This staff also had access to resources and personnel at each of the three organizations. As needs arose, "borrowed" MENC and NARAS staff worked on everything from organizing conferences and meetings, to creating PSAs, to preparing the coalition newsletter, to writing press releases. As part of their job description, staff also took responsibility for making sure all partners were involved in all important decisions.

This informal arrangement continues. The coalition still has no staff of its own; it lives on borrowed time and a borrowed budget. Each partner continues to take responsibility for its share of coalition activity and expense.

- **Figure out financing.** Although the financing pattern adopted by NCME may not be universally applicable, it bears consideration. The partners contributed staff time, space, and office overhead; a separate office housing the coalition effort was not necessary, nor was a separate budget. Each coalition partner simply created one or more line items within its own budget.

In the case of NCME, running a National Commission on Music Education and its hearings, mounting two national conferences, producing several videos, sustaining a continuing publications effort, and supporting coast-to-coast travel have not been a low-budget exercise. But even though the time and monetary contributions of the partners were sometimes unequal, the differences never caused anyone to pull rank. From the outset, all the partners recognized that creating a new organizational bureaucracy and budget could become counterproductive. Instead, they determined to make NCME a priority for each association's mission and to support it from within their own organizations.

- **Learn to laugh.** The wall of pride surrounding each organization was broken through early on, as all three partners realized that the true gift of partnership is greater flexibility and its true grace is laughter. These truths became evident with the first conference sponsored by the National Commission on Music Education. Not only did a keynote speaker—an international music personality—fail to show but the hotel's lunch turned out to be a disaster. And 20,000 reports came back from the printer on the morning of an important conference with an error and had to be replaced that day. With that conference behind it, the coalition knew it could survive.

- **Stay focused on the issues.** Early successes were followed by others, particularly a National Summit on Music Education, which NCME held in 1994 together with a new partner, the American Music Conference. It brought together more than 100 association presidents and executives and business leaders to develop strategies for building on gains already made in professional development, teacher preparation, curriculum, opportunity to learn, and partnerships for advocacy.

And, in 1996, NCME orchestrated special screenings of *Mr. Holland's Opus,* a feature film that focuses on music education. Leading decision makers, educators, community leaders, and representatives from the arts community were invited to attend the premieres, which were used both as information sessions and to recruit these individuals to the cause.

The coalition has endured because of its emphasis on "kid issues" (learning about and experiencing music and the other arts) rather than "grown-up issues" (teachers' jobs, a music store's profits, or protecting organizational and academic turf). What brought the associations together in the first place continues to inspire them.

NCME's success does not mean that the coalition strategy will work for everyone, although it will probably work for many more than have tried it. But clearly, what the associations have achieved together could never have been achieved separately.

References

Bovet, Sara Fry, "Leading Companies Turn to Trade Associations for Lobbying," *Public Relations Journal,* Vol. 50, No. 7 (August 1995).

Bruhn, Karl, "Advocacy: Getting to How-To,'" in Bruce O. Boston, ed., *Perspectives on Implementation: Arts Education Standards for America's Students,* Music Educators National Conference, Reston, Virginia, 1994.

Ornstein, Norman J., *Interest Groups, Lobbying, and Policymaking.*

Wilson, James Q., *Political Organizations.*

John J. Mahlmann is executive director of the Music Educators National Conference, Reston, Virginia.

CHAPTER 21

COMMUNITY SERVICE

RANDY SCHOOLS, CAE

The needs of your association and society go hand in hand: If society is better, your association will be better. Given the pervasiveness of the problems affecting society, neither government, nor business, nor the nonprofit sector on its own can make the world a better place. Yet if all the sectors become involved, each bringing its own management style and creativity to the table, the team can effectively address the problems.

The American Red Cross and the Salvation Army are just two of the well-known nonprofit organizations dedicated to serving people in need. More than 1 million other organizations exist throughout the United States, addressing issues that range from child abuse to homelessness, from education to disaster relief, and many others.

Trade associations and professional societies have a special responsibility to their philanthropic "sister" organizations—their members often have the expertise, resources, and contacts that community-based groups need to survive and grow. By getting involved in these organizations—whether by serving on the board or volunteering at an event—association staff and members can bring a valuable business orientation. In return, they'll be personally enriched by the experience of helping others, have opportunities to develop their leadership skills, and will become more capable citizens.

The association itself benefits through enhanced visibility within the community, improved morale and camaraderie among volunteers and staff, and the development of an internal value system that puts a premium on giving something back to the community. Too, the association will become stronger because volunteers and staff will have faced the challenges associated with developing new skills and having new experiences.

Some associations provide direct financial support to philanthropic organizations, either by matching employee contributions or providing in-kind services such as public relations or legal advice. Other in-kind services might include assisting with printing costs or handling newsletter design and production.

Doing Good

Many members of the corporate community have developed long-term relationships with nonprofit organizations—for instance, General Electric and Mobil have sponsored many series on public television, while Coca-Cola and Kodak have given continued support to the Olympics. Associations may not have the same name recognition, but the projects they support are equally important. Here are just a few examples:

- In 1988, the American Apparel Manufacturers Association (AAMA), Arlington, Virginia, created the Apparel Foundation to facilitate and increase donations of surplus apparel to homeless people in this country and to disaster victims around the world.

- The Minnesota Medical Association (MMA), Minneapolis, launched its "Stop Violence" campaign to teach consumers about the unique role physicians can play in domestic-abuse situations.

   The campaign recruited a local celebrity as a spokesperson; developed posters, billboards, and bumper stickers; and aired public service announcements on more than 90 radio stations. Their message: Victims should talk to their physicians when confronted with domestic violence. Additionally, diagnostic guidelines and referral numbers were sent to all state physicians, clinics, and hospitals, and judges were trained on what to look for in court.

- "Reaching Out '91," sponsored by the Georgia Society of Association Executives (GSAE), Tucker, challenged every member to volunteer at least eight hours. To facilitate placement of volunteers, GSAE created a matchmaker program that paired members and suppliers with service organizations seeking assistance. Members pledged a total of 48,000 volunteer hours, exceeding the goal by more than 3,500 hours.

A Broad Base of Needs

Here are just a few of the many community groups with which associations could get involved:

1. Youth
   — Boys and Girls Clubs
   — Big Brothers and Big Sisters
   — Child Welfare League
   — Boy Scouts and Girl Scouts
   — Junior Achievement
   — YMCA and YWCA

2. Arts
   — Arts councils
   — Theater groups
   — Community theaters
   — Opera company
   — Youth in the arts programs

3. Senior Citizens
   — Meals on Wheels
   — Nursing homes
   — Senior partnership programs

4. Environment
   — Wilderness protection groups
   — Zoo programs
   — Recycling campaigns

5. Society at Large
   — Homeless shelters
   — Shelters for victims of domestic abuse
   — Habitat for Humanity
   — Free clinics

- Through Project Our Home, members of the Wisconsin Manufactured Housing Association, Madison, donated old mobile homes to state prisons. After inmates had refurbished the mobile homes with both purchased and donated materials—learning job skills in the process—the renovated units were given or sold to low-income families.
- When it learned that the state had 4,000 backlogged cases related to child welfare, the Oklahoma Public Employees Association (OPEA), Oklahoma City, coordinated statewide hearings to increase awareness about resources available to protect children. Testimony from more than 200 citizens convinced the state's youth commission to hire nearly 100 additional child-welfare employees. The State Department of Human Services agreed to pay overtime to other social workers to bring cases up to date, and within 30 days the backlog of cases had disappeared.

Getting Involved

"To help assist society with its needs" is not a phrase that appears in many association mission statements. Therefore, whatever an association undertakes is done out of responsibility to the local community and society at large. Here are some suggestions for launching a community service program:

- **Appoint a leader.** Look for a staff member or volunteer who is talented, creative, and ripe for leadership responsibility. Choose someone who will expect, and therefore foster, success. He or she typically works with a committee of staff or volunteers.
- **Select committee members.** Committees are an excellent training ground for future leaders within the organization. Members should make a commitment to developing a long-range strategy that will allow the association to be known for its innovation in solving problems.
- **Involve the leadership.** Staff leaders, as well as the executive committee and board of directors, should support the concept of community service and be willing to devote the labor and financial resources to initiating a project.
- **Select a project.** The committee should investigate numerous possibilities before deciding who and how the association can assist. Some types of projects may prove too controversial to consider, while others might offer a natural fit. A group of professional communicators, for instance, might address literacy issues; an association representing foodservice establishments might get involved with food banks.

For ideas, the community service committee could check with the local United Way or volunteer clearinghouse to find out which groups have the most significant needs for volunteers. The community service committee should meet two or three times to discuss possibilities before selecting a project and setting up a timetable for its implementation. Some associations work with the same nonprofit or for the same cause year after year, while others designate a new project each year or two.

The committee should also consider whether assistance will be ongoing or a one-time effort. Some associations, for example, sponsor a volunteerism-oriented "work day" in conjunction with their annual meetings; during the rest of the year, these groups encourage staff and members to become involved on their own.

- **Be flexible.** Community service volunteers may have a definite idea of how they'd like to be involved—which may not match what the philanthropic or social service organization really needs. Be prepared to assist with these types of activities:

  — Addressing envelopes, creating posters, and typing information.

  — Marketing the organization through telephone calls to possible members.

  — Providing direct service, such as cooking or serving food or being a companion.

  — Offering operational and financial expertise, especially in the area of fund raising.

  — Publicizing the nonprofit by contacting local television, radio, and newspaper reporters.

  — Planning special events, which might range from a black-tie dinner and dance to a chili cook-off. A silent auction, a popular fund-raising effort, can benefit greatly from an association's contacts with local businesses and suppliers.

- **Publicize the commitment.** Not only members want to know the good that their association has done. Word should also reach the local community and the association community through traditional public relations vehicles.

- **Evaluate your efforts.** By gathering information on the strengths and weaknesses of a community service program, you'll be able to make better decisions regarding continuation or modification. In addition, the board of directors may be interested in the return on the association's investment of time and possibly resources. True, benefits can be difficult to measure in dollars and cents, but focus on results such as skills development, public relations, and volunteers' satisfaction levels.

When considering whether to change or adjust a community service program, other questions to answer are:

— Was the environment safe for participants and staff?

— Was the length and timing of the program appropriate?

— Did the program attract and maintain people's interest?

— Were enough financial resources allocated to the program so it could reach its goals?

— How can the committee be designed better for next year?

Randolph R. Schools, CAE, is president and chief executive officer of the Recreation & Welfare Association in Bethesda, Maryland. He is the co-founder of three nonprofits: Special Love—Camp Fantastic, Friends of the Clinical Center, and Children's Inn at NIH.

CHAPTER 22

EDUCATION PROGRAMS

RALPH J. NAPPI, CAE

The very purpose of an association—enabling people to achieve common goals, meet common needs, or solve common problems—is realized through the sharing of information, networking, or joining together for a common good. In many associations, education programs help achieve that purpose. Through their educational efforts, associations help members to better comprehend complex issues, learn the latest information shaping their business or profession, hear about developing trends, and have a source for the continual learning needed to keep pace with today's fast rate of change.

Adult Learning

Malcolm Knowles, a researcher and scientist, noted that adults and children need to be taught differently because they have different approaches to learning. He identified the adult approach as *andragogy*, which directly involves the student in the design, implementation, and evaluation of the learning experience. *Pedagogy* is the approach used with children; it emphasizes the role of the teacher in designing, delivering, and evaluating the educational process.

Additional research by Knowles identified these distinctions between children and adults:

1. **The need to know**—When adults set about learning something, they have a desire to know what they will gain by learning it.

2. **The learner's self-concept**—Adults are more intentional in their learning.

3. **The role of experience**—Adults bring a wealth of experience to the learning event, whether from a life experience, career advancement, or professional development.

4. **Readiness to learn**—At a particular moment, a unique set of factors converge to create an environment that prepares adults to learn.

5. **Orientation of learning**—Children's education is subject-centered. Adults, however, approach a learning event seeking solutions to problems they've experienced and answers to questions they have.

6. **Motivation**—Adults are personally motivated to learn due to varying aspects of their respective environments.

The term *education* refers to the system and process in which learning takes place—in other words, the form of learning. In an association, education often ranges from conferences and seminars to workshops and expositions. From a marketing perspective, one advantage associations have is that they can provide knowledge and skill training specific to an industry or profession, which may not be met through other sources such as on-the-job training, schools, home-study courses, and computer-based studies.

Another advantage for associations is that the members learn with their peers—they share the same profession or industry and have similar expertise and backgrounds as the other learners.

Needs Assessment

There's a difference between what your members need and what they want—a distinction that's important when determining what type of education programs your association should offer, when, where, and in what format. Industry trends, the sophistication level of respondents, and environmental forces can help determine the difference. You'll need to factor them in when interpreting and analyzing the data from a needs assessment.

The most common way to assess educational needs is to conduct a mail survey. Whether developed internally or outsourced, the survey instrument should contain questions that are free of response bias. Other survey methods include focus groups, personal interviews, and telephone interviews (for more information on conducting research, see Chapter 15).

Consider using a combination of approaches, as no one method of data collection is as credible as a mix. Also, when selecting a sample size, favor a larger and more varied sample; the more responses you have, the more ways you can divide the data for analysis and discussion.

Demographic data to be gathered may include type of member (or nonmember), job function, number of years in the trade or profession, number of employees, geographic location, and other associations in which currently involved. This type of data may help determine inconsistencies or similarities among the sample group. Also, questions relating to logistics, budget, and education delivery are helpful in determining how the association should provide the program and in what format. Consider having survey participants prioritize their needs so you'll know what programs offer the best chance for success.

While it is important to acknowledge the opinions of nonmembers or inactive members (those with a low participation history), placing the same weight on their responses as on those of active members would skew the data used for decision making.

When analyzing the results of the needs assessment, you may find that respondents aren't necessarily aware of trends in their field or know how to prepare for the future. Then you must interpret the results and offer programs that will fulfill those unanticipated needs.

Program Design and Development

This step challenges you to:

- Select a program topic that meets the needs identified by the member assessment.
- Create measurable learning objectives and outcomes.
- Select an appropriate delivery system. Education and training can be provided through seminars, workshops, conferences, short courses, symposiums, computer-based learning, institutes, and forums.
- Determine instructional strategies. A variety of instructional techniques can be employed, including lectures, role playing, demonstrations, and case studies. You'll also have a choice of instructors, ranging from speakers and facilitators to consultants and skill trainers. If motivation is a program objective, consider hiring a professional speaker; if relaying information germane to the industry or profession is the primary objective, members can serve as speakers.
- Design a program that also accounts for such factors as budget, logistics, site, and format.

In designing a program, remember that you are dealing with adult learners. They will have varying degrees of expectations, depending on their background, experience, type of employer, and personal objectives for participation. Adult learners comprehend and retain information better when it is gained through informal and experiential-based learning.

Assisting Speakers

Even if he or she is an expert in the subject area to be addressed, a speaker isn't necessarily familiar with the target audience. By providing speakers with the following information, you can ensure their presentations will match the needs of attendees:

- **General background on the industry or profession.** Describe current challenges and opportunities, specific terminology or buzzwords, and any audience sensitivities, such as topics to avoid. Also provide historical background about the association. An excellent way to familiarize speakers with the association and the field it represents is to have them talk with several members in preparation for their presentation.
- **Context of the presentation.** Describe the meeting's or program's theme, purpose, and objectives. Mention other speakers and their topics, specific objectives the speaker should meet, and how the program was promoted.
- **Audience profile.** Offer information on members' education level, experience, average age, gender, and job titles. Also anticipate the size of the audience, along with any special guests who may attend and thereby affect the speaker's message (for instance, media representatives or government officials).

To increase the audience's retention of information, encourage speakers to reinforce their messages with handout materials and audiovisual aids—such as slides or computer-image projections for larger groups, overhead transparencies or videotapes for smaller groups, or flip charts for interactive sessions. For larger meetings, the availability of "ready rooms" allows speakers to prepare and review their slides and notes before the actual presentation.

Budgeting

Before finalizing any aspects of an education program, the association must determine if it will be a subsidized, break-even, or profitable activity. The financial framework for this decision making consists of fixed costs and variable costs.

Fixed costs include items such as room rental, audiovisual equipment rental, speaker honoraria, travel expenses for speakers and staff, and promotional materials. *Variable costs*, which depend upon the number of participants, are primarily related to food and beverage expenditures and handouts, such as conference proceedings and copies of presentation visuals.

Speaker fees can represent a substantial portion of the overall fixed costs. However, a presenter (especially the sole speaker for a workshop, seminar, videoconference, or audiotaped program) who is also involved in marketing the program may be interested in negotiating a tiered honoraria schedule based upon the number of actual participants.

Marketing and Promotion

Attention should be paid to the marketing and promotion component early in the program development phase, along with the needs assessment and choice of delivery system. The identification of the audience and how the program is packaged and priced are integral parts of the marketing plan.

In the past, many associations have enjoyed the position of being the only or the primary source for their industry's or profession's adult education. A more competitive marketplace has evolved, however, which requires a proactive approach to getting members to attend programs.

Although brochures and direct mail remain the core of most education marketing and promotion plans, telemarketing and direct sales have grown in importance. In an effort to control the escalating costs of developing and offering educational programming, some organizations use beta sites (test markets) to try out new topics and approaches.

Targeted marketing via computer-generated data can be effective for associations because they already have specific demographic

ADA Requirements

Although individuals with disabilities may experience limitations in some areas, they are not limited as learners. Their needs are as important as those of any other learner. In fact, under the Americans with Disabilities Act (ADA), the association has the responsibility to make "reasonable accommodations" for participants with disabilities.

Reasonable accommodations may include sign language interpretation, Braille handouts, special meals, and aides for the hearing impaired, to name a few. The meeting planner is required to make a reasonable attempt to provide such accommodations. The person with the disability has the responsibility to provide adequate notice so that the necessary arrangements can be made. Most associations request that attendees highlight such needs on their registration materials.

information about their members and customers. Associations also have the advantage of a high level of credibility among members, who have already demonstrated a commitment to the organization by paying dues.

Implementation and Management

All the best planning, needs analysis, and marketing can be negated if attention to details and on-site logistics are not properly handled. Many associations employ professional meeting planners to concentrate on this area, which encompasses site selection, room set-up, registration, air and ground transportation, shipping, food and beverage functions, and audiovisual contracts. It also includes instructor orientation and training and contracting with hotels, convention centers, or other meeting facilities.

Room set-up, like the meeting location, will vary depending upon the objective of the meeting and the number of participants. For larger and more formal meetings, classroom and auditorium-style arrangements work well; smaller or interactive groups usually prefer a roundtable, U-shaped, or conference-style set-up. (For specific information on meeting planning, see Chapter 27.)

The person charged with planning meetings must be detail-oriented and have the physical and mental stamina necessary to deal with the last-minute changes—such as medical emergencies, speaker no-shows, inclement weather, technological glitches, and transportation difficulties—that inevitably arise during education programs. Extensive planning makes a program successful, but even the best-laid plans are susceptible to adjustments and changes.

Evaluation and Review

It's easy to breathe a sigh of relief once the program has concluded and you've packed your bags to head home. But an important activity still remains: evaluating and reviewing the educational program.

The evaluation process identifies, collects, interprets, and provides information for the purpose of judging effectiveness and the future of the program. Questionnaires and surveys tend to be the most popular vehicles for gathering feedback, but interviews and focus groups also provide useful results. Evaluations can also be done with written examinations, performance tests, and general observation.

Whatever its format, the evaluation instrument should ask about how well objectives were met, the presenter's level of competence, and the items needed for program improvement. More specifically, here are nine areas of an educational program to evaluate:

1. Program content
2. Instructional methods
3. Handout materials
4. Instructor/speaker diversity

5. Facility

6. Design and structure of the program

7. Knowledge gained

8. Attitude behavior changes of the participant

9. Effect on the participant's organization

In general, there are two types of evaluations. A *summative* evaluation focuses on the program's overall effectiveness; it enables you to document program accomplishments, determine the degree to which program objectives and member needs were realized, justify the allocation of staff and financial resources, provide opportunities for membership participation, identify program weaknesses and strengths, and assist in future programming decisions. A *formative* evaluation deals with program improvements, particularly during the event itself.

In addition, evaluation takes place at four different levels. *Level 1* involves participants' reactions—how well did they like the program? This is generally where most associations stop. *Level 2* addresses the knowledge gained; it assesses what principles, facts, and techniques were learned. *Level 3* analyzes behavioral changes. It documents changes in behavior resulting from the program. *Level 4* examines organizational consequences by studying the tangible benefits of the program to the participant's business or employer.

Although evaluations can occur before, during, or after a program, many associations find that on-site evaluations at the end of the program provide the highest return. This method, however, may also involve a greater level of subjective responses as compared to responses from a mailed evaluation. On-site participants tend to be affected by the "motivational high" that occurs immediately following a speaker's closing. A mailed survey allows participants time to reflect on the program and might render more realistic evaluations.

The results of evaluations provide a basis for continuing, adjusting, or eliminating the program. Although program evaluation is the final phase of the education cycle, it is not complete until the data have been compiled and the program enhancements determined. Many associations provide the results to the staff, leaders, and attendees as a courtesy and to promote further discussion for future programs.

Trade Shows

Association-sponsored trade shows enable marketers to display or demonstrate their goods and services to prospective buyers. This type of informal education program may be held independently or in conjunction with an association meeting or convention. It may range from a half-day "table top" event meant to educate more than sell to a multi-day event that provides exhibitors with major marketing opportunities. This is often a good opportunity for organizations to provide educational programs to exhibitors; such programs generally focus on marketing and sales techniques for trade shows or on trends specific to the industry or profession, which are provided to assist vendors in marketing their products.

Although many educational programs are subsidized by associations as part of their overall mission, trade shows tend to be financially rewarding. In fact, excess revenues help to underwrite many other association programs and services. Trade shows offer many opportunities to conduct business and have become an important time for decision making and purchasing. These activities supplement the educational aspects that trade shows have always provided, particularly by identifying new products, services, and technologies available to the trade or profession. (For more information on trade show planning and logistics, see Chapter 27.)

The Use of Technology

New technologies can provide a multitude of advantages, including quickly disseminating urgent information, reducing participants' costs, and enlarging the reach of educational programs. But before making a commitment to using technology, consider members' receptivity; your association's ability to manage new technology; and the fact that not all topics, speakers, and information lend themselves to technological applications.

Options include the following:

- **Computer-based training.** The computer screen may display just text or the latest in high-resolution graphics, sound, and video. Usually the computer presents displays to the learner, then responds to his or her input in various ways.

- **CD-ROM (Compact Disk-Read Only Memory).** This offers a means of storing vast quantities of computer data, particularly the large files needed for video and audio.

- **CD-Interactive (CDI).** This specialized version of CD-ROM can be played on ordinary televisions, using special equipment. The advantage is that people without home computers can use multi-media CD-ROM programs to make television viewing more interactive.

- **Virtual reality.** Together, a computer and multi-media create the illusion of being inside a world that actually exists in the bits and bytes of computer software.

- **Video-based training.** Many instructors show videotapes in their classes to explain information, demonstrate skills and techniques, or establish a starting point for discussions.

- **Satellite communications.** This technology enables you to simultaneously send educational programs to groups of people all over the country. After the broadcast has concluded, an on-site facilitator or teacher engages each site in active learning activities. Or, computer networks or electronic bulletin board systems can be used to supplement the satellite teleconference; experts and teachers can be available online to answer questions or lead discussions.

- **Videoconferencing.** Using telephone lines, you send video pictures from point to point or even link several sites at once.

- **Electronic networks.** The Internet, World Wide Web, and commercial online services are examples of how personal computers and other technologies can be linked and controlled via computer.
- **Desktop conferencing.** Similar to videoconferencing, this technology connects two or more people via their computers. It is similar to a telephone conference call, but in addition to a voice connection you are able to send computer data over the same lines at the same time.

In considering these technologies as possible delivery systems, the message, speaker capability, participant receptivity, facility arrangements, and costs are all important considerations. In fact, the message to be delivered—not the technology itself—is the primary reason driving the use of one of these technologies.

References

Convention Liaison Council, *The Convention Liaison Council Manual,* 6th ed., Washington, D.C., 1994.

American Society of Association Executives, *Association Education Handbook,* Washington, D.C., 1984.

——, *The Association Educators Tool Kit,* Washington, D.C., 1995.

——, *Principles of Association Management,* 2nd ed., Washington, D.C., 1990.

Cox, John B., and Andrew Cohn, "Continuing Education Goes On-Line," *Association Management,* June 1996, American Society of Association Executives, Washington, D.C.

Ingram, Albert L., "Teaching with Technology," *Association Management,* June 1996, American Society of Association Executives, Washington, D.C.

Ralph J. Nappi, CAE, president of the American Machine Tool Distributors Association (AMTDA), Rockville, Maryland, entered the association field in 1981. He previously served as AMTDA's vice president and as director of education and communication.

CHAPTER 23

PUBLISHING PROFESSIONAL MAGAZINES, BOOKS, AND OTHER MEDIA

DEBRA J. STRATTON

Association publications have power—the power to create and maintain an association's image, enhance its credibility within the industry or profession, and establish it as a valuable source of information. Publications link an association with its members, keeping the association viable and visible as competition for members' time and attention grows more intense. And as the need for nondues sources of income also grows, publications can provide added revenues from advertising, subscriptions, sponsorships, and more in both print and electronic form.

The most effective association publishing programs develop a variety of publications that appeal to members' special interests and needs. Arriving at the right mix of publications means adapting to the ever-changing interests and concerns of association members, whether they require a comprehensive textbook on the profession, an in-depth magazine, or an electronic online newsletter. It also requires an understanding of members and their information needs, a clear vision of the association's goals and overall mission, well-defined publishing objectives, and a strategic marketing plan for achieving those objectives.

General Guidelines for a Publishing Operation

Most professional societies and trade organizations promote their publications as the major benefit of membership—with good reason. When asked to rank important association services, members typically place publications at or near the top of the list. The association's newsletter, magazine, or journal represents a tangible benefit to members and reminds them of what the association accomplishes on their behalf. Publications may, in fact, be the only link some members have with an association or society. Given their important role, publications need to be timely, authoritative, credible, well-designed, highly readable, and carefully focused on members' needs.

Understanding those specialized needs begins with an objective and fundamental understanding of your readers: Who are your members? What kind of information do they need and want from your association? Too many associations rely on gut feelings or the views of their leaders in deciding these critical issues instead of regularly conducting basic research to objectively understand readers' needs.

A comprehensive membership or readership survey will provide basic information, including a profile of the average reader and his or her preference for various types of information, such as late-breaking news, developing trends, or issue analyses. Focus groups, informal surveys, letters to the editor, conversations at meetings, and other less formal vehicles for getting feedback can further clarify information needs and help the editor shape a publication that fills a special niche, rather than duplicating what other publications already provide.

Publishing with a Purpose

Every publication—whether a magazine, a fax newsletter, or a book—needs a written statement of purpose: three or four sentences that describe the target audience, the types of information to be included, and the overall goals of the publication. The editorial mission statement might include statements such as, "To keep members up to date on legislative and regulatory developments," "To help members improve job performance by providing practical information," or "To inform members about association activities."

While three out of five associations lack any written publishing objectives, according to the 1991 *Association Publishing Procedures* survey commissioned by the American Society of Association Executives (ASAE), Washington, D.C., successful publications are careful to define their purpose for both readers and advertisers and to communicate the purpose to top management, staff, and elected leaders. A statement of purpose is the basis for determining what goes into a publication and measuring how effective a publication is in meeting its objectives. A vague understanding of publishing goals leads to unfocused editorial content and confusion among readers, advertisers, and outside audiences. Worse yet, it can lead to battles between staff and volunteers over what is appropriate for the publication.

To avoid misunderstandings and unneeded conflicts, and to ensure staff know what is expected of them, develop a written statement of purpose for each periodical, review and update it regularly, and share it with readers, staff, and volunteers. Then use it to judge what does—and does not—belong in the publication.

It is not uncommon for association staff and leadership to disagree on a publication's purpose, especially if the publication is advertiser-supported. Some prefer a "house organ" that reports on association activities and services, while others believe strongly in the need for an independent trade or professional publication. Often a general membership newsletter serves as the house organ, reporting on association activities, advocating the association perspective, and promoting association services and programs, while the magazine or journal focuses exclusively on the trade or profession. Reports of association activities, if included at all in the magazine or journal, appear in an "Association News" column rather than in the feature well.

Clarifying the distinction between a house organ and an independent magazine is critical for publications that carry advertising and serve a broader audience than just members. Is the publication primarily promotional, reporting on the association, or is it independent, reporting on the industry or profession? The more clarification that can be made initially, the more effective the publication ultimately will be.

Matching Needs and Formats

The type of information and the frequency of communication needed help determine a publication's format. If members are looking for the latest legislative news affecting their profession or their companies, a one-page, fax newsletter distributed to members each Friday, for instance, might be the perfect format. But if members want in-depth case studies on how to apply practices in their own settings, a bimonthly or monthly magazine may be more on target. Consider the function of the communication vehicle as you review your current publication mix or consider launching a new publication then match information needs to the appropriate publication format.

Newsletters are the most common format used by associations, with two out of five organizations reporting they rely on a newsletter as their primary publication (ASAE, 1991). Many associations publish a dozen or more newsletters, each directed to a specialized segment of the membership or to nonmember subscribers. Newsletters are fairly brief—usually ranging from two pages to 16 pages—often simple in design, printed in one or two colors, and written to be scanned quickly. Generally, newsletters do not include paid advertising.

Magazines are a more formal means of communicating with members. With 41 percent of associations using magazines as their primary publication (ASAE, 1991), this format nearly matches newsletters in popularity. Although magazines may contain news sections, their primary purpose is to provide in-depth coverage of selected topics. They vary in size, from as few as 24 pages to more than 200 pages, and often are supported by advertising and less frequently by subscriptions.

Depending upon the publication's purpose and the changing needs of readers, an association may select a different format. **Tabloid newspapers,** for instance, are the primary publication for a relatively few associations (7 percent), yet they appear to be gaining ground. Sometimes referred to as "magapapers" or "newsazines," tabloids typically carry short news items up front and longer feature articles in the back. When publishing budgets tighten, this news/magazine format often proves appealing to smaller associations that cannot produce two separate publications. Medical societies also favor tabloids because the format offers a newsy complement to technical periodicals.

Other print formats include **bulletins**—usually reserved for up-to-the-minute updates on legislative or technical matters—and **journals** that explore technical, scientific, and scholarly topics and report research findings.

The special needs of members may necessitate developing new formats that go beyond traditional print communications, such as **online publications, Web pages,** and **home pages.** In recent years, an online newsletter or an online version of the association's magazine has become increasingly common among associations. The advantage of online publications is their timeliness; the disadvantage may be that the majority of members may not yet be equipped to access the Internet. However, that is quickly changing.

Other formats are also tested. For instance, an association of insurance salespeople found its members spending more time on the road than in the office so it began publishing an **audiotape** version of its monthly journal for members to listen to in their cars. Medical societies, whose members are interested in learning the latest techniques but are not always able to travel to meetings, may opt for a video version of their journal, or a **videojournal,** complete with advertising and printed supplements. More common, especially among technical and medical societies, are **CD-ROM** versions of the scholarly journal, which make searching and accessing research papers much more accessible.

Every organization has different communication needs at different times. The formats and frequencies selected must balance members' needs with the association's financial and staff resources. Furthermore, what's valuable to members must also be efficient for the association. A society of professional photographers, for example, may sacrifice other publications to produce a monthly, four-color magazine that showcases its members' work. An organization of scientists, on the other hand, might have staff produce a bimonthly newsletter but rely on volunteers to prepare a book containing specialized research findings.

Is It Still Relevant?

A publication's format, and even its reason for being, may change over time and must regularly be assessed to ensure the publication remains on target. Publishing staff should periodically review each publication to determine relevance and effectiveness: Is this publication still needed? Would another format better suit members' needs? Or has the publication outlived its purpose? Should it be published more often—or less frequently? Would the information presented in a newsletter be better suited for a magazine? How could the publication be repositioned to be more effective?

Regular, systematic review helps ensure that publications remain healthy. This may include using an outside specialist to conduct a readership study every two years or so or to perform a broader audit of publishing operations. An objective outsider can provide insights into how to structure a publishing program to be more effective.

Periodicals

The average association publishes five types of periodicals, from journals and newsletters to magazines and bulletins, according to a 1989 study conducted by the Society of National Association Publications (SNAP), McLean, Virginia.

Some associations publish twice as many newsletters as magazines, with many of those periodicals sent to fewer than 3,000 readers. No matter what the number produced, the staffs of all successful periodicals must first establish an editorial niche and develop appropriate editorial content to fill that niche.

There are several ways an association can identify industry trends and information of interest to readers. For example, staff can track the information requests the association receives to learn what members ask for. Readers can be interviewed in person by conducting focus groups or taking a "straw poll" at conventions or meetings. And by reading other trade publications, association publishers can stay one step ahead of the competition. This informal research, combined with editorial brainstorming sessions as well as more formal readership research, will help identify the topics and article formats that readers find most useful and appealing.

Other publications may opt to use an editorial board to keep it in touch with a technical field or to serve as a sounding board. Scholarly, scientific, or technical journals commonly use an editorial board, whose members function almost as editors to "peer review" articles before publication. Scholarly journals usually require at least three qualified reviewers to look at a manuscript before sending it to the editor—often a paid outside practitioner—for a final decision. This peer review process helps protect a publication's credibility and integrity.

Even some nontechnical publications turn to an advisory board of volunteers for help in developing editorial content and locating expert authors and interviewees. A board, however, can't effectively manage a publication. Ultimately, the decision on what is published rests with a well-qualified, professional editor and staff—the people who know the readers and know the publication the best.

Building Editorial Content

Just as a publication's statement of purpose serves as its foundation, the articles filling its pages represent the bricks. Consistently well-written, high-quality editorial content builds reader interest and loyalty more than award-winning designs and colorful graphics. To generate the editorial content, an association may rely on a staff of editors and writers, freelance writers, members and suppliers, academicians, government leaders, and others. The content-development process should be continual, with the editor always on the lookout for new topics and different angles.

Editorial content should provide an appropriate mix of articles that appeal to readers with different interests and at different levels of experience. "How to" articles, for instance, may attract readers who are new to the industry or profession or who are investigating the uses of new technology, products, or systems. Case studies examine one person's or organization's problem and how it was solved. One association leader, author, or expert might be the focus of an in-depth interview, while several people might share their opinions in a roundtable discussion or open forum.

Although feature articles are the main attraction in a magazine or journal, departments devoted to ongoing issues are equally important. Departments, or standing columns, form the framework for a newsletter or magazine, giving the reader a familiarity and consistency that helps build reader loyalty. Readers know they can turn to a regular department each month for the latest on legal issues, book reviews, or a calendar of events.

Whether the association has a centralized approach to publishing or whether each division handles its own publications, accuracy and consistency of style is critical for the credibility of the organization. Establish style guidelines for the entire association, and adhere to them in all printed communications. Identify a dictionary and a style guide for grammar and usage that all staff members use as a reference source.

Some associations directly adhere to the standards of one source, such as *Chicago Manual of Style* or *Associated Press Stylebook,* while others identify a basic source and then develop their own modifications or even write their own style guide. Consistency in application is more important than which dictionary or style guide is used. Also, if you frequently use outside contributors to your publications, develop author's guidelines governing an article's length, format, tone, and audience.

Design for Readability

Packaging and presentation of publications—layout and design, paper stock, type face, use of photos and illustrations—are critical to readership. Good design and layout gets a publication noticed; solid editorial content keeps readers. A good design provides the publication with a "personality" that remains consistent from one issue to the next. It relies on an easy-to-read typeface, effective use of white space, and other design elements—such as color, headlines, and sidebars—to draw readers into the publication and keep them moving from one article to another.

Every publication needs a professional design as a starting point. When launching a new publication, for example, the initial design should include a logo/masthead, a front-page treatment, feature article treatments, and treatments for recurring departments and columns. And because design can easily become dated and bore readers, reexamine each publication's design every few years to ensure readers do not become complacent.

Larger associations often hire a full-time graphic designer or art director. Smaller associations that cannot afford this luxury can still produce attractive, readable publications by contracting with a design firm for each issue or by hiring an outside designer to develop a format and design look. The association then implements that design with in-house editorial/production assistants, according to the strict specifications established by the designer.

The in-house, do-it-yourself approach to design has proliferated with the advent of desktop publishing. The advantages to it are increased control, reduced costs, and quicker turnaround. The down side to this technology is that it tends to put design in the hands of untrained editors and production personnel. Mastering the system takes time, and desktop publishing often turns already-overworked editors and production managers into typesetters and designers. It's important to provide staff with appropriate training and continue to seek the advice and services of professional designers to create templates and overall formats that can then be used by in-house production staff to execute the layout.

Production

Decisions related to paper stock, scheduling, and distribution are the responsibility of the production manager. This area of publishing represents a key financial function and requires knowledgeable staff to identify and work with typesetters, printers, color separators, illustrators, and fulfillment houses. The production manager is responsible not only for selecting the most cost-effective ways to produce and distribute publications but also for ensuring quality publications that are distributed according to schedule. To fulfill these needs, production managers need appropriate financial and publishing training to prepare and compare print specifications, determine press runs, and keep current with continually changing technology, as well as with postal and distribution issues.

To maintain credibility with their members and compete with commercial publications, associations must base their production decisions on financial data and strictly adhere to schedules. Making last-minute alterations to camera-ready copy, for example, can dramatically increase production costs and delay distribution. A realistic production schedule accommodates many factors, allowing time for submissions from volunteers and outside writers, fact checking, proofreading, and alterations. Acquainting the entire editorial staff with the production process also helps; seeing firsthand how a magazine is printed should reinforce to staff writers the importance of meeting their deadlines.

Financial Management

Association publishing is a business. Like any business, it needs a financial plan to set goals and to help determine how well the publications department meets those goals. The financial well-being of the publishing operation must become the responsibility of all professional staff involved. Ultimately, however, it is the publisher—often called the editor or executive editor—who is responsible for ensuring the publishing operation meets its financial goals.

Financial management begins with preparing a budget that establishes financial goals for each publication. Although their parent organization may operate as a nonprofit, most association publications seek to generate a profit. Clarify the financial goals to avoid misunderstandings:

- Is the association's intent to break even or to make money?
- How much revenue is expected?
- What level of investment in an existing publication or a start-up publication is the association willing to make over how many years to ensure a high-quality, valued publication?

Build a budget for each publication that takes a fresh look at the entire operation each year. Zero-based budgeting—as opposed to factoring in an across-the-board increase in income and expenses—makes staff reconsider each year how they are approaching the publishing process. To be effective, get as much input from staff and outside sources as possible, review the past performance of established publications, and keep well-informed on possible developments that could affect overall costs or income during the coming year.

For publications that include advertising income, break out the publication budget into two sides—advertising and editorial. The advertising side includes all advertising income and all the costs associated with generating that income. The editorial side includes income from nonmember subscriptions, royalties, reprints, and so forth, as well as all the costs of producing the editorial portion of the publication. To reduce potential tax liabilities, ensure that appropriate expenses are charged against the advertising portion of the publication, including a percent of printing and distribution costs, salaries, overhead, and direct sales expenses.

Once the budget is established, use it as a management tool for controlling expenses and making key decisions. At any given time, the editor should know total production costs for each publication, the per-copy cost, and how each publication is financed (for example, fully subsidized by member dues or partially covered by advertising revenues). Hold key staff accountable for performance by comparing actual and budgeted figures each month, along with projections for year-end. Require staff to explain significant deviances from budget and what is being done to correct any shortfalls.

Some associations offer incentives to key staff for reaching or exceeding budgets. They may employ a Management by Objectives system that provides quarterly reviews of goals, along with revised year-end budget projections. Regardless of the system, the director of publications (or publisher or editor) is responsible for all financial aspects of the publishing operation, including the development of realistic budgets and strategies for meeting those budgets. For instance, if advertising sales dips because of an overall slump in the economy, the director of publications must take steps to reduce the size of issues, to economize on paper stock, cut back on the use of color, and so forth.

Adhering to a predetermined advertising-to-editorial ratio in periodicals ensures advertising revenues will help offset production costs. Even if a magazine or journal does not rely solely on advertising to meet its income goals, having an established advertising-to-editorial ratio (some variation of 50 percent advertising to 50 percent editorial) adds structure and balance to a publication.

Advertising Sales

As pressure mounts to expand nondues sources of income, selling advertising becomes an increasingly popular way to partially or totally underwrite the costs of publishing. Nearly nine out of 10 associations (87.4 percent) sell advertising in at least one of their periodicals (SNAP, 1989). In addition to generating more revenue for the association, advertising lends a look of professionalism to a publication and provides readers with information on the latest services and products available in their field.

The decision to sell advertising is a complex one, based on the market, the interest among prospects in reaching your market, competition for readers, perceived value of the editorial content, and demographics of readers. If you are considering selling advertising in a publication, conduct a feasibility study first to determine whether the potential revenue would sufficiently offset the investments of time and money involved in launching an advertising program.

With the pressures to sell advertising, conflict frequently develops between the editorial and the advertising portions of the publication. The greatest conflict is over issues of editorial integrity and whether to run editorial that is in some way supportive or promotional to advertisers. Credible association publications avoid any suggestion of advertising influence in editorial, however general topic areas of interest to advertisers as well as readers are usually identified in an editorial calendar and promoted to advertisers. To avoid conflicts, clarify editorial and advertising policies in advance.

In addition, here are some other areas where conflicts may arise:

- **Ad Placement.** Will all the ads be "stacked" in the back pages of the publication or integrated into the editorial pages? Will ads and editorial be clearly separated?

- **Positioning.** Some publications sell premium positions for a 10-percent increase over regular space costs to ensure placement opposite a popular column or editorial content. Determine if you will offer this and how to structure and promote premium positions.

- **Pricing.** Associations often undervalue their publications when setting advertising rates. Ensure you are selling a quality publication and then price advertising space for value and sell your specialness—your exclusive niche—to potential advertisers. Although association staffs and resources may be considerably smaller than a commercial counterpart, associations have a number of advantages over general trade publications. Price and position your publication to take advantage of the association's inherent strengths:

  — *Clout of organization:* As the official publication of the nonprofit organization, the periodical not only enjoys the recognition and visibility of the association but can also draw on its many resources. Promote this tie-in.

  — *Highly targeted readership:* Association members form a highly specialized group of potential buyers. Advertisers are willing to pay a premium to reach the top players in the industry or profession.

  — *Quality of editorial and level of readership by members:* Traditionally, association publications are well-read. Conduct research to back up this claim and sell it to advertisers.

  — *Paid circulation (by virtue of membership dues) as opposed to controlled circulation:* Association publications that are distributed as a part of membership dues are considered paid and therefore represent a higher quality of circulation than controlled or free circulation trade and professional publications.

Audited circulation—a program whereby an outside firm regularly verifies the quality and accuracy of circulation figures—is even more desirable. As competition for ad dollars intensifies, more associations are moving to Audit Bureau of Circulations (ABC) or Business Publications Audit (BPA) auditing of circulation.

Marketing and Business Plans

To compete successfully, associations must do more than decide to "accept" whatever advertising comes in. Instead they must develop a strategy for aggressively soliciting advertising.

Incorporate a strategy for sales growth into a marketing plan that honestly assesses the strengths and weaknesses of your publication as well as the strengths and weaknesses of competitive publications. Based on this assessment, outline a strategy for long-term growth (over the next three to five years) that will maximize your publication's strengths and minimize its weaknesses to ensure growth in advertising, circulation, and editorial. The annual publication budget then becomes the short-term (one-year) plan for implementing the strategic plan and realizing long-term growth.

To implement the sales plan, hire experienced, well-trained salespeople or contract with an outside sales representative firm. Many associations begin by using a sales rep firm, paid on commission only. Once a publication is established and billing substantial revenues, many associations choose to bring some or all of the ad sales force in house. Usually, advertising sales people on staff receive a base salary, plus commission. Both arrangements have advantages, depending upon the size of the publication, the geographic areas to be covered, and the revenue generated by the publication. A careful analysis of the costs and benefits of both options will help a publisher decide which is best.

In addition to including display advertising, many publications sell print or electronic classified advertising, sponsorships in print publications or monographs, buyer's guide listings, and convention program advertisements. And association publishers are beginning to tap into the Internet with the sale of banners and logos placed on an association's Web page, as well as hot links to the advertisers' home page. This foray into electronic advertising may prove lucrative eventually, but is still in its infancy today.

Tax Considerations

Adding advertising to a publication introduces tax and legal issues. Advertising sold by tax-exempt organizations is currently considered unrelated business income, that is, unrelated to the purpose for which the organization was granted tax-exempt status. It is therefore subject to the Unrelated Business Income Tax (UBIT). Selling advertising does not jeopardize the tax-exempt status of an organization, but it may make the association liable for taxation.

According to regulations issued by the Internal Revenue Service in 1976, an association must allocate a portion of membership dues as subscription income. The allocation is not arbitrary but calculated according to a sequence of steps. In general, these regulations require taxation of net advertising revenues after expenses; editorial income is not subjected to taxation and therefore must be separated from advertising income.

Many nonprofit organizations, including the American Society of Association Executives and the U.S. Chamber of Commerce, have vigorously opposed the regulations, characterizing them as unfair; they can result in allocating so much of membership dues as subscription income that the publication shows a net profit when, in fact, it suffered a loss. Although the UBIT regulations continue to be tested in the courts, associations must still comply with them. Discuss the regulations with an accountant and legal counsel well-versed in association tax and legal matters. It is critical that an association's financial records clearly differentiate between advertising income and expenses and editorial income and expenses. The more that can be legitimately claimed as an advertising expense, the more net advertising revenue can be offset.

Circulation and Distribution

While most commercial publications rely on subscription income to help underwrite the costs of publishing, associations usually equate circulation with membership. Typically, a member's dues entitles him or her to receive a basic newsletter or magazine. However, seldom does the publishing department receive part of those dues to apply toward the publication.

In recent years, however, more association publishers are looking to nonmember subscriptions as a means of not only expanding their reach but also generating additional revenue. Nearly two-thirds of association magazines and 90 percent of journals have expanded their circulation to include nonmembers (ASAE, 1991). Several factors should be reviewed before embarking on a campaign to solicit nonmember subscribers, including:

- **Competition with the membership department.** The keenest competition for prospects usually arises between an association's publishing department and its membership department. The membership department may believe that selling an association benefit separately undermines membership recruitment. Often, however, when nonmember subscriptions are offered, subscribers convert to membership within the first year.

- **Not limiting promotions to potential members.** Suppliers to the industry or profession, government officials, the media, universities, libraries, and members of related organizations are all potential audiences. Purchasing commercial mailing lists will help define the universe of prospective subscribers.

- **Conducting a small sample mailing to test the potential for subscription sales.** Increasing nonmember circulation in increments, such as 10 percent per year, may be more realistic than a one-time effort to increase it 30 percent.

- **Evaluating additional expenses.** The cost of boosting circulation goes beyond a larger print run and increased mailing costs. Adjusting or expanding editorial content to attract nonmembers might require additional staff or outside writers, in addition to the costs of producing and sending direct-mail promotion pieces, purchasing mailing lists, entering subscriber data, and sending renewal notices.

- **Analyzing the long-term pay-offs.** Paid subscriptions translate into more revenue, and higher circulation figures attract more advertisers—but not right away. Can the association wait several years before its investment in nonmember subscriptions pays off?

A program to attract nonmember subscribers forms just one component of a publication's overall marketing plan. Although the plan will vary according to the type of publication and its audience, the plan should include an analysis of the market (including the competition), an analysis of the product (the publication), short- and long-term objectives, and strategies for accomplishing those goals.

Books

Unlike periodicals, which contain news that quickly becomes dated, books have a sense of permanence. An association that publishes books can influence a trade or profession for years to come by setting standards, preparing members for the future, and establishing itself as the main source for information. Books can also be an expensive undertaking, if they are not well-planned and marketed.

Before accepting or rejecting any idea for a book, association staff members, in conjunction with a publications or special-projects committee, should follow several steps:

1. **Assess the need.** Many book publishing projects have their roots in other association activities, such as the results of a professional research survey, requests to the information department, or comments made during informal and formal discussions with members. What is the reason for publishing a book? What can a book do that an article in the association's magazine or journal cannot?

2. **Define the potential market.** Before any work begins, understand the proposed book's market. Is the book targeted exclusively to the association's members or other audiences as well? How large is the potential market? What is the book's shelf life—will the topic still appeal to buyers three or five years later?

3. **Examine the financial considerations.** As a business, a book publishing operation needs financial goals. Can the association afford to heavily subsidize or break even on the project? Some associations are willing to lose money on one book, calculating that sales of another book will more than offset the losses. In addition to financial resources, does the association have enough staff to devote to producing and marketing the final product?

The type of book published greatly affects production time and costs. **Collections** are the easiest to assemble and produce because they contain previously published articles or papers presented at a meeting or symposium. This "greatest hits" format is often popular among members but may have limited appeal outside the trade or profession.

Reference books, including manuals, handbooks, and glossaries, take longer to produce because they involve original submissions and a more rigorous approval process. Once published, however, such books often become the "bible" in the field and remain in print for several years.

Consumer-oriented books have the widest appeal and, consequently, the largest potential market. However, the costs of consumer marketing will be higher.

Among their members, associations have a natural resource for book authors. People who serve on the publications committee can identify experts in the field, or they may wish to write a chapter themselves. Members who are well-known in the field add to a book's credibility, even if they write only one section.

For long-term projects, associations often turn to outside contributors, such as consultants and freelance writers to draft original copy. To ensure consistency in copy, provide manuscript guidelines that discuss deadlines, style, length, tone, and the book's target audience. And require signed copyright release forms from all contributors and paid authors.

A staff member or an outside expert coordinates the book project. Typically, this editor ensures deadlines are met, keeps copy moving through the review process, and assembles all the book's pieces before production. If your association does not wish to maintain complete control of a book project, sign a publishing contract with a book manufacturer. The numerous companies that specialize in these book-publishing partnerships usually give the association editorial control but handle all the other production, distribution, and promotion details.

Whether working with a publishing company or venturing into book publishing on your own, address key issues in advance:

- **Timing.** Associations often schedule a book's release to coincide with a major convention or media event, allowing 12 to 18 months for development and production. If the book's topic is in the news, however, accelerate the production schedule.

- **Review and proofreading processes.** Determine who has the responsibility for approving final copy. Do all members of a publications committee need to review the book, or can that task be delegated to a subcommittee? Do authors have the opportunity to review or challenge changes to their work?

- **Copyright.** Clarify who holds the copyright for books, especially those that are a compilation of chapters written by volunteers. Generally, the association, as publisher, holds all copyright to the book once the authors sign the release form. This way, the association is free to reprint the materials, as needed, and use the information for other educational and information purposes.

- **Print run.** When considering how many copies to order, determine whether the topic or information will change or easily become dated. If that's the case, updates or revisions of the book may need to be scheduled and a smaller print run should be considered.

Printing more than one year's supply can lead to storage problems and expenses. Determining factors may include the subject matter, marketing plans, members' purchasing habits, and response to pre-publication offers. Many associations use "print-on-demand" services where much smaller quantities can be printed quickly and relatively inexpensively.

- **Royalties and commissions.** Payment of contributors varies widely, depending upon factors such as the importance of the publication, the stature of the author(s)—consultants, well-known experts in the field, volunteers, and so forth—the size of the association, and the shelf life of the book, as well as the potential sales revenues anticipated from the publication. Authors may be paid a set amount based on the scope of work or a royalty based on sales revenues or net profit—or they may not be paid because the work is considered a professional contribution to the field.

When determining pay arrangements, clarify when contributors will be paid—upon acceptance of their work or upon printing of the book? Is compensation tied to the number of books sold? If the association has a co-publisher, what is the payment schedule?

- **Order fulfillment.** Does the association have the space, staff, and time to process book orders? How are orders shipped within the United States and abroad? If you anticipate high sales volume or offer numerous titles, consider contracting with a book distribution company. Agreements with co-publishers typically require customers to send their orders directly to the publishing company, bypassing the association completely.

Preparation and Printing

Options available for producing books vary widely, from a hard cover with acid-free paper and a sewn binding to a saddlestitched soft cover. Consider the budget, the size of the manuscript, and the image to be presented with the book. Projects with quick turnaround times (less than six months), tight budgets, or short life-spans might use spiral binding or offset stock with little or no color.

Technology has considerably changed the way books can be produced, speeding production time and reducing costs. Still, printers that specialize in books will provide the best value.

Setting the Price

Book pricing depends on demand for the material, the size of the market, production costs, and the association's goals. Most associations start with the book's direct costs—author's fees, typesetting, illustration, design, and actual printing—and calculate the per-copy cost. Next, they apply a multiplier that ranges from three to 10 times the per-copy cost. Because their smaller print runs represent higher per-copy costs, associations usually use smaller multipliers.

For example, 3,500 copies of a typeset, hard-cover book cost $45,000 to produce, or just under $13 per copy. Having researched what the market will bear, an association may price the book at $39 (a multiplier of 3) or at $65 (a multiplier of 5). Or, it may use both prices: It's common to establish different prices for members and nonmembers, with the latter group paying no more than double the member price.

As with subscription and advertising rates, book prices should be competitive in the marketplace. Pricing a 150-page soft cover book at $3.50 to encourage sales could have the opposite effect. Would-be purchasers may not perceive value in a book that carries a low price tag.

Marketing a book begins long before it rolls off the presses. In fact, the level of response to a pre-publication sales offer can help determine the final print run or the book's price. A marketing plan should be in place while the book is still in outline form; the design of the cover, the popularity of contributors, and the title itself can all contribute to increased sales.

The marketing plan might also include these activities:

- Displaying the book at conferences.

- Cross-marketing or advertising the book in the association's publications and catalogs as well as in the publications of related organizations.

- Printing excerpts or news items in the association magazine and newsletter to pique readers' interest.

- Sending news releases to the press list and arranging interviews with authors.

- Sending review copies to specific people at key organizations, government offices, universities, and so forth.

- Organizing speaking tours for authors, members, or association staff to give presentations at regional conferences or chapter meetings. For consumer books, arrange interviews on local radio and television talk shows.

- Developing a direct-mail campaign to members and targeted outside audiences.

Considerations for the Future

Association publishers who enjoy long-range success—both financially and in terms of member satisfaction—are those who practice "smart publishing." That means they use the most innovative and cost-effective methods available to produce and distribute their publications. Some new technologies and management approaches to publishing are emerging as trends that warrant further investigation by association communicators:

- **Online publishing.** In this faced-paced world, members are increasingly asking for more information provided faster. In response, many associations deliver information electronically, through the Internet. While not all members may not yet be equipped to access information electronically, associations are pioneering this area and preparing for the day soon when electronic newsletters and magazine supplements will be commonplace.

Clearly, the advantages of electronic publishing are both speed and cost.

Electronic bulletin boards and newsletters or magazines allow association members to access news and information instantaneously, thus eliminating the cost of printing, mailing, and distribution. In addition, with online publishing, specialized newsletters to meet the targeted needs of a diverse membership group are less costly and less time-consuming to produce. Electronic communications may never replace traditional print formats, but they help supplement an association's offerings.

- **Outsourcing or contract publishing.** When a turbulent economy pressures association publishers to reduce costs and even eliminate staff, many consider alternative outside publishing arrangements, including contract publishing. This is an arrangement whereby an association agrees to turn all, or some, of its publication management to an outside publisher in exchange for a fee or shared equity. A contract publisher may, for example, manage all aspects of the publications—from editorial and design to printing, ad management, and circulation—or only parts of the operation. The association may continue to develop editorial content, for instance, while the outside firm handles production and advertising sales.

Usually outsourcing or contract publishing offers a major cost savings in salaries, benefits, equipment, and overhead and may reduce or eliminate the risk involved in launching a new publication. As the costs of staffing and equipment continue to escalate, more associations may consider the contract publishing alternative.

A Strong Link

A well-planned and highly integrated publications program strengthens the link between an association and its members. To vie for members' attention in this world of increasingly sophisticated communications, associations must make professional communications a priority and regularly take a critical look at every area of operations, being willing to make changes to strengthen their publishing program. A successful publishing program can ensure a healthy association.

Debra Stratton is president of Stratton Publishing & Marketing, Inc., Arlington, Virginia. Her company provides consultation, research, marketing, and publication management services to associations and other clients.

CHAPTER 24

ASSOCIATION MARKETING

ALAN R. SHARK, CAE

I n an association, marketing involves all the same principles used by modern profit-oriented corporations. There are differences, however, in the way nonprofit organizations carry out their missions. For-profit companies exist primarily to seek profits for their shareholders and, generally, have distinct products and services. Associations, by comparison, view their members as stakeholders. They exist to meet the needs of their members—whether by advancing a cause, promoting an industry, or serving as a collective force to fight for or against laws and regulations that affect the industry or profession. Their products and services are not always clear-cut.

Just because an association is deemed nonprofit does not mean it can survive without using the latest marketing concepts to realize revenue above and beyond expenses. In the past, dues income provided the main source of revenue for associations. But most associations have had to turn to other revenue streams to survive. For many organizations, conferences, expositions, publications, and research services account for at least a third or more of total association income.

As associations have grown in size and sophistication, so too have member needs and expectations. Furthermore, associations have discovered that they are also dependent on customers who, for many reasons, are not members. These customers actively purchase association products and services even though they are usually paying a higher nonmember price. Associations also have found themselves in competition with the ever-growing service sector in terms of providing publications, information services research, training, conferences, and consulting.

Marketing is as critical a component for associations as for-profit corporations. No body of association management knowledge can be complete without a fundamental understanding of what marketing is, who is responsible for it, and why marketing planning is vital to an association's existence.

Understanding Marketing

Marketing is the discipline where ways are found—through the introduction of a product or service—to satisfy a need within a targeted group of customers, whether they are members or nonmembers. Satisfying needs is achieved through market research, distribution, product development, promotion, and pricing strategies.

The function of marketing examines the offering (*product* or service), determines the relative value that one may be willing to pay *(price)* and the method it should best reach customers (*place* or distribution), and plans the best way to make the product or service known and desired by the intended customers *(promotion)*. These elements are referred to in marketing as the four Ps.

In 1989, the Foundation of the American Society of Association Executives created a Market-Driven Study Task Force. Its report provides a working definition of a market-driven association: A market-driven association is directed by the needs of its members and other constituents or customers that members wish to serve. Depending on the particular association and its members' desires, it also may be directed by the broader needs of a profession, by philanthropy, or by society. A market-driven association actively scans the environment for changes that will affect its members and other constituencies. It makes decisions on strategy, products, services, and organizational processes based on constituents' perceptions of their own needs.

In addition, the market-driven association is proactive, not reactive. It aggressively engages in marketing research and strategic planning to define the present and future needs of its members and other constituents and offers a program of services tailored to those needs.

The task force concluded that all associations can become "market-directed." (The term "market-directed" emphasizes the proper role of marketing as one of the key instruments that supports the need of management, rather than being an end in itself.)

The Management of Marketing

What does management have to do with marketing? Quite a bit. While most textbooks focus on the principles of marketing—what it is, what it involves, and its terminology—little has been written about who is responsible for marketing. Is it the chief executive officer (CEO), a deputy, a marketing professional, selected department heads, a committee, a board, or all—or a combination—of the above?

Association marketing is the responsibility of every association staff member and volunteer. But this statement, taken alone, leaves a vacuum of confusion, because staff and volunteers already play many roles in association management. If an organization wants to become market-driven, how would staff help achieve this transformation? What would be the role of volunteers?

Like any corporate structure, associations typically are divided by both function and department. Each function or department carries out some marketing on its own. In a typical association, the membership department seeks new members or looks for new services to satisfy existing members. The meetings and conferences department seeks better programs and promotions to increase attendance. The publications department attempts to find timely material that will attract loyal readers and thus advertisers. Public relations attempts to promote the association or a particular cause or position in a way that makes members want to continue their support. Even top management strives to make its administrative procedures and policies more appealing and user-friendly to members. But the effectiveness of each department's marketing efforts is multiplied if the departments are woven together in a strategically cooperative group.

Achieving association-wide marketing requires a high degree of orchestration throughout the organizational structure. Ideally, someone should have the responsibility of coordinating departmental efforts to ensure that members and customers feel they are dealing with one association and not a collection of uncoordinated groups. A strong commitment from the highest levels also is required for meaningful change.

The Role of the CEO

The chief executive officer must assume responsibility for association marketing. Realizing the magnitude of what is involved with becoming market-driven strengthens the argument for the CEO to be more fully aware and involved. Specifically, here are 10 ways association CEOs can help create or improve on a marketing environment:

1. **Serve as the central marketing staff person.** More and more CEOs now have marketing management experience, a skill that's especially needed in small and mid-sized associations. Because market-driven management differs from more traditional forms of association management, it stands to reason that such leadership must come directly from the top.

2. **Provide for appropriate staff and reporting relationships.** Many associations, especially large ones, require CEOs to have talents in areas other than marketing, such as government relations. In such cases, someone else should be assigned the marketing task and be given abundant support and commitment from the top.

3. **Provide the necessary staff support and budget.** It takes considerable staff resources, time, and financial resources to plan and conduct research and to develop, implement, and evaluate strategic plans.

4. **Create an environment in which marketing receives high priority in decision making.** Association-wide marketing should not be hidden in some obscure area of management. Everyone on the staff and the volunteers must understand what is required of them.

5. **Set realistic goals and objectives.** Market-driven management is not magic. Membership will not double overnight nor will income suddenly come pouring in.

6. **Ensure that market planning is synchronized with other planning.** For example, market planning should tie in with the association's strategic- and budget-planning cycles.

7. **Reward marketing achievement.** Market-directed management is everyone's business. One strategy is to link marketing accomplishments to a bonus incentive plan, which provides extra funds for staff when the association has met or exceeded certain financial goals.

8. **Insist on sound market research as the basis of strategic planning.** Associations that conduct market research, but then do not reflect what that research reveals about members' needs in all important decisions made by the board, staff, and volunteers, are not achieving their full potential as market-driven associations.

9. **Monitor and evaluate results of marketing plans and revisions.** Even the best of plans needs to be routinely evaluated against new information, so view a marketing plan as fluid. Adjustment is ongoing.

10. **Understand that the best of plans can fail when poorly executed.** Proper execution requires an emphasis on planning and evaluation. Staff need to understand that great ideas, new products, and services must have solid follow-through. Carefully consider distribution and administration: Can the new product or service be produced in a timely fashion? Can you deliver what you promised? More important, can you guarantee what you deliver? Many details need to be thought of in advance and all possible contingencies provided for.

Evaluating Marketing Structures

Each organization needs to assess what type of structure will best support a market-driven environment. Six basic models exist; all but one assume that the CEO has delegated the primary, day-to-day responsibility for marketing management to someone else. Some of these models, whose pluses and minuses are spelled out below, can be intermixed to best meet an association's needs.

- **Model 1: Membership Orientation.** Marketing frequently falls to the person who is primarily responsible for membership marketing.

  Opportunities: Membership-oriented staff are usually closest and most familiar with overall membership needs. This knowledge, combined with marketing training, can be valuable in identifying new products and services or improving existing ones. This person also may be the most familiar with individual members and, therefore, able to personally recruit volunteers for the marketing project.

  Limitations: The membership marketer usually has no authority over other departments' efforts and does not play a key role in the association's strategic planning. The position carries marginal responsibility for market research and assessment and has little direct involvement in product or service planning. Membership marketers usually view nonmembers as opportunities for membership, not as potential customers for other association offerings.

- **Model 2: In-house Consultant.** This staff person provides consultation services to the various program departments throughout the association. For instance, he or she assists departments in writing or editing promotional copy, planning for new products and services, reviewing plans and concepts, and assisting with developing marketing strategies. This person may also take responsibility for conducting market research to support other departments.

Opportunities: An in-house consultant provides association staff with important professional resources. Friction is minimized because he or she is not threatening to the departments' status quo.

Limitations: This person is kept quite busy responding to staff needs; he or she more often reacts than coordinates and initiates. Sometimes, little use is made of this individual's sophisticated marketing skills.

- **Model 3: Separate Marketing Department.** Staff have responsibility for developing, implementing, and coordinating all or most of the association's marketing activities. The department usually has considerable budget responsibility not only for promotion and distribution but also for revenue generation.

Opportunities: This department can be very effective when it has both the responsibility and authority to carry out a coordinated marketing program, including developing plans and making final determinations on budget projections on either side of the ledger.

The Role of Volunteers

Volunteers should not be excluded in creating a market-driven organization. Here are some ways they can help:

1. Support an ongoing strategic planning process.

2. Support market research as a central means of evaluating membership and customer needs.

3. Set an example of participation in strategic planning committee events.

4. Resist pet projects and ideas and be open to an inclusive planning process.

5. Provide leadership by taking part in member and customer focus groups.

6. Help foster a positive and open planning process.

7. Ensure that the goals set are realistic and obtainable.

8. Reward success in the form of praise, monetary bonuses, and other forms of recognition.

Limitations: Usually this department is positioned at the same level as program departments. In effect, the director of marketing has little formal authority in relation to the responsibility given. Considered a peer by other department heads, the marketing department's director spends considerable time negotiating or bargaining with others to accomplish goals. Other departments tend to ignore marketing unless they see a direct benefit.

- **Model 4: Senior Marketing Staff Person.** This person has the responsibility and authority to plan, coordinate, and execute an association-wide marketing plan and program. He or she works closely with all program departments, finance, administration, the CEO, and the board and usually belongs to the CEO's "cabinet."

Opportunities: This structure can be quite effective when the position enhances the effectiveness of various program departments and when department heads realize it is in their best interest to support and participate in the marketing program.

Limitations: Marketing professionals are considered relatively new players in association management. Their roles usually are misunderstood, and the expectations placed on them often are unrealistic. Also, there usually is insufficient staff to effectively carry out all necessary tasks and activities.

Rarely does an association hire a marketing professional when it perceives that all is well. More typically, it hires the marketer in an atmosphere of low-grade panic. If, in a very short time, sales or membership revenue goes down—despite many other contributions he or she makes—the marketing professional's position is in jeopardy. Instead of regarding the marketing professional as a luxury that can be justified only by immediate results, associations need to see it as a necessary position that requires a long-term investment in patience.

- **Model 5: Outside Consultant.** This person is given the task of developing a marketing program within a specified time. The plan might be for a particular department or product line or for the entire association. The consultant will make recommendations and may be asked to stay on to help implement the program.

  Opportunities: Consultants can provide analysis, objectivity, and strong marketing skills. They also can reduce staffing requirements within the association and fulfill the need for high-level marketing expertise on an as-needed basis. Unencumbered with internal politics, they usually can move freely among departments.

  Limitations: A consultant usually does not have sufficient time to really get to know staff, the specific project, or member needs. Even if the consultant's recommendations are well-received, execution remains a problem: Who will carry out the plans? What happens once the consultant has gone?

- **Model 6: The CEO as Marketing Director.** A small association may have no choice but for the CEO to also wear the hat of marketing director.

  Opportunities: Regardless of staff size, the CEO is viewed as an association's principal orchestrator, leader, innovator, and motivator. When the CEO is also the marketing director, there is no doubt who is in charge. Acting as the head marketing person enables the CEO to quickly steer the association in new directions as opportunities arise. And, if true market research is indeed a cornerstone for any type of planning or action, the CEO will have valuable information to substantiate his or her policies or programs.

  Limitations: The CEO may have been hired more for his or her skills in lobbying or knowledge of a profession. This person may feel uncomfortable—even resentful—about being burdened with the responsibility of strategic marketing, a skill in which he or she has no or limited training. Plus, given the nature of a CEO's responsibilities, he or she may simply not have enough time to perform the required duties.

The Planning Process

Good marketing stems from good planning. In turn, good planning begins with a strategic plan.

Strategic plans and strategic marketing plans often refer to the same document. In large organizations, the strategic plan gives a "big picture" view of the association and its future. In contrast, the strategic marketing plan may focus on specific association functions—usually products and services.

A strategic marketing plan is a program of action for reaching members, prospective members, and customers or nonmembers. It addresses all association operations—from membership and meetings to exhibits, education, and publications—whether they entail products or services or communicate a message.

The budget is the association's overall strategic plan represented in financial terms. Accounting for all sources of revenues and expenses, the budget is the clearest indication of how and where the association allocates its resources. If the budget is the most important plan an association has, then the marketing plan rates a close second. It prompts the association to rely on market research to develop a database for information, which provides tools for well-reasoned decision making.

Properly used, the marketing plan puts an end to old-fashioned, incremental decision making that frequently plagues an association budget process. Instead of arbitrary "cut the budget across the board" decisions, strategic plans provide for sound business decisions that focus on revenue with as much certainty as expense.

The marketing plan drives much of the budget process. With the plan, an association states operating assumptions, such as trends in membership and conference attendees, and ties them to the budget. The antithesis of a marketing plan is a system that merely counts up all the known expenses, adds a percentage factor to cover the unanticipated, and arrives at a revenue figure to cover the known expenses. In other words, budgets that take into account marketing plans focus on revenue and revenue potential. Budgets developed in a vacuum emphasize expenses; they focus on the past rather than on the future.

Key Components of a Marketing Plan

A strategic marketing plan can be as short as 10 pages or as long as 100, depending on the association's size and complexity and the amount of available data. Whatever the plan's length, it should include the following elements:

- *Introduction.* This section states overall marketing goals and discusses how the plan ties into the association's mission statement or general strategic plan. Given the amount of information disclosed, it's wise to include a statement of confidentiality and nondisclosure.

- *Business summary.* This section explains the marketing environment in which the association operates. It covers areas such as the overall business outlook as determined by inflation, interest rates, the association's competitors, its business partners, public confidence in the economy, and association-specific indicators.

The general business climate needs to take into account the nation or state, compared to that of the industry or profession the association represents. State any and all aspects of the association affected by the business climate: Is membership up or down? What about publications sales? Did the organization lose an important staff person? If so, might it take time to complete a search and bring a new staff person up to speed?

Next, describe the members, nonmembers, or customers the association is trying to target and the rationale behind those decisions. The rationale generally takes the form of a judgment call by the CEO or marketing professional, in concert with board or committee input.

Each membership segment needs to have a unique strategy and message; you might, for instance, make some offerings available only to targeted members, such as chapter leaders or new members. One year, the plan may call for more resources devoted toward an emerging membership class, such as international members. Sending one message to all members is not effective. The more you can identify subgroups of members, the more effective the association will be in customizing its appeal to specific classes of members and customers, thus leading to more effective marketing of products and services.

The business summary should also describe the association's product mix. List the various membership categories, along with the product offerings and services for each. Mention new products and services that are in the works as well as those due to be discontinued. Describe the market position and sales revenue for each category. In some areas, the association may have no real competition and will be the primary source; in other areas, its market position may be secondary if competition is heavy.

Understanding market share or position helps the association focus on its strengths and weaknesses. If an association has a market penetration of only 20 percent of members in a given membership category, for example, it may want to develop strategies to increase that number through more aggressive recruitment programs and membership offerings.

- *Research.* In this section, which constitutes one of the most critical aspects of a sound marketing plan, delineate characteristics of the overall markets or segments in which the association competes. What does the competition charge for its products and services? How many members belong to other organizations or purchase the services of others? What else is known about the association's members?

All too often associations spend an inordinate amount of time surveying members to determine how well they rate its products and services. It is even more important to ascertain membership's preferences and needs with respect to others' products and services. For example, what publications do they read? How often? What industry meetings do they attend? What other associations do they belong to? What do they want and need that is not being offered?

To be truly effective, marketing research must be ongoing and its results used to update the marketing plan regularly. The fluid nature of the plan, which stems from continual research, ensures its viability. The more that is known about members, nonmembers, and customers, the more effective decision-making tools will be available for developing strategies. Yet market research need not be expensive. You can use simple telephone surveys, focus groups, and fax-back surveys to obtain information about members and customers alike.

- *Marketing strategies and projections.* This section of the plan lists the product and service line, including each offering's strengths and weaknesses. It outlines objectives and strategies for each component of the product mix (product, promotion, distribution, and price). The section also presents the marketing budget, noting how marketing dollars will be spent and what is expected in return.

Most associations find the promotion budget the most challenging. They wrestle with questions such as: How much should be allocated for membership recruitment? What are the anticipated results? How much will be spent on direct mail, advertising, public service announcements, telemarketing, and other related activities? Listing previous results for each product and service will help build more effective plans.

Strategic decisions that require additional resources for developing new or improved products and services must be linked to an association's mission statement and strategic plan. Although generally focusing on the bottom line, marketing plans must sometimes allow for some products and services to be offered at a loss. Some products and services that accomplish the goals of the association and fill an important need may never be able to "make a profit." Some intangible benefits may be necessary to recruit or retain members.

Of course, if it has too many intangible benefits that lose money, the association may need to develop strategies for turning losses into goals. For instance, one association offered a "free" six-month membership that entitled people to member discounts on an upcoming conference. On the surface, it would appear that this association would stand to lose six months' worth of membership plus the difference between member and nonmember conference fees. But the strategy was to provide trial memberships while at the same time increasing conference attendance (which would make exhibitors happy). The strategy worked in the long run. Half of those who took advantage of the trial membership renewed, and the conference gained about 50 new attendees.

As another example, consider two associations that created web sites on the Internet. The first association did not see itself as making any money up front and viewed the web site as a loss. On the other hand, the association successfully promoted the industry; made existing members feel good; and promoted membership, publications, and conferences. Later, the association learned that the web site helped achieve its goal of recognition, with some evidence of increased interest in its activities.

The second association considered its web site a failure: It had projected measurable results from increased online sales of memberships, publications, and conference registrations. Each association had a different strategy. While both endeavors appeared similar, one was considered a success and the other a failure.

The rationale for developing a strategy helps to determine whether it is considered a loss or a success. Each association must pursue its own rationale. Not every activity can be expected to bring in direct financial results—some strategies acknowledge that certain activities can lead to other goals.

- *Monitoring and evaluation techniques.* General progress reports on the marketing plan should be issued monthly or quarterly. The frequency will depend on the size, complexity, and scope of the association. Remember, a marketing plan is not a static document, so it can be modified at any time.

If, for example, meeting attendance appears to be down compared to prior years, the association may want to try new marketing techniques (if time permits) or adjust its revenue projections and scale down costs. If the association

---

Pitfalls to Avoid

Several pitfalls commonly plague a strategic marketing plan. Avoid a plan that:

- **Lists only goals, not strategies.** Such plans often fail to support assumptions with factual research.

- **Lacks support from the top.** Adequate resources have not been allocated to make the plan work. Perhaps the person in charge of the planning process has not been given sufficient authority to move ahead or lacks support staff.

- **Is out of sync with the budget cycle.** If the plan is completed after the budget has been approved, it will be of little use to association managers.

- **Disenfranchises staff.** Even if the marketing planning process is a centralized effort, staff from every department must provide input and support. A sound centralized function is open and embraces coordination and facilitation. Every staff member has some responsibility for marketing, regardless of the association size.

- **Is based on flawed assumptions.** A good marketing plan must be more than a wish list or goal statement. Successful plans contain information about how conclusions were derived. Financial data should not be accepted without supporting information as to how and on what basis assumptions were drawn.

- **Relies on poor quality market research.** Some staff leaders fall into the trap of believing that market research will be too costly or take up too much time. Associations must be willing to commit to ongoing, quality market research. Remember the old saying: No research is better than bad research.

- **Is not comprehensive.** If a plan is developed for a one-time event or opportunity, it may do more harm than good. The plan must be integrated with all activities of the association.

- **Gives no one the responsibility for marketing planning.** Another old saying to keep in mind: If everyone is in charge, no one is in charge.

envisions a long-term trend versus an isolated situation, it may want to adjust price. Some associations can raise their registration fees without too much political fallout, while others have actually increased attendance by lowering fees or by offering large discounts on multiple registrants from the same organization. Still others have found that offering low-cost alternative lodging helps boost attendance.

Marketing budgets usually require modification within the fiscal year: Numbers must be changed to reflect outcomes related to the success or failure of certain strategies. When this is accomplished, confusion can arise concerning the association's overall budget: Should it be changed, too? The answer is no. Just add notes to the budget to reflect important changes in the strategic marketing plan. Making notes to the budget may mean marking a budget line item and adding a corresponding note at the end of the budget document. This technique preserves historical data while alerting staff and board members to changes.

A good strategic marketing plan presents many opportunities to evaluate results. For example, expected revenues from specific programs and services should be broken out into fiscal quarters; any product or service that falls short of projections needs to be reevaluated. Were the strategies to blame? Did some unintended event cause a shortfall (for example, was a meeting canceled because of a blizzard)?

Although the strategic marketing plan can continue to change, at some point it should be presented as a new model. The best time to unveil such a plan is well before the budget process begins.

Marketing by Department

For larger associations, or those with separate subsidiaries, it makes sense to have each product- or service-driven department create its own marketing plan. For instance, an association might develop a separate marketing plan for large conventions or for its publications department.

Any plans that segment information need to be part of a larger marketing information system: Membership should be able to access information about meetings, meetings should be able to coordinate with publications, and so forth. A centralized database with information about members and customers helps pinpoint purchasing trends and proves invaluable for planning.

Departmental marketing plans contain all the elements of the association-wide plan and are rooted in the overall strategic plan. The best method for generating departmental plans is to give each program and service department general guidelines for substance and format. Each departmental plan is incorporated into a master plan: Goals and objectives are coordinated among departments for the CEO's approval.

In today's fast-moving business world, the trial-and-error marketing methods of the past won't work. Without an ongoing marketing planning system, an association will base its decisions on past information, making assumptions that are groundless and highly subjective. With well-orchestrated plans, however, associations can count on noteworthy results.

References

Foundation of the Greater Washington Society of Association Executives, *Marketing the Nonprofit Association,* Washington, D.C., 1992.

Kotler, Philip, and Alan Andreasen, *Strategic Marketing for Nonprofit Associations,* 4th ed., Prentice-Hall, Inc., Englewood Cliffs, New Jersey, 1991.

Norris, Donald M., *Market Driven Management: Lessons Learned from 20 Successful Associations,* American Society of Association Executives Foundation, Washington, D.C., 1990.

Alan R. Shark, CAE, is president and chief executive officer of the American Mobile Telecommunications Association and president and chief executive officer of the newly created International Mobile Telecommunications Association. Both associations are located in Washington, D.C.

CHAPTER 25

MEMBERSHIP RECRUITMENT AND RETENTION

CYNTHIA A. DAVIS, CAE, PH.D.

Membership is at the heart of any association—and not just because members are the association's reason for being or because member dues represent an important source of revenue. Rather, membership development activities are often a member's first or primary point of contact with the association. Every contact a member or potential member has with the association—from registering for the annual conference to submitting an address correction—affects that person's view of the organization.

Consequently, membership development proves effective only if integrated with all association activities. In turn, the data and experience derived from membership activities are invaluable guides for shaping other association roles and programs. Membership exists in a symbiotic relationship with all other functions of the association.

Effective membership recruitment and retention go in a cycle: from information collection and analysis to planning, from planning to implementation, from implementation to evaluation—and back to analysis, to start the cycle again. At every stage, membership activities must maintain an active interchange with other aspects of the association.

Information Collection and Analysis

The membership cycle begins with a careful analysis of current and prospective members' needs in the context of the association's mission and objectives. For this step, you'll need to collect and review demographic, historical, and environmental information about current and prospective members and the association.

It does not take a huge survey to gather all this information. Much of the data may already be available. For example, information about competition and changes in the industry may have been collected as part of the strategic planning process. By coordinating with other association departments, the membership manager can identify any gaps in information and consider whether conducting a survey or employing another research instrument may be a necessary part of the membership plan.

Starting the Cycle

This is the type of information you must collect to begin the membership recruitment and retention cycle:

- Current number of members
- Percentage of members in each membership category
- New-member recruitment rates and trends (changes over time)
- Retention rates and trends
- Size of potential pool of members (all those eligible for membership), current penetration (ratio of current to potential members), and trends
- Differences in recruitment and retention rates among different categories of membership
- Dues and other costs of membership
- Typical or average characteristics of members (for example, age, occupation, and income for individual members; number of employees, size of budget, and number of branches for corporate members)
- Trends in those characteristics (for instance, is the average age increasing or decreasing?)
- Geographic patterns (Are most members on the East Coast? In small cities?)
- Relative proportions of members with different characteristics (for example, average age alone would not show that members fall into two dominant age groups, versus an even distribution)
- Services most often used or requested by current members
- Most frequent member complaints
- Changes in the industry or profession
- Other changes in the external environment (political, social, economic)
- Competition (other organizations, other demands on the time and resources of members)

Not all useful data are quantitative or quantifiable. Results of focus groups, individual interviews, or conversations with members may give qualitative yet in-depth information to supplement statistical information.

As information is compiled, patterns immediately appear. One membership category may be growing, another declining. The average age of members may be increasing or decreasing. Retention rates may be higher in some parts of the country than others. External forces, such as economic trends or government policies, may be provoking new member concerns or causing changes in the industry.

Some patterns require deeper analysis. Is the age of the average member rising because more older people are joining or because younger ones are not? Are geographic differences related to economic trends? Is the penetration rate (of the potential member pool) declining because of lower retention rates or because of the appearance of a new type of potential member?

Ultimately, through information collection and analysis, you want to paint a clear picture of the needs of current and prospective members and determine how well the association currently meets those needs. The analysis then lends itself to a statement of problems (or gaps) and opportunities.

Of course, no single plan can address every member need, fill every gap, or seize every opportunity. The next step, then, is to set priorities for plan development: What gaps are the most important? What are the most promising opportunities? Which should be addressed immediately, and which need more research, preparation, or resources before they can be tackled?

The association's overall mission and focus should guide the setting of priorities. A membership campaign, no matter how sophisticated, will not succeed in the long run if it runs counter to the fundamental interests or focus of the association. A slick campaign or an attractive special offer may attract new members, but they will not renew if the association does not serve their needs and address their concerns. Even a large pool of potential members might not become a priority if pursuing them would shift the association's focus in unacceptable ways. Conversely, a new pool of prospective members might *require* a change in focus for the association to remain representative of its constituency.

Therefore, membership priorities should be determined in context of the association's goals and be consistent with the larger strategic plan. Certainly, the information collected for membership planning must feed into strategic planning, and vice versa. When goals are established for the membership plan, they should flow from and be explicitly linked to the association's strategic plan.

Developing a Plan

Discussions of membership development often deal primarily with recruitment, because new members provide a continuing flow of volunteers and resources for the association. However, a recruitment campaign cannot function in isolation. Recruitment and retention must intertwine; long-term members represent a much bigger return on the association's investment of resources.

In *Strategic Marketing for Nonprofit Organizations*, Philip Kotler and Alan Andreasen define the marketing mind-set as putting "the customer at the center of everything one does." The needs-based approach, centering as it does on current and prospective members, makes membership development a marketing function. Thus, modern membership campaigns naturally employ marketing techniques and concepts such as segmentation, targeting, and testing.

The plan for a membership recruitment and retention program includes these elements

- **Target Audiences.** It is impossible to develop a "universal" membership appeal that will work on any and all potential, or even current, members. Instead, you must divide the larger audience into specific, identifiable categories (segmentation) and market to them with the most appropriate strategies, messages, and offers (targeting). The emphasis should be on selecting segments that are large enough to justify spending resources on marketing to them. In addition, they should be "mutually exclusive" and "conceptually separable"; in other words, each segment should have distinctive characteristics, needs, and motives for joining or staying in the association. That specificity enables you to customize the membership message.

Segmentation and targeting determine membership strategies. Suppose your association has identified a growing demographic segment as people between the ages of 20 and 29. A campaign targeting them would use language, images, and offers with proven appeal to that segment. This might mean photos of that age group, "youth-oriented" language, and premiums such as clothing or merchandise appealing to that generation.

Or suppose current members fall into two main interest categories: informational services and lobbying. Renewal appeals to the first group might highlight the newsletter as a member benefit; for the second group, a checklist of the association's legislative accomplishments might be more appealing.

Effective segmentation requires reliable sources of data, including lists with appropriate background information. For current members, a demographic database or record of services used may delineate some basic segments. For prospective members, mailing lists can be obtained from other associations, from subscriber lists of related publications, or from attendee lists at conferences. Tracking returns from contacts with specific segments (mailings, calls, exhibits, meetings) will provide even more data for future efforts.

A systematic membership plan must include concrete, measurable objectives, such as a specific percentage or numerical increase in membership or retention rates. Segmentation and targeting allow for more closely defined objectives (for example, increased representation of a target group), thus enabling the membership plan to address specific issues such as member diversity or geographic representation.

- **Content.** The message of the campaign must be appropriate for the target audience. It should focus on the identifiable concerns of that group, use appropriate language and images, and highlight the member benefits that will have the most resonance with those people. It must also appeal to the strongest motives the group has for joining or renewing membership.

Any special offer should fit the basic

Getting Specific

Here are various ways you can segment current and prospective members:

- Individual demographics (age, location, gender, ethnicity, income)

- Corporate characteristics (size, budget, employees, branches, range of corporate activities)

- Interests, hobbies, tastes

- Relation to the association (former member versus never belonged, long-time versus new member, specific member category)

- Use of association services (conference attendee, subscriber, purchaser of other services)

- Length of time in the profession or industry

target and message; for example, the target group most interested in lobbying activities might be offered a free legislative update. A group of current members that already has a strong attachment to the organization might be offered an extra month's membership for early renewal or a sign of affiliation such as a membership pin.

- **Vehicle.** Likewise, a direct-mail package should have a "look" appropriate to the target audience and message. If the message is serious ("Join now to relieve world hunger"), the package may take a somber appearance or use a news format to convey urgency. On the other hand, if the message is more upbeat ("Join for provocative publications and exciting programs"), the package might have a livelier look. In either case, reinforce the message through the use of color, paper, design, illustrations, and photos.

If telemarketing is used, the caller's script should convey not only the information but also the message and tone appropriate to the audience. In fact, the choice of vehicle is influenced by the target audience. Many association executives do not like to use telemarketing for recruitment, for example, on the theory that nonmembers may resent "cold calls." Current members, however, are more likely to feel connected to the organization and to appreciate the call.

Direct mail and telemarketing are the most commonly used vehicles for recruitment and retention. They reach a wide audience at a relatively low cost per contact yet can easily be personalized or customized. Other vehicles, though, may be desirable for specific targets and messages. For example, radio or TV ads reach a wide yet relatively unsegmented audience; they are often used for visibility campaigns or public-interest messages. Print ads in trade papers can reach specific corporate segments. Exhibits at trade shows or personal visits can be useful for highly segmented markets that need high levels of face-to-face personal contact.

Computers and the Internet have opened up new avenues for membership development and communication. A simple but informative home page can provide basic information about the association, offer further resources, and invite online inquiries—and might, by its very existence, modernize the association's image. Depending on the technological sophistication and accessibility of your markets, you can offer even more interactive contacts, from electronic bulletin boards and forums to product purchase or affiliation by computer. You might distribute resources like the membership directory on computer disk or CD-ROM. Like any strategy, these possibilities should be carefully planned and evaluated for cost-effectiveness and appropriateness to the target audience.

- **Logistics.** Once you've determined the target, message, and vehicle, attend to the logistics of the plan. Who will develop the concept and write the copy? Who will assign and approve the artwork, photography, layout, and scripting? Will in-house staff handle the logistics, or will everything be outsourced? What is the role of association volunteers? Then there are production issues, which include arranging for printing, filming, recording, phone banks, assembly of an exhibit, and pricing (requesting proposals, analyzing prices, signing contracts).

For the plan to come to life, all these activities must be coordinated so the message can be effectively delivered by mail, phone, exhibits, or meetings. It's helpful to formulate a calendar with dates and deadlines marked for each step along the way.

Many logistical factors derive from data gathered during the information-analysis stage. For example, a renewal mailing could be scheduled to coincide with a time of year when retention rates are traditionally high. Other factors relate to timing of other association projects. A membership mailing may have to be scheduled when no other major mailings are planned so the recipient's attention isn't divided; alternatively, a renewal or recruitment appeal might be "piggybacked" with another mailing to save postage.

- **Testing.** The targeted approach to membership development demands testing to identify which appeals, messages, offers, designs, or vehicles register the greatest success. Samples from target audiences are tested to determine whether their response justifies a more large-scale effort. Regularly reviewing test results can produce more effective campaigns. This does not necessarily mean devoting extensive resources to special tests. Every element in the campaign *is* a test, whose results can be used in designing the next step in the campaign.

  Whether done for a pilot or the full campaign, testing demands careful tracking of results. For example, a target group might be divided in two, with each group receiving different mailings. The group with the higher response rate would point to the more effective appeal. Or, small portions of several target groups might receive the same mailing: The most responsive segments would then be targeted in a bigger mailing. As another example, an association could compare retention rates of new members when half of them receive a six-month follow-up survey and the other half receive a special "new member" offer.

  Successful testing must be built into membership planning. A response form (membership application, member sponsorship form, or survey) can be coded to show which mailing produced it or which target group it represents. With telemarketing or personal contacts, the contact record provides the tracking. Test results will identify the most responsive targets, the most successful messages and vehicles, and the most effective timing.

Integration with Other Activities

When coordinated and integrated with other association activities, membership campaigns not only maximize the use of resources through shared mailings and events but also reinforce association goals and membership incentives. After all, members join and stay because they like what the association does for them.

Renewal and recruitment appeals should remind members of the association's most successful products and services. In turn, association products and activities should convey the membership message whenever possible. The annual report, the annual conference, member surveys and reports, and press conferences are all opportunities to tell current and prospective members why membership is valuable. The newsletter should carry membership information, recognize members who contribute or volunteer, and encourage active involvement. Does the association have a major public relations event coming up? Membership materials should be available there, and a membership campaign should follow up on the increased visibility.

No membership mailing or renewal invoice can have as much effect as regular, conscious contacts that reinforce how much the association values its constituency and how well it serves it. The membership manager has the responsibility to watch for these opportunities and work with other staff to rein-

---

Following Up with Non-Renewals

No association has a 100 percent renewal rate. What should you do about members who do not renew? Try these strategies:

- Send at least three renewal reminders, timing them for maximum effect.
- Personalize renewal mailings as much as possible.
- Vary the message and appearance of each renewal notice to catch the member's attention.
- Increase the urgency with each message, moving from a friendly "Time to Renew" to "Last Chance—You're Missing Out on Important Services!"
- If the member has failed to renew after the first three notices, send a "Why did we lose you?" letter with a brief survey. Offer check-off options to capture the major reasons for non-renewal. Make one option, "Oops! I forgot! Please DO renew my membership!" Include space for further comments, and ask for the respondent's name and address (their option).
- If the survey is returned and you can reply, call or send a friendly letter. If the member has a complaint that can be fixed, do so. If not, explain why. In the worst cases, offering a free year's membership as an apology might win the member back for life.
- Use volunteers for follow-up activities. A local member can follow your renewal mailing with a reminder phone call or more personal letter and help respond to some complaints. Personal contacts carry much more weight than form letters.
- Analyze non-renewal patterns. Are they concentrated in geographic areas, industry segments, or demographic groups? Are there repeated complaints on the follow-up survey? This information should go back into your membership planning.
- Keep track of former members. They may be willing to rejoin later on, if appropriately targeted. After a year, try a "We've missed you" appeal.

force membership messages through other activities. Such links should be built into the overall plan.

Legal Issues

The association must be confident that its membership categories, distinctions in dues and services, policies for member admission and expulsion, and membership applications conform with legal requirements.

As Jerald Jacobs notes in the *Association Law Handbook,* "the greater the competitive advantage derived from association membership, the more closely scrutinized will be the membership requirements." If membership confers a competitive advantage, membership materials must clearly spell out the open and objective requirements for membership. Individuals or companies cannot be excluded from membership on grounds that would constitute restraint of trade. If the association conducts credentialing or certification activities, those must also be open, objective, and fairly administered. Similarly, membership appeals should not describe the benefits of affiliation or credentialing in ways that suggest collusion or other violation of antitrust laws.

Depending on the association's tax status, certain activities (for example, lobbying) may be restricted, prohibited, or subject to unrelated business income tax. Tax status also affects whether member dues are deductible as charitable contributions or business expenses. The legitimacy of certain categories of membership (for example, supplier or vendor members) may be questioned if their membership rights and responsibilities are not carefully defined.

In addition, laws limit the deductibility of member dues based on the association's lobbying activities. It is the responsibility of the membership manager to be familiar with these restrictions and to make sure that applications, dues notices, and other membership materials provide appropriate and accurate notices to members. (For more information on legal issues, see Chapter 5.)

Resources

Few, if any, associations have unlimited resources for conducting membership campaigns. In fact, it may be difficult for the membership manager to persuade the association to divert money from other activities in order to recruit and retain members.

An honest assessment of needed and available resources must be incorporated into the membership plan. The budget should cover not only the expenses of the immediate recruitment effort but also related activities, such as welcome letters, orientation programs, renewal invoices, and follow-up contacts with nonrenewing members. To justify these expenses, project the revenue to be received from new and renewing members. It is not necessary for the campaign to pay for itself immediately—for dues collected in the first year to cover all costs—but the cost should be recouped over a reasonable period of time. You can use the average retention period to weigh the cost of acquiring and keeping a new member against the anticipated revenue over the life of the membership.

The plan should also address expenses other than cash, such as the time of member volunteers, in-kind services that may be donated, and alternative costs (for example, the use of rentable space for the telemarketing team).

Implementation and Management

Now you're ready to put the plan into effect. But the membership responsibility does not stop when the recruitment letter hits the mail. Follow-through is essential and consists of continuously tracking results and involving members and other staff in membership efforts.

Given the importance of targeting and testing in any membership marketing campaign, devote a great deal of attention to tracking and reporting results. Develop reports on each test, each mailing, and each segment targeted, and regularly update and review them. Also monitor membership recruitment and retention rates and any attitudinal changes that may surface through surveys and staff contacts with members.

Membership is everybody's job. Everyone from the switchboard staff to the chief executive officer must be able to answer basic questions and encourage membership. A customer service attitude should permeate all staff behavior and association activities. The membership manager can lead this effort, working with other staff to help create a customer-service orientation and to ensure that member contacts and concerns are high on the agenda when staff make decisions.

Expense Areas

The budget should cover the following areas:

- Design and production (brochures, letters, scripts)
- Purchase of lists
- Data entry
- Mailing (postage, mailhouse costs)
- Telecommunications (phones, space, cost of creating and maintaining home page, electronic mail)
- Premiums, incentives, discounts
- Supportive programs (for example, new member orientation)
- Staff time
- Consultants
- Reimbursed volunteer expenses
- Indirect costs

But staff alone should not drive a membership campaign. Members are the reason for the campaign and in many cases it's the involvement of "experts"—current members—that determines success. If properly recruited, trained, and recognized, members can assist in every step of membership development by:

- Analyzing the information collected. In chapter-based associations, members may themselves distribute and collect surveys and help tabulate the results.
- Participating in setting priorities and selecting target audiences.
- Reviewing campaign messages and timing for effectiveness.
- Recruiting friends or colleagues by expressing their personal reasons for affiliation with the association. Member volunteers can be the most effective renewal callers or can reinforce renewal appeals with personal letters. In printed materials, member testimonials provide a special support for the basic message.

Evaluation and Revision

After implementation comes perhaps the most neglected aspect of membership development: evaluation and revision. Evaluation usually is divided into two main areas: "control tools" (measures such as revenue, attendance figures, and market share) and measures of customer satisfaction.

If you have built appropriate tests and tracking into the plan, a wealth of information will be available in both areas. Reviewing that information, evaluating how well the elements of the plan worked in practice, examining internal systems, and constantly monitoring member attitudes and participation all constitute a full evaluation—not only of the specific campaign but also of the membership development program in general. Based on this evaluation, membership strategies must be revised.

At this point, the process has come full circle. The evaluation feeds back into the fact base, expanding the information available for analysis and plan development. Experience with implementation of the plan as well as changes observed help in setting new priorities and membership objectives.

Facing new patterns, new problems, and new opportunities, the membership manager begins again the adventure of seeking, serving, and keeping members—the life of the association.

Checklist for Success

You can use the following items to measure the viability of a membership development program. It must include:

- Responsive system of member records
- Realistic appraisal of potential for membership growth
- Updated list of potential members
- Membership development and retention plan with specific strategies and goals
- Follow-up on lapsed members
- Adequate funds for membership development and retention
- Regular progress reports
- Communication to members about association programs and services
- Monitoring of changes in membership attitudes and needs
- Demonstration of member interest through volunteering, attendance, and contributions
- Staff responsible for membership development
- All-staff understanding of responsibility for member relations
- Procedures for handling member requests
- Volunteer involvement in membership development
- Due process procedures where appropriate

Source: Association Peer Review Program, American Society of Association Executives.

References

Butler, Wilford A., "The Volunteer in Membership Activities," *Attracting, Organizing & Keeping Members,* American Society of Association Executives, Washington, D.C., 1989.

Coursey, James W., Kathleen R. Lane, and Kenneth E. Monroe, "Membership Marketing," *Attracting, Organizing & Keeping Members,* American Society of Association Executives, Washington, D.C., 1989.

Faulkner, Michael, "Membership Development Techniques I: Direct Mail and Telemarketing," *Attracting, Organizing & Keeping Members,* American Society of Association Executives, Washington, D.C., 1989.

Jacobs, Jerald A., *Association Law Handbook,* 3rd ed., American Society of Association Executives, Washington, D.C., 1996.

Kotler, Philip, and Alan R. Andreasen, *Strategic Marketing for Nonprofit Organizations,* 4th ed., Prentice Hall, Englewood Cliffs, New Jersey, 1991.

Levin, Mark, "Segmentation and Targeting," *Marketing the Nonprofit Association,* Greater Washington Society of Association Executives Foundation, Washington, D.C., 1992.

Webster, George D., *The Law of Associations,* Mathew Bender and Company, Inc., Oakland, California, 1995.

Cynthia A. Davis, CAE, is executive director of the National Association of Workforce Development Professionals (NAWDP), Washington, D.C., and its Partnership Education Fund. She previously served as membership director at the American Association of University Women and as issues management director at the National Federation of Business and Professional Women's Clubs.

CHAPTER 26

GOING INTERNATIONAL

CAROLYN A. LUGBILL, CAE

The world grows smaller by the day. And thanks to technology and the many ways available to communicate with members (fax, broadcast fax, fax-on-demand, electronic mail, home pages/web sites, chat rooms, and listservs), associations have an unprecedented opportunity to capitalize on their international potential.

For example, a presence on the Internet enables an association to frequently (and inexpensively) contact its members located virtually anywhere in the world. In addition, potential members can discover the association exists and see the wealth of information and resources available.

The various kinds of communication technology available have thrust associations into the global arena whether or not they want to be there. To capitalize on the opportunity, the association must be ready and know how to position itself in the global marketplace.

What It All Means

What does the phrase "going international" really mean—conducting an off-shore meeting every two years? Creating specific products and services to serve international members? Establishing an international federation? Changing the association's name to include the word *international?* Revising the association's governance structure to allow international representation on the board? Or, in the case of a trade association, providing statistical data to help members penetrate new markets?

Going international can encompass all these activities or focus on just a few of them. For one association, it may mean expanding its educational programs to reach groups of overseas members. Another association might go through a complete top-to-bottom restructuring, enabling it to engage in global activities in all areas.

The definition will also differ for a trade association, a professional society, and a philanthropic organization. For a professional society, for instance, going international may involve building a relationship with its overseas counterparts so members can exchange technical expertise and experiences through meetings; it may also include translating the association's publication into several languages as a way to recruit and serve international members. In a trade association, going international may translate into regularly holding export seminars on specific target markets or organizing U.S. pavilions in other countries, so members can showcase their products and services at trade shows.

Going international affects every functional area of the association, from education and finance, to marketing and publications, to communications and chapter relations. For example, if your U.S.-based association holds a meeting outside domestic borders, the education and convention areas aren't the only departments involved. The finance department will have to become skilled in assessing exchange rates, making payments in a foreign currency, and possibly opening up an overseas bank account. The marketing department must consider printing the meeting's promotional brochure in one or more languages and give careful consideration to promotional techniques.

An association has truly gone international when it has integrated a global dimension into all its activities, so a separate department doesn't have to exist to handle all activities abroad. This level of integration is the goal to which any association should strive.

Determining Potential

Whatever the definition of "going international," an association should not attempt it before completing a comprehensive needs analysis that looks at membership, the internal and external environment, and the competition. Only through the process of conducting this audit will the association be able to determine if international activities fit into its mission and strategic plan, how such activities will benefit its membership, and how to accomplish this new objective.

The international audit can be an extremely valuable exercise, especially when a board member or other volunteer leader suggests that your association conduct an international activity. Rather than succumb to the personal interests of a volunteer leader, you will have the proper research on hand to identify whether a need really exists. The audit provides the supporting evidence to help a board make wise decisions about the organization's international potential and possible international activities.

Conduct the international audit on two levels. First, assess the extent to which your association represents an industry or profession that is international in scope, and determine the nature of its international character. Second, evaluate your association's current international standing. The following questions—to be answered by the board and volunteer leaders, in conjunction with association staff—will guide you through the process.

1. *Is the industry or profession identifiable and quantifiable by country, region, or continent?* Are there specific areas of the world where members of the industry or profession are grouped or where they are virtually absent? What is the geographic nature of the industry or profession?

   Initially, you may find it feasible to target only one or two countries before deciding to research a whole region or continent such as Europe, Asia, or Latin America.

2. *Are there significant differences in the operation and sophistication of the industry or profession by country, region, or continent?* Are there geographic imbalances in the dissemination of information or application of technology upon which your segment of the economy is based? What are the reasons for these differences, and what are the consequences—both negative and positive—of changing the balance?

For example, in some parts of the world where you'd like to distribute your publications, the postal system may be very slow or unreliable. You may have to look at using an international mail distribution company to ensure timely and accurate delivery.

3. *Does the industry or profession have counterpart or related organizations in other countries?* What cultural and regional differences exist among the industry or profession in various countries? How do members of the profession or industry communicate, share information, network with their peers, and lobby their government? Is it possible to benchmark other associations in closely related industries?

It is almost a given that a counterpart association in Europe or Latin America will have a different *modus operandi* than one in Asia. You'll need to develop different strategies for working with the various groups.

4. *Is your country generally considered the world leader in the profession or industry?* Will members of the profession or industry outside your country recognize what they have to gain by affiliating with your existing members? Or are they likely to feel threatened by potential competition?

5. *Will your members benefit from their counterparts in other countries?* How? By sharing expertise and information? What might your domestic members lose if the counterparts have equal access to your association's benefits?

6. *Does the industry face significant international competition?* Who are your members' competitors? Will international liaison with those competitors strengthen the industry or profession as a whole, or might it damage your members' ability to do business?

7. *What percent of worldwide market share do members of your profession or industry in your country enjoy?* Why? What is the potential worldwide market, and what factors influence it? To what extent is the world market saturated?

8. *Does the industry or profession depend upon raw materials or other resources that are not readily available or competitively priced in your country?* Are there sources outside your country that could be tapped to the advantage of members—but aren't because of shipping, customs, technological difficulties, or other problems? Can the association help alleviate these problems?

9. *Does the association currently have members from other countries?* What percent of the membership and of total dues do they represent? Are the international members active? How?

10. *How are members from outside your country represented in the association?* Do they pay equal, lesser, or greater dues? Can they (and do they) serve on committees

and in other leadership positions? Are there any special restrictions or problems associated with their involvement?

11. *Do members of your profession or industry outside your country seek out your association's products and services?* Do your conventions, meetings, and educational seminars attract international members? Do they subscribe to your periodicals or buy your materials? Do they communicate with you electronically or access your web site regularly?

12. *Do you actively market the association's products and services to international members and nonmembers?* Are market data available that would shed light on whether domestic and international members have different interests and needs? Have you surveyed the market potential or conducted trend analyses?

13. *Is any other organization—association, company, or government agency—supplying competitive goods and services to the international members of your profession or industry?* How do the quality, accuracy, price, and delivery system compare to what your association can offer? Is there an advantage in working cooperatively? To what extent have other organizations penetrated the particular market? Could members in your country benefit from their products and services? Is national pride or identity a significant factor that will influence your ability to compete?

14. *Do members in your country oppose membership from international firms or individuals?* Why? What percent of your members share this feeling? What would be the consequences of proceeding despite this opposition?

15. *Do legal or regulatory impediments to technology transfer exist between your country and some (or many) others?* If so, can you control the flow of information through journals, trade shows, electronic communications, and so forth?

16. *Can your association's structure and culture accommodate international involvement?* Can the budget handle the variances in currency value, mailing costs, overseas meetings, and the possibility of additional staff? In addition, can staff adjust to the language and cultural differences of international members? Will your association's mission have to change? Might outside assistance be needed to help redesign or redirect your governance or staff structure?

17. *Whose idea is it to consider expanding internationally?* The board? Other volunteer leaders? The chief executive officer? What is the motivation—additional revenue for the organization, access to new markets, or exchange of information or expertise?

Thoughtful and thorough responses to the audit questions will provide the blueprint for determining any international objectives. In some cases, the audit will lead an association to rethink its mission and revise its long-range or strategic plan.

For instance, as a trade association representing U.S. manufacturers, your association may want to remain U.S.-based and have U.S. members only. Still, members might benefit from an office in Brussels that would provide advice on regulations, standards, and distribution networks for members' products in Europe. Even a U.S.-based association, with only U.S. members, can have international aspects to its services.

Or perhaps your association is currently U.S.-based, has members inside and outside the U.S., and gears its services primarily to a U.S.-based audience—but wants to move toward providing unique services to international members. Steps to take may include conducting a needs assessment then, depending on the outcome, determining whether to modify certain U.S.-based services or develop new international ones. You'll also need to assess whether these new services could be cost-effective and bring in additional revenue. As another example, your association may wish to become an international or global organization that serves the unique needs of its non-U.S. members. That would require significant international representation and activities at the board and committee level; the choice of a common language; identical dues and a similar level of services, conferences, and publications, for all members; and a mission and objectives that reflect global trends.

The more clearly your association can define its objectives, the stronger the possibility that the money and time invested in going international will build toward an inevitable payoff. If your association doesn't know how much it can realistically accomplish, go slow in outreach and investment: Try one international activity before launching several simultaneously. Continuously monitor the feedback and results and review and revise the association's strategic plan annually.

An Array of Activities

Suppose your association has conducted an international audit and concluded it should become international in some form or at some level. Here are some international activities to consider pursuing:

ASSOCIATION LEADERSHIP

- Analyze your association's governance and staff organizational structure. Consider other types of associations as models (an international federation or global association, for example).

- Form an international committee or advisory council within the association. Invite international members to serve on committees or the board of directors.

- Incorporate a globalization goal in the association's strategic plan.

- Change the association's name from "national" or "American" to "international".

- Establish a lobbying function to contact foreign governments on behalf of your industry or profession.

- Open an office overseas, or contract with an association management company to represent your association.

- Update the board regularly on progress of international goals.

MEMBERSHIP AND MEMBER SERVICES

- Identify and develop relevant services for international members based on needs assessment.

- Market membership and your association's products and services (journals, meetings, educational programs, certification programs, web site, and so forth) to international prospects and members.

- Ensure that your membership database will accommodate longer overseas addresses and country or city codes for phone and fax numbers.

- Survey your international members about delivery systems of member services.

- Develop a separate category of membership for international members.

- Analyze your association's membership dues structure.

- Produce a directory of members who have international expertise or experiences in a given subject area and could serve as speakers, authors, and consultants.

- Serve as a clearinghouse for all international inquiries and requests.

- Conduct and provide customized research on international requests and markets.

- Establish an awards program that recognizes members' "best practices" of operating in the international arena.

- Provide recognition or eligibility for special prizes to international members who recruit other international members into the association.

COMMUNICATIONS

- Start a regular international column in your monthly publication.

- Write feature articles on various international topics and issues.

- Include international events in the calendar section of the association's monthly journal or newsletter.

- Appoint an international editorial advisory board.

- Translate publications and association materials into other languages.

- Contract with an international distribution company for overseas mailings.

- Publish and offer international titles in your publications catalog.

- Develop publications solely for your international audiences.

- Include a listing of your overseas counterparts and other international organizations in your membership directory.

- Access foreign media to become knowledgeable about specific country trends and issues.

MEETINGS AND TRADE SHOWS

- Provide international programming at your annual convention and other smaller meetings.

- Establish an International Welcome Center or "lounge" at your annual convention.
- Recruit overseas exhibitors and attendees to your trade show.
- Ensure that your registration materials are internationally friendly.
- Designate an International Pavilion for international exhibitors on trade show floor.
- Recognize international members at your meetings with a reception, flag ceremony, song, speaker, and so forth.
- Provide "international" ribbons, language buttons, or flag pins to designate overseas attendees.
- Arrange for a group photo opportunity of all overseas attendees; publish it in your conference daily or monthly publication.
- Hold special events such as breakfasts and receptions for international exhibitors.
- Develop an international conference that either is a stand-alone or is part of a larger association meeting.
- Find speakers outside the U.S. who can present papers at your annual convention.
- Provide simultaneous interpretation at your meetings.
- Consider videoconferencing at your meetings to allow for more international participation.
- Translate promotional meeting materials and presentation papers into one or more languages as appropriate.
- Highlight international activities and seminars in a special section of your pre-conference publicity brochure.
- Expand your press program to overseas press contacts.
- Provide a special welcome letter to international members in registration packets.
- Provide "buddies" on site to welcome overseas attendees.
- Consider having a special registration area for overseas attendees.
- Market and hold meetings outside the country where your organization is headquartered.
- Prepare an information booklet for members traveling to an overseas meeting.

TECHNOLOGY ISSUES

- Make your fax-on-demand system accessible to international members.
- Develop an international component to your web site that provides helpful resources and links to related organizations.
- Make your web site cross-culturally reader-friendly and useful to international members.

- Link your counterparts' web sites to yours.
- Encourage other domestic and internationally oriented web sites to link to your site.
- Allow your international counterparts to post their own schedules of events, directories of members, and other contact information.
- Provide a listing of international counterparts' addresses, phone and fax numbers, and e-mail addresses on your web site.
- Develop listservs for domestic and international members who want to exchange ideas and information.
- Automate membership sign-up and renewal processes so international members can easily join and renew.
- Promote conference attendance, exhibits, and educational programs through your web site. Automate registration procedures for conference attendees.
- Create an online version of your publications catalog.
- Automate ordering of documents.
- Create online version of your membership directory.
- Allow domestic and international members to update their own membership profile data. Provide "members only" access to selected information.
- Establish an online job bank. Allow members to post their own notices.
- Display pictures of key association staff, and provide e-mail access to each person.

EDUCATION AND TRAINING

- Consider expanding your certification program offshore.
- Hold an education program for association staff and volunteer leaders on meeting the needs of your association's international members.
- Produce an internal newsletter several times a year that will "globalize" the thinking of staff in a fun, engaging way.
- Make sure your educational programming includes an international component.

FINANCE

- Open an overseas bank account to handle international member payments for dues and other financial transactions.
- Contract with a foreign currency exchange firm to process international wire transfers, handle forward contracts, and make foreign currency payments.

LEGAL ISSUES

- Consult legal counsel in the relevant countries (in addition to the United States) concerning any potential legal problems that may arise in connection with international activities. Issues include—but are not limited to—corporate registration and compliance, tax status and treatment of revenues, antitrust, contracts, affiliate relationships, and protection of the association's intangible property (such as the association name, copyrights, and trademarks).

- Initially provide complimentary legal consultation for members operating in the international arena.

CHAPTER RELATIONS/AFFILIATES

- Identify and form international chapters or affiliates.

- Consider alternatives to international chapters, such as affiliating with an existing organization, establishing an independent local group and then affiliating, or working through another association's chapters.

- Produce guidelines for chartering of new chapters or affiliates.

- Draft chapter affiliation agreements.

- Develop a "Chapter Self-Assessment Tool" to measure and enhance chapter's programs and services.

INTERNATIONAL TRADE

- Develop and monitor international standards.

- Participate on international standards-setting bodies.

- Hold export training seminars.

- Develop international data about various foreign markets.

- Sponsor an export trading company.

- Conduct trade or study missions.

- Participate in overseas trade shows.

- Organize U.S. Pavilions at overseas trade shows.

- Participate in a foreign government assistance project, such as the U.S. Agency for International Development or the U.S. Department of Commerce's Market Development Cooperator and Foreign Buyer programs.

- Provide business links and networking opportunities.

- Publish market research.

- Provide government financing information.

- Develop a logistics program that saves your members money by consolidating shipments of products exported overseas and providing centralized warehouses.

ASSOCIATION HEADQUARTERS

- Hire part-time or full-time staff dedicated to the association's international activities. Ensure they have foreign language capabilities.

- Provide international resources in your association's library.

- Internationalize your association's letterhead and all other materials.

- Restructure your association's membership database to allow for international addresses, phone, fax, postal, and country codes.

Classification Options

Here are the different ways that associations classify themselves, in terms of who they serve and their level of international activity:

- U.S. association with U.S. members only.

- U.S. association with members inside and outside the U.S., with services essentially designed for U.S. members and offered to all members.

- U.S. association with members outside the U.S. whose unique needs are served.

- International association—significant portion of membership based outside one region, or members headquartered in one region with significant interests in other regions.

- Federation—several (regional) associations as members; also called an umbrella association.

- Global association—direct membership spread over two or more regions of the world, more or less equally, and not one country majority on the board.

- Host international members at the association's headquarters and networking events.

- Develop contacts at foreign embassies, tourist boards, and government agencies.

- Provide members with a list of staff who speak foreign languages.

- Assess whether the association should be located in the same country where it currently operates.

STRATEGIC ALLIANCES/COUNTERPARTS

- Use *Gale's Encyclopedia of Associations* to research who your counterparts are. Contact them.

- Offer training to your association counterparts on the fundamentals of managing a private voluntary association.

- Develop Memorandums of Understanding and Agreement with your counterparts outlining the issues on which the organizations will cooperate and work together.

- Provide complimentary registration to leaders of overseas counterparts at your association's meetings.

- Provide forums for leaders of overseas chapters or counterpart associations to meet at least once a year.

- Cosponsor a meeting with a counterpart.

- Publish a newsletter at least twice a year that solicits and compiles the activities and issues of each of the counterparts.

- Let your members know that you can provide access to overseas associations in their field.

- Publish a directory of overseas associations and association leaders in your field.

Moving into the international arena requires a global mind-set, a lot of hard work, determination, cross-cultural awareness, flexibility, and, most of all, the desire to build and maintain long-term relationships with international members and counterparts.

Recommended Reading

American Society of Association Executives, *Going Global: An Association Primer*, Background Kit, Washington, D.C., 1994.

Digh, Patricia, "Twenty-five Steps to Get You Started Going Global," *A Sharing of Expertise & Experience*, vol. 11, American Society of Association Executives, Washington, D.C., 1993.

Fazio, Carolyn, "Defining the International Association," *International News*, May/June 1992, American Society of Association Executives, Washington, D.C.

Fazio, Charles R., "Going International: Effective Strategies and Resources II," *A Sharing of Expertise & Experience*, vol. 10, American Society of Association Executives, Washington, D.C., 1992.

Ferguson, Henry, "Going International: Effective Strategies and Resources I," *A Sharing of Expertise & Experience*, vol. 10, American Society of Association Executives, Washington, D.C., 1992.

Lindner, Randy, "How the Internet Can Benefit Your Association," *International News*, March/April 1996, American Society of Association Executives, Washington, D.C.

Meyer, Jill, "Working with International Chapters," *International News*, March/April 1996, American Society of Association Executives, Washington, D.C.

Romano, Gerry, "Boosting Members Exports," *Association Management*, October 1995, American Society of Association Executives, Washington, D.C.

——, "The World According to Shuster," *Association Management*, February 1996, American Society of Association Executives, Washington, D.C.

Siegl, Theresa, L., "How to Mobilize to Globalize Your Board," *International News*, March/April 1996, American Society of Association Executives, Washington, D.C.

Svevo-Cianci, Kim, *Associations and the Global Marketplace: Profiles of Success*, American Society of Association Executives, Washington, D.C., 1995.

——, "Soul-Searching Your Organization with an Audit," *International News*, July/August 1996, American Society of Association Executives, Washington, D.C.

Westgeest, Alfons, "Managing the Truly Global Association," *International News*, July/August 1996, American Society of Association Executives, Washington, D.C.

Carolyn A. Lugbill, CAE, MAM, is international activities director for the American Society of Association Executives (ASAE), Washington, D.C., and also manages the ASAE International Section. Previously, she was manager/director of government and industry affairs and manager of member services at the National Glass Association.

CHAPTER 27

MEETING PLANNING AND MANAGEMENT

DAWN M. MANCUSO, CAE

"...Bless, then, the meeting and the spot;
For once be every care forgot;"

—Charles Sprague (1791-1875)

O ur society's increasing use of technology would make the casual observer conclude that the importance of face-to-face meetings for conducting business affairs was waning. Interestingly, statistics prove otherwise.

Conventions, expositions, and meetings constitute a significant industry; in fact, they contributed more than $80 billion to the gross domestic national product in 1994 alone. Association-sponsored meetings generated a large majority of this figure (approximately $56 billion), and the number of annual conventions and meetings held by associations steadily increased throughout the 1990s. Likewise, these meetings and conventions have great importance for their sponsors: They can account for approximately one-fourth of an association's annual income.

Meetings play a key role in an association's ability to fulfill its mission because they deliver educational programs to members. For example, professional societies often hold educational conferences as part of their credentialing program. Meetings also bring together members to conduct personal, professional, and association business. They establish forums for the development of industry and association policies or for the airing of controversial issues and concerns. Recognizing volunteers, rewarding professional or industry excellence, enhancing member relations, and providing a showcase for products and services are other functions. In terms of member recruitment, meetings create an opportunity for prospective members to "test drive" the association before making the decision to join.

Additionally, the bylaws of most associations call for at least one annual business meeting of members, usually to elect board members and vote on bylaws amendments. While alternative methods of balloting are frequently used—including casting votes by mail, fax, and online service—none has, as yet, rendered the traditional annual meeting obsolete.

Program Development

What makes a meeting or convention successful? One survey identified these factors for success: stimulating programs, well-planned and executed logistics, knowledgeable moderators and chairpersons, a good physical environment, and the opportunity to meet one's colleagues and exchange ideas. On the flip side, meetings that lacked clear objectives, had poor presenters, or were in an inadequate facility were deemed unsuccessful.

The key to hosting a successful meeting lies in the advance work. Adequate planning will streamline costs, maximize revenues and participation, and simplify the on-site logistics.

The objectives of the meeting should be clearly delineated and in keeping with the association's mission. Around these objectives, develop a program and format that will deliver an event (or series of events) that meets participants' needs. To elicit excitement and entice attendance, you'll need a solid understanding of the needs and expectations of all groups within your intended audience. For instance, a trade association whose members are businesses is more likely than a charitable organization to emphasize an exposition. On the other hand, many professional societies emphasize comprehensive meetings featuring multiple, concurrent training sessions. Regional groups may find their members most value the networking and social parts of their programs, while international groups may find their participants more interested in working on joint business challenges or learning from top-flight management experts.

The most common method for deciding on a meeting's program and format is to use a volunteer committee or task force. This group, comprised of members from various membership or audience sectors, carries different titles, depending upon the governance structure of the association and the event being planned: convention planning committee, education committee, special events task force, expo committee, exhibits advisory council, and so forth. In some cases, numerous committees have responsibilities for different aspects of the meeting; other committees involved might include those related to awards, the host city, certification, marketing, and fund raising.

Program content should be based on information gathered through a number of research techniques. Valuable input may come from program or education committees, member (and nonmember) surveys, focus groups, sampling techniques, evaluations of previous events, and association departments that have special insight into "hot" topics or new trends. Other sources of information include industry suppliers, the association's credentialing program, computer bulletin boards, responses to a call for presentations, chapter meeting agendas and evaluations, and the programs of meetings held in complementary industries or professions.

Planners often find a common theme underlying many of the educational topics identified through the research process. A logo designed to incorporate this theme can become an important part of the marketing for the meeting.

Finding a Format

The next step in planning is to design a meeting format that will deliver the chosen content in the most interesting and effective way. Consider the learning objectives identified during the needs-determination process, how interactive the format should be to foster this learning, the demographics of the attendees, the meeting's overall objectives, the character of the destination (once chosen), budget, and available delivery systems.

Typical format options are:

- **General Sessions.** *Formal* lectures usually highlight one expert or a celebrity speaker, who addresses a topic of general interest to all segments of the audience. *Plenary session* is another name for a general session, although some associations use the term *plenary* to describe an interactive session following a formal lecture.

   An *audience reaction* team refers to a group of members (usually three to five) seated on stage; they query the speaker with typical audience questions. A *panel discussion* includes a small group of experts, who discuss an issue from a variety of perspectives, while a *colloquium* involves a panel of experts and a panel of members, all of whom discuss and debate various issues related to a topic.

   An *interview* may involve a presenter being questioned by a moderator or a team of members; it is an especially effective presentation format if the presenter is a controversial or visionary figure. Finally, a *debate* often makes a thought-provoking general session because it positions two individuals or teams on opposite sides of an issue.

- **Expositions and Trade Shows.** Standardized 8' x 10' or 10' x 10' *display booths*—the basic exhibit spaces—face an aisle on one side, with an 8'-high drape as the back wall and two 3'-high drapes as side walls. Some exposition managers organize the exhibits by product or service category; others ensure competitive exhibitors are not close to one another on the exhibit floor.

   Other common configurations include *island booths* (bordered by aisles on all four sides) and *peninsula booths*. The latter normally consist of two or more standard booths and are bordered by aisles on three sides and neighboring booth(s) on the remaining (fourth) side. Peninsula booths usually require special height regulations to protect the visibility of neighboring booths.

   Product demonstration sessions provide company representatives the opportunity to show a crowd of attendees how a product or service works. Some trade shows set aside space on the exhibit floor for *model facilities*, such as a futuristic store, a model warehouse, and so forth. Many times these models incorporate and showcase the products or services of several exhibiting companies.

   Association information centers give many associations a way to use their trade show to promote their benefits and services to attendees. In these centers, associations display information and sample products (books, tapes, and so forth) in or near the regular exhibits.

- **Educational Sessions/Breakouts.** In addition to general sessions, many meeting planners appeal to certain segments of attendees by scheduling multiple, concurrent sessions that cover more customized topics. These breakout sessions may follow the traditional general session formats noted above (formal lectures, panel discussions, and interviews, for instance), as well as these alternatives:

— *Workshops or roundtables,* where a moderator leads a small audience in discussing one or more topics.

— *Teams or buzz groups,* where the audience is broken down into small units and given assignments.

— *Hands-on demonstrations,* during which participants actually learn to use equipment or practice a new technique.

— *Simulations,* in which a trained facilitator leads attendees through hypothetical exercises.

— *Poster sessions,* whereby presenters provide written materials that are affixed to large display boards and exhibited in an area where all attendees may review them. Sometimes, authors also give short presentations.

— *Fishbowl,* in which an inner circle of members debate an issue while an outer circle observes the interchange.

• **Guest Programs.** Many associations schedule activities for spouses, companions, guests, children, and other family members who accompany meeting participants. Active guests are less likely to draw the regular attendees away from your core programming. Plus, encouraging their participation in your meeting could lead to higher ticket sales for evening and social functions and boost overall meeting attendance.

To understand the interests of these guests, consider conducting a survey. Talk to the area's convention and visitors bureau, a local destination management company, or a tour operator to find out what attractions are available in the vicinity for group tours. In addition, educational programming on topics such as personal finance, self-improvement, physical fitness, relationships, and new technologies are often popular. Just be careful not to over-schedule guests; they also like to have some unstructured time for their own pursuits.

• **Tours and Other Social Events.** A meeting delegate typically wants some social time mixed in with the educational or business events. In fact, many planners find they must schedule some visits to local attractions or risk losing attendees' participation at other functions. Aside from the obvious mental break they provide, such events offer attendees a means to network with old and new friends and to learn something about the local area.

Receptions are the traditional way of helping members network in a social atmosphere. *Tours,* whether incorporated into the regular program or offered as options (with a separate fee), may include local area "hot spots" or stops at the business facilities of local members or suppliers.

Fund raisers and *sporting events* are two more options to consider. Many groups hold fund-raising auctions, black-tie dinners, or special lectures to benefit the organization's foundation, scholarship fund, or a designated charity. Golf or tennis tournaments are also popular ways of involving participants in social functions outside the meeting room.

Once you've decided on the right mix of events, you need to set a schedule or agenda that includes the number of days the meeting will be held, the start and end times for each event, and the program format for each event.

Budgeting

The basic components of a meeting budget are income (or revenue), expenses, and net return.

It is crucial to set reasonable expectations for each revenue source: delegate registration (number of participants, minus any complimentary registrations offered, multiplied by the registration fee), special event ticket sales (including tours and guest program), exhibit space rental, exhibitor registrations, sponsorships, and other miscellaneous income (such as sales of convention proceedings or seminar CD-ROMs or tapes). Detailed historic information about past meeting results will provide a good basis for setting realistic goals.

Meeting expenses typically fall into one of two major groupings: direct or indirect. Direct expenses are those owed for goods or services provided by outside suppliers. These include food and beverage costs (paid to the hotel, convention center, or an outside caterer), audiovisual equipment and labor, staff travel and accommodations, speakers fees, entertainment, photography, decorations and signage, exhibition decorating services, printing of convention programs, facility rental, security, and insurance.

Indirect expenses are incurred by allocating salaries, benefits, and office expenses against the event. Indirect expenses are as much a part of the cost of putting on any event as direct costs; they must be taken into account to get an accurate picture of an event's effect on the association's bottom line.

Net return is the difference between income and expenses. Most associations rely heavily on their conventions and meetings to bring in a surplus; in fact, conventions and meetings were the largest source of non-dues revenue for nearly one third (32 percent) of associations in 1995.

The budget, along with information gathered on expenses during the logistics planning stage, should be used to set participant prices for the meeting. Calculate full registration (which includes all events), individual event ticket prices, meal prices, optional tour prices, guest program prices, and exhibit booth rental. Many associations offer a discounted price for early reservations and charge a premium for registrations received on-site.

Site Selection

Identifying the most appropriate facility type, location, and time of year to hold a meeting requires some basic information on the potential meeting audience.

Does the group comprise corporate CEOs looking for opportunities to network or individuals very interested in sports? A resort facility would offer lots of informal activities to foster that networking or fulfill recreational needs. A trade association with members who conduct much of the buying for their businesses at its trade show should entertain using a first-rate convention center or hotel with substantial facilities to house exhibits. Airport hotels offer the convenience of location for smaller, shorter meetings, but they usually do not have meeting facilities big enough for a large annual convention.

Members' pocketbooks also affect their preferences: a five-star hotel in a large city would probably not be the best choice for a budget-conscious group. Locale, too, plays a big part in site selection. Many national groups rotate their conventions around the country so that no one group of members is required to travel long distances every year. Some groups prefer large cities, while others feel more comfortable in suburban or rural settings. Furthermore, some regions of the country may hold special significance to the members of a group; for example, the members may wish to visit an area where business is growing rapidly or where they hope to vacation after the meeting has concluded.

Timing may come into play as well. Conventions for educators may need to be held during the summer months or school breaks, while most lifeguards probably prefer to wait until their off-season to attend a convention.

Once you've zeroed in on a location or two, the local convention and visitors bureaus (CVBs) can assist in your quest for an appropriate meeting facility. Compile all the information on the meeting's schedule, format, history, and preferred locations and dates into a Request for Proposal (RFP) and distribute it to the CVBs. The bureaus will identify and contact the most appropriate facilities for your meeting. Bureaus sometimes collect the proposals and put together a citywide bid to host an association meeting that's likely to require multiple facilities to hold all the events.

Historical data will be crucial in determining whether a facility is right for a meeting. Collect information such as the number and type of sleeping rooms used per night, the number and types of food and beverage functions held, the number and size of meeting rooms used each day, the number of hospitality suites utilized, the amount of space required for registration/ticket sales/information desks, and the number of exhibit spaces rented. Given this data, the dollar value of a meeting to a host city can be calculated—an important bit of information to use when negotiating with the facility.

Conducting a Site Inspection

The next step is to personally visit the most promising facility. Once again, the local CVB can help arrange a site visit.

Most meeting planners conduct their own site inspections. Some, however, rely on site-inspection teams of volunteers. No one is as familiar with a meeting as the meeting planner, so delegate this function only to those who are qualified, dependable, and as impartial as possible. Explicit job descriptions for these volunteers should be written and adhered to, and final contract negotiations should remain a staff function.

When selecting a meeting site, consider rates (prices for sleeping rooms, meeting rooms, food and beverage costs, and exhibit space), dates (exact days

Site Inspection Checklist

Consider these issues when conducting a site inspection:

Sleeping Rooms

- Will the hotel commit a sufficient number of sleeping rooms to your group for the meeting?
- Are you being offered a single (flat) rate, or does the rate vary based on the type of accommodations (single, double, triple occupancy)? Most hotels in the United States quote room rates on a European plan, which doesn't include meals. Outside the U.S. and at some resorts, rates are for a Full American plan (including three meals daily) or a Modified American plan (including breakfast and dinner).
- Can you fit your entire sleeping room block in one hotel, or must you use multiple properties?
- Are there sufficient hospitality suites for your industry suppliers?
- What is the condition of the sleeping rooms? Will they be a good value for your participants?
- What amenities are offered (hair dryer, makeup mirror, iron, in-room safe, snack bar, cable television, telephone, computer modem hookup, voice messaging service, video check-out, parking, and so forth). What are the charges for these services?
- Will other groups be holding meetings at the same time? Will there be any conflicts over public space (lobbies, lounges, foyers)? Are the sleeping room rates for the other groups comparable to yours?
- Historically, what has been the hotel's occupancy rate over the dates being considered? Is this the high season, shoulder season, or off-season?
- Are security and safety high priorities with the hotel? Does it have working smoke detectors, fire alarms, sprinklers, and adequate lighting? Are there sufficient fire extinguishers, and does the hotel meet the Hotel-Motel Fire Safety Act, as well as local fire and safety codes? Does the hotel have an emergency plan, an on-site security force, and a chain of command for emergency situations?

Meeting Space/Exhibit Hall

- Does the hotel or convention center have sufficient space to hold your various events at the times you want? Compare an actual room with the figures given on the facility's diagram. Many times these figures originate from architectural drawings or projections and do not account for any alterations made to the floor plan or for set up of additional staging or audiovisual equipment. More accurate figures are usually available from the manager of convention services or catering.

continued

- Will the flow from one meeting room to another be comfortable for your attendees, or must they do lots of extra walking to get from place to place?
- Are the meeting facilities in good shape? Are the air walls clean and in good repair? Do they provide sufficient soundproofing for your meeting? Will any other functions be held next door to your meeting?
- Is the lighting sufficient? Can the lighting system be controlled individually in each room?
- Is there a sound system in each room, and does it work well?
- Is the ceiling height in each room sufficient for your audiovisual needs? For example, will the chandeliers interfere with any audiovisual presentations being planned?
- Is the temperature in each meeting room individually set? How is the thermostat controlled?
- Are the public facilities, especially the restrooms and foyer areas, clean and neat?
- Is the freight door or elevator large enough to accommodate exhibits? What is the weight limit for the exhibit floor?

Complying with ADA

According to the Americans with Disabilities Act (ADA), your association becomes a "public accommodation" when it leases a hotel or other facility for a meeting. Thus, the association is responsible for leasing a site that is accessible to disabled individuals covered by ADA, including the visually impaired, deaf or hard of hearing, and those in a wheelchair or with some mobility impairment.

- Do the meeting and exhibit facilities meet ADA requirements? Check for ADA compliance in parking lots; walks, curbs, and ramps; entrances, corridors, and stairs; the front desk; public restrooms; accessible guest rooms and meeting rooms; restaurants and lounges; elevators; and public telephones and water fountains. Facilities should also have specialized emergency procedures for disabled guests.
- Will the facility agree to comply with the ADA in its contract? Will it agree to hold the association harmless against any claims made against the association for the facility's non-compliance?

Finally, it is always wise to talk with other meeting planners who have held events at the facility you're considering, to hear first hand how the property performed and what challenges can be expected on-site. The hotel, convention center, or CVB can provide the names of planners who have held recent meetings at the properties in question.

for which sleeping rooms and meeting space are available to the group), and space (amount and configuration of meeting space being offered and the flow of that space from one event to another). In concert with the visit, review the meeting specifications or request for proposal and the hotel or facility's proposal and floor plan.

Signing on the Dotted Line

With the site inspections completed, it is time to narrow the field to one or two top choices, place a tentative "hold" on the space, and start contract negotiations. While not all meetings require a formal contract, every meeting should involve at least a letter of agreement signed by representatives of both parties (the hotel or facility and the association). Putting the agreement in writing helps clarify the terms and makes the terms binding and enforceable.

A clear offer must be made and accepted by both parties involved in the agreement. In layman's terms, the contract must detail what the hotel or facility will provide and what the association or its members will pay. Both parties must agree in writing to this offer. As with all contracts, consult legal counsel before signing any agreement on behalf of your association.

Negotiate fairly with a hotel or other property so the finished product—the contract—provides a fair profit for the services and facilities provided. Some meeting planners have discovered that driving a property to agree to a one-sided contract results in poorer quality service during the convention or a lack of interest in hosting future meetings. Remember, everything is negotiable: Concentrating on additional services and amenities can be a good alternative to strictly focusing on price. (For tips on effective negotiating, see Chapter 9.)

In addition to rates, dates, and space—the three main negotiating points of all meetings contracts—address these issues:

- Does the contract cover a single meeting, or does it cover multiple meetings during the course of a year or more?

- How will room reservations be handled—by rooming list, reservation cards, housing bureau, or phone-in reservations? What is the cut-off date for reservations, and what happens to rooms in your block after that date? How can reservations be made after that date and at what cost? Will the hotel assure the association that its meeting participants will receive the lowest room rates available to any guests at the time of the meeting? Are special rates available for a small number of staff rooms? Will the hotel agree to give the association the right to approve any requests for suites during the dates of its meeting?

- Will the association earn complimentary sleeping rooms for use by staff or VIPs, based on actual rooms used? The industry standard is 1 complimentary room for every 50 paid rooms, although some properties may use a 1-to-40 ratio under certain circumstances. Find out if comp nights are calculated on the total number of room nights blocked or on a night-by-night basis.

- What rules will govern the establishment of a master account for the association? Are any deposits required, and are they put into escrow? What are the payment terms? How will billing be handled? Make sure the payment terms require the association to pay only for undisputed charges within the prescribed time (normally 30 days) and that payment is contingent upon the association's receipt of a full post-convention report from the property.

- Confirm the availability and cost of additional services, such as parking, airport transfers, in-room telephone service, package receiving, fax services, and concierge services.

- Name the exact meeting, exhibit, and public space being held for the association and the costs associated with the use of that space.

- Agree on specific food and beverage quotes, a percentage discount off the published catering menus, or a date by which food and beverage prices may be negotiated.

- Include a paragraph confirming the hotel's or facility's compliance with the terms of the Americans with Disabilities Act as well as any fire, safety, and building codes.

- List the responsibilities of the hotel should a meeting delegate with a confirmed reservation be turned away because the hotel is filled or oversold. Most times, the hotel will agree to find the guest alternate accommodations of equal or better quality, provide transportation to and from the association's meetings, and offer a room amenity, until it can once again offer a sleeping room.

- Address what the property is required to do when and if any renovations are planned. Also note whether any concurrent meetings sponsored by other groups may be booked.

- Hotels may require performance or "attrition" clauses for sleeping room pickup or food and beverage revenues in their contracts. Associations need to be careful that the performance levels set by the hotel are reasonable, attainable, and clearly listed. Any payments from the association required by the hotel should be based on lost profits; for some meetings, specifying damages in actual dollars will help to avoid disputes over profits that may or may not have materialized.

- Watch the wording of any cancellation clause. Usually, cancellation is permitted if it results from an Act of God (such as a hurricane), strikes, epidemics, or declarations of war. If penalties apply to the association for canceling a meeting of substantial size or economic value within a set period of time (usually one year) for other reasons, similar penalties should be applied to the property that cancels the group's contract. The contract should clearly stipulate when cancellation fees must be paid.

    Cancellation clauses should require the hotel to attempt to resell the rooms and state that revenue from resold rooms will be deducted from the amount owed by the canceling association. Again, any payment due for a canceled meeting should be set as a specific dollar amount based on lost profits, not gross revenues. Special cancellation policies may apply in cases where the hotel management changes, the meeting outgrows the meeting space, the meeting requires space or sleeping rooms at more than one property, the property is facing bankruptcy, or the property does not perform satisfactorily at an earlier meeting.

The contract should address appropriate notification policies in each of these cases, clearly state the procedures to be followed when disagreements occur, and designate the state given jurisdiction in cases involving such disagreements. Many planners stipulate that contractual disagreements be referred to the Alternative Dispute Resolution (ADR) program administered by the meeting industry's Convention Liaison Council.

• The indemnification clause should say that the hotel will pay the legal fees and any judgments against the association if someone names the association in a lawsuit for something within the hotel's scope of responsibility. Likewise, it should say that the association will hold the hotel harmless if the lawsuit concerns something under the association's control.

• Convention center contracts often have stipulations that apply to events other than typical association meetings, such as sporting events and concerts open to the general public. Be sure to eliminate the provisions that do not apply to your meeting.

• Insurance clauses can require the association, the hotel, or both to carry a minimum amount of liability insurance and to name the other group and its representatives as additional insureds on the policy.

• The contract should specify that the people signing have the authority to do so on behalf of their companies. It should also spell out that the contract and any signed addenda constitute the entire agreement between the parties.

Most associations set up a master account at the host hotel or meeting facility. Against this they charge meeting expenses such as food, meeting room rental, and labor. A master account is set up by filling out a credit application and getting approval from the property in advance of the meeting. Be explicit with the hotel about what will and will not be charged to the master account and who has authority to charge items. Once on site, review the charges made to the master account each day.

Specialized Services

Many planners contract with additional suppliers, such as airlines, car rental agencies, destination management companies, travel agents or tour companies, caterers, entertainers, audiovisual companies, and trade show decorators for specialized meeting services. For instance, an airline might offer attendees a discount on travel to and from a meeting when the association names it the "official airline" for the meeting and helps promote travel on that airline. The association usually receives a complimentary ticket for use by staff or VIPs every time the number of airline tickets sold to members reaches a certain threshold. The standard formula is 1 complimentary ticket earned for every 40 to 50 tickets sold.

Because most planners are not experts in overhead projectors, VCRs, and laptop computers with LCD projectors, they typically hire an audiovisual firm to provide, set up, and operate the equipment. When choosing a firm, ask about equipment inventories, the firm's location (an in-house firm is likely to have a larger supply of labor and equipment available on the spur of the moment), labor costs, overtime policies, and any additional charges incurred for use of the hotel sound system.

Working with entertainers requires special expertise as well. Be sure to give the performers guidelines for appropriate entertainment (acceptable language, for instance), background information on the audience, the event start time and length of performance, and any expenses covered by the association beyond the arranged performance fee. Booking agents can recommend appropriate acts and offer additional services such as on-site coordination; they can also be helpful in emergency situations when a last-minute replacement is needed. Whether using an agent or booking the entertainer directly, always preview the act before confirming the booking.

Remember that providing any entertainment that includes the use of copyrighted music will require the sponsoring association to secure the necessary performance licenses from organizations such as the American Society of Composers, Authors and Publishers (ASCAP) and Broadcast Music International (BMI).

Contracts with suppliers should be carefully reviewed to ensure the terms of the agreement are clear and equitable. Like contracts with facilities, they should include clauses on indemnification, performance, cancellation, assignability of the contract, and compliance with the ADA and other pertinent regulations.

Booking Speakers

One group of service providers—speakers—merits special attention. When choosing a speaker for a general session or educational workshop, consider whether the speaker's message will help the association satisfy the meeting's objectives, if the speaker's participation will stimulate attendance or press coverage, if the audience will recognize and respect the speaker's expertise, and whether the speaker's style of delivery will hold the audience's attention.

Many associations find talented speakers through local and national speakers bureaus that represent both the famous and the not-so-famous. Other speaker sources include professional organizations (such as the National Speakers Association), convention and visitor bureaus, universities and colleges, destination management companies, other associations, and association members and suppliers. Whenever possible, preview the speaker by seeing him or her give a presentation or by sending a committee member to do the preview.

Speaker contracts should cover the usual items, such as day, time, location, program length, and presentation format (lecture, Q&A, and so forth), as well as the following: liability issues (copyright/slander), security requirements of high-profile speakers, substitute speakers provided by the speakers bureau, expenses covered in addition to the arranged speaking fee (for example, coach versus first-class travel), whether the speaker may market any ancillary products (books or tapes), preferred attire, audiovisual equipment needed, approval to tape the presentation, cancellation by either party, and the type of background information to be provided to the speaker.

For any speaker to be successful, he or she needs to be briefed on the audience—its demographic profile, perspective on the topic, the industry's or profession's general concerns and jargon, and topics to avoid. Additionally, educate the speaker about the meeting itself, such as its theme, format, and program.

Marketing Your Meeting

An association may host the best meeting in history, but it won't be a success if no one attends. The elements of a marketing plan will vary based on the type of meeting. Annual conventions with expositions, for instance, require at least two separate marketing campaigns: one to potential exhibitors and one to potential delegates. Other potential audiences are past attendees, government employees, university professors and other instructors, and representatives from allied industries. Some of the marketing budget and resources should also be set aside for publicizing the meeting to the trade and consumer media.

Once again, an association's market data will help determine how much promotion to do and how best to do it. Factors that will help in the decision-making process include the purpose of the meeting, the budgeted attendance goals, the attractiveness of the meeting program and location to target audiences, the accessibility of the meeting location, the appropriateness of the meeting dates, the cost for attendees, the amount of competition for the audience's training and travel dollars, and the meeting's marketing budget.

As a point for comparison, most associations spend 10 to 15 percent of their meeting's expense budget on marketing. The convention planning committee can be an excellent resource in identifying new target audiences and promotional vehicles, as well as boosting the meeting's profile through word-of-mouth advertising.

Technological advances offer new ways to deliver the marketing message to prospective audiences. Many associations promote their meetings to members via fax-on-demand systems and web pages in addition to direct mail, advertising, and press releases.

Regardless of how the message gets out, meeting promotions should include the benefits an attendee can reasonably expect to gain by attending; the schedule of events, including their exact time and location; registration instructions and fees; information on air travel, sleeping room accommodations, airport transfers, car rentals, and other travel arrangements; recommended attire; other local activities or attractions that may prompt a person to want to visit the meeting location; and who to call for more information.

The best way to manage the marketing function is to establish measurable goals, develop a marketing plan to meet those goals, design a budget, and set a calendar of deadlines for each activity in the marketing plan. For example, many associations start a year in advance with a "hold the dates" promotion for an annual convention and space out the other mailings and promotions throughout the year.

Marketing the convention does not stop the day the meeting begins. In fact, many meeting planners set up a newsroom for media that cover the meeting, provide special information kits and story lists, plan media-only events such as press conferences, and offer interviews with well-prepared volunteers and staff who serve as spokespeople for the association.

Exposition Management

If an exposition or trade show accompanies the meeting, a basic tenet must be understood: A buyer-seller relationship exists between the companies exhibiting and the people attending (or the companies they represent). The stronger that relationship, the greater the odds that the exposition will be a valued part of a meeting.

Big or small, trade shows should not be treated as an afterthought in the meeting planning process. From the beginning, the exposition should be an integral part of the meeting's objectives. For instance, a meeting facility with sufficient space to hold the planned exhibits must be selected. Larger trade shows and those featuring large products—such as vehicles or heavy equipment—may not be able to find a hotel with adequate exhibit space. In these cases, the association may hold its trade show and some events in a convention center—a facility with meeting and exhibit space but no sleeping rooms that's usually operated by a public entity.

When picking a site for exhibits, consider these factors:
- Amount of space available
- Quality of the space (column-free, contiguous, well-lit?)
- Ceiling height
- Floor load capacities and any weight limitations
- Size of freight doors, elevators, ramps, and other entrances
- Union work rules and rates and other facility regulations
- Availability of T-1 and ISDN telephone lines
- Any exclusive contracts for suppliers you are required to use (electricians, caterers, security, drayage, and so forth)

Keeping exhibitors happy requires delivering a good supply of buyers to them on the exhibit floor. That means designing the meeting agenda so delegates have time to visit the trade show without the interruption of other sessions or seminars. To ensure high buyer turnout, many associations conduct advance marketing promotions and offer incentives for delegates to walk the show floor and place orders (such as free meals, prize drawings, and giveaways in the exhibit hall).

The Catch-22 of putting on a successful trade show is that while exhibitors will evaluate the show on the basis of the buyer turn-out, delegates will evaluate the show on the basis of the quality and quantity of products and services on display. Thus, any exposition marketing must use a two-pronged approach.

The marketing materials sent to potential exhibitors should include details about the show (show hours, set-up and tear-down times, floor plan, booth assignment procedures, and booth personnel registration arrangements), a buyer profile, an exhibit space rental agreement, and show rules. The contract should cover space price and payment terms; cut-off dates for deposits, payments, and cancellation refunds; cancellation due to acts of God; booth restrictions (size, perimeters, sight lines, display materials, performance of copyrighted music, excessive noise or heat); labor union requirements; assignability of contract; exclusive suppliers; a hold-harmless liability clause; restrictions on certain sales activities; insurance requirements for exhibitors; and restrictions on sharing exhibit space. Once again, consult legal counsel when developing this contract.

It is important to note that nonmembers of the association do not have to be solicited for booth rental; it's also legal to charge nonmembers a premium price if supplier dues are regularly used to defer exhibit show costs. The courts, however, view exhibiting privileges as a competitive advantage, so restricting exhibit space rental to members may open the association to the risk of an antitrust suit.

Almost all meeting planners organizing a trade show hire a trade show decorator, or exhibition service contractor, to assist in the planning and on-site logistics management. These contractors, for a fee, provide and set up the pipe and drape that creates the individual booth spaces on the exhibit floor, aisle carpeting, signage, lounge and booth furniture, registration counters, and special decorations.

In addition, the decorator creates and distributes a manual for exhibitors, which highlights the rules associated with show move-in and tear down and markets a number of services, such as drayage, furniture and equipment rental, and labor. The decorator usually makes most of its money by providing these services directly to exhibitors; make sure that these services are fairly priced so exhibitors find participation in your show to be a good value.

Housing

There are several ways to handle the sleeping-room reservation process:

A *rooming list* includes the name of meeting participants along with their arrival and departure dates and any special needs (roll-away bed, crib, accessible facilities, and so forth). The association—or a destination management company employed by it—typically compiles this information and sends it to the hotel. Reservations are usually confirmed by the hotel and guaranteed by the association.

Participants are sometimes instructed to reserve rooms directly with the hotel, either by phone or mail. If using a *reservations form* or card, which is typically provided by the hotel and distributed by the association, be sure to collect information the hotel needs to comply with the Americans with Disabilities Act.

A *housing bureau* is a centralized reservation service operated by the association or outsourced to the local convention bureau or a destination management company. This option is often used for meetings that require sleeping rooms at more than one hotel or for associations that want to control the assignment of sleeping rooms (for example, by giving reservations only to those delegates who have preregistered for the meeting). Maintaining a housing bureau within the association requires a commitment of staff and other resources, which can be offset by collecting advance deposits (usually one-night's room rate) on reservations.

Whatever the housing process used, the meeting planner should assign any VIPs to special rooms (upgrades or suites) before the room block becomes available for general reservations and make sure that those who register receive confirmations. Additionally, the planner should consider reserving a few extra sleeping rooms before the cut-off date in case a speaker, staff person, board member, or other participant forgets to make a hotel reservation for the meeting.

Food and Beverage Functions

These events often prove the most visible and memorable of functions. They also require close scrutiny on the part of the planner in order to safeguard the meeting budget.

Rooms holding meal functions should be the appropriate size: not so small that participants are uncomfortable, but not so large that empty space in the room overshadows the event. Additional space should be allowed for food stations, bars, dance floors, staging, and walking room for participants and wait staff. Check that restrooms are nearby and, if the event is scheduled for outdoors, have an indoor location reserved in case of inclement weather.

Local attractions often provide unique and memorable backdrops for a meeting function; be sure to alert the host hotel not to include the off-premise function in the list of meals it will provide. Preferably, give this notice to the hotel before contract negotiations commence.

The most common types of meal functions are:

- **Coffee/Refreshment Breaks.** Either held right in the meeting room or in a separate but adjacent area, these allow people to socialize freely while taking a break from attending sessions. Pricing for these functions varies. Coffee prices may be based on per-person or per-gallon consumption, while soft drinks (in cans or bottles) may be charged on a per-item price based on actual consumption.

- **Breakfast/Brunch.** This meal can be economical to serve. Because of increasing diversity in menu preferences among attendees, many planners offer a buffet for this meal. Plated breakfasts, however, are still an option.

- **Lunch.** Priced either by the plate or per person, lunch can be a plated function or a buffet.

- **Receptions.** These can range from simple networking events including drinks and conversation to elaborate mini-meals featuring hors d'oeuvres, entertainment, and decorations. They are priced either by the person (per hour) or by ordering a set quantity of food and drink.

A hosted beverage service—where the association pays the cost of all refreshments—is usually priced either by the head (person per hour), by the bottle consumed (or opened), or by the drink. Cash bars, which require attendees to pay for their own drinks, operate on a per-drink basis; in addition the association will sometimes incur a labor charge for bartenders and cashiers. It is also important to know if the hotel will serve house, call, or premium brands of liquor, or what types of beer, wine, and soft drinks will be served—particularly if the meeting attendees have strong preferences. If paying for beverage service by the bottle, remember to take an inventory of bottles before and after the event to make sure you're being charged appropriately.

Associations concerned about the liability associated with serving alcoholic beverages should work with the catering director to limit consumption. Options include decreasing the size of glasses, giving participants a limited number of drink tickets, or limiting the time the bar remains open.

• **Banquets.** When making arrangements with the catering staff for a sit-down meal function, consider the type of service required. Typical events use *plated service* (each plate is prepared in the kitchen and presented to an attendee), but fancier events could use *French service* (the wait person serves each item separately to each person at the table) or *Russian service* (diners serve themselves each item from a platter held by the waiter). The room is either set up for open seating, where attendees choose seats upon entering the room, or for assigned seating, which is done before the meeting.

Banquet meals are priced according to the actual number of people served (called a "per plate" charge); thus, they require the planner to "guarantee" the number of meals to be served. Because hotels usually require guarantees 48 to 72 hours in advance, the planner must be adept at forecasting actual attendance. The idea is to guarantee the exact number of people to be served so the association doesn't pay for meals that aren't consumed; if the planner underestimates attendance, however, the hotel may not have sufficient food or table space to serve everyone wishing to attend. Hotels usually prepare a small number of meals over the guaranteed figure (5 percent of the total guarantee is standard), but ask about the exact percentage before deciding upon the guarantee.

Meal functions can be priced on a per-ticket basis. In this scenario, the meeting participant receives a ticket for a meal function upon registration. The server waiting on the table or working at one end of a buffet line collects this ticket, and the association pays for the number of meals based on tickets turned in. Usually the association must still give a guarantee to the hotel so the catering staff knows how much food to prepare. If tickets are required for a food function, be sure to have a staff person or volunteer on hand to assist delegates who have forgotten or lost their tickets.

Selecting appropriate menus requires a good understanding of the meeting delegates. Younger, adventurous delegates are likely to appreciate trendier, more exotic menu items, while older attenders may prefer traditional fare. Menus can be tailored to fit any type of cultural or religious profile and are often picked to match an event theme. Frequently, participants are looking for lighter, healthier food such as low-fat meats, fruits, and vegetables.

The catering staff can assist with menu design and planning, the most effective room layouts, and ways to get the most amount of food for the association's budget. Most hotels and facilities will negotiate food and beverage pricing three to six months before the meeting dates; if a budget amount is needed further in advance, you may be able to negotiate a set percentage off the menu prices or a cap on price increases for a set menu. Remember to include taxes and gratuities when calculating costs—and find out if gratuities are taxable.

Finally, it is the meeting planner's responsibility to make sure adequate dining facilities exist to serve delegates when meal functions are not planned. Find out, for instance, if the hotel has sufficient restaurant capacity for a mid-day luncheon or if your group of early-risers will put a heavy demand on the room service staff in the morning.

Registration

The first experience participants have with a meeting is the registration desk. Long lines, misplaced registration packets, and missing tickets or materials will not give delegates a positive first impression. Be sure to staff your registration desk adequately, offer separate areas for pre-registrants and on-site registrants, provide training for the desk staff, streamline registration procedures as much as possible, and make sure all participants are treated courteously.

Security

Awareness of safety and security measures during a site inspection will help a planner choose a facility that will meet participants' expectations. Look to see whether the facility has smoke alarms, well-lit hallways, and marked exits.

To minimize the possibility of theft, use bonded personnel, put all receipts in a safe deposit box, and reconcile registration receipts and other sales every evening. By hiring a security company you can provide a secure environment for exhibitors during move-in, exhibit days, and tear down. Remember to get competitive bids, check references, and ask about company policies on overtime, breaks, employee longevity, dress code, and whether the guards are armed.

As another security measure, associations often require meeting participants to wear a name badge at all events.

Insurance Considerations

Meetings expose their sponsoring associations to a higher level of liability and risk. Among the areas of risk generally accompanying meetings are general liability (bodily injury and property damage), fire, medical expenses and malpractice, product liability, burglary and robbery, workers compensation, accidental death and disability, exhibitor property loss, show cancellation, and liquor liability.

Periodically review your association's insurance coverage to ensure it is adequate. Also, have the association named as an additional insured on policies maintained by third-party vendors, such as exposition decorators and bus charters, and collect proof of insurance from all exhibitors.

Printed Materials

A plethora of printed items must be produced for most meetings, especially large conventions. They range from imprinted specialty items (registration portfolios, bags, and pens) to direct mail marketing materials, from exhibitor contracts and manuals to printed meeting programs, exposition directories, convention proceedings, and evaluation forms. You might also produce registration and hotel reservation forms, badges, tickets, daily convention newspapers, and speaker handouts.

Meeting planners have devised alternative methods of providing many of these printed materials. For instance, proceedings can be available on computer disk, CD-ROM, or association web site; educational seminars can be distributed on audiotape or videotape. Attendees might access promotional information via a fax-on-demand service or a web page.

Team Management

Meeting planners require the assistance of many people—other association staff members, committee members and other volunteers, hired temporaries, hotel/facilities staff, and staff from other suppliers such as show decorators and tour companies. Orchestrating all these people so that no detail is overlooked and that events run smoothly requires a lot of time, attention to detail, and coordination of resources.

Common wisdom says that volunteers are the most productive when they serve in an advisory capacity. For instance, they might identify customer needs (educational programming and site preference) and unique resources (potential exhibitors, speakers, or entertainers). Some associations also find it helpful to involve volunteers in the on-site management of functions, especially staffing welcome desks, hosting new members, and operating on-site tours of member facilities.

Before the meeting begins, the planner should develop job descriptions for each of the roles assigned to volunteers. This means that the convention planning committee, volunteer speakers, and the evaluation team (and everyone in between) have a clearly stated mission and list of activities for which they are responsible. These job descriptions help volunteers understand and accomplish their goals in relation to the meeting and clarify the working relationships between staff and volunteers.

Both volunteers and staff should know exactly what to do should an emergency strike. The emergency plan should include the chain of command, actions to take for various situations, and important telephone numbers to use on site.

The staff of the hotel or meeting facility needs to be involved in developing the emergency plan—one of the many roles they fill during the course of planning a large convention or meeting. Typically, the meeting planner conducts contract negotiations with a sales representative; once the contract is signed, the planner usually begins working with a convention services manager to plan the logistics. While most convention services managers serve as the main point of contact for a planner, sometimes the planner works directly with various department heads, such as the front desk manager (for reservations and special check-in arrangements), the catering manager (food and beverage functions), the security director, room service director (for small functions in hospitality suites), and so forth. With so many people involved, a detailed contract and accurate record keeping are essential.

For smaller meetings, or in smaller properties, the sales representative may assist with all arrangements for the meeting.

Convention Planning Tools

The meetings industry has developed a number of standard tools to assist with the management of planning and to simplify communications between the members of the meeting planning team.

The *meeting profile and specifications report* delineates the meeting's arrival/departure pattern, meeting room and sleeping room requirements, food and beverage functions, and exhibit space needed. It also includes historical data on past meeting locations and dates. The profile and specifications are the heart of a Request for Proposal when searching for a meeting site.

The *meeting timetable* or *activity calendar* is a schedule of beginning dates, deadlines, and names of the people responsible for each task related to planning the meeting. Project management techniques and tools, especially software programs, can streamline the creation of this calendar.

The *convention resume* is what planners use to communicate the specific work plan for each event during the convention. It includes a narrative overview of the meeting (with background on the meeting participants), contact information, VIP arrangements, master-account billing instructions, expected shipments or deliveries, special security requirements, anticipated outlet usage (restaurants, room service, lounges), lobby services requirements (bellmen and concierge), front desk instructions, planned use of the facility's public space, day and time of on-site pre-convention meeting between hotel staff and planner, and the function sheets for each event planned.

Function Sheets compile the myriad details surrounding each event at the meeting. Each sheet should carry the name of the association, the event name, the day and date, beginning and ending times, meeting room and floor number, desired set-up, a diagram of floor layout (if necessary), expected attendance, the person in charge of the event, audiovisual equipment needed, food and beverage needs, and any special requirements.

Other items to communicate to the convention services manager about room set-ups include: staging; head tables; lecterns or podiums (tabletop or free-standing); audiovisual equipment such as screens, projectors, and stands; special lighting requirements (darkened house lights, spotlights); entertainment scheduled in the room; centerpieces desired; smoking/non-smoking sections; and room and food station decorations.

The proliferation of affordable computer software has simplified coordination of meetings. Software programs can record and track registrations and ticket sales, print badges, diagram a meeting room set-up or exhibit show floor, maintain mailing lists, record pertinent sales information, create transcripts of continuing education credits, and schedule and organize the planning and management functions (project management).

On-Site Management

Despite the long hours associated with planning, work days during the meeting itself can become grueling for the meeting planner, association staff, volunteers, and hired suppliers. Meetings place association staff in a highly visible position, where members and nonmembers alike watch and evaluate how the staff interacts with volunteers, customers, and each other. Staff's behavior becomes a reflection of the association itself. Proper rest, a positive attitude, and healthful meals go a long way toward making the on-site experience rewarding for everyone involved.

An organized on-site operation is crucial for the meeting to appear well-planned. The planner should arrive at the site one to three days in advance to set up the association's office, verify that all materials shipped to the hotel have arrived, meet with the hotel staff at a pre-convention meeting (commonly called the *pre-con*) to review all plans and provide updated counts and guarantees, arrange for a safe-deposit box or local bank account for daily receipts, conduct an orientation with staff and volunteers, and monitor exhibit hall set-up and move-in.

During the meeting, the planner needs to oversee all events and support

Standard Set-Ups

When specifying room set-ups, using common industry jargon will ensure clear communications with the hotel's set-up crew. Such terms include:

- *Theater style*—chairs are set in a succession of rows. These rows can be placed straight across, in a semicircle, or in a chevron (V-shape), with or without a center or side aisles.
- *Schoolroom* or *classroom style*—narrow tables are set in front of the chairs so participants have a place to put books, writing tablets, and so forth. Again, this set-up can be in rows straight across or in a V-shape.
- *U-Shaped* regular-width tables are set out with chairs in a U-shaped configuration.
- *Hollow square or rectangle*—a U-shaped configuration where the open end has been closed off with tables. Chairs are placed all around the outside edge of the square, looking in toward the center.
- *Conference style*—a large table, or series of tables pushed together to create one large table, is set in a rectangular shape with chairs around the perimeter. Unlike the hollow-square set-up, there is no space in the center of the configuration.
- *Banquet style*—5' or 6' round tables that each seat 8 or 10 people around the circumference. As the name indicates, this set-up is typically used with food and beverage functions.
- *Cocktail rounds*—small round tables and few chairs, used mostly for receptions and other social functions.

If you're using an unusual layout for a function, a floor diagram becomes imperative. Meeting planner templates and specialized computer software programs are available to help you design your own diagrams.

International Destinations

Meetings held outside the United States pose special challenges. First and foremost, the association should determine whether the tax-deductibility of the meeting is an important consideration for participants. If so, the planner should choose a site in a country that meets IRS regulations. In general, the IRS denies tax deductions for travel expenses to meetings outside the North America area unless attendance relates directly to the conduct of business by the participant or unless it is as reasonable for the meeting to be held outside the North American area as within.

This "as reasonable" test incorporates several issues usually applied by the IRS in reviewing deductibility questions: the purpose of the meeting, the activities taking place during the meeting, the mission and activities of the sponsoring association, and the home country of the association's members and meeting participants. In other words, the meeting program should incorporate an international focus—through special study tours, involvement of professional colleagues from the host country, and other educational offerings that could not be easily duplicated in the United States.

The IRS has, however, expanded its definition of "North American area" to include any U.S. possessions, Canada, Mexico, and a number of Caribbean countries (Bermuda and Jamaica, for instance). Any meeting held in these areas does not have to meet the "as reasonable" test in order for travel expenses to be deductible. Still, check with a tax attorney before planning an international meeting to verify the tax-deductibility status of the host country being considered.

IRS regulations are not the only challenge to planning a successful meeting abroad. You'll also encounter language and cultural differences, substantial mailing and shipping costs and delays, customs and immigration regulations, duties and taxes, currency exchange rates, special insurance requirements, electricity and other utility systems disparities, and labor union regulations. Because of these added concerns, planners usually lengthen their planning timetable considerably and seek outside help from U.S. consulates, customs brokers, freight forwarders, professional conference organizers, and travel agencies. Members residing in the host city and local convention bureaus are generally good sources of additional assistance.

services, such as registration and information desks; check that the hotel's information systems (such as the reader board and in-room video services) correctly list the daily events; check each meeting room's set-up at least 1 hour before the event start time; check all food and beverage set-ups 30 to 60 minutes before the function begins; set up cash boxes for each registration worker; make sure the cash boxes are balanced every day; have signs posted in appropriate places; make sure handouts, awards, and other items are in the right place; review the hotel's daily report on sleeping rooms; monitor on-site registration numbers and adjust guarantees; verify that speakers, entertainers, and VIPs arrive on time; and count attendance at each event for a historical record.

Just before returning home, the planner needs to spend time with the convention services manager and the accounting department to review the master account bill; prepare thank you notes and gratuities to hotel staff and other suppliers; make arrangements to return rented equipment such as computers, copy machines, and walkie-talkies; conduct a post-convention meeting with volunteers and suppliers; pack up the remaining registration, office, and other materials for return shipping; and make arrangements to handle the cash receipts via wire transfer, cashier's check, or a credit on the master account. Planners often find it necessary to stay a day or two beyond the meeting dates to finalize all these arrangements.

Clearly, it would be impossible for one person to personally handle all the details of a large meeting. Planners regularly rely on other staff members, assistants hired from the local convention and visitors bureau or destination management company, and association volunteers. Because the planner cannot be everywhere at once, associations typically rent beepers, cellular phones and walkie-talkies to keep staff in touch during the meeting, especially when concurrent events are taking place.

A detailed plan of action that assigns specific duties to individuals helps ensure that all meeting events go smoothly. To implement this plan of action, the association chief executive officer must give the planner the authority to direct the on-site operations.

Evaluating the Meeting

No planning process is complete without a thorough evaluation of what transpired. This evaluation should tell the planner not only what happened, but *why* it happened. Include each audience segment—delegates, exhibitors, speakers, and members of the press—in the evaluation process.

Methods of evaluating a meeting range from small, single-event surveys distributed and collected on site to comprehensive, post-convention surveys mailed to meeting participants. Others include special focus groups, an evaluation team or committee, and personal interviews conducted on site or afterward by telephone.

Consider all aspects of the meeting when designing the evaluation tool: the meeting site, facility, events, speakers, registration desk procedures, entertainment, exhibits, schedule of events, convention timing/dates, pricing, use of audiovisual aids, optional tours, official suppliers (travel agent, airlines, car rental agency), pre-convention promotions, and the printed program booklet.

The data collected in the evaluation process, along with the financial results and statistical data provided by the association, the hotel, and the CVB, should be compiled into a meeting history report. Those data will prove useful when planning future meetings.

Emerging Trends

Societal trends related to the quality of the environment and the importance of communities have prompted planners to make meetings more environmentally friendly and socially conscious. For instance, they use recycled paper products in their convention materials, have recycling bins available for discarded handouts, collect badge holders at the end of a meeting to reuse or recycle, conduct fund-raising and community service projects in the host locale, and distribute food remaining from banquet functions to area food banks. Likewise, some hotels and other members of the hospitality industry sponsor outreach programs in their local communities.

Ethics has also become a watchword. Because of the industry's focus on hospitality and the competitive relationship among suppliers, meeting planners and their professional organizations have established guidelines related to accepting familiarization trips, site inspections, gifts, and rebates and to booking cancellations.

On the legislative and regulatory front, the challenges include local governments' increasing taxation of tourists to offset general budgetary deficits, the deductibility of spouse travel to meetings, and the deductibility of meeting and travel expenses for meetings held abroad or on cruise ships. Some of these threats have spurred planners and their professional societies to become proactive about educating legislators and the public about the role associations play in American society.

The future undoubtedly holds many changes for the meetings industry. Already, the Internet has changed how associations market their meetings, and the medium will continue to influence how planners obtain site information and communicate with hotels and vendors.

The methods of delivering educational programming to members may change as well. Meetings proceedings are frequently offered on CD-ROM as well as on audiotapes and videotapes, and talk abounds about the possibility of "virtual trade shows" overtaking traditional expositions. Associations may also turn to teleconferencing, digital and high-definition television, and other technological advancements to send the meeting to the member instead of having the member come to the meeting.

No one really knows how consumers will use the burgeoning technologies. Associations and their meeting planners must keep abreast of the changes or risk getting left behind.

References

Jarrow, Jane E., and Ciritta B. Park, *Accessible Meetings & Conventions,* Association on Higher Education & Disability, Columbus, Ohio, 1992.

Nadler, Leonard, and Zeace Nadler, *The Comprehensive Guide to Successful Conferences & Meetings,* Jossey-Bass Publishers, San Francisco, California, 1987.

Shure, Peter, "Conventions, Expositions, Meetings, and Incentive Travel: Red-Hot Industry Outpaces Growth of a White-Hot Economy," *Convene* 10 (November 1995).

———, "PCMA's Fifth Annual Meetings Market Survey," *Convene* 11 (March 1996).

Smith, Robert H., *Association Meetings and Conventions in the 1990s*, American Society of Association Executives, Washington, DC, 1985.

Dawn M. Mancuso, CAE, is the executive director of the Association of Air Medical Services in Alexandria, Virginia. Formerly, she served as senior vice president of the National Association of RV Parks & Campgrounds.

CHAPTER 28

SETTING STANDARDS

M. LAUCK WALTON, CAE

E arly on, trade associations in the United States realized that by cooperating they could ensure fair competition. Unfortunately, some associations took their cooperative programs too far and effectively excluded competition, fixed prices, and controlled distribution channels. Such activities led to increased government scrutiny and influenced the current environment in which association standards programs operate.

The early trade associations correctly saw the advantage to setting standards, an activity whose importance has grown in an increasingly global society.

Voluntary product standards focus on the continuation of the most desirable products and services by creating definitions, terminology, symbols, and abbreviations that can be then used in setting criteria for design, material, performance, and procedures. Standardization occurs through the development and setting of specific, reasonable guidelines that state how a product will be measured or analyzed and the desired outcome in terms of safety, health, strength, size, construction, or output.

In the past, these programs were divided into two categories: product standardization and simplification. Through the years, these differences have diminished and all of these types of programs now are called voluntary standards. Examples of voluntary standards were used to make light bulbs, batteries, fax machines, VCR tapes (Beta or VHS), and many other day-to-day products work. An example of the use of voluntary standards in the service industry are accounting and auditing standards.

Benefits of Standards Programs

Standards programs benefit a variety of audiences:

- **Producers and suppliers.** Product standardization programs allow for the interchangeability of parts and items; this means that manufacturers can focus their innovative efforts on achieving greater consistency and usability. Standardization reduces the number of available options, which increases the volume used and reduces production costs. Furthermore, because more product or service is used, it is easier to determine the effectiveness of a standardized item. Evaluation of the product or service is fostered through the consistent expectations set by the standards. Finally, standardized products provide greater information about quality, safety, and performance than non-standardized ones.

- **Customers.** Standardized products are expected to perform a particular way; therefore, consumers can more easily evaluate performance and price. Because most standardized products meet minimum standards for quality, the consumer can have confidence that the product will fulfill certain requirements. In addition, the existence of the standards makes customers better informed and able to speak the supplier's language. Sometimes standardized products become synonymous with the variety of products that they may have replaced over time.

- **Society at large.** Because standardization is a voluntary process, it may obviate or reduce the need for government regulation, saving taxpayers money in the process. Often, standards set by industry experts are likely to be more comprehensive, specific, and attainable than those set by a government bureaucracy.

Also, voluntary standardization programs are able to react faster to technological change because of the close linkage among the association, its standards committee, and the suppliers of the product or service. When these groups work together, technological change can be managed to the betterment of all parties. When these groups fail to work effectively, governments may become involved. Government-controlled standardization, by its nature, is a slow process that requires legislation, approvals, rule making, and implementation. Also, once a government entity creates law, standards are no longer voluntary. A static law often has the effect of preventing creative solutions to complex problems and inhibiting the application of new technologies.

Associations, by their nature, are more able to coordinate international standards than a government entity. Associations that include international members have an opportunity to receive input from more sources than the legislative/rule-making process permits. A government process sometimes helps the most effective constituents without consideration of the greater good. Well-defined and operated association standards programs have safeguards (including antitrust considerations) to prevent the same results.

Government regulations often are quite narrow in scope because they typically are created to prevent a problem. Association standards programs tend to be written with the producer or supplier in mind and provide more detail to assist the end user. Society benefits greatly from this additional detail as new producers and suppliers enter into competition with established firms. New competition, in addition to simply abiding by the prevailing law, has access to technical specifications that have been found to ensure a quality product. In many cases, this can lead to improved competition for customers.

As opposed to government regulation, permitting the market to dictate successful products and services is an important benefit to society as well. Government intervention often can result in an inefficient entity's continuation and the stifling of competition. Association standards programs allow sufficient flexibility for producers to innovate and to make a better mousetrap.

Finally, association standards programs may result in the elimination of inferior products and services. Products that are eliminated can be those that are upgraded because of a standards program, made obsolete by new technology, or those that are never introduced because they are unsafe or undesirable.

General Cautions

In setting up a standards program, associations must be vigilant about preventing antitrust violations. The standards, for example, must be no more stringent than necessary to ensure that applicants have attained the minimum competency or quality levels. Associations are at greater risk for antitrust when the economic value of the product being standardized is substantial. Any hint of price fixing or back-room discussions of what constitutes a fair price raises antitrust red flags. Guarding against antitrust must be a written and stated objective of any standards program. It is essential that all staff and volunteers are consistently counseled as to their responsibilities in this area and that the association's governing board rigorously review and enforce these expectations.

Any combination of *performance outcomes* can be used to create reasonable standards. It is extremely risky to regulate the manufacturing process, which is not the desired outcome in standardization programs. For instance, a program cannot establish criteria that actually, or appear to, limit competition or exclude particular manufacturers or methods. If the standards result in the practical boycotting of a particular manufacturer or supplier, antitrust litigation may be successfully prosecuted against the standards-setting association.

Creating a Program

Here are the steps necessary to establishing a standards program:

1. **Form a standards committee.** One committee may be appointed to oversee all phases of a program. When complex technical standards are involved, however, it may be more appropriate to appoint a separate committee for each stage.

   Avoid the temptation to select committee members exclusively from within the association. The greater the association's reliance on "insiders" who have a vested interest in creating standards, the greater the risk of antitrust problems. It's important to include representatives of the public, as well as nonmembers of the association who are likely to be affected by the promulgation of the standards.

   Public members may be educational or credentialing experts, consultants, representatives of business and industry, or anyone with sufficient knowledge of the activity being standardized who can objectively participate and broaden the knowledge base of the committee. In addition, public members may serve as "referees" between industry representatives; because they do not have a vested interest in the committee's decision, they often are more practical and unemotional and can therefore listen to all sides of an argument, narrow the choices, and arbitrate disputes. Their presence assures outsiders that the process was essentially fair and equitable. Likewise, should vacancies arise on the committee, ensure that the membership remains broad, with no likelihood that members could be accused of self-promotion and self-interest.

The setting of standards requires comprehensive knowledge of the product and a great deal of time to convert objectives into an appropriate program. As a result, the exercise requires adequate staff and professional resources. Standards that rely heavily on specialized technical language, for example, require staff or consultants who are not only conversant in the specialty but also capable of writing clearly enough to present the criteria to all audiences. The committee also should have access to legal counsel. Ideally, counsel will participate in an early session with the committee to review antitrust concerns, including prohibited activities.

2. **Environmental Scan.** Once the committee is in place, it is critical to attempt to determine the external environment that may affect the proposed standards programs. The environmental scan seeks to identify trends within the trade and to ascertain the continued relevance of the products or services for which standards are proposed. There is little purpose in creating standards for a product that will be replaced by more advanced technology in the near term, but there may be an opportunity and a need to begin considering standards that might incorporate the successor technology.

An important facet of the environmental scan is to consider that other organizations may already have standards in place or in production. This may lead to an opportunity to work with another affiliated or related organization. In a standards program it is not necessary to have to do all of the work in-house. Many standards programs are created by groups representing more than one association and may have government representation as well. Joint standards development is an effective vehicle to have a broader base of knowledge and to share the risk and expense of the standards program.

Organizations such as the American National Standards Institute (ANSI) and the National Institute of Standards Technology (NIST) have been assisting with the implementation of voluntary standards programs for many years. These organizations should be contacted as a part of the environmental scan process.

ANSI also can help organizations seeking information about ISO9000, which is a set of quality management tools designed to bring organizations and customers together despite any number of barriers, including language, customs, culture, and business practices.

3. **Establish program objectives.** Clearly articulated objectives are essential for measuring a program's effectiveness. The greatest error made by organizations that create inappropriate, unused, or illegal standards programs is rushing the process, so take the time to define appropriate objectives.

Appropriate objectives are compatible with the association's mission or exempt purposes, are not set just for the benefit of association members, and reflect a complete understanding of the product or service. This understanding is gained by thoroughly researching the product or service.

Asking this series of questions can help guide the development of objectives:

- Would the standard exclude potential competitors, including foreign competition, from the market? If so, search for foreign manufacturers or service providers to include on the committee.

- Who will be affected by the standards program? Have these groups been informed that the association has begun to study standardization or simplification?

- Do the objectives promote free and fair competition among competitors—or might it appear that the proposed standards limit competition to the benefit of the members of the association?

- Based on its objectives, does the program offer compelling potential benefits? If not, what is the purpose of proceeding? If so, where do the compelling benefits lie?

- Is the general public a beneficiary? If not, the association board would be well-advised to scrap the effort immediately.

If, after thoroughly investigating the program's effect on every possible audience, the standards committee concludes the program would help the association meet its mission, the board of directors (or other governing body) should ratify the objectives and permit the process to continue.

4. **Draft initial standards.** This time-consuming step involves designing the minimum qualifications of performance and quality to be attained. Avoid standards that would limit competitors to a specific process or raw materials.

In general, the standards should enable an objective person to evaluate each potential product or service against a predetermined set of guidelines; therefore, ensure that every standard is written clearly, concisely, and in language not subject to varied interpretation. The standard should state the minimum acceptable level of performance.

5. **Call for comments.** Seek comments on the first comprehensive draft from all interested parties, not just association members. For instance, nonmembers, industry experts, academicians, and perhaps even government regulators should be afforded a reasonable amount of time to comment on the proposed standards. Even though the standards are voluntary in nature, manufacturers or service providers who receive early notice of the proposed standards may reap significant economic benefits; therefore, it is necessary to distribute proposed standards as broadly as possible.

6. **Review the comments.** After the comment period has ended, the committee should reconvene to systematically and objectively review all the responses received: Staff should remain alert to any favoritism or "horse trading" demonstrated by members of the committee. A revised standards document that incorporates suggested changes should then be prepared for distribution. Retain the comments that are not incorporated into the second draft, and

record the rationale for their being passed over. It also is good practice to respond to each comment in writing. This will preserve written evidence that the standards-setting body was thorough and reasonable in its deliberations and eliminate the possibility that an aggrieved person can later complain that the committee had not considered his or her comment.

The committee may seek additional comments on the revised standards, especially if the changes are substantial. If the changes are merely editorial and do not change the meaning of the standards, the comment phase can be closed and the final standards sent to the association's governing board for approval.

7. **Obtain approval.** The association's governing body, in conjunction with legal counsel, should review the standards program before proceeding. At this point, the board must not attempt to change the standards but rather ensure that the standards-setting activity has been performed properly. Specifically, the board should review the process to determine whether the program has incurred any risk of antitrust violation or litigation has arisen and whether the various audiences have had the opportunity to comment on the standards and participate fully in the committee's deliberations.

8. **Test the standards.** Before the program can be officially promulgated, some companies must agree to test their products against the standards. In many cases, the committee members and other interested parties already have done this as part of drafting reasonable standards and providing appropriate comments. Still, additional volunteers are needed to objectively evaluate the proposed standards.

The number of companies that participate in the pilot needs to be large enough to determine whether the standards work in the field as well as they do on paper—but small enough so that the program can be supported by staff and the feedback easily evaluated. In highly concentrated industries, the number of participants may be small, whereas industries or service areas with many competitors would require a larger number of participants.

It's preferable to open the pilot study to both members and nonmembers, particularly if implementation of the standards program will give a competitive advantage to participants. If an insufficient number of companies volunteer for the pilot program, this indicates that errors have been made in selecting committee members, setting the objectives, or determining the relevance of the program to product manufacturers or service providers. Another possibility is that implementing the program appears too costly or too complicated to justify joining a pilot study.

It is likely that the pilot program will not verify the efficacy of the proposed standards to the letter. Any changes made to the standards as a result of the "field testing" must be distributed broadly for comment. Again, the committee should review the comments and possibly revise the standards before submitting them to the governing board for ratification.

9. **Finalize the results.** As before, the governing board does not judge the standards themselves but the process that produced them. If antitrust or liability

concerns arise, the board may refer the program back to the committee or to legal counsel for review. But if the board determines that the program has been implemented properly, the outcome of all the comments, revisions, and testing can be sent to all interested parties as "final" standards.

Maintaining a Program

The work of the standards committee never ends. Once the standards are in use, the more difficult task begins: keeping the standards up to date. Many associations have created standards programs that had all of the best intentions, but as time passed, the aging standards became less utilitarian and appropriate; in some cases, they prevented new competitors from entering the field.

To prevent well-crafted standards from becoming obsolete, take the following actions:

- Constantly review and monitor the standards.

- Propose changes to the standards whenever appropriate but always check with all parties, both members and nonmembers, for comment before implementing final changes.

- Maintain and nurture a strong independent standards review body that rises above association politics while respecting the board of directors' responsibility to monitor the standards program. The review body or committee should include people who do not have a vested interest in the standards.

- Periodically review the standards to see if any have become unnecessary. Also look closely at the industry or profession to determine whether a more efficient way to deliver the product or service has been developed. If these new methods violate the standards, but work as well as or better than the old methods, strongly consider revising the standards.

- Encourage new participation and leadership on the standards committee. Having one or two people dominate the committee for many years will sap the group's creativity and encourage complacency.

- Carefully train the staff, especially those who must explain the standards to others. Ensure that they are absolutely certain they can apply the standards fairly and consistently.

- Set up an appeal or grievance mechanism that will permit those adversely affected by the standards to explain why their product or service should be acceptable. If someone makes a reasonable case for change, revise the standards quickly and efficiently so as to minimize any impairment to competition.

Standards that are static are not necessarily wrong, but if they are not carefully and periodically reviewed, they may subject the association to needless litigation. In some cases, it may be better to withdraw standards that no longer appear effective and start the process over, rather than maintain flawed standards and edit them as time passes. When it becomes clear that the standards no longer are useful, the association should publicly retire the program. Notify everyone affected by the discontinuation of the standards—members, nonmembers, and the public.

Antitrust Cases

The standards committee, the association's governing body, and staff members must clearly understand the risks as well as the rewards of undertaking a standards program. Violations of antitrust regulations carry stiff penalties, including treble damages and even criminal prosecution in some cases.

Case law is well-developed in this area. Legal counsel can provide numerous cases that appear to advocate or oppose the creation and maintenance of standards programs. In general, however, associations have the right and, in fact, are encouraged to create voluntary standards programs for the benefit of a variety of audiences—as long as they avoid limiting competition and create a level playing field for all producers and suppliers.

The case that has a direct bearing on association standards programs is *American Society of Mechanical Engineers v. Hydrolevel Corporation* 456 U.S. 556 (1982). In this case, ASME was found liable for antitrust when junior-level staff and the standards committee incorrectly interpreted a standard, which resulted in a reduction in competition. The program was apparently designed appropriately, and the standards allowed the new boiler in question to meet the standard. Unfortunately, a staff liaison and some members of the standards committee interpreted the standard incorrectly and harmed an entity. As a result of these errors in judgment, the court attached a significant liability to the association.

When an association intentionally or accidentally limits competition through a standards program, it can become embroiled in serious antitrust litigation. But when its standards program fosters an environment of quality, fair play, and rigorous application, an association is able to fulfill part of its mission to the industry, the nation, and the world.

References

Lad, Lawrence J., *Current Principles and Practices in Association Self-Regulation*, American Society of Association Executives, Washington, D.C., 1992.

Jacobs, Jerald A., *Association Law Handbook*, 3d ed., American Society of Association Executives, Washington, D.C., 1996.

M. Lauck Walton, CAE, is director of operations for the Accrediting Council for Independent Colleges and Schools, in Washington, D.C.

CHAPTER 29

CERTIFICATION AND ACCREDITATION PROGRAMS

MICHAEL S. HAMM

As the world grows in complexity, more people seem to be searching for reliable ways to measure the performance of individuals and institutions. The association world strives to meet this demand—and exhibit leadership in their respective fields at the same time—through the development of certification and accreditation programs.

Some confusion surrounds the meaning of these terms. *Certification* usually implies the measurement of competency for individuals; *accreditation* usually refers to a process of standards setting and compliance measurement for systems, organizations, or institutions. According to *Policies and Procedures in Association Management 1996*, a survey conducted by the American Society of Association Executives, the two top reasons that associations develop certification programs are to ensure professional competence and to enhance the prestige of the profession. While typically developed for the same reasons, accreditation programs have traditionally been viewed as a regulatory and quality-enhancing mechanism for the educational world, although a variety of businesses and trades have implemented the concept as well.

Certification and accreditation programs are also referred to as *credentialing* activities, a broader term that encompasses the various licensure programs administered by government agencies. Education and training organizations also grant credentials, but these forms of recognition are not traditionally viewed as certification programs. The certificate programs offered by some colleges and universities can create confusion as well. *Peterson's Guide to Certificate Programs at American Colleges and Universities* (1992) defines certificate programs as: "A sequence, pattern, or group of courses or contact hours that focus upon an area of specialized knowledge or information and that are developed, administered, and evaluated by the institution's faculty members or by faculty-approved professionals." Some organizations refer to completion of one of these programs as demonstrating certification in a particular field or discipline. In general, however, satisfactory completion of acceptable educational programs is only one component of a valid and reliable national certification program.

Questioning the Need

Certification and accreditation programs tend to be long-term commitments that an association should enter into only after careful evaluation and thought and with demonstrated evidence of membership support. Any organization considering the development of such a program should first conduct a thorough strategic analysis. During this analysis, raise the following questions:

• Does the proposed credentialing process fit into the current or new mission and objectives of the association?

• Do the volunteer leaders understand all of the ramifications of initiating a credentialing program?

• Is your association the best organization to meet this need? Should you seek partners or pursue this project as a joint venture with other national organizations respected in your field or discipline?

• Could your field or discipline accomplish the goals of a credentialing program with an alternative system?

• Will volunteer leaders commit the appropriate level of resources to develop a credible and defensible program? "Half-baked" credentialing efforts frequently create more problems than benefits for all of the parties concerned.

A credentialing program developed without adequate planning and design can backfire when stakeholders and applicants question its basic validity and reliability. These issues may not be apparent in the beginning, but they certainly will arise if the credentialing process assumes a high stakes role in the field or discipline. It is always easier to develop a program based on this assumption, rather than assume that the process can be redesigned in the future if challenges develop.

• How will your association address the needs of all of the stakeholders who will interact with the credentialing system? Examples of stakeholder groups that frequently need to be considered include:
— Association members
— Members of similar and even competing organizations
— The public and consumers of the goods or services provided by your members
— Employers and businesses involved with your field or discipline
— Government agencies (local, state, and national)
— The media
— Educational organizations
— International interests (in some fields)
— Entities and organizations unique to your field or discipline

• What methods or means will you use to assess the competence of individuals or the performance of organizations in an accreditation program?

• How will a proposed private-sector credentialing effort supplement or work with existing or potential future licensure programs in the field of interest?

Credentialing systems can lead associations to a new and broader role in their respective fields. One of the most challenging aspects of developing a new credentialing system is adjusting to the fact that active standards-setting organizations will interact with a variety of stakeholders in the development of these programs; to be effective, a credentialing system must address the varied needs of these groups in some fashion. In this sense, credentialing initiatives can quickly move beyond the traditional membership service focus of many associations. There is no legal requirement that a certification or accreditation program serve the particular needs of a broad community of stakeholders, but volunteer leaders will quickly understand that the program's credibility will suffer if its focus is limited to association members.

Benefits to Associations

Well-developed certification and accreditation programs can become the premier vehicles for defining excellence, quality, and acceptable performance in a field. In this sense, these programs have the potential to become one of the most important initiatives undertaken by a national association. Credentialing programs can enhance the reputation of the association, provide a valuable public service and, in some cases, minimize or prevent government regulation of a field or discipline. The major stakeholder groups frequently rely upon and use strong credentialing programs.

In the final analysis, a strong credentialing program has the potential to become an highly valued service for members. In some fields, the credential has become so important that members would give up their association membership before they would consider losing their certification or accreditation status. Keep this potential in mind during all aspects of the planning and evaluation of these programs.

Unfortunately, the potential power of these programs can lead to some abuses. Some stakeholders may place more importance on credentials than is warranted based upon an objective analysis of the outcomes achieved or the exaggerated claims made in promotional literature. For example, some people assume a certification guarantees that the individual who earned it is competent or believe an accreditation guarantees an organization will provide high-quality service. Credentialing bodies usually clarify the limitations of their recognition, but this "fine print" sometimes gets lost in promotional literature extolling the virtues of the credential.

Common Misconceptions

These seven misconceptions often arise in the course of program development:

1. **Credentialing programs are large sources of revenue for associations.**
   While certification programs can grow into strong revenue streams, there are no guarantees. Sound certification programs are expensive to develop, market, and operate, and the ultimate financial performance often depends upon a

variety of factors related to the credential's importance within the workforce or job market. Generally, certification programs developed for larger target audiences have the best chance of generating profits.

Accreditation programs sometimes take more time to develop, and the review process is usually more expensive and time consuming than that of a typical certification program. These factors tend to increase the costs of accreditation efforts and may create financial barriers for potential applicants. Larger programs can generate considerable amounts of revenue but, again, profitability depends upon a variety of factors related to the economics of the discipline or the field. Sometimes an association will develop an accreditation program for a small universe of applicants with the understanding that the effort may need to be permanently subsidized.

2. **"If we build it, they will come."** Associations often assume that a certification or accreditation program will thrive and grow based upon the group's sterling reputation rather than the real value conferred by the credential. This dangerous perception is increased when the "blue ribbon" leadership of an organization is involved in creating and implementing the program.

   While a strong organizational reputation and a well-respected standards-setting body can enhance interest in a credential, even the best programs need to invest in marketing and publicity efforts. No national association can assume that its strength and reputation are enough to persuade the market to accept a new credentialing effort.

3. **Our credentialing program can easily be managed by a staff member responsible for education or training.** Associations frequently underestimate the amount of time, money, and staff resources required to develop a sound certification or accreditation program. These false assumptions often lead an association to assign development and implementation responsibilities to a manager who already has a full plate of other duties, such as the director of education or membership. This person may quickly become overwhelmed upon realizing the magnitude of the challenge and the importance of the credentialing program to the sponsoring association. Association leaders need to allocate sufficient resources (both staff and dollars) if they expect to develop a credible and respectable credentialing initiative.

4. **If it doesn't work, we can end the experiment and move on to other projects.** Certainly, any service can be discontinued if it does not fulfill basic performance objectives. Credentialing programs, however, present some unique challenges in terms of their life cycles. Once your association has made a commitment to accredit organizations or to certify individuals, a growing population of stakeholders will come to rely on this service. Discontinuing this recognition raises a host of legal, financial, and public relations issues.

   To an association, launching a new credentialing program is akin to a couple having a baby: The fundamental structure of the family changes forever, and the parents must assume the responsibilities and risks inherent in raising a child.

5. **The association will always control all aspects of the program.** The majority of credentialing efforts begin with the assistance of a parent association. Many programs evolve to the point where stakeholders' needs prompt the credentialing body to seek a separate and independent status. This issue is of particular importance when the credentialing body serves a significant population outside of the association membership.

Credentialing bodies also find it helpful to dissociate themselves from some of the lobbying and political concerns of the parent organization. While some association leaders would argue that management and control of standards-setting bodies is one of the highest priorities of a national membership organization, the public and other key stakeholders tend to be more comfortable with credentialing programs that are separate from the economic and political agendas of their respective associations. In many cases, it is best to plan for an independent status from the onset, to avoid the later complications of organizational change.

6. **The credential should be limited to members only.** While most credentialing efforts are developed to meet a need of the members, the most effective ones are not tied to any membership criteria for participation. The credibility of the credentialing effort is enhanced if it is viewed as a service to the public rather than a self-serving membership service.

Of course, members should be encouraged to participate in their association's credentialing program, and it is appropriate to offer discounted fees to members when an association is the primary sponsor of the effort—but no national certification program should limit participation to its members exclusively. Competency, quality, and acceptable performance have nothing to do with the payment of dues to an association or professional society.

7. **Credentialing will increase demand for other association services.** Certification and accreditation programs have the potential to boost interest in other services such as education and training, but they should not be developed for that purpose. A credible national credential should accommodate multiple concepts of quality, competency, and performance. This usually means that the parent association's educational resources are only one of many avenues available for achieving and maintaining competency or a level of performance in a particular field or discipline.

Associations cannot assume that competence can only be demonstrated by satisfactory completion of their particular course or educational program. You can build a certification or accreditation program around one association's or educational organization's model, but the reputation of the credential will never transcend this limited foundation.

Developing a Program

Here are the basic steps to follow:

- **Collect background information.** While the concept of credentialing is being considered, gather written materials and information from other association executives whose organizations sponsor similar programs. Staff as well as volunteer leaders can attend continuing education programs related to credentialing, and consultants can also assist in the information-gathering process.

- **Conduct market research.** After the governing body has made a commitment to pursuing a credentialing program, quantify the potential demand for the service and identify specific issues and concerns that need to be addressed during the development and implementation phases. Market research can include focus groups; individual conversations with members and representatives of the various stakeholder groups; and a formal feasibility study conducted by mail, fax, or computer. The feasibility study is, in essence, an insurance policy—it protects against "finger pointing" should a credentialing effort fail because of insufficient demand for the service.

- **Develop a business plan.** This document includes the relevant assumptions about the projected market for the credentialing activity, its place within the existing organizational structure, and assumptions about the expenses and revenues related to launching and sustaining the effort. Board approval of the business plan is usually secured prior to implementation of the program.

  The business plan should include strategies for marketing the credential—not only with the intention of telling the target audience and key stakeholder groups about it but also to create positive perceptions about the credential.

Key Questions

Here are five key questions to answer in your market research aimed at determining members' need for and interest in an accreditation or certification program:

1. What is the reaction of the potential target audience to the concept?
2. How does each stakeholder group view the association's proposal?
3. What assessment or measurement methods are deemed acceptable or desirable?
4. What is the target audience's specific level of commitment to the credentialing effort?
5. What are the unique characteristics or demographics of the supporters and of the opposition?

Even a well-developed and credible certification or accreditation program can fail if it is not perceived properly by the target audience. Because the meaning of certification and accreditation often creates confusion, information regarding these concepts should be included in speeches, newsletters, journals, and annual meeting programs to help pave the way for this new service.

Given the wide range of efforts required to reach the desired audiences, adequate funding is necessary in this area. Associations may use their existing marketing staff or bring in specialized consultants with expertise in certification or accreditation marketing.

Additional actions to take during the planning phase include the following:

— Analyze the legal implications of launching a credentialing program, including the tax status of the new credentialing organization or its potential effect on the parent association's tax status. Consider consulting a specialist if your legal counsel does not have experience in credentialing issues.

— Review your directors' and officers' liability insurance to make sure that the policy covers this new service and the increased liability exposure it brings.

— Develop an appeals process and a supporting set of policies and procedures for its use. Legal counsel should, at a minimum, review all the appeals policies and procedures.

— Have legal counsel review promotional literature to make certain it does not misrepresent the true meaning of the new designation. An example of misrepresentation would be a statement within the promotional literature claiming that certified individuals are more competent than practitioners who do not possess the credential. While this statement may be true in some cases, a certification organization could get into trouble if it became involved in a legal challenge and had no evidence to back up the claim.

— Decide what type of examination, assessment instrument, or format for the review process will be used.

— If applicable, incorporate the standards of government agencies or private recognition bodies into the credentialing initiative.

— Develop a policy for dealing with requests for "grandfathering"—waiving requirements for a selected group based on the assumption that the group's members have demonstrated some level of competence that merits special treatment.

Obviously, grandfathering can potentially pose trouble for any new credentialing effort. Before waiving requirements for a large number of applicants in an attempt to build "buy-in" for a new credentialing effort, consider the likely reactions of the various stakeholder groups. The practice could influence the credential's credibility and acceptance by other recognition bodies.

— Establish policies for continuing competence. Most reputable certification and accreditation programs require holders of the credential to demonstrate ongoing compliance with certain criteria and standards.

— Develop a method for dealing with individuals or organizations that fail to demonstrate the qualities that permit continued maintenance of the credential. This discipline concept adds credibility to a credential, yet the legal aspects of removing a credential are significant. Give this matter careful attention and study.

Structure and Governance Issues

Some associations handle accreditation and certification services internally through a committee or special office. While this option may seem most desirable from a management and control perspective, the credibility of the credential will be limited if it is viewed as just another membership service.

Independent credentialing boards or commissions can be more credible in the world beyond the membership arena. Sometimes an association will develop an external board or commission but stay involved in the program by providing financial and staff support.

Management staff support for credentialing efforts can be provided by hiring a new CEO with credentialing experience or assigning this responsibility to a senior manager within the parent association. Another alternative is to contract with an association management company or a consultant to provide this service; this sidesteps political problems that might arise when the interests of the credentialing body and the parent association differ.

Governance is another critical area to address as part of a credentialing effort. The governing body of a credentialing program has a powerful role in the field. The success or failure of the effort depends, to a certain extent, upon the reputation this group has among the target audience and other key stakeholders.

Members of the governing body should be selected for their ability to ensure that the credentialing effort maintains the highest standards of performance and accountability to the stakeholder groups, not for political reasons. Their role is challenging at best, but even more so when the credentialing effort is primarily aimed at protecting the public. Including public members on the governing body is important to any credentialing effort; ideally, those members should not have any political or economic ties to the profession or field of interest.

Evaluating Program Performance

Any new association program or service should be developed with some form of evaluation in mind. Certification or accreditation programs should be given a reasonable amount of time to achieve the goals set forth in the original mission statement, with periodic reports on progress provided to senior management and the governing body of the association. Appropriate follow-up should take place depending upon the unique circumstances of each program.

Collecting feedback from the stakeholder groups is the most important aspect of performance evaluation. This can be done through surveys or focus groups conducted either by association staff or an external evaluator who has no direct stake in the results reported.

Developing successful credentialing programs is complex and time-consuming. The amount of time will depend upon the unique circumstances of each discipline or field, but most new programs require at least one to two years to achieve a break-even status. In some fields, this time frame may be much longer if a lot of promotional work is required to build widespread acceptance of the credentialing effort's value.

Although the benefits of a strong and credible credentialing program are many, the original cast of staff and volunteer leaders may not see the fruits of their labors because of the lengthy life cycles these programs tend to have. That's why all individuals involved in the planning of these programs should adopt a philosophy of "taking the high road"—their efforts will have a long-lasting influence on key stakeholder groups and perhaps even the public.

Resources

ORGANIZATIONS

American Society of Association Executives (ASAE)
1575 Eye Street, N.W.
Washington, DC 20005
Phone: (202) 626-2723

Clearinghouse on Licensure, Enforcement and Regulation (CLEAR)
Lexington Building, Suite 410
201 W. Short Street
Lexington, KY 40507
Phone: (606) 231-1909

Council for Higher Education Accreditation (CHEA)
One Dupont Circle, Suite 800
Washington, DC 20036-1193
Phone: (202) 955-6126

National Organization for Competency Assurance (NOCA)
1200 19th Street, N.W., Suite 300
Washington, DC 20036-2401
Phone: (202) 857-1165

PUBLICATIONS

Council on Licensure, Enforcement and Regulation, and National Organization for Competency Assurance, *Principles of Fairness: An Examining Guide for Credentialing Boards*, Lexington, Kentucky, 1994.

Hamm, Michael S., *Fundamentals of Accreditation*, American Society of Association Executives, Washington, D.C., 1997.

Hamm, Michael S., and Larry A. Early, "Certification: Yes or No?", *Association Management*, December 1994, American Society of Association Executives, Washington, D.C.

Jacobs, Jerald A., *Certification and Accreditation Law Handbook*, American Society of Association Executives, Washington, D.C., 1992.

National Commission for Certifying Agencies, *NCCA Guidelines for Certification Approval*, Washington, D.C., 1991.

Pare, Michael A., ed., *Certification and Accreditation Programs Directory*, Gale Research, Inc., Detroit, Michigan, 1995.

Professional Examination Service, *Guidelines for the Development, Use and Evaluation of Licensure and Certification Programs*, New York, 1996.

Michael S. Hamm is the principal of Michael Hamm & Associates, a Rockville, Maryland-based consulting organization specializing in meeting the unique planning and operational needs of certification and accreditation organizations. Hamm has more than 15 years' experience in association management.

CHAPTER 30

AFFINITY PROGRAMS

MATTHEW J. ROWAN

The Dilemma

Association members are expecting an ever-increasing level of benefits and service, but without increases in dues. With limited options to support new member benefits, more and more associations have turned to non-dues revenue from affinity programs as part of the solution. Through sponsorship of affinity programs, associations can generate non-dues revenue, decrease the pressure to raise dues, and provide valuable benefits to members.

What Are Affinity Programs?

Affinity programs generally involve the association's sponsorship of a commercial company's product or service being marketed to members through the use of the association's name, logo, or mailing lists. The essence of a properly structured affinity program is the association licensing its intangible property (i.e., name, logo, and mailing lists) to the vendor company and receiving a royalty in return.

HISTORY AND TRENDS

Pioneered in the United States by the insurance, car rental, and credit card industries, affinity marketing activity has exploded in recent years. Affinity programs have grown in popularity and acceptance to the point that it's rare to find an association without some type of sponsored program. Fueled by the demand from the large number of associations that have experienced the benefits of affinity programs, an increasingly diverse list of benefit programs are now being offered to associations. Joining the trend toward mass-marketed, consumer-oriented products and services, companies specializing in a particular industry are also expanding into affinity marketing. Publishers, education providers, and other industry-specific vendors have discovered the target marketing opportunities and the value in the marketplace of an association sponsorship. They benefit from the access, credibility, sales, and reduced costs that come with an affinity marketing program. The programs available to associations have grown to include office products, long distance telephone, mutual funds, consumer loans, overnight shipping, paging, and home mortgages, among many others.

Royalties and other licensing fees are paid to associations by companies willing to provide a service to members. The nature and characteristics of the compensation is somewhat complex, and is influenced by consideration of rules applicable to unrelated business income tax (UBIT), as described further below. Other associations couple sponsorship programs with in-kind services; one professional group had their World Wide Web (WWW) site developed and maintained by a publisher who is active in the same industry. This saved the association the time and expense of establishing their Web site, enhanced member service, and generated more Internet traffic for the publisher.

Creating The Win-Win-Win Situation

The appeal of affinity marketing is that it represents a "win" situation for the association, the company offering the affinity program, and the association members.

HOW ASSOCIATIONS "WIN"

For associations, affinity programs enable associations to offer new services for members that generate non-dues revenue with little investment of money or staff resources. By licensing the association's name, logo, and mailing list to an affinity program provider, associations benefit from the specialized expertise, financing, and delivery systems of the company administering the affinity program. The affinity program company also takes full responsibility for marketing and customer service. By sponsoring existing products and services, the association can focus its resources on satisfying member needs.

Affinity programs also help reinforce the bond between the association and the member. When members use an association's sponsored credit card, for example, it is a tangible reminder of their commitment and loyalty to their association. It also builds awareness by reminding members that the association is providing a good value and a useful benefit.

By generating non-dues revenue, affinity programs can reduce pressure on associations to increase membership dues. Avoiding or minimizing dues increases has a direct impact on increasing membership retention and recruitment. It can also help avoid the organizational turmoil that can accompany dues increases.

HOW AFFINITY MARKETERS "WIN"

For companies offering affinity programs, the primary benefit of an association's sponsorship is greater sales efficiency: generating more sales per promotional dollar. The association's sponsorship gives a company enhanced credibility and recognition in the marketplace. Companies realize additional sales by tapping into the members' loyalty to the association and the association's credibility with its membership through the licensing of the association's logo, name, and mailing lists.

A direct mail promotion mailed using the association's logo is much more likely to be noticed and read by the members. Resistance to sales and consumer skepticism can be greatly reduced by the stamp of approval the association sponsorship represents. This results in higher response rates to all promotions, especially direct mail and telemarketing.

Association memberships are a ready-made target marketing opportunity for companies. Associations tend to be formed around homogenous groups with common characteristics such as level of education, profession, income, age, or interests. These demographics can be used to estimate potential member acceptance of an affinity program. Using these targeting techniques, the affinity marketer can generate profitable sales with reduced promotional costs. Since promotions include the association logo familiar to members, affinity marketers avoid the difficult and expensive process of establishing themselves in a new market.

Receiving the sponsorship of an association also serves to differentiate a company's product or service from its competition. Many affinity programs are offered on an exclusive basis which can pre-empt the affinity marketer's competition.

Affinity program agreements give the company a license to use the association's name and logo on all marketing material directed at the association's membership, which can greatly improve the effectiveness of sales and marketing activity. A concrete reflection of the association's sponsorship, the association logo is a powerful tool that gives the product or service being sponsored a "foot in the door" with members. Envelopes, brochures, and other promotions with the association logo are more likely to be read, members may be more open to the affinity program's product offering, and the likelihood of a purchase is increased.

Affinity marketers find association members tend to spend more money, create less bad debt, and turn into longer term customers than non-affinity customers. Member loyalty is demonstrated by the fact that many associations experience membership renewal rates in excess of 85%. This established link between members and their associations spills over into the relationship between the member and the affinity program. The potential for long term profits from loyal customers increases the attractiveness of affinity marketing for the company offering the affinity program.

HOW ASSOCIATION MEMBERS "WIN"

Association members benefit by the opportunity to receive a "better deal" on a product or service that is available to them only as a member of the association. This preferred service represents a better value either through a price discount, a special, value-added package of products or services, or both. The member receives the benefit of the group purchasing power represented by the entire membership to which he or she belongs.

Being part of a larger block of business can result in better customer service for the member. Members can also rely on the leverage of the association sponsorship to be an advantage in settling any disagreements or customer service problems with the company providing the affinity program.

Non-dues revenue from affinity programs can help minimize the pressure to raise membership dues. When membership dues increases can be postponed, reduced or eliminated altogether, it provides a direct benefit to the individual member.

Affinity programs also represent a convenience for members who often trust their association to compare the affinity program to similar products or services in the market, negotiate on behalf of the association's membership using their group purchasing power as leverage, and select the best value for its members.

Affinity Programs and UBIT

Unrelated Business Income Tax (UBIT) applies to income generated through activity typically outside the association's tax-exempt purpose. Activities that constitutes a "trade or business," unrelated to the exempt purpose, and that are "regularly carried out" are subject to UBIT. UBIT has special implications with regards to revenue from affinity programs.

The Internal Revenue Service (IRS) considers a broad range of activities to be unrelated marketing and promotion services subject to UBIT, such as advertising and promotions. However, "royalties" from the use of intangible property are provided a special exemption from UBIT, along with other passive income such as dividends and interest. The exemption has implications for how an affinity agreement is properly constructed and implemented, so it is advisable that associations consult with their financial and legal advisors to calculate a program's potential UBIT implications before the affinity program contract is signed.

PASSIVE INCOME IS TAX EXEMPT

In general, the key distinction for characterization of revenue from affinity programs for tax purposes is whether the conduct of the association is "active" or "passive" in the affinity program. If the association is an active marketer of the affinity program, some or all of the income likely would be viewed by the IRS as a trade or business unrelated to the association's tax exempt purpose and, therefore, subject to UBIT. If, on the other hand, the association is merely licensing its name, logo, and mailing lists (i.e., intangible property) to the company running the affinity program, and not an active promoter of the program, the income would not be subject to UBIT.

For income to be considered passive, the association must not participate in the program's marketing activity. "Active" conduct such as free advertising, promotional letters from the association's officers, and insertion of marketing materials in mailings to members can cause the IRS to consider the association's income derived from that affinity program subject to UBIT.

If the association does become actively involved in promoting the affinity program, the association's expenses related to advertising, marketing or promotion may be used to offset UBIT income, so the tax is paid only on the "net revenues." However, an excessive amount of UBIT could jeopardize an association's tax-exempt status, so it is advisable for the association to closely monitor its UBIT obligations and seek professional advice from financial, tax, and legal experts.

UBIT Considerations When Establishing Affinity Programs

Some helpful tips to apply in constructing a tax-free revenue stream from affinity programs include:

1. The agreement for an affinity program should be called a "Royalty Agreement" or "License Agreement" and the fees clearly referred to in the agreement as "royalties."

2. To maintain "passive" involvement in the affinity program, the contract should not require the association to assist the affinity program company in marketing its products or services.

3. The association should include provisions that permit prior review and approval of all marketing materials or documents that include the association's name or logo to protect the association's goodwill.

4. It is preferable to base royalties on gross proceeds, and more risky to contract for a percentage of net profits from the activity.

5. The association should not share expenses with the affinity program provider and the provider should pay fair market value for advertisements in newsletters or magazines and exhibit space.

6. Avoid use of the term "agent" in the agreement. Neither party should be referred to as the agent of the other.

7. The agreement should affirmatively state that it is not intended to create a joint venture or partnership between the parties.

8. The program should always be referred to as the outside service provider's program, and should not be referred to as the association's program.

Roles And Responsibilities: Who Does What?

THE ASSOCIATION

In sponsoring an affinity program, the association agrees to sponsor a product or service to be marketed to its membership by licensing the use of the association's intangible property such as its name, logo, and trademarks. The association agrees to allow its logo to be used on all promotional material, including brochures, envelopes, letterhead, flyers, and advertisements. Announcements may be run in association magazines and periodicals.

For administrative purposes, often associations are also asked to identify a staff person to serve as primary point of contact. Usually a responsibility of the membership services, marketing, or membership development departments of the association, this staff function may serve as liaison, reviewing and approving use of the association's name and logo, and seeking member or committee approval as appropriate for new affinity marketing plans. Once programs are launched, their responsibilities include monitoring performance, executing the marketing plan, coordination with the affinity marketer and evaluation of member satisfaction. Of course, any active marketing assistance provided by the association staff member—beyond permissible advance reviewing of the use of the association's intangible property—could jeopardize the tax-free status of revenues received. To avoid this, the association may want to consider having the affinity marketing conducted through the association's for-profit subsidiary, or to construct the marketing contract with the affinity program such that it is split into two agreements, a royalty agreement and a marketing agreement.

COMPANIES OFFERING AFFINITY PROGRAMS

Affinity marketing companies are responsible for developing a high quality product or service. The affinity marketer usually pays the costs and handles the logistics of administering, operating, and promoting the program. This includes development of marketing materials, executing the marketing plan, providing customer service, general account servicing, sales tracking and reporting, and payment of royalties due the association.

Promoting Affinity Programs

The majority of the costs of promoting affinity programs is generally borne by the company offering the affinity program. This includes printing of materials, graphic arts, copy writing, postage, mailing services, and telemarketing. All promotions bearing the association's name or logo should be approved by the designated association contact before they are printed or mailed; the legal reason for this is to protect the "style and quality" of the association's trademarks.

The marketing plan and schedule the affinity program company plans to implement should be clearly spelled out in the contract between the company and the association. The affinity program company should have experience marketing its program to other groups and that experience should be reflected in the marketing plan. Samples of mailings, advertisements, and other marketing materials should also be provided to the association to illustrate the quality of promotional materials and exact display of the association logo.

DIRECT MAIL

Associations rely heavily on direct mail to promote their educational programs for the same reasons affinity marketers do: it is pro-active, cost effective, and can be closely targeted.

For most affinity programs, direct mailings to the association's membership are the primary means of promotion. Catalogs, brochures, letters, and other materials may be mailed to the membership by the affinity program company using the association's logo. Marketers prefer direct mail because it allows for market segmentation and target marketing. Age, education level, income, job title, and past purchases are among the demographics most often targeted by affinity marketers. Targeting allows promotions to be tailored to the market segment most likely to purchase the product or service. The affinity marketer can avoid the expense of mailing to other market segments that are less likely to have purchasing responsibility or an interest in the product or service. Direct mail also has the advantage of being very cost effective. Sales can be accurately tracked to evaluate and monitor the promotion's effectiveness.

The downside of direct mail is member complaints about receiving too much "junk mail." This can be minimized by closely monitoring the number of direct mail promotions members receive. Mailings can also be spaced out so the membership receives these promotions at regular intervals. In some cases, several different affinity program companies may bundle their promotions in a single mailing to reduce the number of individual mailings.

TELEMARKETING

Calling an association's members to promote an affinity program can create extreme results, both positive and negative. For this reason, it's understandable that many associations are often reluctant to provide affinity marketers with member lists that include phone numbers.

Experienced affinity marketers, however, have trained their telemarketers in a softer, less aggressive approach that has made telemarketing a more viable promotional vehicle for association affinity programs, and associations should review and approve any telemarketing scripts that use the association's name.

Telemarketing has some built-in advantages over other promotional vehicles. The first advantage is speed. A telemarketing program can launch a program promotion in a matter of weeks as opposed to the months it takes for mailings and advertisements to reach members. Should telemarketing generate complaints, it can be halted at a moment's notice. The second advantage is that a telemarketing campaign can be monitored "live" as it happens (of course, in accordance with applicable telemarketing and "privacy" laws). The association's affinity program liaison can monitor the telemarketing calls to ensure that members are not being harassed or receiving a "hard sell." They can also participate in telemarketer training sessions to further sensitize them to the unique needs of the membership.

ADVERTISING

Advertising in the association's publications is another popular promotional vehicle because of its low cost and high visibility. Advertisements of various sizes are developed and prepared by the affinity marketing company and approved by the association representative. Affinity program ads in the association's official publications further communicates to the membership the association's endorsement and commitment to the affinity program.

"TAKE ONE" BROCHURES

"Take ones" are small brochures or flyers produced by the affinity marketer to communicate discount offers and other special values. Take ones are very cost effective because the cost of printing is low and they can be used in a variety of settings.

Choosing Affinity Programs

SELECTION PROCESS

The process of selecting, evaluating, and launching affinity programs varies with the association. For more staff-driven associations, the decision making process requires the staff to do much of the research and report its recommendations to a committee. In more member-driven associations, a committee of members become intimately involved in the evaluation and selection. It is important to recognize that the failure to exercise "due diligence" in selection of the vendor could give rise to tort or other liability (such as "negligent selection") if loss or damage is experienced by the members as a result of negligence by the vendor. In addition, if the association becomes too actively involved in the vendor's activities, it can be liable for "negligent supervision" or other negligence if the members suffer loss.

Member Demand

Anticipated member demand for an affinity program should be the primary driving factor in the association's decision to endorse an affinity product or service. If the program offers a valuable, tangible product or service that is in strong demand from the membership, revenue generation and membership retention will be enhanced. Should the member demand for the affinity program's offering be low, the benefits of affinity marketing will not accrue to the association.

Affinity Marketer Commitment

The affinity marketer's commitment to the association's sponsorship is also key. Does the company have many association clients or just a few? How long have they been involved in affinity marketing? The answers to these kinds of questions can help the association determine if the company has made the long-term commitment to provide top-notch service to the association's members. If the affinity marketing company appears to be looking for quick, short-term profits, securing association sponsorship may not be productive for either party. A visit to the affinity marketer's facilities may be one way to ascertain the company's commitment to the association market.

Reference Checks

An affinity marketing agreement is a long-term arrangement and the association should have in-depth discussions with other association clients of the company offering the affinity program. The company should have a proven track record in product delivery, marketing, and customer service, and a reputation as a reliable provider and administrator of affinity programs for associations. If an affinity marketing company has a track record of paying royalties on time and has numerous satisfied association clients, it is probably a good indicator of future performance as a affinity marketing partner.

Legal Protection

Basics of Affinity Marketing Contracts

All association affinity marketing contracts should be reviewed by legal counsel to be sure the association has adequate protection. The contract should specify the exact responsibilities of the affinity marketer including marketing plans and schedule, discounts to be offered to members, performance standards, member pricing, royalty calculation, and payment schedule. Limits on the association's legal obligations and liability should be clearly detailed in the agreement, particularly through a comprehensive indemnification clause. Any and all ambiguities should be questioned, resolved, and appropriate changes made to the contract to accurately reflect the responsibilities of each organization in the affinity program.

Contract language regarding royalties should be clearly spelled out as payment for use of the association's logo, name, and mailing list, and not as compensation or fees for services rendered. As indicated, one strategy for protecting the tax-free nature of royalty income is to run marketing through a for-profit subsidiary; splitting the agreement into two, a royalty agreement and a marketing agreement, may also be a useful approach for this purpose.

TERMINATION

A termination clause is particularly important for affinity marketing contracts. In the event that either party elects to end the affinity marketing relationship, the association's members would be accepting service from a company who has lost the sponsorship of the association. For this reason, the termination clause should specify the disposition of the members' accounts, make arrangements for continued servicing of members, and provide for any ongoing royalties to the association.

Particularly with insurance and other long-term financial products, the contract should specify whether the association's block of business stays with the affinity marketer or can move with the association to a new provider. It's best to investigate the association's options prior to signing a contract.

Conclusion

Affinity programs bring the product and marketing expertise and experience of corporations together with the market power of the association's sponsorship. By reinforcing the loyalty and bond between the member and the association, affinity programs have become a substantial source of revenue and goodwill for associations and corporate America. As association members continue to demand higher levels of service at a constant dues rate, affinity programs will play an ever-increasing role in the future success of associations.

References

Glassie, Jefferson C., "Summary of Legal Aspects of Association Corporate Relations," Jenner and Block, Washington, DC, 1997.

Goedert, Paula Cozzi, "Update on Association Tax Issues," Jenner and Block, Chicago, IL, 1997.

McBride, J. Scott, "GWSAE Marketing Survey: Evaluating Your Association's Marketing Success," Greater Washington Society of Association Executives, Washington, DC, 1996.

Slaughter, Jodie Hirsch, "Managing Affinity Marketing Within the Association," McKinley Marketing, Chevy Chase, MD, 1996.

Slaughter, Jodie Hirsch, "Success in Association Affinity Marketing," McKinley Marketing, Chevy Chase, MD, 1996.

Slaughter, Jodie Hirsch, Paula Beste Cleave, and Henry Chamberlain, "Creating Profitable Affinity Relationships with Associations," presented at the School of Association Management: Understanding and Selling to the Association Market, American Society of Association Executives, Washington, DC, 1996.

Teagno, Gary C., *Profiting Through Association Marketing*, Irwin Professional Publishing, Illinois, 1994.

Matthew J. Rowan has over 12 years professional experience in association publishing, membership, and marketing. He is currently Deputy Director for Publishing and Marketing at the Water Environment Federation (WEF), where his responsibilities include development and implementation of the association's strategic plans for product development and marketing. He also serves as Publisher for WEF's 180 book titles, three magazines, four newsletters, a World Wide Web Site, and other electronic publishing programs.

American Society of Association Executives

CAE EXAMINATION CONTENT OUTLINE

T he Content Outline (CO) serves multiple functions for the CAE program. First, and most important, it provides guidance to candidates for test preparation. The degree of detail informs candidates of the scope of content that may be expected, and the range of numbers adjacent to each major content heading indicates the relative emphases. Certainly, candidates should devote greater effort to the content areas that contain more items (e.g., Management & Administration), than to the content areas that have less (e.g., Leadership Processes).

Second, the CO provides the framework for each candidate score reports. In addition to an overall score and pass-fail decision, each candidate will receive subscores indicating the number of multiple-choice questions (MCQs) answered correctly in each major content area. Referencing these subscore data against the CO is very useful in aiding candidates to understand their relative strengths and weaknesses, and in charting continuing education courses that may eliminate any subject matter deficiencies.

Finally, the CO is a statement, both within and outside the association management profession, of the skills required to function effectively as an association executive. This compilation of knowledge helps in the growing recognition of association management as a distinct profession.

The CO is the result of an extensive survey of association executives. This survey, conducted by one of the leading testing companies in the U.S., evaluated the criticality of the wide array of knowledge for satisfactory association management, and the frequency with which this knowledge is used. Content that respondents indicated was more critical and more frequently invoked has greater emphasis on the CO than content that was noted to be less critical and less frequently used. As a result, the CO has an empirical foundation and relevance to the knowledge used by association executives that contribes to effective management.

As the CO indicates, association management is built on a vast base of knowledge. Some areas of the CO (e.g., personnel, accounting) overlap with the knowledge of other professions, some of which require an advanced, professional degree for practice (e.g., law). However, the level of knowledge tested on the CAE examination will be three years of experience as chief staff executive, five years of experience as senior management staff or a combination of these two. For example, effective association executives must be knowledgeable about specific legal imperatives such as the Americans With Disabilities Act (ADA), but their level of knowledge is below that required of an attorney, a reflection of the need to be aware of specific legal responsibilities, while also being aware of when to retain an attorney for legal advice.

In addition to the usual test preparation advice such as reviewing relevant professional literature, all candidates are urged to review the CO thoroughly. Study groups also provide useful preparaton and peer exchange of ideas for test preparation that many candidates value significantly. Regardless of the method(s) of preparation selected, ASAE extends its best wishes to all candidates for success on the examination.

CAE Examination Content Outline

DOMAIN 1: GOVERNANCE AND STRUCTURE (16–20%)

A. Volunteer Structure
  1. Establish, integrate, and maintain an effective and representative governance system (e.g., officers, board of directors, executive committee, nominating committee, house of delegates) to guide the mission of the association.
  2. Establish and maintain an effective system of organization units (e.g., committees, task forces, sections, special interest groups) to develop and/or implement the mission of the association.
  3. Establish and maintain an appropriate volunteer recruitment, training, recognition, and accountability system.
  4. Serve as liaison with the board and executive committee to achieve the association's goals.

B. Policy Development (Public Policy and Internal Operations)
  1. Identify and analyze the need for policy development, such as foundations and subsidiaries.
  2. Recommend, adopt, and implement approved policies.

C. Planning (e.g., long-range, visioning, strategic planning, work plans)
  1. Ensure that the association has a focused and well-articulated mission that is communicated to members, staff, and the public.
  2. Assess the current status or position of the association.
  3. Identify methodology to establish a planning process and guide its implementation.
  4. Develop effective monitoring and evaluation of the plan and process.
  5. Review plans and recommend revisions on a periodic basis.

D. Legal
  1. Develop policies and procedures to ensure compliance with local, state, and federal laws.
  2. Maintain required documents (e.g., articles of incorporation, bylaws, minutes).
  3. Maintain appropriate insurance coverage to protect the fiduciary interests of the association, members, and staff.

E. Parent/Chapter Relations
  1. Develop and implement an effective partnership, delineating lines of authority and responsibility of various components.
  2. Identify strategies for mutually advantageous programming opportunities (e.g., education, government relations, and membership).

F. Subsidiary Corporations
  1. Identify and implement, when appropriate, other corporate entities to further the parent association's mission (e.g., foundations, service corporations).

DOMAIN 2: LEADERSHIP PROCESSES (12–16%)

A. Mission
   1. Motivate the staff to incorporate the mission in all their work activities.
   2. Coalesce the association around its mission.

B. Interpersonal Relations, Group Dynamics, and Group Facilitation
   1. Identify and appropriately resolve interpersonal conflict.
   2. Inspire individuals to strive for greatest potential (e.g., mentoring, career counseling and advancement, leadership development).
   3. Promote and facilitate consensus building.
   4. Provide opportunities to develop interpersonal and cross-cultural skills.
   5. Promote a healthy sense of personal and professional balance for self and others (e.g., number of overtime hours worked per week; using allotted vacation time).
   6. Promote and facilitate individual participation, contributions, and ownership toward group efforts and decisions).
   7. Use effective oral and written communication techniques.

C. Negotiating
   1. Acquire and ensure the use of effective and ethical negotiation skills for self and others.

D. Diversity
   1. Advocate and utilize diversity (e.g., gender, race, age, sexual orientation, cultural, geographic) to maximize results, to benefit all constituencies.

E. Ethics
   1. Identify ethical dilemmas and demand highest standards of self and others.
   2. Lead by example through maintaining highest degree of personal integrity and professional ethics.

F. Analysis and Synthesis
   1. Take decisive action and make the difficult and sometimes unpopular decision in the best interests of the association.
   2. Recognize and integrate both intuitive and analytical decision-making processes for self and others.
   3. Identify and, when appropriate, take risks.
   4. Analyze the association as a whole, its elements and environment, and their relationships.
   5. Integrate the interests and goals of stakeholders to achieve success for the association.

DOMAIN 3: MANAGEMENT AND ADMINISTRATION (22–28%)

A. Management
   1. Translate appropriate management theories into effective management of the association.

B. Budget and Finance
   1. Develop, recommend, implement, review, and manage a budget.
   2. Develop systems to monitor and manage financial performance.

3. Develop long-range funding and needs plans.
4. Ensure that finances are audited on a periodic basis.
5. Develop, recommend, implement, review, and manage investment policies.
6. Report financial information to appropriate constituencies.
7. Integrate budgeting within the mandates of the strategic plan.
8. Identify, recommend, and secure adequate revenue sources (e.g., member-ship dues, sales, programs, grants).

C. Fund Raising
1. Identify motivating factors associated with giving and incorporate these factors into fund raising strategies.
2. Identify and incorporate the economic and environmental issues impacting donors' giving patterns.
3. Utilize the various fund raising vehicles (e.g., annual and capital campaigns, special events, grantsmanship), and develop strategies to incorporate them into revenue planning.
4. Develop a management plan specific to fund raising (e.g., volunteer, impact, costs, risks, recognition, legal aspects).
5. Determine the criteria for establishing foundations and endowments within the non-profit legal structure and philosophy and strategies of your associa-tion.

D. Human Resources
1. Establish a work environment to foster staff teamwork, communications, efficiency, and effectiveness.
2. Recruit, provide job training for, supervise, evaluate, counsel, coach, disci-pline, retain, and terminate staff.
3. Develop, implement, and evaluate personnel policies and procedures.
4. Comply with legal requirements.
5. Develop, implement, and manage salary administration program.
6. Provide opportunities for professional development.
7. Promote flexible and adaptable approaches to work and interpersonal rela-tions (e.g., home office/telecommuting, family leave, Americans With Disabilities Act [ADA], flextime, compressed time).
8. Develop and implement crisis prevention and safety programs.
9. Analyze the need for, and content of, employment contracts.

E. Research and Evaluation (e.g., needs surveys, marketing analysis, salary classi-fication).
1. Identify research needs, implement research, and evaluate research out-comes.
2. Report research outcomes to appropriate constituencies.

F. Technology and Facility Management
1. Use technology (e.g., computers, communication systems) to maximize efficiency and effectiveness.
2. Maintain an efficient and safe office environment.

Domain 4: Internal and External Relations (17–23%)

A. Member Relations
   1. Strategically position members in relation to the media, government, and public affairs.
   2. Provide information, education, and resources to help members maximize their potential.
   3. Recognize and reward best practices.
   4. Guide the members in the formulation of ethical standards that are consistent with the public good and supportive of association interests.

B. Government Relations
   1. Plan, implement, and evaluate government relations programs, as appropriate.
   2. Monitor city, state, and national legislation and regulations, as appropriate.
   3. Report to appropriate constituencies the impact of proposed and enacted legislation.
   4. Implement, manage, and report the actions of appropriate regulatory bodies as they relate to the membership and to other interested parties.
   5. Plan and implement procedures and preventive education to help members maintain compliance with laws and regulations.

C. Self-Regulation
   1. Foster an environment in which members are encouraged to identify and adhere to high standards of ethical behavior.
   2. Plan and implement procedures and preventive education to help members maintain compliance with the association's ethical standards.
   3. Monitor and evaluate the impact of professional and industry practices on the public good.

D. Public Relations, Education, and Information
   1. Identify the target groups and individuals that must be positively influenced to achieve the goals of the association.
   2. Identify and transmit appropriate messages to target groups.
   3. Plan, implement, and evaluate a public relations education and information program to positively influence groups and individuals (e.g., use of advertising; identifying, training, and positioning an effective spokesperson; crisis management).

E. Coalition Building
   1. Identify and bring together groups with a common interest to develop a plan to reach mutual goals.
   2. Integrate the interests and goals of stakeholders.

F. Community Service
   1. Identify opportunities for community service programs and develop materials, plans, and procedures for the implementation of those programs.

G. International Relations
   1. Identify opportunities and potential for global outreach.
   2. Analyze the impact of global, social, cultural, and economic trends on the

association.

3. Plan, implement, and evaluate international programs and activities, as appropriate.

Domain 5: Programs and Services (20–26%)

A. Credentialing (Certification, Accreditation, and Licensure)
   1. Identify and prioritize need for credentialing program.
   2. Plan credentialing program (e.g., resources; logistics; audiences; design and content; pilot testing; integration with other programs and services; legality).
   3. Promote credentialing program.
   4. Develop, implement, and manage credentialing program.
   5. Evaluate and recommend maintaining, improving, or eliminating credentialing program.

B. Educational Delivery Systems (e.g., conferences, seminars, and expositions)
   1. Identify and prioritize need for educational delivery system.
   2. Plan educational delivery program (e.g., resources; logistics; audiences; design and content; pilot testing; integration with other programs and services; legality).
   3. Develop, implement, and manage educational delivery program.
   4. Promote educational delivery program.
   5. Evaluate and recommend maintaining, improving, or eliminating educational delivery program.

C. Publications and Other Media
   1. Identify and prioritize need for publications and other media.
   2. Plan publications and other media program (e.g., resources; logistics; audiences; design and content; pilot testing; integration with other programs and services; legality).
   3. Promote publications and other media.
   4. Develop, implement, and manage publications and other media.
   5. Evaluate and recommend maintaining, improving, or eliminating publications and other media.

D. Information Services (e.g., libraries, resource centers, clearinghouses)
   1. Identify and prioritize need for information services program.
   2. Plan information services program (e.g., resources; logistics; audiences; design and content; pilot testing; integration with other programs and services; legality).
   3. Develop, implement, and manage information services program.
   4. Promote information services program.
   5. Evaluate and recommend maintaining, improving, or eliminating the information services program.
   6. Identify and use appropriate technology to disseminate information (e.g., electronic bulletin boards, fax, database, CD-ROM).

E. Promoting the Profession, Industry, or Cause
   1. Identify and prioritize need for public information/education program.
   2. Plan for, develop, implement, and manage public information/education program (e.g., resources; logistics; audiences; design and content; pilot testing; integration with other programs and services; legality).
   3. Evaluate and recommend maintaining, improving, or eliminating public information/education program.

F. Affinity Programs (e.g., endorsements, joint ventures, sponsorship)
   1. Identify and prioritize need for affinity program or service.
   2. Plan affinity program (e.g., resources; logistics; audiences; design and content; pilot testing; integration with other programs and services; legality).
   3. Market the affinity program.
   4. Develop, implement, and manage affinity program.
   5. Evaluate and recommend maintaining, improving or eliminating affinity program.

G. Membership Recruitment and Retention (Domestic and International)
   1. Identify and prioritize need for membership recruitment and retention program.
   2. Plan membership recruitment and retention program (e.g., resources; logistics; audiences; design and content; pilot testing; integration with other programs and services; legality).
   3. Develop, implement, and manage membership recruitment and retention program.
   4. Evaluate and recommend maintaining, improving, or eliminating membership recruitment and retention program.

H. Research and Statistics
   1. Identify and prioritize need for research and statistics program.
   2. Plan research and statistics program (e.g., resources; logistics; audiences; design and content; pilot testing; integration with other programs and services; legality).
   3. Develop, implement, and manage research and statistics program.
   4. Promote research and statistics program.
   5. Evaluate and recommend maintaining, improving or eliminating research and statistics program.

I. Standards
   1. Identify and prioritize need for standards program.
   2. Plan standards program (e.g., resources; logistics; audiences; design and content; pilot testing; integration with other programs and services; legality).
   3. Promote standards program.
   4. Develop, implement, and manage standards program.
   5. Evaluate and recommend maintaining, improving, or eliminating standards program.